Samuel + Evelyn Kaplan B10
Aug. '63

CHAIM
WEIZMANN

A BIOGRAPHY BY SEVERAL HANDS

CHAIM
WEIZMANN

A BIOGRAPHY BY SEVERAL HANDS

WITH A PREFACE BY
DAVID BEN-GURION

EDITED BY
MEYER W. WEISGAL
AND
JOEL CARMICHAEL

ATHENEUM NEW YORK

1963

To Vera Weizmann

CONTENTS

vii

ILLUSTRATIONS

A portrait of Chaim Weizmann by Oswald Birley, RA

*Photograph No 6 is by D. Yaffo, 14 by Lasar Duenner, 16 by Korngold, London,
21 by Associated Press, 22, 24 and 25 by Keystone Press. Others from the
Weizmann Archives.*

EDITORS' NOTE

IN PRESENTING this biography of Dr Weizmann by several hands, we have aimed at producing a composite portrait that would encompass the totality of his life. The task has not been easy: creative writers seldom fit readily into a preconceived design. Each author has expressed his own views. There is some overlapping, but we hope it does not impair the essential unity of the book.

In the case of Sir Isaiah Berlin's contribution, the Editors point out that it was conceived and executed as an objective and factual review of Dr Weizmann's life and not as a personal assessment or appreciation of his life and works. It will appear, in Hebrew, in a coming volume of the *Encyclopaedia Hebraica*.

The Editors are indebted to The Weizmann Archives in Rehovoth and its Curator, Mr Boris Guriel, for providing hitherto unpublished source material to several of the authors of chapters in this book.

M.W.W. and J.C.

CHAIM WEIZMANN

A BIOGRAPHY BY SEVERAL HANDS

PREFACE

DAVID BEN-GURION

TWO GREAT MEN rose in the cause of Zionism—Herzl and Weizmann. It is difficult to find, in the history of any one nation, two men who had so powerful an influence over the lives of their fellows, yet who were so very different, not only in their capabilities, but in the relationship they bore to their people.

Herzl came from the outer world. He was a typical assimilated Jew with no knowledge of his people's culture nor any acquaintance with the Jewish masses. He was, surely, moved by an inherent Jewish feeling, but it was only through reaction to external events that he returned to the Jewish people and conceived the idea of the Jewish State. It was just this alien quality that fascinated Jews. It is questionable whether a Jew from the East could have aroused among the the Jewish masses the Messianic fervour stirred by Herzl's appearance—the spectacle of a prophet who had seemingly arisen from another world. Yet Herzl came as the emissary of Jewish history to awaken his people to self-realization, and to regard themselves as a Jewish force. Despite his unfamiliarity with the way of life of the Jewish masses in Eastern Europe, Herzl knew that suffering could be not only a debilitating force, but an instrument of renaissance. He recognized the suffering of the Jewish people and manipulated it for the purposes of Zionism. But Herzl's feeling toward his fellow-Jews was one of compassion and love—the feeling of a distant relative standing aloof from his kinfolk. He had no idea of the faults of the Jewish character. Even if he had, he would never have dared to criticize them: for he was not one of their kind and would have been chary of giving offence.

Weizmann was the exact opposite in a number of essential respects: for one thing, he was first and foremost a *Jewish* Jew. He was born in a small hamlet within the Pale of Jewish settlement in Russia; he was bred in the lap of Judaism, amongst the masses of Israel. He was

I

nurtured in his people's qualities of insight, humour and intelligence;
and, although he later settled in Western Europe where he studied
and acquired the ways of European culture and became its scion,
speaking its principal languages—German, French and English—as
fluently as he spoke Russian, Yiddish and Hebrew, the intimate
medium in which his keenness, humour, alertness of mind and
straightforwardness found their best expression was Yiddish.

Herzl found his way to Eretz Israel through the idea of a Jewish
State, the territorial idea; Weizmann, on the other hand, found his
way to the State of Israel through an inward and Messianic tie with
the Land of Israel. This love of country he had acquired with his
mother's milk, in religious school, through the Hebrew language,
through Hebrew prayer; it was an organic part of his nature. That
was why he opposed the Uganda proposal so passionately, in spite of
his practicality and realism. To his mind Eretz Israel as such stood
above State and Land.

For this reason, Weizmann was the greatest Jewish emissary to the
Gentile world. He was an ambassador to the Gentiles, the most gifted
and fascinating envoy the Jewish people ever produced. There was
no other Jew in whom the non-Jewish world perceived the embodiment of the Jewish people, with their ability, their will, and their
longings. He was perhaps the only truly great ambassador produced
by the Jewish people throughout the generations.

Weizmann fascinated the Gentiles with his *Jewish* grandeur, his
Jewish profundity, his genius for depicting for them the deepest and
most intimate emotions of the people of Israel.

I was not prominent in Zionist councils at the time of the Balfour
Declaration; I know only from reading of Weizmann's tremendous
personal influence and charm during his encounters with men like
Balfour, Lloyd George and others; but later, when I was privileged
to be Weizmann's aide in the Zionist Executive, I had the opportunity of attending a number of meetings at which Weizmann spoke
to Englishmen of all political parties, Tories, Liberals and Labourites,
and I was able to see in what esteem he was held by people of all
strata. They felt that generations of the Jewish people at its noblest
were addressing them.

Weizmann was known as a man of moderation, a man of compromise, as it were, and for that reason many opposed him within the
Zionist movement; but I do not know whether they were aware that
Weizmann's moderation was evident only when he spoke to us, to his
brethren, to the Zionists, at our Congress, for he knew our limits. But
Weizmann was neither moderate nor humble when he spoke to the
non-Jewish world. I was often present when he spoke to Cabinet

Ministers and to those in high places, and I was always astounded by the inner forcefulness, sometimes even aggressiveness, of his manner. It was a different Weizmann from the one who appeared on Congress platforms: the full force of Jewish anguish, the historic humiliation of our people, the profound truth of both our miseries and our hopes sprang from his throat; and that was why whatever he said was heard with respect though not always accepted, since the Jewish message is not easily accepted by this world.

Weizmann was the seer and man of action; he had to grapple with all the hindrances that confront the man of action. There were those who accused him of lacking foresight. They did not know him; foresight was not enough for him: he bent all his immense abilities toward the realization of the vision. It was, therefore, inevitable that all those whose strength lay entirely in verbal prowess, and who made and unmade worlds by the power of mere speech, should look upon Weizmann slightingly. His greatness as a Zionist lay in the fact that he strove, and built, and laid foundations. There are no bounds to the lofty spirit of those who live in a world peopled by fancies, nor any limit to their loquaciousness; Weizmann was a man of action, and he was consequently required to show patience, stubbornness and a deep understanding of difficulties.

Weizmann was the only practical man among all the Zionist leaders, and the only one among them who left the Diaspora not through external persecution or edict, or catastrophic upheaval. He had a proud and assured position in England such as was given to few Jews in the world, but he belonged to a family of outstanding pioneers and men of action. He identified himself personally with the undertaking in Eretz Israel and settled in this land.

When Hitler came to power Weizmann realized more than anyone the scope of the approaching calamity. The moderate statesman, who had believed in gradualness, in slow but steady progression, who urged patience and restraint, himself ceased to exercise self-restraint and became intolerant of delay.

In 1936, it will be remembered, a British Royal Commission under the chairmanship of Lord Peel came to this country in the wake of the anti-Jewish terrorism that had been organized by the Mufti of Jerusalem with the aid of Hitler and Mussolini. Dr Weizmann's testimony before this Commission was, perhaps, the most profound and penetrating analysis ever given of the plight of the Jewish people and their position in the non-Jewish world, coupled with the strongest and most vigorous claim ever put forward for the immediate creation of the Jewish State as the only deliverance from the danger threatening the Jewish masses. I do not think there is in the whole of Zionist literature anything as profound, as awe-inspiring, as penetrating, or as true. It is interesting that Weizmann did not speak of the sixteen million Jews in the world, but dwelt only on the six million Jews in Europe, devoid of hope and facing imminent danger. He expressed this theme of direct and urgent danger with deep Jewish emotion and the prescience of a prophet of doom; his statement made a tremendous impression upon his listeners. For the first time we then heard fall from the lips of statesmen in whose hands lay the fate of Palestine the explicit term, 'Jewish State'.

There is no need for me to dwell on the well-known episode of the Peel plan, the internal polemic, the hesitancy within the British Government. The second World War broke out. The six million Jews of whom Weizmann spoke and whose speedy rescue he sought, were exterminated by the Nazis who dominated Europe. This catastrophe, the scope and significance of which we are still incapable of assessing, had among other things the effect of undermining the very foundations on which the Zionist movement had stood.

With his intuitive perception Weizmann had felt that these six million were the mainstay of the Zionist cause at this period. He wanted to save them for their own sake, for the sake of their people, and for the sake of the future Jewish State. Those in whose hands lay the key to their deliverance closed their ears; the destroyer did his work without hindrance; the mighty tree of European Jewry was felled.

A second tragedy, the political tragedy of Weizmann's life, then overcame the great emissary to the non-Jewish world, and especially to Great Britain, the nation chosen as the world's representative in Eretz Israel. England withdrew from her mission. The years 1937-38 witnessed the termination of Britain's desire, and perhaps even ability, to assist the Jewish people in establishing their national home. This was, perhaps, the crowning disaster in Weizmann's political career, because he cherished a deep faith in the British people. Indeed, his entire political creed was built upon Jewish-British co-operation. But his Zionist and Jewish convictions triumphed even over this blow, though not immediately or easily; from the White Paper of 1939 until the UN decision in 1947 Dr Weizmann was beset by a gnawing inner confusion and stress, and I believe that he failed to find his way.

But even in these years we witnessed his human greatness. He performed his Zionist tasks with complete dedication, although officially he seemed to be no more than one of the rank and file. I use the term 'seemed' because he always towered head and shoulders above the people, serving the movement loyally and doing nothing to obstruct those who had chosen a new course, although he was for a long time sceptical of its correctness.

Weizmann found himself again with the creation of the State; rarely in history does a creator achieve his reward. Moses died when he saw the land from afar. Herzl died on alien soil whilst the dream of his life was still remote from realization. Weizmann was privileged to see the fruits of his life's toil; the State of which he had laid the foundations and which he had spent his years building. And the State of Israel was proud to elect Weizmann its first President. His presidency enhanced the glory of our State and nation, just as the State was the crown of his life's work.

I know that I shall not be doing full justice to Weizmann's great personality if I limit these words to his Zionist aspect. Weizmann was a man of spirit and an illustrious man of science, and his scientific achievements entitle him to an honourable place in the history of the Jewish people and mankind. He was a rare example of the synthesis of the Jewish spirit with the highest European culture of our times. In himself he blended vision and fulfilment to a degree achieved by none before him. He was the man of intellect and of science, who not only understood the value of science in the resurgence of Israel and the creation of our new life, but who had himself made a tremendous contribution to scientific advancement, laying the foundations in this country for its institutions of higher learning—the Hebrew University in Jerusalem and the Weizmann Institute in Rehovoth.

Weizmann had such vitality that I feel reluctant to write about him in this rather impersonal and remote form, which I am afraid sounds almost like a eulogy. I should like to quote from a letter I wrote him after the Zionist Congress in 1937, where, for political reasons, I had been fighting him as vigorously as I could. This letter, written in the heat of battle, is a more accurate, because more immediate, testimony to the feelings I and millions of other Jews always had toward him, than any philosophic summing up of his career:

Dear and venerated Chaim:

I am very, very sorry, much more than I can express in words, for having caused you yesterday, before the close of the Agency (session), distress and suffering. I have loved you all my life; all Jews have loved you since those great days of the Balfour Declaration. But you were sevenfold dearer to me when I saw you after the 17th Zionist Congress (1931). In your distress and humiliation a new Weizmann revealed himself to me then—not Weizmann the leader, the magician and charmer, but Weizmann the man, full of pain, wounded, writhing in his anguish and conquering, with supreme moral heroism, his personal ambition, putting himself as an ordinary, devoted soldier at the service of the Movement that had wounded him.

Your 'exile' lasted four years; during those four years I—and many of my comrades—had a bitter feeling: as if we were partners in the cruel strategem used against you. Your return to the leadership of the Movement seemed to me not only a political need but, first and foremost, a moral necessity. The Zionist Movement was not flourishing; it was burdened by the sin of having 'stabbed its teacher'. From the political point of view you remained the leader even when not elected to the official Presidium, but we felt that we must give back to the Zionist Organization its 'honesty towards itself'. Therefore it was a must that the 19th Zionist Congress should re-elect you.

And after I had the privilege of working closely with you, I saw you in a new light. I never was a blind follower of yours, and I never will be. I did not always agree with you; whenever I felt that I had to oppose you, I did so; if in the future I again see a need to oppose you, I shall do so again.

But even in the fury of battle my feelings of love and veneration for you were not diminished by one iota. I know that you are the champion of the Jewish people, not because you have been elected (to this post) by a majority, but because you were born for it; the 'Shechinah' of the Jewish People rests upon you. And, during the last few months, when the great hope of establishing a Jewish State began to glimmer, I saw this 'Shechinah', shining over you with a great and new light, and a new power of youthfulness, revealed itself in you, with grace and charm to an extent invisible to my eyes before. And, although even in those months, I have sometimes disagreed with you about one detail or another, I know that this time you are bearing upon your shoulders a historic burden not borne by any other Jew for the last two thousand years. I also know that every one of us now, more than ever before, stands by you with all his heart and with all his might so that you may succeed in carrying out the stupendous task imposed on you by the historic destiny of our people—the renewal of the Kingdom of Israel.

The task imposed on you now, is in my view, greater and more difficult than the burden of the Balfour Declaration. The hindrances and pitfalls on your road are now more manifold than ever. There are more objective hindrances and there are also more enemies, not only from the outside, but also from the inside. Our enemies have been joined by the cowards and the blind. But if the number of our opponents has grown, so has our strength—our strength in the country, our strength in the Jewish people, and our strength in the world. And you are the personal focus of this strength. There is no other man or circle of men in the Jewish people that can compare with you. I do not believe the superficial theory that history is made by personalities. But I do believe that unique personalities are the emissaries of the collective energies of nations and of classes in history. The Zionist enterprise and Zionist vision have beamed all their light on their supreme emissary, and this light is growing apace. . . .

There are in Eretz Israel one hundred thousand Jewish workers, and I am one of them—and no more than that. As one of them, you are dear to me as the Chosen One of the people; as one of them, I know that I must stand by you, and as one of them I pray for your success.

I am sorry that I caused you grief. When I saw you yesterday in your anguish I was unbearably sorry because I love you with all my heart and with all my soul. I want you to know that I had not intended to grieve you. Let us hope that we shall soon have a more satisfactory state of affairs.

With love and confidence,
D. Ben-Gurion

Prime Minister David Ben-Gurion of Israel has been in the front rank of the world Zionist leadership for more than a generation. He became Israel's first Prime Minister in 1948 at the birth of the New State, in which he played a decisive rôle.

INTRODUCTION

MEYER W. WEISGAL

TO THE EXTENT that one can pinpoint the exact moment at which a book starts to take shape, this one, I suppose, dates back over more than eighteen years, to 1944; and to another not entirely dissimilar project which was its literary ancestor.

Dr Weizmann's seventieth birthday was approaching, and even in the midst of all the horrors that had begun seeping out of Nazi Europe it seemed to me essential to observe it. I thought it appropriate to record the reactions of a number of illustrious statesmen, scientists, and philosophers to one of this century's most fascinating personalities. The book was published in 1944 under the undramatic title *Chaim Weizmann—Statesman, Scientist, Builder of the Jewish Commonwealth*.

It was to be a birthday present for Dr Weizmann and should of course have been a surprise. But as the publication date approached I began to worry. It was more than possible that Dr Weizmann might not appreciate my failure to ask his permission. My association with him at the time was particularly close, even intimate; I was his personal representative in the United States. I felt I really had to tell him.

On the other hand, I was afraid he might oppose the entire project. I particularly dreaded his lethal and familiar use of the word 'Bilge!'

I sent him a painfully worked-over letter, and in trepidation waited for his reply. When it came it was couched in a characteristic *mélange* of irony, admonition, and charm; it ended as follows: 'If you *must* publish this book, please make molehills out of mountains!'

The phrase was so wholly Weizmann that I used it as the motif of that book in 1944, and today, after assembling material again for another approach to Weizmann's life—to be sure, under vastly different conditions—I find it is very much on my mind. Understatement was an integral part of Dr Weizmann's personality all of

9

his life—his political career as well as his scientific achievements were guided, primarily, by his overwhelming insistence on the exact, the accurate and the minimized fact. He was severe with those around him, but equally so, at least, with himself. His aversion to loose claims drove him to test and retest a thousand times—whether in the arena of *realpolitik* or in the chemical laboratory.

In many ways, this trait served him ill. Those who opposed him, within the ranks of the Zionist movement, frequently charged him with deliberate underplaying, with a kind of caution so extreme that in itself it was perilous. Just as he responded with acerbity and some annoyance to the idea of a birthday book in 1944, so, were he alive today, I am sure he would oppose the publication of *this* volume— oppose it but none-the-less permit its publication. He would argue that only ten years have passed since his death; that the movement he led is still in turmoil; that many people who helped him and fought him are still alive; that the time is far from ripe for any sort of literary monument. And he would be right—as usual.

The time has *not* yet come for a stately literary monument to him; nor for an official biography, exhaustively detailed and documented; nor for a rounded scholarly assessment of the man and his multi-faceted career.

The Life of Chaim Weizmann will take some years to write and until then the material for such a definite work is being made ready, slowly and painstakingly, at the Weizmann Archives in Rehovoth.

In the decade that has passed since 1952, much has been written and said about Chaim Weizmann. Despite his nomadic life, extensive records were kept throughout most of his productive life and all of those collected are preserved in the archives. So are his voluminous correspondence in many languages, his political memoranda, his scientific papers, the mountains of newspaper clippings and photographs which recorded the various stations of his public life, even reels of motion pictures and recordings—all these are filed away in great vaults constructed to withstand time and climate. They are indispensable records, and they await annotation and analysis: the final arrangement of fact and interpretation that constitutes a meaningful and authoritative biography. But that gigantic task is not our present responsibility.

This is an informal glance backward, an image in mosaic created, respectfully, but without paralysing reverence, by a panel of Weizmann's friends, disciples and even critics. It does not pretend to be more than this. Its purpose is simple and modest: to pause and to reflect on the occasion of the tenth anniversary of a great man's death.

For this reason, we have decided to let this book take the form of a chronological narrative of Dr Weizmann's life. Its contributors are varied; as varied as were their experiences and the rôles they played in the dramatic story of Zionist fulfilment. They vary also in the degree of the closeness of their personal relationships with the subject of this book. In common they have their knowledge of him; the fact that they were spellbound in their different ways; and most profoundly impressed by him. It is Dr Weizmann's impact on each of these writers which essentially qualifies them to appear on these pages. None was chosen at random. All were involved in a specific period of Dr Weizmann's life; either directly and personally involved, or involved as experts of that long and exciting era during which the State of Israel was in the making.

Without question, the life of modern Israel is the real expression of Dr Weizmann's astonishing gift for creation. Perhaps more than any other statesman of our time, he succeeded in effecting an organic fusion between the abstractions of the mind and the practical activities demanded by man's physical existence. This fusion is reflected in the very core of life in Israel today. It is part of the flavour of Israel's politics, part of the cacophony of its unflagging discussions, of its intellectual posture, of its argumentativeness, of its addiction to theoretical formulæ and its adoration of dedication. In all these, one recognizes easily two major and familiar chords—the spiritual turbulence of pre-revolutionary Russia and, perfectly parallel with it, the basic values of Anglo-Saxon democracy.

Just as these were the twin paths along which Weizmann's political concept developed, with no disharmony or clash ever interrupting their growth—so Israel itself is an organic coalescence of both types of social organization.

I would not like to be misunderstood. There is much about contemporary Israel that Weizmann would certainly have disapproved of, or that in any case would have distressed him. He would have been affronted by the overwhelming preponderance of sectarian and partisan influence. He himself represented a Jewish nationalism that was always global; his dislike for dogma and narrow allegiances was deep-rooted and basic. He would have disliked everything in the State that is parochial, and everything that is most tolerant of expediency.

But the basic tenet of Weizmann's political and moral beliefs was his conviction that the character of a human being or, for that matter, of a nation, mattered more than anything else. In all his important statements, this theme reappears, implicitly or explicitly: 'What a man *is* means more in the long run than what he *does*. The same is true of Nations.' And I am sure that the essential character of the Jewish State, in 1962, towards which he contributed so much, consciously and unconsciously, would have been not only acceptable but cherished by him.

It was the qualitative character of this State which concerned him most during the last years of his life—those months when, exhausted and spent, he lay chained to his bed in the high room of his Rehovoth home overlooking the Judean hills he loved.

When I saw him then, shortly before he died, he talked about science, about freedom of inquiry, about the sacredness of work for its own sake, and not for the sake of some trivial reward. In his last moments, characteristically, his dual concern remained national morality and the universal scope of science. I had the feeling that through me he was pleading with the Jewish people not to abandon its prophetic values or its standards of morality.

Now it occurs to me that he never said *Israel* or *the Israelis*, that he spoke only of the Jewish people. This, too, was characteristic of his philosophy. To him, World Jewry and the Jewish State were an integral entity. The Jewish people, and not Israel's citizens alone, constituted the generating power that would make his vision a reality.

Weizmann always envisaged a coalescence of the best minds and heart of Israel and the Diaspora in the joint striving of the Jewish people as a whole for self-realization. He never believed in the existence of any profound or insurmountable dividing line between Israel and the Diaspora.

To him both Israel and the Diaspora were expressions of the Jewish personality. Israel had, after all, been established to redress the imbalance of the Jewish community as a whole. Once established, it was to enable the Jews, as a group, to live in inner harmony. Fundamentally, Zionism represented a synthesis of the creative energies of the entire Jewish people. These energies were to function harmoniously both in the one centre where Jews controlled their own fortunes directly and in the numerous centres outside Israel where Jews were bound to remain subject to Diaspora influences. In Weizmann's view these different centres, both within Israel and beyond its borders, would inevitably be linked by bonds of the deepest emotional and intellectual identification.

This was the reason for his overriding concern with the launching of intellectual life in Israel along the proper lines. It goes without saying that the creation of an economically viable community had a certain fateful priority. But this was only on the economic plane. A viable economy was a meaningless phrase to him if it did not represent a community with high spiritual standards. And that *community*, that feeling of creative mutual kinship, could have only a spiritual and intellectual basis.

He saw a cultural life, in the broadest sense, as a vital prerequisite for the fertile expression of the creative energies of rejuvenated Jewry. And the cultural foundation had to be well and truly laid. It had to underlie the conjunction—and ultimately the fusion—of the activities of both Israel and the Diaspora that alone could lend historic significance and contemporary effectiveness to the State of Israel.

Weizmann had a profound faith in the possibility—indeed, the indispensability—of a close interaction between the Jews in Israel and outside. Hence his constant preoccupation with the establishment of basic cultural institutions in Israel. His interest in them was never that of a mere man of learning, of a high-brow (as has occasionally been maintained). No whim or foible or fantasy made him ascribe a rôle of paramount consequence to institutions of learning. He was guided by his unwavering conviction that only through the development of the characteristic Jewish contribution to civilization —which may be summed up as mind plus feeling—could Israel in the long run survive at all. And only thus would its survival have historical value.

This conviction stands out as another instance of that fusion, so marked within him, of traditional Jewish values and the accumulated knowledge of Western civilization—science in the broadest sense of the term.

As a realist, Weizmann by no means underestimated the practical aspects of Israeli-Diaspora relations. He respected money, but he never equated it with wisdom. Until his last breath he felt that Israel must return to the concepts of classical Zionism—the unity, the indivisibility of the Jewish people, once again predominantly in the spiritual sense.

But he recognized no conflict between the spiritual and the practical. On the contrary: he always believed that a purely material partnership, with no moral basis, was inherently ephemeral.

The quintessence of Weizmann's feelings about the Jewish people was perhaps best expressed by himself in February 1949, in his opening address to the first Knesseth in Jerusalem.

'Having taken part in the great battles of the human spirit, having shed our blood for the liberation of many peoples, we have finally won the right to toil and labour in order to give expression to our distinct national identity, and to make our contribution to the spiritual treasure of the world. Let us strive to strengthen among us the constructive resources of science and research, which are the basis of human achievement. Yet, for all the decisive importance of science, it is not by science alone that we shall win through. Let us build a new bridge between science and the spirit of man. "Where there is no vision the people perish." We have seen what scientific progress leads to when it is not inspired by moral vision. . . . All my life I have laboured to make science and research the basis of our national endeavour. But I have always known full well that there are values higher than science, the only values that offer healing for the ills of humanity—the supreme values of justice and righteousness, peace and love.'

It is this thought that should be kept in mind by the reader as the *leitmotif*, so to speak, of the book that follows.

Mr Meyer W. Weisgal, publicist and editor, is the head of the Weizmann Institute of Science in Israel.

1874–1952

CHAPTER ONE

THE BIOGRAPHICAL FACTS

ISAIAH BERLIN

CHAIM WEIZMANN was born, according to his own account on 17 November[2] 1874 (8th Kislev, 5635) in the small town of Motol in the district (Ouyezd) of Kobrin in the Department (Guberniya) of Grodno in Western Russia, on the borders of the kingdom of Poland, the third child of Ezer, son of Chaim Weizmann (also known as Fialkov) from the village of Serniki, and of Rachel Leah, daughter of Michael Tchemerinsky, a tenant of the Counts Skirmunt who kept an inn in Motol. Ezer Weizmann was born into a Jewish family typical of the Russian Pale of Settlement in the nineteenth century. His own father Chaim was a man of small means, but, as was usual among the Jews of Eastern Europe, any child who showed the slightest capacity for Jewish learning was vigorously encouraged to pursue it. Educational possibilities were limited in the village of Serniki, and the neighbouring townlet of Motol offered somewhat wider opportunities. As was the custom at that time, the boy Ezer Weizmann came with a recommendation to the relatively prosperous Tchemerinsky. Soon after his arrival, his host's daughter, Rachel Leah, fell in love with him and the marriage was easily arranged, Ezer being then sixteen years of age, his bride a little under fourteen. Fifteen children were born to them in the course of the following twenty-two years, of whom three died in infancy; the rest for the most part survived to old age. In order to earn a living, Ezer Weizmann, after trying other forms of business, became what among the Yiddish-speaking Jews of those days was known as a 'transportierer' —that is to say, a timber merchant, responsible for assembling and

[1] This biography was, in the first place, commissioned by the *Encyclopaedia Hebraica* of Jerusalem, and constitutes the English original of the Hebrew version due to appear in that work. The author would like to take this opportunity of thanking Mr Boris Guriel, Mr Harry Sacher, Mr Israel Sieff, Mr Leonard Stein, Mr Robert Weltsch and Mrs Vera Weizmann, to whom he submitted his original draft, for corrections and valuable suggestions.

[2] According to his British passport 27 November. His Russian school-leaving certificate gives the date as 12 November 1873.

floating rafts of logs to and along the Vistula to its mouth in Danzig, where it was sawn and whence it was duly exported.

Despite his strictly orthodox upbringing, Ezer Weizmann had been touched by the modernist tendencies then alive among the Russian and Polish Jews. Western enlightenment had begun to seep into the Russian empire in the eighteenth century; stimulated by a sense of backwardness vis à vis the West and by wounded national pride, it led to a sporadic and unbalanced, but spectacularly rapid, development of Russian culture, which by the middle of the nineteenth century had begun to penetrate even the large insulated enclave within which Eastern European Jews lived their traditional, semi-mediæval lives. The liberal reforms instituted by Tsar Alexander II (1856-81), had raised the hopes of the Jews, as of other oppressed minorities in the Empire, that the ancient obstacles which stood in the way of any modification of their social, economic and political condition might be crumbling at last. The desire for democracy and national self-determination, especially among the subject nations in the Austrian Empire, which culminated in the European revolutions of 1848-49, did much to bring home to individual Jews in the West the full anomaly of their own ambivalent status, and in due course this awareness affected the more sensitive and educated among the Russian Jews also. Men like Peretz Smolenskin, Yehuda Leib Gordon and others raised the banner of Jewish nationality. They boldly began to use Hebrew, hitherto confined to purely sacred purposes, as a vehicle for secular literature; they wrote poems, essays, pamphlets, in which they called upon their brothers to break out of the frozen religious establishment which cramped their reason and petrified their feeling, yet avoid the other, even more humiliating and equally fatal extreme, the effort to shed their Jewish characteristics and forget themselves in the surrounding Russian culture, to achieve 'assimilation' to a foreign way of life by deliberately suppressing everything that was their own. They called for a Jewish cultural renaissance by a deliberate policy of reviving the national language and national tradition, the sense of national and historical identity, in a spirit, though they may not have known it, similar to that which, earlier in the century, had animated patriotic historians and scholars in Germany, Italy, Bohemia, Hungary and other nationalities long ruled by men of alien language and culture. Other Jewish writers went further still: Lilienblum and Pinsker had independently reached the conclusion that a Jewish national rebirth, without which the Jews were doomed to an ignoble decadence, could not take place without a territorial base. Pinsker said that the Jews were but the spectre of a murdered nation, haunting the living, causing everywhere uneasiness, fear and hatred; it would not be laid until the homeless wanderers acquired a land of their own, whether it be in Palestine or elsewhere. Lilienblum preached that historical memories could not be altered; for good or ill, every man had but one set of parents and could not exchange them for better ones: Palestine was the land to which the Jews were attached by every fibre of their spiritual being, thither they must go to create an independent life upon a soil of their own.

These early nationalists had few converts among the Jews of Russia, but they had some. A thaw had finally set in the great Jewish glacier of Eastern Europe. While the majority remained immovable and insulated in the ice of the ancient tradition, a minority had begun to drift off; some into assimilation or semi-assimilation, fed by liberal hopes of the growth of enlightenment whereby the Jewish inhabitants of Russia would gradually be emancipated and treated as fellow-citizens by the dominant nationality. Others put their hopes in socialism which, by ending class war, would cure all forms of social injustice; since the Jewish problem was but a patholo- gical form of general social abnormality, it would automatically be solved in the revolutionary transformation of society: those who believed this tended to join or support clandestine revolutionary movements. Still others looked for a more immediate answer in immigration to America and other countries where Jews could live in freedom, dignity and peace. But there was a handful of men who, moved by the wave of national feeling then rising to a new height in Europe, obstinately believed in a Jewish culture and a Jewish national existence, whether as an independent nation on a land of its own, or as a unit in a free federation of nationalities within a multi-national empire. Finally, there were those—of necessity the majority—who did not think a great deal, but remained absorbed in the immediate problems of physical survival in a violently hostile world. There were, of course, many combinations and blends of all these attitudes and views.

Ezer Weizmann was one of the few who inclined towards the nationalist solution. He read the 'forbidden' modern tracts written by the *Maskilim*,[1] and educated his growing family in this spirit. The period was one of great cultural ferment among the Russian Jews. Poets, painters and musicians of original gifts, scholars and scientists, lawyers and historians, revolutionary socialists and national leaders grew up in this *milieu*—the names of Soutine and Pasternak, Dub- now and Bialik, Trotsky and Martov, Vinaver and Berenson, will

[1] A group of nineteenth-century writers both in Hebrew and Yiddish en- gaged in spreading secular culture among the Jews of Russia and Poland.

serve to indicate the variety of gifts and of social and cultural patterns. It was in this rapidly altering, transitional phase—between the end of one tradition and the beginning of another—that Chaim Weizmann grew to manhood. He received an orthodox Jewish upbringing. At the age of three he was taken into his house by his maternal grandfather Tchemerinsky, who, so he is said to have recalled in his old age, told the child stories of the humiliations inflicted upon his own father and grandfather in the early part of the century by wild and tipsy Polish magnates. The boy was taught the rudiments of the Bible by a typical *melamed*[1] of the town, Zvi Bloch-Blumenfeld; he was followed by Shlomo Sokolovsky—the boy's teacher until he was sent to school in the neighbouring city of Pinsk. A letter by Weizmann is still preserved, written in 1885 (occasioned perhaps by the death in that year of Sir Moses Montefiore, the well-known Anglo-Jewish philanthropist an oleograph of whose head was to be seen in many houses in Eastern Europe) in which the eleven-year-old boy says that the kings and nations of the world are plainly set upon the ruin of the Jewish nation; the Jews must not let themselves be destroyed; England alone may help them to return and rise again in their ancient land of Palestine.

Weizmann showed ability from the beginning. He did well at the *Realschule* in Pinsk. The science master of the school noticed the exceptionally intelligent and bright boy, took him under his wing and induced him to specialize in chemistry. Ezer Weizmann never achieved prosperity, and the boy added to his meagre means by giving private lessons to the children of the more prosperous Jews of the town. In return for board and lodging he taught the brothers Saul and Ovsei Lourié, sons of the prosperous owner of a chemical factory in the city, and they and their friends and relations, Georg (Gad) Halpern, Isaac Naiditch, Judah L. Berger and others, became his lifelong friends and allies. He divided his time between his chemical and Hebrew studies, the latter under Shlomo Vilkomir in Pinsk and Abraham Motolyanski in Motol. In 1895 his entire family moved to Pinsk. Three years before this, Weizmann matriculated; he obtained the highest marks in every subject, save drawing. His contemporaries at this time recall him as combining luminous intelligence and uncommon capacity for thorough and continuous work, with a strength of character, vitality, gaiety and a biting wit which gave him an easy ascendancy over his milieu. The natural course for a brilliant Jewish schoolboy was to try to enter a Russian university. Under the *numerus clausus* then in operation, few of the Jews who passed the required examinations were admitted: they were not to

[1] Teacher of sacred writings.

exceed 10.5 per cent of the student body in the provincial Russian universities, or 3 per cent in the universities of Petersburg and Moscow.

National feeling was strong among Jewish students at this time. The great pogroms of 1881 which followed the assassination of Alexander II, and were a mere prelude to a general intensification of anti-Semitism both in official circles and the popular press, greatly stiffened the resistance to russification on the part of the prouder and more sensitive among the educated Jews in the Empire. Mass emigration to America, the creation of agricultural settlements by the Khovevei-Zion[1] in Palestine (later supported and augmented by Baron Edmond de Rothschild from Paris), clandestine revolutionary agitation, terrorist activity—all these were characteristic reactions of a national minority to the open repression practised by the Russian Government. In later years Weizmann spoke with bitter feeling of his own experiences at the hands of the Tsarist police. Whether from national pride, or because the natural sciences were far better taught in the West, he decided to go to Germany. The family was not well off, and he declined to take more than a minimum from his father. In 1892 he travelled on one of his father's rafts to East Prussia, stayed three nights in the city of Thorn, arrived in Darmstadt and enrolled as a student in the local Polytechnic. In order to supplement his means, he taught Russian in a Jewish school in the neighbouring town of Pfungstadt, kept by a Dr Barness. His memories of this establishment—a mixture, as it seemed to him, of pedantry, patriotic conformism and hypocrisy, permanently coloured his view of a certain section of German Jewry. The daily journeys between Pfungstadt and Darmstadt, followed by giving private lessons in the evenings, proved too exhausting. After two terms, in 1893 he moved to Berlin and continued as a biochemist in the Institute of Technology (Technische Hochschule) in Charlottenburg.

Berlin at this time was a nursery of future Zionist leaders, as, half a century before, it had been of the Russian liberal intelligentsia. Weizmann here found himself in the midst of a lively circle of Russian Jewish students, bent on resisting Jewish 'assimilationism' both socialist or liberal. His friends included Leo Motzkin, Isidor Elyashov (who wrote under the name of Baal Makhshoves), Victor Yakobson, Nachman Syrkin, Selig Soskin, Judah Vilensky, and other young intellectuals—Zionists before the term had come into existence. The dominant influence on these young men for some years

[1] The 'Lovers of Zion' movement constitutes the immediate pre-history of Zionism: it was inspired by an ideal of an autonomous Jewish culture rooted in a territorial centre in Palestine, and owed a good deal to Russian populism and Mazzinian nationalism.

was the teaching of the most celebrated of all the ideologists of the Jewish national revival, Asher Ginsberg, who wrote under the name of Ahad Ha'am. This thinker, whose ideas were closely related to those of 'Lovers of Zion', preached that the sporadic creation of small colonies in Palestine by town dwellers turned farmers, noble as their motives were, would prove of small account unless it sprang from, and gave concrete expression to, a spiritual regeneration which the invention of new institutions could not by itself create, a state of spirit which each individual must effect within himself. Unless the dry bones of traditional Judaism were covered with living flesh again, Judaism would not recover a sense of its past, of its place among the nations, and especially of the meaning and purpose of its unexampled martyrdom during the centuries of the Dispersion. The principal task—even more important than the return to the ancient homeland—was psychological self-emancipation, a new realization of the values for the sake of which alone Jews had lived and died, of what alone constituted their unique contribution to human culture, of which the highest was the idea of justice. In a series of essays which made a profound impression on founders of modern Jewish nationalism, Ahad Ha'am stressed over and over again that colonization or other forms of social and political action would prove abortive unless they were animated by a historically rooted, specifically Jewish, vision of what men were and could and should be. This vision could be incarnated only in a spiritual centre built in Palestine, the only authentic soil in which Jewish culture could achieve a new birth.

In 1896 a Viennese journalist, Theodor Herzl, who had been a correspondent of the *Neue Freie Presse* in Paris, burst upon a startled world his *Judenstaat*—a fiery pamphlet demanding the creation of a Jewish state by political action—public recognition by the great powers of the claims and rights of the homeless Jewish nation. The Dreyfus case had destroyed a good many optimistic delusions about the condition and prospects of the Jews, and led to their radical reappraisal. The book was acclaimed and assailed with equal passion: Herzl was looked up to as an inspired prophet and denounced as a mad and dangerous demagogue.

The little Russo-Jewish colony in Berlin, of which Weizmann was a member, had in fact accepted Herzl's basic propositions before he had advanced them; they had a deeper understanding than Herzl himself of the Jewish cultural tradition and the part it must play in the kind of political transformation for which he was calling. They were not as sceptical or as gradualist as Ahad Ha'am, who declared that one institution of higher learning in Palestine,

irradiating the Jewish Diaspora, was of greater value than ten agricultural settlements, but neither did they, like Herzl, believe in
the possibility of creating a Jewish State or colony by the dramatic
intervention of saviours from without—the Kaiser, or the Sultan, or
the Prince of Wales or the British Parliament—or by drastic political
acts, bold and spectacular diplomatic activity by Jewish 'notables'
or groups or parties. They accused Herzl of a purely visionary faith
in the possibility of a miraculous transformation overnight of the old,
withered Jewish nation into a young and beautiful political state by
the mere waving of a magic wand by emperors or millionaires. They
insisted on the slow and painful but, as it seemed to them, indispensable process of education and cultural work. The fact that
Herzl was an exotic figure, remote from the pious Jews of Eastern
Europe, coming to them like a Messiah from another world, raised
high above the heads of his followers, indeed his very appearance
and voice and bearing, created a wave of exalted emotion amongst
the Jewish masses. Weizmann and his friends, ironical and sophisti-
cated as they were, despite their reservations welcomed Herzl's
campaign and central ideas with enthusiasm. When in 1898
Weizmann migrated from Berlin to the University of Fribourg in
Switzerland, he, like his Berlin friends, was a convinced Herzlian
Zionist.

Weizmann did not attend the first Zionist Congress in Basle in
1897. He was at this time plunged in his chemical researches, and
had indeed made a valuable industrial discovery (for which he took
out a patent that enabled him to continue with his work). But the
main reason for his failure to go was most probably his poverty; his
father is reported to have offered him his fare to Basle, but his own
circumstances were such that his son could not bring himself to
accept this sacrifice. In 1898 he attended the Second Zionist Congress as a delegate. In January 1899 he obtained his doctorate in
Fribourg with two short chemical dissertations. He sold yet another
invention to the great German chemical firm of Bayer, and felt
financially a little more at ease. In 1901 he went to Geneva where he
became assistant to Professor Bystrzycki, then a demonstrator in
Professor Karl Graebe's laboratory.

His life was, as before, divided between science and Zionist
activity. He was in constant correspondence with his friends Leo
Motzkin, Shmarya Levin, Esther Shneyerson, Berthold Feiwel,
Martin Buber, Victor Yakobson, Abraham Idelson, Joshua Buch-
mihl, Sofia Getzeva, Zvi Aberson and many others. He recognized
Herzl as his leader, but had strong doubts about the possibility of
achieving a Jewish state or autonomous region by a *fiat* 'from

above', by a political act of recognition solemnly entered into by the great Powers, or by a Charter on the lines of those of the East India or South Africa companies. He distrusted any political short cut which omitted or played down the need for a mass movement from below, and insisted on the need for the growth, necessarily gradual, of a widespread consciousness among the Jewish masses of their needs and capacities for collective action, in the first place for practical work in creating an agricultural and industrial base in Palestine itself. Unless this was done the granting of constitutions or the establishment of a political entity would, in the view of Weizmann and his friends, remain mere empty shells, which would merely expose Jewish inability to make use of them, and so tragically demonstrate their unreadiness to establish an independent community. Weizmann did not minimize the need for political action: but the tension between the essentially political Herzl (and later for similar reasons, Jabotinsky) who believed in the primacy of action on an international scale and the creation of public institutions for the Jewish people, as against those who emphasized the need to develop Jewish social, economic and cultural activities, especially of agriculture and education, as a base on which alone a political structure could be built—action for the people versus action by the people—remained a constant source of difference between Weizmann and the Herzlians. There were differences of temperament too. With their ironical, somewhat irreverent attitude, Weizmann and his friends tended to question the value of Herzl's passionate insistence on forms and ceremony in the conduct of the movement. Congresses conducted with appropriate solemnity and discipline, the lofty style in which Herzl spoke and addressed sovereigns and nations—these were his antidotes to the squalor and *Schlamperei*, the chaos, self-contempt and lack of dignity in Jewish life. Later Weizmann himself attached much importance to this, although at heart he remained incurably democratic and addicted to informal methods and habits. Herzl to him remained always a man of dazzling genius, a prophet consumed by a vision, but a figure who bound his spell on his fellows from a distance, a civilized Westerner out of touch with the temper and outlook and feelings of the Jewish masses of which Weizmann all his life retained an instinctive understanding.

In 1901 at a meeting in Basle, before the Fifth Zionist Congress, he and his friends, Zvi Aberson, Martin Buber, Berthold Feiwel, Leo Motzkin and Kogan Bernstein, created the 'Democratic Fraction' within the Zionist movement. This was to be a 'loyal opposition'. Its members believed in responsiveness to the moods of the masses, emphasis on the cultural, educational and colonizing activity; they were sceptical about the effectiveness of *élites* of dedicated leaders engaged in negotiating with European statesmen high over the heads of the people itself; they believed in empiricism, disbelieved in general principles and final solutions, distrusted all forms of rigidity and fanaticism, and wished to keep equally clear of rabbinical traditionalism on the one hand, and of purely secular and western political forms on the other.

Since this was his general approach, it is not, perhaps, surprising that Weizmann, like Ahad Ha'am, conceived a profound admiration for England, as the home of slowly growing constitutional liberties, of respect for tradition and precedent, of capacity for practical action, of adaptability, moderation and instinctive realism, as against the metaphysical romanticism of the Germans, or the addiction to absolute principles and abstract ideas of the French. Weizmann's outlook became formed early in his life, and its fundamentals never seriously altered. For him Judaism was not solely a religion or a culture or a race, but a nation; a unique compound of common civilization and common historical memories, in which the religious and the secular were inextricably interwoven, of common language, outlook and racial kinship, which it was misleading to classify in terms of criteria intended to fit modern, territorially defined nations. He believed in Jewish nationhood all the more easily because the Jewish community from which he himself sprang was, by historical circumstance, geographically welded together into a culturally and ethnically distinct group, inhabiting a more or less continuous area in Western and Southern Russia, in which it formed a self-conscious national minority, forcibly made aware of its sharp differences from the surrounding Russian and Polish populations. He believed, moreover, that to deny this fact—to believe, as some highly intelligent Western Jews were inclined to do, that the Jews were or could collectively become entirely and utterly German, French, English, different from their fellow-citizens only in religious belief, as the Protestants, say, differed from Catholics, or Quakers from Anglicans, was a profound and fatal illusion which the rest of the world did not entertain, and from which, from time to time, it brutally awoke the Jews by treating them as a foreign body—whether with conscious toleration born of liberal principles, or with indifference, or with fear or hatred (to which, as Pinsker had pointed out, nationally self-conscious, civilized nations were even more prone than less self-conscious, barbarous ones) that took the form of persecution and occasional massacre. Zionism for Weizmann as for Herzl meant the need for a conscious effort on the part of the Jews to become aware of their situation and act accordingly, that is to say, cease to

struggle against their historically conditioned national personality
(which was not, in itself, either superior or inferior to any other), but
was what it was and not another thing; for unless they were allowed
to live and think as Jews in the only conditions in which this was
possible—as a free nation settled on its own territory, they would
continue to poison their own lives and those of others, as all those
must who live a conscious or unconscious lie. He accepted the fact that
some dramatic act was needed to make a sufficient impact upon both
Jews and Gentiles to set up the process of emancipation. Herzl, in
his view, partly because he was brought up outside traditional
Judaism and did not therefore appreciate the violent psychological
resistance to his ideas that the spiritual 'alienation' of the Jews
would generate, alone possessed the burning, single-minded vision,
unhampered by too much worldly realism, to administer the required shock capable of rousing the people from the fantasies that it
took for reality or even happiness; at the same time, this act was not,
by itself, enough; unless the Jewish nation, or a large portion of it,
understood the causes of its predicament, the plethora of ineffective
remedies that were constantly offered it from all quarters—Messianic
faith, self-protective separatism, the march of enlightenment, socialism, revolutionary or evolutionary, liberal internationalism, assimilation and so forth, would continue to distract it. He did not, like the
Marxists, believe that the revolutionary transformation of social or
economic conditions, even if it was feasible, would of itself solve the
Jewish question. He thought this too crude an approach to a problem that was at least as much psychological and historical as socio-
logical or economic. He was not an irrationalist. In his scientific
activity as in his life he believed in the power of reason, knowledge,
understanding, judgment, practice founded on observation and
good sense; but with Ahad Ha'am, he believed that a nation can
only be led along its own historical path of development, in line with
the outlook and values which spring from its own unique tradition,
ways of life, sacred books and historical experience. In this respect
his views were close to those of the leaders of other oppressed national
groups in Europe, especially to the ideas and temper of those democratic nationalists who had fought for Italian, Polish and Southern
Slav liberty in the nineteenth century.

Switzerland at this time contained a good many students from the
Russian Empire unable or unwilling to be educated in the universities of the Tsarist regime. The majority of these were Jews, to whom
the doors of Russian universities were all but closed. The leaders of
the young Russian Social Democratic party—men like Plekhanov,
Lenin, Martov, Helphand—and particularly of its Jewish Bundist

section, looked for recruits among the radical Russian Jewish students in Western universities. So, too, did the Zionists. Fierce disputes broke out between these rival fishers of souls both in private and in public. There is good evidence that Weizmann was involved in a public debate with the most brilliant of all the Russian socialists, Plekhanov; it is less likely that he met either Lenin or Trotsky. His principal opponents were the Jewish Socialists of the Bund, Medem and others, who had opposed Herzl, and with whom Weizmann came into conflict in Geneva, Berne and elsewhere. All his energies at this time went into the creation of groups of Zionist students and their sympathizers in Switzerland, Germany and neighbouring lands. Herzl was the inspired leader, seeking interviews with the Kaiser and the Sultan, in an endless effort to obtain internationally recognized rights for the Jews to create a national home in the Turkish province of Palestine. Weizmann and his friends were mainly concerned with creating cadres of young men who would speak in their own language to Jews everywhere, but particularly in Eastern Europe whence the immigrants would surely come.

In 1903 public recognition at last came to the Zionist movement. The British Foreign Office, whose head was Lord Lansdowne, made a tentative approach to the Zionist leaders in England with regard to the Jewish colonization of a portion of the East African Protectorate in the territory of Guas Nigishu-Platan, 5,000 square miles in extent. This proposal, the initiative for which came from the British Colonial Secretary, Joseph Chamberlain, was for the Zionists a cardinal event. It was the first time that the Jews had been recognized as a national entity by a great sovereign state—indeed, the most powerful in the Western world. Earlier efforts to obtain a territory—in British Cyprus, or in El-Arish in the Sinai Peninsula, to which the Turks could offer less resistance—had come to nothing.

The Zionist movement was upset and excited. The proposed territory, commonly, if incorrectly, referred to as Uganda, was not Palestine; but it was a concrete offer. A great debate broke out at the Zionist Congress. Herzl was inclined to accept the proposal as at any rate the first stage in the great Return. Others, for the most part Russian Zionists, were dead against this scheme: Zionism without Zion had no meaning for them. It was to be brought back to Zion that Jews prayed thrice daily. It was only Jerusalem that could create and justify the vast uprooting that the new life involved. At first Weizmann vacillated; his father, himself a delegate to the Congress, voted for accepting the British offer; the Russian delegation, like the others, was divided. In the end Weizmann came down decisively on the side of the anti-Ugandists: it must be Zion or nothing. Herzl had not originally specified the territory in which the state was to be founded: Palestine was the goal: but perhaps East Africa would provide the beginning of statehood—a *Nachtasyl* as Nordau had called it—on the road to Zion. When the delegates from Kishinev, where in the previous year the worst of all Jewish pogroms had broken out, voted against Uganda, Herzl realized what Zionism meant to most of his European followers: 'These people have ropes round their necks, and yet they refuse!' he said. He understood the point of view of Ussishkin and the other intransigents who wanted no temporary solutions nor the slightest deviation from the road that led to Palestine alone, and ceased to press for the acceptance of the miraculous British offer.

In 1904 Herzl died. The movement chose as its head his follower, David Wolffssohn, a Cologne banker of Russian origin, an honourable and devoted but somewhat colourless figure. Weizmann and his followers had, since 1899, turned their attention towards such unpolitical tasks as the organization of a bank to finance colonization into Palestine; propaganda and education, principally among young Russian-Jewish intellectuals; and, more particularly (since 1902) to the foundation of a Jewish university, to act as a national centre of Jewish culture, learning and education. Weizmann wished to create it in Jerusalem; but was prepared to compromise and set it up elsewhere, if the Turkish authorities proved too obdurately hostile. In 1906 he married Vera Chatzmann, a medical student from Rostov on the Don in Russia, whom he had met in Geneva, and with whom he had shared his hopes and anxieties since 1901. His work as a biochemist occupied most of his time. In Geneva the prospect of academic advancement seemed dim. When a post in the University of Manchester fell vacant, he applied for it, and was appointed. He was attracted by the prospect of life in England. His anglophile feeling became a central strand in his life and was destined to play a major part in his triumphs and defeats. His wife took a second medical examination in England in order to qualify to practise as a health officer of the Manchester municipality. At the time of his arrival in England he was thirty years old. For the next ten years he was to be a prominent, but not central figure in the Zionist movement. He was out of sympathy with the faithful Herzlians who still dominated it: he did not belittle the importance of public diplomacy: but he believed that practical work in Palestine and the education of the Jews in the Diaspora mattered more. He found some degree of moral compensation for his political frustration, then and in later years, in the laboratory: scientific papers flowed from his pen in a steady stream. In Manchester he met and deeply influenced young men with Zionist inclinations who were destined to play a part in Zionist history—Simon Marks, Israel Sieff, Harry Sacher (then on the staff of the *Manchester Guardian*), and their friends and allies in London, notably Leon Simon, Samuel Landman and Leonard Stein with whom he was to collaborate fruitfully in later years.

The aftermath of the abortive Russian revolution of 1905 led to a new wave of pogroms in Russia which sent several thousand new Jewish immigrants to Palestine. Weizmann continued on his middle path: political pressure must continue, but unless it was backed by a constant effort of colonization, it would not avail. 'If the Governments give us a Charter today,' he argued at the Eighth Congress held in the Hague in 1907, 'it will be a scrap of paper. Not so if we work in Palestine; then it will be written and indissolubly cemented with our blood.'[1] This doctrine—the chemical mixture of 'political' and 'practical' Zionism—came to be called 'synthetic Zionism'. Not all his friends accepted it. Motzkin aligned himself with the more purely political followers of Wolffsohn. Hot debates broke out between the factions.

In the same year, shortly after the birth of his eldest son Benjamin,[2] Weizmann visited Palestine for the first time, and returned more convinced than ever of the importance of practical work as against purely diplomatic pressure upon the governments of Europe. These governments did not respond; the Turks proved deaf to all Zionist blandishments; hopes revived after the Young Turk revolution, but the successors of Abdul Hamid proved even more suspicious and unwelcoming than the old tyrant. The British government seemed to have lost interest in Zionist aspirations. Neither Germany (despite Herzl's efforts to interest Kaiser Wilhelm II) nor France had shown real interest. The years immediately preceding the first World War remained an arid chapter in the history of Zionism. Many were discouraged. The mockery of the orthodox Jews to whom Zionism was a blasphemous attempt to forestall the Messiah, and the hostility of the cultivated and prosperous liberal Jews of the West, who looked on Zionism as a dangerous attempt to fire the Jews with an artificially fanned chauvinism likely to compromise their relations with their fellow-citizens of other faiths, harassed the Zionist movement on both flanks. By 1911 the sheer impotence of Zionist diplomacy finally won the 'practicals' a majority at the Tenth Zionist Congress. In this year Wolffsohn resigned from his office, which was put in the hands of a Commission headed by Professor Otto War-

[1] *Chaim Weizmann*, ed. P. Goodman (Gollancz, London, 1945), pp. 147-8.
[2] His second son Michael was born in 1915.

burg. This seemed to mark a *détente* between the two trends within Zionism. The powerful philanthropic Jewish bodies—the Anglo-Jewish Association, the Jewish Board of Deputies in England, the French *Alliance Israélite*, the *Centralverein* of the German Jews, the most influential American committees—shied violently from political Zionism.

In 1913 Weizmann was involved in a characteristic conflict with the *Hilfsverein* (of the German Jews) which had materially helped in the foundation and organization of the new Jewish Technical School in Haifa, which it financed. Led by Paul Nathan, the *Verein* wanted the language óf instruction in 'technical' subjects to be German; partly, perhaps, in order to strengthen German influence in the Middle East as against that of the French *Alliance*. Weizmann and his friends conceded that Hebrew did not as yet possess a technical vocabulary adequate for the natural sciences—therefore German might, in the beginning, have to be used; but maintained that to give German a status equal to that of Hebrew as the language of instruction would be fatal to the central purpose of the entire movement—the revival of Judaism as a modern civilization. A culture could only flourish through the medium of its own language; for thoughts and feelings and words are inextricably interwoven, and all languages but Hebrew were to some degree foreign importations, vehicles and symptoms of imitation and assimilation—the deadly enemies of Jewish survival. Among the leading Jews only Baron Edmond de Rothschild of Paris, defying the opinions of most of the rest of his family, showed no hostility to Zionism, and quietly and effectively continued to found and support colonies in Palestine. In later years he is said to have remarked that without him political Zionism might never have been born; but that without Zionism his work would have been dead.

Weizmann continued, under Professor William Perkin the younger, with his chemical work in Manchester and duly became University Reader in bio-chemistry. He felt that he deserved a higher post, but when the professorship fell vacant, he was passed over. Late in 1905 he met the British Prime Minister, Mr A. J. Balfour, in Manchester, and expounded Zionism to him. Balfour, a connoisseur of individuals and ideas, was impressed by the man even more than by his theses: at the time he thought the latter no more than interesting. He remembered the meeting in later years. The influence of his ideas upon English Zionists was not great; such prominent figures as Joseph Cowen and Leopold Greenberg (editor of the London *Jewish Chronicle*) were not impressed by Weizmann's central themes: that the Hebrew University, as he declared in Vienna in 1913, was to be the Jewish 'dreadnought', more powerful than the fortunes of the millionaires; or that to have industrial and agricultural workers in Palestine 'is for us the law and the prophets'. Élites of intellectuals and technical experts, he said over and over again, would not create a Jewish national home. In 1914 Wolffsohn died. The Zionist movement still had no President. Weizmann was now forty or forty-one years of age. His position in the Zionist movement was not a commanding one. He was a member of the Larger Actions Committee, a member and later president of the Standing Committee of the Congress, an acute and prominent critic of the Zionist establishment, and no more. The outbreak of the first World War transformed the situation.

When hostilities broke out, the Zionist Executive, located in Berlin, decided to send Nahum Sokolow to England: Weizmann was evidently not considered senior enough to take charge of the movement there. Occasionally Yekhiel Tchlenov visited London from Moscow for the same purpose. Nevertheless Weizmann, who felt at home in England and was encouraged by his friend and mentor Ahad Ha'am, decided to exploit the new situation independently. The English Zionists of whom he saw most, were Joseph Cowen, Herbert Bentwich, Moses Gaster (the Haham of the Spanish and Portuguese Jewish Congregation), Harry Sacher, James de Rothschild, Leon Simon, Dr Tolkovsky. The gifted, energetic and eloquent Vladimir Jabotinsky had also arrived in London, intent on forming a Jewish legion to fight on the Allied side; he was an intimate friend of Weizmann and for a time they shared a flat in Chelsea in London. In the autumn of 1914, at the house of a common Manchester friend, Mrs Eckhard, Weizmann met C. P. Scott, the editor of the great Liberal journal, the *Manchester Guardian*. Scott was a man of great political influence, a friend and adviser of cabinet ministers and in particular of David Lloyd George. The chance meeting with Scott proved a turning point in the history of the Zionist movement. Scott became a convert to Zionism and brought Weizmann and his ideas to the notice of prominent British politicians: in particular of Herbert Samuel and Lloyd George. Herbert Samuel, at that time head of the Local Government Board in Asquith's Liberal administration, and then, in succession, Postmaster General and Home Secretary in the same government, needed no convincing. He had, quite independently, conceived a warm sympathy for Zionism. Weizmann was greatly astonished to find a firm advocate of the idea of a full-fledged Jewish state in the British Cabinet—in a man, moreover, who by origin and upbringing, belonged to the Anglo-Jewish élite which was in general far from friendly to Zionism. Once the Turks had entered the war on the German side, the question of the disposal of the Ottoman empire became a matter of cardinal interest to the British Government. Early in the war Samuel addressed a memorandum to the Cabinet, advocating as one of the Allied war aims, the creation of a Jewish state in Palestine—the term was loosely used—after the defeat of the Turkish Empire. The Prime Minister, Herbert Asquith, records that he was somewhat surprised by so romantic a proposal from the 'well ordered and methodical brain of Herbert Samuel', and later remarked that evidently, as Disraeli had observed, 'race is everything'. He remained unimpressed and critical of the idea. Weizmann, mindful of his interview with Balfour ten years before, asked the Jewish philosopher, Professor Samuel Alexander, to reintroduce him to Balfour, and wrote to sound him out on Zionist aspirations. Balfour, not then in the Government, responded courteously: he said that Weizmann needed no introduction, since he remembered the earlier meeting, but did not commit himself. The proposal was, however, well received by the Foreign Secretary, Sir Edward Grey; Lloyd George approved from the beginning, on strategic as well as sentimental grounds. Samuel's proposal was consequently not discarded and engaged the intermittent attention of various British statesmen and officials during the first years of the war. At one point Grey sounded out the Russian and French Foreign Ministers along the lines of Samuel's memorandum; the Russians showed no interest; the French before 1917 remained equally non-committal. The indefatigable champion of the idea in the British Cabinet was Herbert Samuel throughout. Hope revived in Zionist circles that England was once more to be the champion of the Jewish cause—the sponsor of that public act to the promotion of which Herzl had sacrificed his life.

On the outbreak of war, Weizmann, in response to a Government circular, offered his discoveries in the field of fermentation to the British scientific authorities. He obtained no response. In 1916, when the prospects of war seemed dark for the Western allies, Weizmann's work was brought to the attention of the Brtish Government scientists by C. P. Scott and others. He was asked by Mr Winston Churchill, then First Lord of the Admiralty, whether he could provide a process that would yield acetone, a solvent needed for producing naval munitions. He successfully accomplished this task. His work with the Admiralty laboratories took him away from Manchester to London. It absorbed his entire time, with the result that he resigned his university post and a new phase in his life began.

His scientific achievement brought Weizmann to the notice of British government circles; and although his official position in the Zionist movement was still relatively subordinate, the singular force of his personality, and his ability to charm and impress eminent Englishmen whose outlook and style of life he found deeply attractive, helped to advance him to the foremost place in the ranks of Zionists in England. He had indeed no serious rivals there: Sokolov spent a good deal of time in France and Italy, countries with which he had a somewhat greater affinity; Tchlenov, Ussishkin and the other founding fathers of the movement found it difficult to leave Russia. The German Zionists stayed in their own country or in neutral states. Victor Yakobson was in distant Constantinople. The rise of England as the leading partner in the war-time alliance automatically lifted the relatively obscure Zionists of that country to a leading position, and Weizmann dominated them all by his political and diplomatic gifts and natural capacity for leadership. Lloyd George recalls that when he was asked what honour he desired as a reward for his scientific service to his adopted country, Weizmann replied that he wanted nothing for himself, only a country for his people. The story is probably apocryphal, and if the Balfour Declaration had no direct connection with Weizmann's scientific services, the mood in which the British offer was conceived clearly owed something to Weizmann's personal position in the eyes of more than one British statesman.

Late in 1916 Asquith resigned. Lloyd George became Premier, and Balfour Foreign Secretary: both had been strongly attracted by Zionist ideas; and in the meanwhile other forces were also at work. The desire to induce America to enter the war on their side was a major pre-occupation of the Western allies. American opinion on the war was divided, and among the pro-Germans and isolationists were to be counted prominent Jews; some among them were of German origin and emotionally inclined to German culture, others came from Russia and Poland, with bitter memories of Russian persecution, and were repelled by any form of alliance with the odious Tsarist regime. The support, or at any rate the neutralization, of American Jewish opinion was deemed of importance in Allied circles. The Russian Ambassador in Washington reported to his government that his French and British colleagues kept drawing his attention to the bad effect that the Russian treatment of her minorities was producing in America. The French government sent Victor Basch, a Jewish savant with Zionist sympathies, to attract American Jewish support. The notion that the American Jews might prove valuable allies, and that the British Zionists could engage their sympathies through their alliance with American Zionists, and especially with the influential Justice Brandeis, began to gain support in British political circles. Sir Mark Sykes, who had in December 1916 been appointed one of the

Under Secretaries of the newly formed British War Cabinet, had sought information about Zionism from Herbert Samuel's friend the Haham Moses Gaster. He met Weizmann at Gaster's house (possibly through the offices of a London Armenian called James Malcolm who later claimed to have effected the encounter). Sykes, a fervent and romantic Roman Catholic and an expert on the Middle East, who had recently concluded the secret agreement with the French about the post-war division of ex-Turkish territories (known as the Sykes-Picot Agreement), was fascinated by Zionism, and became one of its ardent advocates before the Cabinet; Weizmann and Sokolow, whom he had again met in Gaster's house, became his friends and allies. Lloyd George and Balfour were favourable, the Under-Secretary of Foreign Affairs, Lord Robert Cecil, had been earlier converted by Weizmann; so, by now, were Milner and Amery, into whose liberal imperialist dream (not altogether shared by Balfour) the prospect of a settlement of loyal anglophile Jews at a strategic point of the route to India wholly fitted. Rumours, by no means without foundation, that the Germans might forestall the Allies by arranging for a similar offer to be made to the Jews by the Turks, acted as an added stimulus to action. It was rumoured that the British Jews were against this proposal; feelers were put out among their leaders. For the most part, they were not unfriendly. One of the most prominent, Lord Rothschild, declared himself to be, like his younger brother Charles, a Zionist. His relative, James de Rothschild, an army officer, son of the Baron Edmond, had long been a supporter. Samuel, of course, supported the scheme vigorously, although, loyal to Asquith, he had resigned from the Government. But Zionism had violent enemies among the British Jews. Mr Edwin Montagu, soon to be Secretary for India, was outraged by the very idea of a Jewish nationality. It seemed to him to cast doubts on the rights of Jews to consider themselves full Englishmen; 'You are being misled by a foreigner,' he said to Lloyd George. Similar views were held by Claude Montefiore and other prominent members of the Anglo-Jewish establishment. There was hostility in corresponding circles in France. The idea was canvassed widely enough to stimulate a letter in *The Times* in the early summer of 1917, signed by D. L. Alexander and Claude Montefiore, the chairmen of the Conjoint Foreign Committee of the Jewish Board Deputies and the Anglo-Jewish Association, expressing hostility to the idea of a national Jewish entity in Palestine, on the grounds that it might involve the Jews in antagonism with the Arab natives of Palestine, and create the problem of divided allegiance for loyal Jews in the countries of which they are citizens. The principal figure behind this protest was Lucien Wolf, an old enemy of

Zionism. A reply to this letter appeared over the signature of Lord Rothschild; and although the original remonstrance may have affected the ultimate wording of the British Government's proposal (known as the Balfour Declaration) it was not sufficient to kill it. The draft of the proposal to invite the Jews to create a national home in Palestine went through many versions, and led to much conflict within and without the Jewish community. An almost equally controversial issue was that of the Jewish Legion: supported by Jabotinsky and Weizmann, it frightened not only anti-Zionist Jews, but Zionist leaders who feared its effect on the Jews of Turkey and Palestine and the Central Powers. There was much dispute and recrimination in the English Zionist Federation. Head of English Zionism as he had become, and at the height of his powers, with an ever-growing reputation and prestige, Weizmann felt that he was not obtaining the support that he deserved. He encountered, too, repeated obstacles in his work as an Admiralty scientist; he felt excessively frustrated; early in 1917 he wrote to Sokolov resigning his official post as the head of the English Zionist Federation. He thereupon received a letter from Ahad Ha'am telling him that he did not owe his unique position of moral and political leadership to formal election by any body of men; that there was therefore no one to whom he could properly resign; events, his own genius, but above all the historic goals and claims of the Jewish nation laid upon him a task and an obligation given to no other man in modern times; it was morally inconceivable that he should seek to leave his post. Weizmann remained. He was the unchallenged leader of the movement; he marshalled his forces, Jewish and Gentile, against the Jewish anti-Zionists; he was consulted at every turn by British politicians and officials who had begun to draft the document which was to become the Declaration, and worked diligently to give undivided rule over Palestine to England alone, since he feared divided rule such as was contemplated by the Sykes-Picot Agreement. Balfour was deeply impressed by the arguments of Brandeis during his visit to America, and he and Robert Cecil remained Weizmann's firmest allies within the British Cabinet; C. P. Scott was a tower of strength in the larger political world outside. Another factor may also have played a part in forcing a decision. In the autumn of 1917 the situation in Russia, both political and military, was, from the point of view of the Western Alliance, deteriorating rapidly. A move likely to increase sympathy for the Allies not only among American Jews, but among the five million Jews in the Russian Empire, was deemed valuable in London. Exchanges of drafts between Zionist leaders and the Cabinet draftsmen took place. Edwin Montagu, who had rejoined the Cabinet, fought hard against this policy, in part because as Secretary for India he feared its effect upon the Moslems under British rule.

In the midst of these concerns Weizmann was suddenly sent on an abortive sea voyage. In 1917 the elder Henry Morgenthau, who had recently ceased to be US Ambassador in Turkey, conceived a plan for inducing the Turks to make a separate peace. Since his scheme involved the possibility of Jewish settlement in Palestine, Weizmann was sent to Gibraltar by the British Government to confer with Morgenthau and Professor Felix Frankfurter as American representatives. The meeting in Gibraltar came to nothing; the Turks remained in the war, and the identification of Zionism with the Allied cause inevitably made the position of Palestinian and Turkish Jews perilous, and at times tragic. Meanwhile developments in the Zionist world rose to a climax. On 2 November 1917 a letter was finally published, addressed by Mr Balfour, as Foreign Secretary, to Lord Rothschild, declaring that 'His Majesty's Government view with favour the establishment in Palestine of a national home for the Jewish people.'[1] This cardinal act was universally regarded, though its architects were many, as a personal triumph for Weizmann. From that moment his position among the Jews, in virtue of the regard evidently paid him by the rulers and people of Great Britain, itself became dominant. It was to him that Sir Mark Sykes, emerging from the Cabinet meeting which had finally adopted the Balfour Declaration (a document largely drafted by Milner) announced the momentous news. His name became indissolubly linked with this, the greatest event in Jewish history since the destruction of Judaea. Hundreds of thousands of leaflets proclaiming the Declaration were showered upon the Jews in Germany, Austria–Hungary and, above all, Russia. Weizmann had formally welcomed the Revolution that had broken out in Russia, in March in the same year, explaining that it was not to persecution alone that Zionism looked for its chief stimulus, for it was a positive movement, and did not seek to thrive on injustice. The Bolshevik Revolution occurred five days after the publication of the Balfour Declaration; but the majority of the Jews in Russia who came to hear of it were, understandably, more deeply moved by the former event. Weizmann's mother, attending

[1] The relevant text runs as follows: 'His Majesty's Government view with favour the establishment in Palestine of a national home for the Jewish people, and will use their best endeavours to facilitate the establishment of this object, it being clearly understood that nothing shall be done which may prejudice the civil and religious rights of existing non-Jewish communities in Palestine, or the rights and political status enjoyed by Jews in any other country.'

a Zionist meeting in Russia, received an ovation, and was blessed as
one who had given birth to the Emancipator.

Weizmann's position had risen to new height, and he accepted the
power and prestige which he had gained, as his birthright. In a sense,
his rôle was anomalous. What Ahad Ha'am had said in the letter
mentioned above, was true enough: Weizmann had risen to his pre-
eminent position through no act of democratic selection. Some
among the other leaders, who had naturally looked upon themselves
as the duly appointed heads of the movement, looked with incredulity
not unmixed with a certain indignation on Weizmann's new and
undisputed status. He was not even a member of the Zionist executive. But his position, largely owing to his personal qualities, had
become unassailable. He had become clearly the greatest figure in
the public life of the Jews since the death of Herzl, and was recognized as such by Zionists and non-Zionists, Jews and Gentiles, from
the day on which he boldly linked the fortunes of the movement with
British policy. In 1918 he headed the Zionist Commission sent to
Palestine, then being conquered by Allenby's troops, to advise on the
future settlement, and effect the liaison between the Jews of Palestine
and the British authorities. Before he left he was received by King
George V, and came armed with high hopes. He had an affecting
meeting with his old friend Jabotinsky in Cairo, and then, flanked by
Majors James de Rothschild and William Ormsby Gore as British
liaison officers, and with some of his old Manchester friends[1] as
members of his Commission, he arrived in Palestine to be met with
scepticism and suspicion sometimes amounting to hostility on the part
of powerful figures among the British military representatives. The
conqueror of Palestine, Field Marshal Allenby, was himself not unsympathetic. The Jews in Palestine, after suffering indignities and persecution at the hands of the Turks, were nervous and bewildered. The
Arab and Christian communities were uncertain and suspicious. On
British advice Weizmann made his way to the other side of the Jordan
to meet the Emir Feisal, one of the leaders of the Arab revolt, son
of the Sherif Hussein of Mecca, to whom the British had made
promises of Arab independence. The Emir met him with gifts in the
desert, and in his camp near Akaba assured him of his sympathy.
In a letter written in January 1919, when they met in London, he
expressed the wish that Jews and Arabs should co-operate in the
development of Palestine and of the Arab States. He was later quoted
in the press as expressing the opposite sentiments. Later still, in a
letter sent to Professor Frankfurter during the Versailles Conference,
he returned to his original position: Jewish settlement, Feisal

[1] As well as representatives of other Allied Powers.

declared, was an expression of a national need, as the Arab movement also was, and not one of foreign colonization or imperialism; he would respect and welcome it; as in the earlier letter to Weizmann he rested his pledge on one condition that the pledges given him and his father by the Western powers were fully honoured. They were not. He was himself driven from the throne of Syria; his father and brother were expelled by Ibn Saud from Mecca and the Hedjaz; and although he became King of Iraq, he thenceforward regarded the original agreement and therefore, presumably also its pro-Zionist corollary, as having been rendered void by the treachery of the West. But all that still lay in the future.

In 1918, before the end of hostilities, Weizmann solemnly laid the foundation stone of the Hebrew university of Jerusalem, 'in order that the Jewish soul which had been hovering between heaven and earth might here find an earthly habitation' and so the words of the prophets might be fulfilled. The fate of the university henceforth became one of his deepest concerns: its career was a source of alternate pride and anxiety to him until the day of his death. He remained sober in the midst of triumph. In May 1917 he had said 'States must be built up slowly, gradually, systematically and patiently. We therefore say that the achievement of it [a Jewish Commonwealth] lies through a series of intermediary stages.' In an hour of joy and exultation in the entire Jewish world he dwelt on the difficult days to come. He said over and over again that only the people's own labour, slow, dedicated, organized, painful, not the inspiration of a moment, would create the framework of the Jewish national existence. The soil must be conquered by careful and agonizing effort; an unbelievable opportunity had been offered, and if the Jews of the world did not rise to it, the responsibility and shame would be theirs alone. There were dissentient voices. The veteran Max Nordau demanded mass immigration. He thought that for the Jews it was now or never; if they did not pour in in their hundreds of thousands, they would not again ever be offered the chance of fulfilment for their national needs. Jabotinsky, too, thought along similar lines. Weizmann did not think such forced marches feasible, and said so. From this moment the rift between him and those who demanded drastic political action and a swifter and more violent tempo, originally opened by the differences between his *Erfüllungspolitik* and the 'maximalism' of Herzl and his followers, began to widen. But Zionism was still united by the powerful opposition to it within Jewish ranks. In 1919 the Zionist Organization was invited to present its case to the Peace Conference at Versailles, before the Committee of Ten, composed for the most part of the Foreign Secretaries of the victorious Allies. Weizmann, Sokolov and Ussishkin spoke briefly before the Committee. A representative of the French Jews, Professor Sylvain Lévi, an eminent orientalist, also spoke, and echoed the fears of the anti-Zionists, including the British Jews represented in Paris by Lucien Wolf. Lévi spoke of Arab hostility, the dangers of divided allegiance among the Jews, and added a new point of his own about the possible effect of mass immigration into the Middle East by persons infected by the virus of revolutionary ideas from Eastern Europe. Weizmann could hardly contain himself: Lévi's words seemed to him a desecration. But the American representatives, Wilson, Lansing, House, remained no less favourable to Zionism than their British counterparts, who, by now, included Smuts as well as Lloyd George, Balfour and Milner. Lansing asked him what he meant by 'National Home'; he replied that it was hoped to 'build up gradually a nationality which would be as Jewish as the French nation was French, and the British nation British.' (This was later echoed by both Samuel and Balfour.) The Zionists won their case. Weizmann was duly congratulated by Balfour, and declined to accept Lévi's proferred hand, calling him a traitor to the Jewish cause. Lucien Wolf, in his turn, attempted to warn the allied negotiators, in particular Lloyd George, through his secretary Philip Kerr (later Lord Lothian) of the dangers of Zionism, but with little effect. The Mandate for Palestine, given by the League of Nations (in accordance with Zionist hopes and wishes) to Great Britain, incorporated significant portions of the original Balfour Declaration. The Jewish National Home, and the special status of the Zionist Organization in connection with it, had been recognized by 'public law'. Herzl's dream had to that degree been fulfilled. True, the Mandate did not speak of Jewish 'rights' to Palestine, only of 'historical connection'. This was a phrase probably inserted by Lord Curzon who succeeded Balfour as British Foreign Secretary; for (so Weizmann used to relate) he pointed out to him that while rights can be claimed, a connection cannot. 'The temperature of this Office has dropped considerably,' Weizmann recollected saying to him, 'since the time of your predecessor.'

Weizmann was now in undisputed control of the Zionist movement. He was the commander-in-chief in a war on two fronts: against opposition and indifference among the Jews and against opponents among Gentiles, principally in Britain and Palestine. His attitude towards the former remained unbending. He had said in an essay published during the war that 'the efforts of the emancipated Jew to assimilate himself to his surroundings . . . deceive nobody but himself'. From this he never moved, and he mocked and reviled those who disagreed. As for the latter, he had not long to wait. By 1920

Arab riots had broken out in Jerusalem. In 1921 Jabotinsky was arrested in Jaffa and placed in Acre prison. The local British administration could scarcely be described as co-operative or sympathetic, despite the appointment of Sir Herbert Samuel as First British High Commissioner.

At the Zionist Conference held in that year, differences between Weizmann and his allies began to take concrete form. Justice Louis Brandeis, the most eminent of the American Zionists, believed in the necessity for organized economic action to create a solid foundation for Jewish immigration and settlement in Palestine. He wanted a body vested with plenary powers for at any rate three years, backed by private, principally American, Jewish capital, capable of planning systematically, in order to avoid confusion and conflict. In the political field he opposed centralization: the national Zionist bodies were to form a loose federation, each autonomous in its own country: there was to be no world Zionist executive in supreme authority. Weizmann rejected both these policies. Despite his empiricism, his grasp of day-to-day material needs, his freedom from utopianism, he saw in these proposals a danger to the central principle of Zionism. The Jewish commonwealth must be built by the concerted efforts of the entire people; too much emphasis on private capital as against the public funds created by the Zionists—the Keren Kayemeth and the Keren Hayesod; too great a diminution in the power and status of the body representative of the national interest of the Jewish people—the Zionist Organization, and the great design would decline into philanthropy, mere economic activity, and lose its democratic nature and political ideal. His constant emphasis on the importance of the pioneers—*Chalutziuth*—sprang not merely from the natural tendency toward populism by which most Russian Zionists were affected to some degree, but from the belief that a community that is planned for by an élite of experts, however dedicated and efficient, cannot grow organically. He believed that a nation must build itself with all the errors and confusions that this may entail: things cannot, he maintained, be arranged from above: peoples cannot be developed like business enterprises or even colonies by the *fiat* of remote authorities elsewhere. Personal factors also played their part: Weizmann was not too tolerant of other leaders, and Brandeis was a great force; but more important was the genuine difference of principle and approach.

Weizmann's constant pleas for more cultural autonomy and more education did not spring from any explicit system of values in which intellectual interests dominated over others. He was not greatly interested in general ideas, nor, for all his love of music, in artistic activity as such. He was essentially not a theorist but an inventor and builder; he used opportunities as they came. But he possessed singular insight into the nature and value of intellectual and artistic creation, and an instinctive understanding of what makes societies and nations, in particular of the interplay between human and technological factors; and in virtue of this he became a states-man and negotiator of rare genius. Moreover, despite his under-standing and admiration for the West in which he had made his home, he remained to the end a native member of the Eastern European Jewish community, a Jew among Jews, who understood the Jewish masses, and in his own person thought, felt and suffered as they did, and knew out of his own experience what enhanced and what cramped their lives; and this alone gave him an incomparable advantage as a popular leader. He was a deeply impressive public speaker and a most fascinating talker, but not, like Nordau or Jabotinsky, a spell-binding orator; and tended, at times, to grow distant and self-absorbed. In politics he suffered neither fools nor equals gladly. He believed in his own judgment, he was bold, inde-pendent and, at times, deeply disdainful. Yet he remained a man of the people to the end, and was felt to be such by them—not a convert to their cause, nor a figure from another world who had stretched his hand to help the brothers from whom he was emotionally or socially remote.

In 1920 a Zionist Conference was held in London. It had revealed a widening gap between his position and the social and economic doctrines of the American decentralizers. At the American Zionist Convention held in Cleveland in the early summer of 1921, these differences led to an open breach. Brandeis, Frankfurter, Stephen Wise, Mack, Nathan Straus and others resigned. He was supported by a group of American Zionists led by Louis Lipsky, who defended him at the first post-war Zionist Congress, held in Carlsbad in Sep-tember 1921 where the 'American' position was argued by Julius Simon and de Lieme. 'Evidently there is no bridge between Pinsk and Washington,' Weizmann had remarked some months before at a meeting held during his first American visit. He found it difficult to share the direction of affairs with others; Brandeis thought him overbearing and politically ruthless. He had, during his Ameri-can tour, established links both with the American Jewish masses and with some of the financial leaders of American Jewry, over the heads of the Brandeisists. This stood him in good stead when he created the expanded Jewish Agency in 1929.

The Hebrew University had always been the apple of Weizmann's eye. He tried to attract to it the greatest intellectual luminaries among the Jews of the world. Einstein came, but left after a relatively short stay. Weizmann's relationship with Einstein, despite their deep mutual admiration for each other, remained ambivalent; Weizmann was inclined to regard Einstein as an unpractical idealist inclined to utopian attitudes in politics. Einstein, in his turn, looked on Weizmann as too much of a *Realpolitiker*, and was irritated by his failure to press for reforms in the university away from what he regarded as an undesirable American collegiate pattern. Nevertheless they remained allies and friends to the end of their lives. In particular Einstein supported Weizmann's efforts to attract men of first-rate scientific ability to Palestine.

There were periods in Weizmann's life when the pressure of public work caused him to abandon his scientific work. But he returned to it whenever he could, and sought and obtained much solace in it, particularly when obstacles made political activity difficult. He belonged to the optimistic tradition of the enlightenment in his belief that the application of scientific method to life was both inevitable and desirable, and threw the full weight of his authority and expertise behind the various industrial enterprises which rested on the application of scientific technology—Rutenberg's electric station, the potash works on the Dead Sea, experiments in his beloved settlements. It was under his inspiration that his old Manchester friends, the Sieff-Marks family, endowed a scientific institute in Rehovoth in Palestine, that was opened in 1934. This later grew into the Institute that bears Weizmann's own name; he attracted first-rate scientists to it, and personally guided it with characteristic breadth of vision. In it he spent what were, in his own view, the most satisfactory and productive months and years of his life. Nine years before, the Hebrew University in its new building on Mount Scopus was formally inaugurated by Lord Balfour, and Weizmann as its first president delivered an inaugural address. He did not, from the first, see eye to eye with its first head, the Chancellor Dr Judah L. Magnes, from whose political and academic views he strongly dissented; their differences grew greater with time.

In 1921 he became President of the World Zionist Organization. His main work now lay in negotiation and administration. He had to conduct operations on three troubled fronts, Jewish, British and Arab. In the Zionist world, he occupied his customary central position; to the right of him stood Jabotinsky and his followers. Violently opposed to the decision made at the Cairo Conference in 1921 whereby Trans-Jordan was removed from the original territory of Palestine, and by the subsequent White Paper issued a year later by Mr Churchill, then Colonial Secretary, which laid down that

Jewish immigration must be determined by 'economic absorptive capacity' and other limiting factors, the 'Revisionists' wanted, with the example of Ireland and colonial territories in mind, an out and out assault upon the mandatory power using every weapon of political pressure and resistance open to a minority. Weizmann believed this policy to be futile. He placed his faith from the beginning in the British connection both on grounds of sentiment, and because he believed in the community of Zionist and British interests. To his opponents on the extreme nationalist right this seemed a policy of weak compromise tantamount to treason. He had staked his political career on close collaboration with the British administration and remained faithful to this ideal for over twenty years. Weizmann was pragmatic and flexible in his means and methods, but his ends never altered: he remained unswerving in his pursuit of a free, self-governing Jewish commonwealth, preferably under British auspices, in Palestine.

To the left of him he had opponents who pressed for a greater degree of immediate socialism in the Jewish settlement, criticized the 'capitalist' methods of colonization and the Government's immigration regulations which discriminated in favour of richer immigrants, resented what seemed to them undue interference by the British mandatory government, the Zionist Organization and private economic agencies in the social and economic life of the Jewish colonies, and demanded a greater degree both of socialism and of autonomy. Both sides accused Weizmann of anglomania, and in particular of a tendency to appease and yield to his British friends. Weizmann was not a socialist: he professed no economic doctrine and declared himself unskilled in such matters; by temperament he was inclined towards democratic and semi-socialist institutions. However autocratic he could at times be, he distrusted plutocracy, philanthropic paternalism, oligarchy, and other forms of élitism. He saw the building up of Jewish Palestine as a collective effort carried through principally by agricultural and industrial workers in an egalitarian society. Equality and fraternity had deeply penetrated the life of common suffering in the Pale of Settlement whence most of the early immigrants, and he himself, had come; he recoiled against the hierarchies of the Western world as strongly as the immigrants themselves. He felt some distaste for the Rothschild colonies with their tradition of patronage, although he recognized their unique historic services. He insisted on diverting Zionist funds to *Moshavim*[1] and *Kvutsoth*,[2] even though he was not convinced that they were economically viable, and was often told that it was more rational to

[1] Settlements with individually owned land.
[2] Collective settlements.

support a greater degree of private enterprise. He loved best his visits to the settlements—Nahalal, say, or Ein Harod—his *rapport* with the settlers was intimate and happy, happier than his relations with some of the representatives of economic corporations from America or England. The colonists and members of *Kibbutzim* were among his most faithful admirers. His heart was with Eastern Europe and the poor, his brain with the superior resources and standards of Western capital and skill.

As for the Arabs, he was, perhaps, over optimistic about the possibility of peaceful and harmonious relations with them. He insisted from the start that they must not be exploited. The Jews had come to live a national life, not to oppress others or create an Arab proletariat; he placed his hopes in the vast rise in the level of social and economic life which Jewish immigration would be bound to bring to the Arabs of Palestine; he underestimated the countervailing force of Arab nationalism, fed by a mounting resentment of the influx of foreigners who came to settle 'as of right and not on sufferance'. Consequently he had no discernible Arab policy—a fact which his opponents were not slow to point out.

As for the occupying Power, his anglophile feeling seemed to the more critical among his followers to blind him to the British Colonial officials' frequent distaste for the Jews and their moral doubts about their own task under the Mandate. For all his anger with its shortcomings, Weizmann made the British connection the basis of his entire policy. When, in the end, he became convinced that he had been betrayed by Britain, this was the deepest wound, and, indeed, the central tragedy, of his life. It was with the British that his principal business lay. Patiently and persistently, during the twenties, he pressed the Colonial Office for more and more certificates for immigrants, and for land which the Jewish National Fund did not itself have the resources to purchase. He was condemned to perpetual frustration. Since the first flush of war-time enthusiasm, successive British governments inclined to considering the Zionist adventure a piece of romantic folly which was costing the British Government far too dear in the terms of Arab goodwill. The Foreign Office, especially, came to regard the promises to the Jews as morally indefensible and politically embarrassing. It is doubtful whether others could have obtained more from a government and officials steeped in this outlook. About this opinions will probably always differ.

Weizmann's relations with successive High Commissioners naturally varied greatly: even when he was most critical of his policies, he retained much respect and admiration for the first Jewish governor of Palestine since Nehemiah—Sir Herbert Samuel. This feeling was fully reciprocated and grew stronger with the years. He was, however, happiest in his relations with the three soldiers among the High Commissioners: Lord Plumer, Sir Arthur Wauchope and Sir Alan Cunningham. He found men of simple, resolute and open nature easiest to deal with.

The scale of both financial contributions and immigration provided by the Jewish world in the mid-twenties fell far short of Zionist expectations and the economic situation in the Jewish settlement often grew critical. For these reasons and also because he had always conceived of the entire enterprise as one undertaken by the entire Jewish people and not merely by a party within it, Weizmann worked fervently for an expansion of the Zionist Organization to cover as great a sector of Jewry as possible. The greatest blow to these hopes was the disappearance of the great Russian Jewish community of more than three millions behind the Soviet Curtain. Mass immigration from the West had never seemed to Weizmann a concrete prospect. In 1929 his wish was at last partially fulfilled. An expanded Jewish Agency was formed, against criticism by both the right and left wings of the Zionist movement, with the adhesion of Louis Marshall and Felix Warburg in the United States, and other non-Zionist sympathizers in many lands, who were to form fifty per cent of the central body with which the British Government formally dealt in all matters concerning the Jewish national home. Weizmann became the head of the new organization. He had now attained to the highest formal position in the Jewish world, a modern Exilarch, *Rosh Hagolah*, leading his people back to their ancient home. His figure inspired profound respect and interest throughout the world. He had, after the War, established his headquarters in London; his gifted wife and he entertained widely; his circle of acquaintance grew large and varied: it included some of the most eminent, remarkable and influential figures in British social and public life. To some of his old followers he seemed altogether too grand, remote and inaccessible. These were years of peace, and slow, gradual, difficult, unspectacular achievement. His influence in government circles rose and fell, but was never negligible. There was no doubt of his unique status and reputation; although he represented a relatively small group of human beings, and little financial power, the force of his personality was such that he created an illusion, to which the leaders of the Western world willingly succumbed, of representing not only a people but a state, of being the prime minister of a government in exile. It was not as a suppliant but as an equal that he spoke for a great historical nation; he was a figure of formidable powers whose proposals were not to be ignored.

The great array of Jewish solidarity for which Weizmann had worked in a single-minded fashion, frightened and enraged the Arabs. The first result of the creation of the Jewish Agency was the outbreak of violent anti-Jewish riots in Palestine. Jews were massacred in Safed, Hebron and elsewhere, and a Commission presided over by a British Colonial Judge—Sir John Shaw—was sent out to investigate. In November 1930, the Colonial Secretary of the British Labour Government, Sidney Webb (by then Lord Passfield) issued a White Paper in the name of the British Government, which, as on previous occasions, deplored the Arab riots, but tracing their cause to the natural reaction of the Arabs before the dangers of Jewish immigration, called for its curtailment, and a tighter supervision of Jewish activities. Weizmann's entire policy was founded upon the feasibility of fruitful co-operation with British Governments sympathetic to Zionist aims. The White Paper administered a severe blow to Jewish hopes, and was regarded by Jews and their friends everywhere as an act of injustice. It compromised Weizmann's entire position, and he felt obliged to resign from the presidency of the Agency. A volume of protest broke out not only from Jewish organizations but from Conservative, Liberal, and, in part, also Labour benches in Parliament, and outside it. A letter signed by some of the most prominent names in British public life appeared in *The Times*. The Prime Minister, Ramsay MacDonald, bowed before the storm and sent a letter to Weizmann in which he interpreted the White Paper in a somewhat more pro-Zionist sense. Although the position was half saved for the moment, Weizmann never again felt the political ground firm beneath his feet.

A year later, at the Seventeenth Congress in Basle, he was defeated by the combination of parties predominantly of the right. He symbolized the now discredited British connection. British behaviour strengthened the hand of the intransigent right wing which demanded more drastic anti-British tactics. Nor had he made himself more popular by being quoted in a newspaper interview as neither understanding nor sympathizing with the demand for a Jewish majority in Palestine. Whether or not his position has been accurately represented, he was clear that the immediate prospect of increasing the trickle of Jewish immigration did not seem bright: he was inclining towards a temporary solution based on a claim to political parity with the Arab majority. Nahum Sokolow was elected President of the Jewish Agency, and until 1935 Weizmann was out of office. He did not sit with folded hands. He returned to his laboratory which had always served him as a source of moral strength. He devoted himself to the building and organization of the scientific institute in Rehovoth which the generosity of the Sieff-Marks family had made possible. He begged eminent German Jewish scientists to leave their country over which Hitler's shadow daily grew darker, and come to Palestine; some were persuaded; the great chemist Fritz Haber died in Basle while on the way to Rehovoth. At the same time he continued to work in the Zionist movement. He undertook fund-raising journeys for Zionist agencies in South Africa, the United States and elsewhere; he took a vigorous part in the affairs of the central Zionist Bank—the Jewish Colonial Trust founded by Herzl as an English company, which was facing an acute financial crisis during the great worldwide economic slump. He was invited and accepted the Zionist Executive's invitation to help in the urgent tasks created by the new and frightful predicament of the German Jews, caused by Hitler's rise to power in Germany, and threw himself into the work of rescuing refugees. He spoke and wrote; his unseen presence hovered over all Zionist action; Sokolow is said to have remarked that he was a mere umbrella-stand on which Weizmann had chosen to hang his hat. In 1935 in Lucerne, at the Nineteenth Congress, he was returned to power. It was plain to all that he was irreplaceable, his authority in the Jewish and Gentile world unexampled. He was the greatest Jew in public life in modern times and his continuance as a private individual had become too much of an anomaly.

Britain had behaved generously in giving asylum in the United Kingdom to the refugees from Germany. Its Palestine policy was another matter. It had become evident to most observers that in the rising tension between Germany and the Western world, the Arabs had politically far more than the Jews to offer to either side, and that, in consequence, their favours were likely to be solicited by the Western allies at the expense of the Jewish settlement, which, like a foundling, was proving more and more unwelcome to its adoptive British parent. Weizmann slowly came to realize that the Mandatory experiment was set on a self-defeating course. As a result of Hitler's persecution and the growing fears in Central Europe, Jewish immigration into Palestine had risen by leaps and bounds: economic absorptive capacity had proved far more elastic than the British administration and its experts had anticipated. In 1936 widespread Arab riots broke out, this time not merely against the Jews but also against the mandatory power, and developed into a species of guerrilla warfare. A Commission under Lord Peel was sent out to investigate and make fresh recommendations about the future of Palestine. Weizmann appeared before it in Jerusalem, and his testimony, both in form and content, is one of the most impressive documents, both intellectually and morally, ever submitted on behalf of a nation. It contained a survey and an analysis of unsurpassed authority and force, dealing with the past, present and future position of the Jews in the world, historical, social, economic, and political; it formed the basis of thinking on this tormented topic for many years to come. Its prophecies were largely fulfilled. The Commission's report, itself a State paper of the first order and probably, to this day, the best account of British policy and action in Palestine, advocated partition of Palestine into Jewish and Arab self-governing entities, although this was hedged in with important reservations. Weizmann tentatively accepted this plan with his own reservations, as the lesser of two evils. He thought that the Mandate had outlived its usefulness; that British authority both in London and in Palestine had plainly proved unequal to its task. It was a painful conclusion for a man who had cast his lot with Britain, and had paid dearly for his open admiration and love for British qualities. But having reached it, he set himself to persuade the Agency and Congress to accept partition. A storm rose in both the Jewish and the Arab worlds. The Zionist Congress, after passionate debates, accepted the solution in principle, although with radical qualifications. The Arabs rejected it outright. The British House of Commons voted for it by a majority, but the Government slowly and remorselessly sabotaged it, by collecting the inevitably adverse opinions of the Arab states, and by sending out a Commission to advise on the new frontiers, and accepting its conclusions—that in fact no satisfactory frontier could ever be drawn. Weizmann lived through agonizing months. He had accepted the Solomonic judgment with anguish, on the ground that any viable Jewish self-governing territory, however small and insecure, was preferable to the alternative which was perdition. He was attacked from the left and the right as a traitor, an appeaser, a British agent.

In America particularly partition was denounced by leaders of Jewish opinion as the sacrifice of economic viability and prospects of large-scale immigration to the mirage of political independence in an absurdly small area and one too difficult to defend—a retrogressive step in a world of growing economic interdependence, the sacrifice of a vision of a wider world, free from fiercely protected natural frontiers, to an anachronistic and narrowly political nationalistic ideal. For Weizmann the entire future of the Jewish people was at stake at this moment. It seemed to him clear that if they did not seize the opportunity of national independence now, the chance might not come again within the calculable future.

The political situation in Europe rapidly grew darker. Italy had conquered Abyssinia, the civil war in Spain had ended in a fascist victory, the Germans occupied Austria and began to threaten the Czechs.

The Palestine Arabs continued to harass the mandatory power and the Jewish settlements. The Jews formed a semi-legal defence corps of which the *Haganah*, originally formed in 1920, had been the illegal beginning; to some degree it co-operated with the British forces. Towards the end of 1938 came the final *dénouement*. The false hopes engendered by the Munich Agreement faded rapidly. With the prospect of a war with Germany looming, the British Government, seeking to secure its Middle Eastern base, finally decided to yield to Arab demands. A veiled but ominous statement implying this, was issued in 1938. This was followed by the St James's Palace Conference, attended by Weizmann together with Ben-Gurion and other Zionist leaders, in which the Jews were pressed by the Foreign Secretary, Lord Halifax and the Colonial Secretary Mr Malcolm Macdonald, to give up their dream of either a majority or an autonomous establishment, let alone a state, in Palestine. In 1939 a British White Paper was published, which imposed severe restrictions upon the transfer of land to the Jews, and made all prospect of Jewish immigration after five years dependent on Arab goodwill which was clearly not likely to occur in any foreseeable period. No one doubted that the British Government had executed a complete *volte face*: it was intended to liquidate the Zionist experiment for good. The path for Weizmann was now clear. He rejected with dignity and force the death sentence pronounced on the Zionist movement, accused the British Government of turning Palestine from a home into a death trap for the Jews, and prepared to fight. The Zionist Congress held in the late summer of 1939, during the last weeks before the outbreak of hostilities, haunted the memories of those who had been present. Delegates, as they spoke, were conscious that they might soon be cut off from each other, no one could tell when, perhaps never to meet again in this world; those from Eastern Europe knew that they were returning to probable torture and death. Weizmann, according to all accounts, towered over the meeting as the father of his people—its misfortunes were directly reflected in his personal agony. In September 1939 Hitler invaded Poland; Great Britain and France declared war upon Germany. Weizmann immediately promised the Allies all possible aid by the Jewish population in Palestine. A new phase had begun.

In the early months of the war Weizmann again offered his scientific services to the country of which he had now long been a citizen. This time he found little response in official circles. He was appointed honorary chemical adviser to the Ministry of Supply, but this led to nothing. He reflected gloomily about the suspicious and negative official attitude in 1939–40, as contrasted with the more imaginative response in the first World War. He pressed for the formation of special Jewish, and in particular Palestinian, units in the war against Germany. The Government departments, in particular the Foreign, Colonial and War Offices, were, above all, anxious never again to be, or seem to be, under any obligation to Zionists or their friends. Nor was there support from the leaders of the armed forces. Zionist hope was now centred upon neutral America, where the openly pro-Arab policy of the British Government was condemned by large sections of public opinion as part and parcel of the general policy of appeasement, culminating in the Munich agreement of October 1938. Weizmann's second son, Michael, had joined the British Royal Air Force on the day after Mr Chamberlain's triumphal return from Munich, and was now a pilot. Weizmann beat in vain upon the doors of government departments to secure admission into Palestine for Jews trapped in the still unconquered countries of Eastern Europe, fully realizing that the most probable alternative was extermination. Those who suspected him of softness with British officials, could now be matched with those who thought that the fierce words he addressed to the Foreign and War Offices, in which he virtually called them accomplices of Hitler, went too far.

With the German invasion of the Lowlands and France in the summer of 1940, Weizmann renewed his pleas that Palestinian Jews be allowed to fight as an autonomous unit. His wish was not realized until Mr Churchill, whose Zionist sympathies had never been in doubt, finally authorized the formation of this body in 1944. Weizmann remained in London during the bombing of the 'Blitz', and received a more sympathetic hearing from the new Churchill administration than from its predecessor. In February 1942 his son Michael was declared missing by the Air Ministry. Neither Weizmann nor his wife Vera ever wholly recovered from this loss. In 1941 Weizmann went to New York; for the United States had by then plainly become the centre of gravity of the free world. In London Zionists were being treated as, at best, highly embarrassing allies; in Washington minds seemed to Weizmann more open about the organization of the new post-war world. He rapidly became the centre of political activity within American Zionism. Old friends among British officials and politicians were not all unsympathetic. He saved at least one group of Jewish refugees from extermination by a personal intervention: but in general he could do little to modify the immigration policy of the British Government and its High Commissioner in Palestine, which led to the death and suicide of boatloads of Jewish victims of Nazism escaping from central Europe. He fared better in his approaches to eminent Americans. The American Government had declined all responsibility for

Palestine, and could afford a more detached view. The sympathetic attitude towards Zionist aims displayed by such American statesmen as the Vice-President, Henry Wallace, the Under Secretary of State, Sumner Welles, the Secretary for War, Henry Stimson, the Secretary of the Treasury, Henry Morgenthau (who was a Jew), and indeed President Roosevelt himself—as well as officials, journalists and leaders of opinion in every walk of life, owed a good deal to the extraordinary fascination exercised by Weizmann upon almost all uncommitted personalities with whom he came into contact. He continued with his scientific work in which Britain had displayed no interest. He duly took out an American patent for discovering a new process for the production of synthetic rubber. He hoped, perhaps, to repeat the 'miracle' of the first World War, and use the value to the United States of his scientific contribution as a means of enhancing his status, an asset to be used in favour of his cause. His patents brought him royalties which made him financially independent, and this gave him that complete freedom of action which characterized his entire public life. His continued fame as a chemist added to his laurels in American eyes.

As the victories of the West began to point towards the end of hostilities, Weizmann began once more to travel from America to England and back again, in a continuous effort to keep Zionist claims alive before the future peacemakers. Despite varying degrees of suspicion or hostility in the foreign ministries of all the major allies, the old Partition scheme, recommended by the Peel Commission, came to life again in the British Cabinet. The prospect of Jewish autonomy in Palestine was touched upon during the talks between Roosevelt, Churchill and Stalin at Yalta. The Arab rulers remained adamant in opposition: King Ibn Saud of the Hedjaz warned Roosevelt that he would forcibly resist a pro-Zionist solution of the Palestine problem. There were American Jews, too, who feared a Jewish state as being likely to affect their own status, but they were not nearly as influential as their British predecessors had been in 1917. At a Zionist conference in New York the so-called 'Biltmore Resolution' was passed, on 11 April 1942, openly demanding for the first time the creation of a Jewish commonwealth in the whole of Palestine. This became part of the official programme of the movement. The initiative for it came from David Ben-Gurion and the Palestinian delegation. Weizmann did not oppose it, he had indeed written of a Jewish state as a world need in an article published in a New York periodical earlier that year; nevertheless the possibility of a self-governing Jewish dominion within the British Commonwealth still occupied his mind. The opposition to the Biltmore programme took the form of schemes,

promoted largely by left wing and other groups in Palestine and
America, for a bi-national state of Jews and Arabs, an idea which
had originally been discussed in 1931. In the meanwhile the war,
which hampered travel and communication, led to some weakening of
contact between Weizmann and the Jews in Palestine. The growth,
during the war, of underground and terrorist Jewish groups determined on violent resistance to British policy, scarcely impinged on the
consciousness of Weizmann, then busily engaged in discussions with
British statesmen about the future constitution of Palestine. In 1945
the British Minister of State in the Middle East, Lord Moyne, was
assassinated in Cairo by members of the Stern group in Palestine.
Weizmann returned to London and found that Churchill's attitude
had, as a result, stiffened against Zionist demands. The British Cabinet
abandoned conversations about partition, and set itself to suppress
rebellion in Palestine. Anthony Eden, the British Foreign Secretary,
had, some time before this, been instrumental in creating the League
of Arab States, whose antagonism to Jewish hopes was unconcealed.
President Roosevelt's attitude remained ambiguous until his death in
1945. In the summer of that year, in the first election after the end of
the European war the British Conservative Government fell, and the
Labour Party under Major Attlee came into power. Ernest Bevin
became Foreign Secretary and pledged himself to solve the Palestine
problem. His antagonism to Zionist demands increased steadily.
Weizmann found little common ground between himself and either
Bevin or the Prime Minister, Clement Attlee, who thought the original
British Mandate an egregious error. The pro-Zionist election pledges
of the Labour Conference had evidently had little effect. Many
schemes were discussed: division of Palestine into cantons, trusteeship
and partition plans, an independent Arab state with guarantees to the
Jewish minority—all of which displayed a marked anti-Zionist bias.
Meanwhile the American President, Harry Truman, was pressing for
permission for at least one hundred thousand survivors from the Nazi
concentration camps to enter Palestine. The Arabs threatened renewed revolt. An Anglo-American Commission of Inquiry was sent
out to investigate the situation. Weizmann delivered one of his most
memorable addresses before it. After some disagreement among its
members, the Commission recommended a wider measure of immigration than any British Government was prepared to accept. Mr
Bevin was becoming progressively more irritated by Jewish pressure,
especially in the USA. Illegal immigration of Jews into Palestine began
to assume large proportions. Bevin's treatment of Jewish concentration camp victims on board an 'illegal' ship named *Exodus*, who were
compelled by him to return to the refugee camp in Germany from

which they had come, advertised, so it seemed to some, his growing anti-Semitism. Illegal immigration increased by leaps and bounds. Whatever the official attitude of the Jewish Agency, the sympathy with this movement of Weizmann and most other Jewish leaders far beyond the bounds of Zionism, and throughout liberated Europe as well as wide circles in the USA, was mounting rapidly. Resistance to British rule in Palestine on the part of dissident Jewish groups in Palestine grew in violence; the occupying authorities attempted equally strong repressive measures. Weizmann, who had during the greater portion of his political life, believed in the British association, and had indeed hoped that the Jewish community in Palestine would develop institutions, and a social and political temper, not dissimilar to British democracy, grew profoundly disillusioned and embittered. Even the friends of Zionism in England began to say to him that she could not be expected to take on obligations beyond her now greatly reduced powers; its opponents denounced the iniquity of placing the Arabs under Jewish rule in any form.

In 1946 the first post-war Zionist Congress assembled in Basle, and the British connection with which Weizmann's name had been indissolubly identified, was the fundamental issue before it. He had, though without enthusiasm, and in order to avoid a final rupture, advocated acceptance by the Jewish Agency of the invitation issued by the British Government to a conference in London in 1947. This proposal was refused by the Congress largely by the votes of the Palestinian representatives led by David Ben-Gurion, who regarded the entire policy based on co-operation with England as discredited and hopeless. Some of his former supporters now tended to look upon Weizmann as a statesman, who had been great and effective in his day and had rendered major services to the movement, but had become hopelessly bemused by his thirty years of work with the British, and was no longer aware of the new realities, either in Palestine itself or in the power relationships which had arisen after the war. Weizmann returned to London, once again defeated as a champion of the 'anglocentric' point of view, although he had, in fact, no illusions left about the attitude of the British Government.

Notwithstanding the vote of the Congress, a conference with the British authorities did take place in London, but without Weizmann, and duly led to a total *impasse*. The Foreign Secretary decided, in the face of growing Jewish violence, to refer the entire issue to the United Nations whence all authority for British trusteeship in Palestine was in principle derived. The United Nations appointed a Commission of Inquiry (UNSCOP) which visited Palestine in 1947, and before which Weizmann, then back in his home in Rehovoth, gave evidence.

The effect made by Weizmann's measured words on the Commission was, as always, profound. The Swedish chairman of the Commission, Dr Sandström, like his predecessors, had no doubt that Weizmann stood head and shoulders above everyone concerned in the affair. To the painful surprise of the British Government, the Commission recommended partition: the setting-up of an independent Jewish state in a part of Palestine as the only way out of a hopeless deadlock.

In theory Weizmann was now a private citizen occupied in scientific research at the Institute situated near his home in Rehovoth. Even before his defeat at the Congress in 1946, the anti-British military activities authorized by the Executive in Palestine had been conducted largely without his knowledge, and when he, as head of the Jewish Agency, complained about this to his colleagues, it became clear that his advancing years and his reputation as an anglophile and a moderate, and perhaps other differences also, had decided his colleagues to withhold the details of military resistance from him. Nor did the British authorities, on their side, ever look upon him as among their enemies. When most of the members of the Zionist Executive in Palestine were arrested by the British authorities, Weizmann denounced this act of the High Commissioner with bitter scorn. His final political links with England had been snapped. He occupied no official position in the Jewish Agency. Nevertheless when the future of the Jewish establishment once again formally entered into the area of international discussion, no one in the Jewish world doubted that Weizmann alone must represent his people before the nations. His health had long been undermined: he was growing blind, suffered from a chronic infection of the lung and a bad heart, and had been in ill-health for many months. He had no doubt about his course of action. He established his headquarters in New York, and in effect headed the Jewish delegation in the great United Nations debate in the autumn of 1947 which decided the future of Palestine. In November two-thirds of the representatives of the United Nations voted in favour of the establishment of a Jewish state in a part of Palestine. This decision, and, in particular, the fact that the United States Government retreated from its last-minute attempt to substitute a trusteeship scheme for partition of Palestine into independent Jewish and Arab states, owed a great deal to Weizmann's personal interventions with President Truman, who had conceived great sympathy and admiration for the Jewish leader. He enjoyed similar consideration from M. Léon Blum in France, and produced an indelible impression upon other members of the United Nations Organization who met him at this time. He was naturally concerned with the frontiers of the future state. The US State Department wished to detach the Southern

Negev from the prospective Jewish territory, and this plan was put forward by the American representative to the United Nations. In the course of an interview with President Truman at a crucial moment, Weizmann succeeded in convincing the President that King Solomon's port on the Red Sea was indispensable to the new Jewish state if it was to preserve its communications with the Indian Ocean and the Pacific against a possible Arab blockade of the Suez Canal and the Mediterranean Jewish ports. The USA successfully resisted the plan to bisect the Negev, which became an integral part of Israel.

Since 1946 Weizmann had identified himself wholeheartedly with claims to full Jewish statehood in Palestine. When, after the slow departure some six months later of the British authorities (whose government had not given their approval to the UN decision), the desirability of proclaiming an independent Jewish State of Israel was debated in Palestine, he sent messages to Ben-Gurion pressing for its creation. The declaration of Independence by the State of Israel on 14 May 1948, was the fulfilment of his ardent wish. The state had been created in the face of a great deal of opposition and warning by interested and disinterested powers; it was viewed with much nervous anxiety by many friends of Zionism and some Jewish leaders in Palestine who thought that the new state would be crushed by the numerically vastly superior Arab armies. American policy in the United Nations vacillated under the influence of many pressures. the Department of State largely shared the view of the British Foreign Office. President Truman, whose regard for Weizmann's personality and integrity was consistently high, decided to recognize the State immediately on its foundation. This personal act on the part of the President was a moral and political asset of incalculable worth for the new State; Weizmann's decisive part in securing it is not open to doubt.

One of the first acts of the Government of the new State of Israel, headed by David Ben-Gurion, was to offer the Presidency of the State to Weizmann. His right to it was unquestioned. It was a position of high symbolic significance. Weizmann's acceptance of it was signalized by the new flag that was hoisted over his hotel in New York, but it carried with it no real power. His views did not command general assent in the government of the state which he had, by universal consent, done more than any other human being to render possible. He returned to Rehovoth and his Institute, and his house there became his official residence. He was old and his health was failing, but his eyes had seen the fulfilment of the dream of which he had written to his teacher as a boy more than sixty years before.

In 1948 Israel was invaded by the Arab armies and was obliged to fight for its life. Weizmann had no doubt of the outcome. After the war had been won there was universal recognition of Weizmann's supreme achievement in recreating his nation. In his own country he was revered as the father of his people, a myth in his own lifetime. He performed his official functions as head of the State, and spent a great deal of time in scientific work. He was physically almost exhausted. He travelled abroad in an effort to recover his health, but it grew progressively worse. He received foreign ambassadors and other eminent foreign visitors; he heard reports from his ministers, of whom he was at times sharply critical, saw and wrote to old friends, revised and added to earlier drafts of his memoirs, took continuous interest in affairs of state but little direct part in decisions of policy. Towards the end he grew almost totally blind. He died on 9 November 1952 (21 *Marcheshvan* 5713) and he was survived by his eldest son Benjamin, and by his wife Vera with whose existence his own had been most intimately linked. Their deep and happy love, and the complete respect and trust which they felt for one another, was the foundation of both their lives.

He was buried in the grounds of his house in Rehovoth. His grave, like that of Herzl, is at present a place of national pilgrimage in Israel.

Sir Isaiah Berlin is Chichele Professor of Social and Political Theory at Oxford University.

1874–1904

CHAPTER TWO

THE ROAD FROM MOTOL

MAURICE SAMUEL

> 'If thou wouldst know'
> CHAIM NACHMAN BIALIK

AMONG LEADERS of men it is not unusual to find complexity of character side by side with singlemindedness of purpose, but rarely has the contrast stood out as sharply as in Chaim Weizmann. The contradictions in his drives and in his way of seeing life should on a common-sense view have led to a kind of paralysis; he was powerfully drawn towards a public career, and he hankered after the seclusion of the laboratory; he had a quick eye for the comicality of the human scene, and he was deeply involved in the human struggle; he was unawed by worldly success, and was determined to achieve it; he was unimpressed by the trappings of leadership and knew that the two are inseparable; he despised political guile and met it on its own ground; and, finally he alternated between despair of the Jewish people and unshakeable faith in its future. But where in small men contradictions cancel out, in great men they add up.

All of us long to 'understand' the 'great man', and we are undeterred by the fact that we don't understand the small man; we go after calculus before we have mastered arithmetic. Still, the effort has its peripheral rewards; we learn something about ourselves and about the setting which surrounded the subject of our search; the hero is an insoluble enigma but he is a useful approach to the study of history. This essay examines the *Shtetl* background of Weizmann's life. It does not purport to be an explanation or to provide a point-to-point correspondence between the man's character and his early environment; we shall observe many parallels and similarities as well as suggestions of development by opposition. But *why* Chaim Weizmann reacted as he did, and became what he became is another matter; there even his autobiography is of little help.

The *Shtetl*, the Jewish village or rural settlement of East European Jewry, was itself a mass of contradictions. It was in the countryside,

59

but not of it; as an economic unit it was inseparable from its surroundings, as a spiritual phenomenon it was completely disjoined
from them. It had its own institutions, its own way of life, its own
language. We cannot classify the *Shtetl* as just another national
minority village. Poles, Lithuanians, Ukranians did indeed speak
different languages, observe different customs, sometimes belong to
different churches. But it was all within reason; the spiritual and
cultural substance of their lives had much in common; they belonged
to the same civilization; they lived where they were and they lived
contemporaneously. Half the time the *Shtetl* just wasn't there; it was
in the Holy Land, and it was in the remote past or the remote future,
in the company of the Patriarchs and Prophets or of the Messiah.
Its festivals were geared to the Palestinian climate and calendar; it
celebrated regularly the harvests its forefathers had gathered in a
hundred generations ago; it prayed for the *yoreh* and *malkosh*, the
subtropical former and latter rains, indifferent to the needs of its
neighbours, whose prayers had a practical local schedule in view.

   Of his own village, Motol, near Pinsk, where he lived until his
eleventh year, Weizmann writes in *Trial and Error*: 'We were
strangers to their [the non-Jewish villagers'] ways of thought, to each
other's dreams, religions, festivals, even languages. There were times
when the non-Jewish world was practically excluded from our consciousness, as on the Sabbath and, still more, on the spring and
autumn festivals. ... We were separated from the peasants by a
whole inner world of memories and experiences. ... My father was
not yet a Zionist, but the house was steeped in rich Jewish tradition,
and Palestine was at the centre of the ritual ... the Return was in the
air, a vague, deep-rooted Messianism, a hope which would not die.'

   To live physically in one world, mentally in another, is fraught
with psychological peril for an individual. How much more for an
entire people which sustains this condition for generation after
generation, century after century! The *Shtetl* was something of a
freak, the life of its inhabitants correspondingly freakish. The contradictions in its external relations were paralleled by equally perilous
inner contradictions, a fantastic divisiveness within unity, a high
tension between the spiritual destructiveness of class antagonisms and
snobberies and the spiritual creativity of a common dream. Little
wonder that in the folklore and the relevant literature the attitude
toward the *Shtetl* is one of extreme ambivalence.

   On the one hand it is remembered sentimentally. From just below
the horizon—historically speaking the *Shtetl* disappeared only yesterday—it sends up a nostalgic glow for its survivors and for those of
their sons and grandsons who retained some of the tradition; one

would think it had been one of the rare and happy breathing spells of
the Exile, the nearest thing to a home from home that Jews have ever
known. It stands up in retrospect as an impregnable citadel of Jewishness. The Jewish city, the 'mother in Israel'—Vilna, Warsaw, Odessa
—had more Jewish life quantitatively, but it also had its large segment
of defection. In the city Jews were exposed to worldly opportunity
and a respectable non-Jewish culture; in both these respects the
Shtetl was surrounded by uniform inferiority. The city was famous,
the *Shtetl* anonymous; the *Shtetlach* might be called the *lamed-
vovniks* of East European Jewry—the thirty-six anonymous saints
who under the guise of humble ignoramuses stave off in every generation the otherwise merited destruction of the world. The cities are
known by their own names; the *Shtetlach*, if at all, by the names of
the great men who issued from them. On the other hand the *Shtetl*
is remembered with a grimace of repugnance. Forlorn little settlements in a vast, hostile and primitive environment, isolated alike from
the centres of Jewish and non-Jewish civilization, their tenure precarious, their structure ramshackle, their existence a prolonged
squalor to the outer view! Who would want to live there?

The temptation of the sociologist is to strike an objective pose, to
say judicially that the truth no doubt lies somewhere between the two
extremes; but in this case the judicial would be an evasion. It is the
peculiarity of the *Shtetl* that the truth lies precisely in the two
extremes. The *Shtetl* may well serve as a symbol of Jewish life in the
Exile, not a mixture which fuses into grey but a checkered pattern of
black and white, of the ignominious and the inspiring.

The close of Yal Peretz's wonderful story *Between Two Cliffs*,
though pointed towards another theme, may serve here as a parable.

Reb Noachke, the gentle and dreamy Chassidic *Rebbi* of Biale
receives a visit from his former teacher, the learned and implacably
orthodox Rabbi of Brisk. They have not seen each other for many
years; chance has brought them together, and the Rabbi of Brisk
hopes to rescue his former pupil from the abomination of the Chassidic heresy. The young devotee of Reb Noachke, the intermediary
and the instrument of the chance, thus describes the outcome:

'He of Biale—his memory be a benediction—followed a custom
of his own on the day of the Rejoicing of the Law. He would send his
Chassidim out of the Study House and tell them to go strolling in
the open air; he himself would sit on the verandah and take pleasure
in the spectacle.

'The verandah was on the second storey, and below it the village
and its surroundings lay as in the palm of your hand, enclosed

between the hills on the east and the river on the west. The *Rebbi*
sits up there and looks down. If a group of Chassidim passes without
singing, he throws them the opening notes of a melody, which they
take up and carry away with them. So group after group goes by
and, singing, spreads out into the fields, filled with true happiness, as
is proper on the day of the Rejoicing of the Law; and the *Rebbi*
would remain up there and never stir from his place.'

Into this setting comes the rigorous Talmudic master, he of Brisk,
all intellect and erudition, and begins a discussion with his former
pupil, the mystical adept. But rather than explain himself in words,
Reb Noachke invites his former teacher to step out on the verandah,
and with him the narrator, who continues:

'I saw the wide, enormous heavens, infinite in extent, and blue,
radiantly blue, so that the eye was filled with delight. A host of little
silver clouds floated up there, and if one looked closely one could
really see that they quivered with happiness, as if they themselves
were dancing in the Rejoicing of the Law. Below, within the circle of
the hills and the river, the townlet lay imbedded in green, a dark and
living green; one would have said that a living spirit breathed among
the grasses . . .

'On the meadows, among the trees and grasses, little groups of
Chassidim walked to and fro. Their satin gabardines, and even those
of cotton, glittered like mirrors—all of them, even those that were
ragged. And the flames that danced among the grasses touched the
festive attire of the Chassidim and played with it; it was as if every
Chassid were surrounded with exultant, joyous fire. And the Chassidim turned their longing eyes to the verandah, and the light in their
eyes was drawn from the eyes of the *Rebbi*. And as the light grew
their songs became louder, gayer, and even more sacred . . . and not
they alone sang; the heavens sang, and the earth under their feet;
the soul of the world sang, everything sang.

'Lord of the world! The sweetness of it melted my heart.'

And there the Rabbi of Brisk stood, erect, majestic, hard, unseeing.
Suddenly he broke in with the sharp command: 'It is time for
evening prayers.'

'In that instant', says the narrator, 'everything vanished. I looked
and saw an ordinary sky, and under it ordinary light. On the fields
wandered beggarly Chassidim in tattered gabardines.'

What you saw in the *Shtetl* Jews depended on which of two pairs of
glasses you happened to be wearing. Of neither pair could you say
that it distorted the picture, but you could not wear the two pairs
simultaneously. Every Yiddish writer who has described the *Shtetl*—

which means practically every Yiddish writer—keeps putting on and taking off his glasses according to mood; which pair he favours depends on his temperament.

Weizmann, not a writer, but a leader and state-builder, also made use of both pairs, but in public he seldom gave utterance to his negative moods.

All national literatures and nearly all serious recorders of a people's life alternate in their use of the glasses, but no other national literature has the schizophrenic quality of the Jewish—from the Bible down to our own day. The Jewish people loves and hates itself, admires and despises itself, with pathological intensity. It is either God-selected or God-rejected, and it cannot be the second without the first. Certainly no other people robbed of its homeland and sent into exile by nations no better than itself would go on repeating for millennia: 'Serves us right!' But then no other people goes on existing for millennia after expulsion and dispersion, and no other people has associated its ultimate purification and rehabilitation with the destiny of the human species as a whole.

This aspect of the psychic environment in which Weizmann the child and youth grew up is best reproduced, among moderns, by Mendelle Mocher S'phorim, *der zeide* or granddaddy of Yiddish literature. He juxtaposes with unique starkness the negations and affirmations of *Shtetl* life and Jewish life in the Pale generally. Quantitatively the negations predominate in Mendelle; from the bulk of his work the *Shtetl* emerges with such repulsiveness that one is put in mind of Swift's country of the houyhnhms, or rather of its arboreal yahoos; but on the same subjects he has passages so loving and tender that they border on the mawkish.

He dwells with bitter gusto on the beggarliness of Jewish life in the Pale, its shlimihl-ishness, its cynicism, its complacency in misery.

'If you were suddenly to ask a Jew of Tuniadevky how he managed to make a living, the man would stand stock still in confusion, with no idea of what you are talking about. Then, coming to after a while, he would answer with a kind of daft artlessness: "How do I make a living? How do I support myself? There's a God in heaven, isn't there? And He doesn't forsake His creatures, does He? There's your answer, right there!" "But still," you insist, "what do you actually do? Have you a trade, a business, a profession?" His face lights up. "Praised be the Holy Name! To begin with—take a good look at me, Mr Jew—I have a gift from Him, a sweet voice for prayer, I'm in great demand hereabouts, among the villages, for the High Holy Days. Not for the main prayers, you understand, but for the supplementary prayers, the in-between prayers. And that's only a beginning. I'm a first-class circumciser, and on top of that there isn't my equal in these parts for putting holes in *màtzos* when Passover comes round. And what about playing the matchmaker now and again, and collecting a little commission? Wait! I'm not through yet. I've got what you might call a kind of inn, and I milk that from time to time; I have a goat that milks well, and a rich relative who can be milked from time to time. So, as I was saying, there's a God in heaven, and there are our Jews—aren't they the merciful sons of merciful fathers?" '

He describes the *Shtetl* market-place, the 'merchants' and their merchandise—a basket of vegetables, a few hens, a handful of rags, a couple of prayer-books. The synagogue is in ruins, the Talmud Torah —the community school—a farce . . . a life of misery and decay.

'I call up in my mind's eyes our little prayer-houses, dirty, disorderly, malodorous, filled with loiterers and loungers who lie stretched out on the benches puffing at their pipes and sneering at everything and everybody. . . . Idlers, loafers, cadgers, cripples . . . and suddenly a sound of music, a wedding procession, a boy bridegroom and a child bride, grandmothers clapping hands, the crowd rejoicing . . . *Mazaltov*, Jews! Good luck to your brand-new paupers, your candidates for the mendicants' club . . .'

In *The Travels of Benjamin the Third*, we wander with the hero through *Shtetl* after *Shtetl*, each meaner than the other. Everywhere an absence of economic foundation and simple sanitation, everywhere rancours, pride of descent, exploitation. In a later novel, *Shlomo Reb Chaims* Mendelle depicts the appalling social discrimination. The hand of the *baalebatim*, the 'well-to-do' householders, lies heavy on the poor. A worker is forbidden to wear a silk gabardine or a *shtreimel* on the Sabbath—it's not for the likes of him. In the synagogue his place is on the rear benches near the door. When called up to a reading from the Torah—which is seldom enough, and only when the minor honours have not been distributed among his betters —he is announced as *chaver* (member) and not with the honorific title of teacher. At community gatherings his opinion is not sought; if he protests he is answered with insults; he can even be dragged into the lobby and flogged. The children of the workers are '*chapped*' (snatched) and sent into the army, so that *a tatten's a kind* may go on studying or pretending to study in the *beth ha-Midrash*. A curious phrase, that, '*a tatten's a kind*', a-son-of-a-father, denoting the offspring of the upper class. Who or what was supposed to have fathered the offspring of the poor?

And the women, God help us, the women! Harridans whose mouths are filled with lyrical imprecations (the wives of 'Benjamin the Third' and of his companion, his Sancho Panza, Senderl), whose hands deal out slaps among the children and do not spare even the husbands. It is these wives who provide the 'livelihood' for the family in the market-places; being the breadwinners they are the bosses of the household.

Oddly enough, *Shlomo Reb Chaims* stands out among Mendelle's novels for its predominantly affirmative tone, its sentimentality. He wrote it after the persecution of Russian Jewry was renewed, following the assassination of Alexander II in 1881. He could hardly free himself from the pattern he had established in *Die Klatche, Die Taxe, Fishke der Krumer* and *Maasos Benyomin Ha-shlishi*; but here, for the most part, he wears the rose-tinted glasses and sees the *Shtetl* as an extraordinarily beautiful phenomenon. The very aspects which had moved him to satirical fury take on a glamour and wistfulness which seem to belong to another world.

The hideous poverty of the *Shtetl* fades from the centre of his attention, which focuses instead on the spirit of high idealism accompanying it. He does not deny the poverty; indeed, he makes it the springboard for his enthusiastic encomium on the lofty spiritual standards of *Shtetl* life. 'Let our grandchildren and *their* grandchildren know what the house of a Reb Chaim was like in the village of Kapulye, and how it was contrived to meet all the needs of a human being. There was really only one room, *die shtub*. It served as kitchen, dining-room and bedroom, and the sleeping was done mostly on benches shoved together against the wall near the stove. All week long this room was also a kind of saloon for the poor peasants, who would drop in for a jigger of whiskey and a beigel. For market days there was a supply of hard-boiled eggs, pickled herring, fried fish and fried livers. During the goyish winter festivals, the village girls came in their best dresses, the peasants in their best suits; they drank and played and cracked nuts, till they had to be driven out—sometimes you had to drench them from head to foot with a bucketful of water, there was no other way of getting rid of them.'

But wonder of wonders, this house in Kapulye, and its owner Reb Chaim, and Kapulye itself, shine for the writer with an unearthly radiance. '*A sheiner, yuster baalabos*' was Reb Chaim, a fine householder, one of the distinguished figures in the *Shtetl*. 'And to be that it wasn't enough to have a *shtub* and a cow. With these alone you were merely rich, and if you had ten times as much but were unlearned you were still *a grober yung*, a coarse nobody. Of course the rich man is worshipped everywhere, but the inner respect of the community did not go to such. . . . In Kapulye it was scholarship that counted, and so it was throughout Lithuania in those days; and

Kapulye had been a place of learning from of old—*an ort fun Toireh fun eibige yohren*—where nearly all the inhabitants were by nature bookish, where the *shuhl* and *Beth ha-Midrash* were full, early mornings and late evenings, with householders, fathers of families, sitting and studying . . . and there were hot arguments and fiery sermons and flaming interpretations, sharp anecdotes and epigrams and parables which filled mind and heart with love toward man and God.'

More remarkable still is the transfiguration of the market-women, the Chantzies and Yentes. A moving chapter is devoted to a 'wick-drawing' bee, something like a quilting bee, but religious in character. The village women assemble in one of the houses to draw out wicks for synagogue candles while they improvise prayers to the God of Abraham, Isaac and Jacob. Hardly one of them can read or write; the only Hebrew they know consists of words that have gone over into Yiddish. One must think of this pious company sitting by candle-light in a primitive cottage, around them a world completely alien but for a handful of cottages like their own. They sway to and fro as they repeat the words of the improvisor, and the thoughts and images they invoke go back through centuries and millennia to a place of prophecy and palm-trees and psalmody.

'Judge of the world, merciful God! These candles which we are making for the synagogue, for your dear and Holy Name's sake, and for the sake of the souls of all the holy ones, these candles—may they awaken the sainted patriarchs and matriarchs, and cause them to rise from their graves to intercede for us, that no evil, no pain and no suffering be visited upon us; that the light of our husbands and of our children be not put out before their time, God forbid. . . . As I draw out this wick for our Father Abraham, whom You saved from the fiery furnace of Nimrod, so shall You purify us from sin, so that our souls may come before You unspotted as on the day when they entered our bodies. And for the sake of the thread which I draw out for our Mother Sarah, remember, O God, her anguish when her son Isaac was led to the sacrifice. Let her be a good pleader for us, so that our children may not be snatched away from us, and that they shall not be scattered far away like lost sheep. And for the sake of this thread which I draw out for our Father Isaac, have mercy on us, O God, so that we may be able to bring up our children and afford a *Rebbi* for them, so that they may shine and learn and have knowledge of Your beloved Torah. . . . For the sake of the thread which I draw out in the name of our Father Jacob, whom You delivered from his enemies, standing by him in the hour of his need —for his sake help us as You helped him, against all slanderers and betrayers, so that they may become dumb, and be unable to plot against us and blacken our name. . . . Help us, so that on the Day of Judgment a good sentence may be pronounced for us, and for our husbands, so that we shall not become widows and our children orphans. . . . And for the sake of Solomon, who built the Temple, and implored You that when a stranger, the son of an alien people, offers up prayer in it, You shall hear and heed him too—for the sake of Solomon, O Judge of the World, keep open the gates of prayer, and let me be remembered to the good, with my husband and my children and all good people: Amen.'

At this point Mendelle breaks in passionately: 'Let him laugh who can, let him, if he can bring out the words, say it is all foolishness. No! May there be more such candles, many of these pure utterances of love for Torah and for all mankind.' He goes on to reflect: 'And where do you find all this, I ask? Among women who, seen from without, are coarse and ignorant, little souls of small account, women you will pass by in the market-place without glancing at a second time. . . .'

He becomes indignant: 'Let the mockers hear them, let them know what a Jewish heart really is.' And if the astonished reader were to protest: 'But you are the biggest of the mockers,' Mendelle would answer: 'I mock them out of love, for their improvement; not so the others.'

Whatever his mood and however extreme, no Jewish observer could deny that the education of the young was a central preoccupation of the *Shtetl*. Weizmann writes: 'There was, in every townlet of the size of Motol, a government school, but attendance was not compulsory. Some of the peasants sent some of the children to school, irregularly; most of them grew up quite illiterate. By contrast the Jews, who did not make use of the government schools, and who had only the *cheders*, had a high degree of literacy. But there the education was entirely Hebrew and Yiddish. Those who wanted to give their children the beginnings of a Russian and modern education engaged a special teacher, usually of third-rate ability.'

But on the subject matter of the education there could again be strong divergence of opinion. In Mendelle it is difficult to say what, on balance, he wanted. He was a lover of Jewish knowledge and tradition, he surely believed one could not start a child early enough on the traditional path; yet he was uneasy contemplating the divorce between the traditional Jewish education and the realities among which Jews lived, whether these were the neighbouring realities of the countryside or the wider ones of modern civilization.

'All right, nature-shmature,' says a grown-up to a youngster, 'I

suppose it's not too bad—though if you want to look at the whole
thing it's just foolishness, and.it's silly to waste a moment on it. Still,
though a grown-up with wife and children and a living to make has
no business to be fiddling around with nature, I suppose you can forgive it in a youngster.... Go ahead, then, take your walks in the
wood at the back of the house . . . and look up at the birds-shmirds.
But remember, you rascal, don't over-do it. Don't forget, you little
hooligan, that a boy of your age has to be busy with the Talmud.
Nature here, nature there—but the important thing is the Tractate
on Seeds!'

What was the result of this attitude? 'Little Shlomo had accumulated, long before his *bar mitzvah*, as much experience as if he were
of Methuselah's age. Where hadn't he been and what hadn't he
seen? Mesopotamia, Egypt and the Nile, Persia, Shushan, the capital
of Ahasuerus's empire, the deserts and the mountains. It was an experience unknown to the children of other peoples. For the Jewish
child sat in his place and his studies had nothing to do with his surroundings. He could not tell you a thing about Russia, about Poland,
about Lithuania and its peoples, laws, kings, politicians.... But you
just ask him about Og, King of Bashan, and Sihon, King of the
Amorites, and Nebuchadnezzar, King of Babylon! Ask him about the
Euphrates and the Jordan. He knew about the people who lived in
tents and spoke Hebrew or Aramaic; the people who rode on mules
and camels.... He knew nothing concerning the fields about him,
nothing about rye, wheat, potatoes, and where he got his bread from;
he didn't know that such things existed as fir-trees, pines and oaks.
But he knew about vineyards, date palms, pomegranates, locust-trees.
. . . He knew about the dragon and leopard, the turtle dove and the
hart that panteth after the living waters—he lived in another world.'

This was little Chaim Weizmann's early education, as it was of
hundreds of thousands of others. He says: 'I myself knew hardly a
word of Russian till I was eleven years old.' Some of these youngsters
repudiated the tradition when they grew up; others stayed rooted in
it all their lives. Every individual had his own reasons; what we have
here is a statistical and not a personal explanation. We begin to
understand the general difference between East European Zionism
and Western Zionism. Western Zionists like Herzl and Nordau saw
only or chiefly the sufferings of Russian Jewry; *Shtetl*-born and
Shtetl-bred Zionists were moved by more than hatred of the Exile;
they were drawn irresistibly towards Palestine.

We also get a glimpse into the mental composition of the Russian-
Jewish students in Berlin, Montpellier, Vienna, Basle and other
Western university towns who were the founding fathers of Zionism

before the coming of Herzl; we understand something of the compulsions of which they were the victims, and their ability to withstand
the hostility and derision of their contemporaries. When, in 1914, I,
a youth of nineteen, Western-educated though not Western-born,
turned to the movement, Zionism was still a poky, hole-in-the-wall
phenomenon, associated in the mind of intellectuals with Rosicru-
cians, the search for the lost Ten Tribes, and similar esoteric absurdi-
ties. Yet by 1914 at least famous men like Nordau and Zangwill had
declared for the movement; Herzl had left his indelible stamp on it;
the Encyclopaedia Britannica of 1911 devoted two whole pages to it
(and, incidentally, not much more to Communism). There were
dozens of Jewish colonies in Palestine. But in the eighteen nineties
there were only the faintest beginnings of colonization, and in the
Western world the movement, which was not yet a movement but
an obscure, formless though powerful agitation among the East
European Jewish masses, must have looked correspondingly odder.
Yet there they were, these Russian Jewish students, particularly the
members of the *Judisch-Russisch Wissenschaftliches Verein* of Berlin
(to which Weizmann, Leo Motzkin, Shmarya Levin, Nachman
Syrkin belonged) talking big, but big, about the Jewish State-to-be,
about international diplomacy, the buying off of Turkey, etc. A
Westerner like me could have occasional doubts, not as to the
rightness of the enterprise, but its feasibility. Not they. They knew
themselves to be makers of Jewish history.

Within this uniformity of outlook and inspiration Weizmann was set
apart from his fellow-students, not by superior dedication, and not
alone by the superiority of his gifts—this was not yet evident—but
by an intuitive consistency of long-range method, by a personal programme which he understood only in part. His fellow-students had
brought with them out of the *Shtetl* and out of the Pale generally
some of the negative as well as the positive features, most of all an
impracticality which was to hamper their usefulness to the movement
in later years. Weizmann came to Berlin in 1895, at the age of
twenty-one, and he studied there till the age of twenty-four. He says:
'When I left Berlin for Switzerland, in 1898, the adult pattern of my
life was set. Of course I learned a great deal in later years; but no
fundamental change took place; my political outlook, my Zionist
ideology, my scientific bent, my life's purposes, had crystallized.'
    Those three years he sees as crucial. Against the background of
the *Judisch-Russisch Wissenschaftliches Verein* he learned what he
wanted and did not want to be. 'At first,' he writes, 'I was greatly
overawed by my fellow-students, among whom I was the youngest.

Fresh from little Pinsk, with its petty Zionist collections and small-town discussions, I was staggered by the sweep of vision which Motzkin and Syrkin and the others displayed. There was also a personal detail which oppressed me at the beginning. I was only a student of chemistry; they were students of philosophy, history, economics, law and other "higher" things. I was immensely attracted to them as persons and as Zionists; but gradually I began to feel that in their personal preparations for life they were as vague as in their Zionist plans. I had brought with me out of Russia a dread of the "eternal student" type, the impractical idealist without roots in the worldly struggle, a figure only too familiar in the Jewish world of forty and fifty years ago. I refused to neglect the lecture hall and the laboratory, to which I gave at least six or seven hours a day. I read on my subject, I studied consistently. I acquired a taste for research work. In later years I understood what deeper motives impelled me in those days to attend strictly to the question of my personal equipment for the life struggle. For the time being it was enough for me to make up my mind that I was going to achieve independence.'

We do not find anywhere in the pages of *Trial and Error* a hint as to the 'deeper motives' which Weizmann thought were at work in him during the Berlin years. We know how magnificently the programme worked out, but Weizmann does not imply that he foresaw his role as Zionist-Scientist or Scientist-Zionist, or that he thought, in Berlin, of high scientific status as one of his important recommendations to British and American statesmen in two world wars. He all but acknowledges that he became a scientist by accident. There happened to be among his teachers in the *Gymnasium* or *Realschule* of Pinsk, Kormienko, a man of exceptional gifts, and, for Russia, of exceptional devotion to his vocation. Kormienko taught chemistry, and 'to him,' writes Weizmann, 'very possibly, I owe whatever I have been able to achieve in the way of science.' If Weizmann had come to Berlin as a general student, without this 'bent', would he have failed to make his way to the leadership of the Zionist movement and rendered it less signal service?

The familiar question of the day is before us. Are the skills of a scientific training transferable to other fields? Was de Valera an abler statesman for being a mathematician, Berthelot for being a chemist? The fact seems to be that the strain of practicality in Weizmann goes farther back than his scientific training. He was deeply influenced by his father, who, besides being a student of Maimonides, was in his way a thoroughly practical man. Ozer Weizmann was one of the 'well-to-do' householders of Motol ('it may give some idea of the standards of well-being which prevailed in Motol when I say that our yearly budget was probably seldom more than five or six hundred roubles—two hundred and fifty or three hundred dollars—in all'), He was a 'transportierer' in the timber trade. 'He cut and hauled the timber and got it floated down to Danzig. . . . It was hard and exacting work, but on the whole my father did not dislike it, perhaps because it called for a considerable degree of skill. It was his business to mark out the trees to be felled and he had to be able to tell which were healthy and worth felling.'

Ozer Weizmann's worldly strain showed itself in other ways. He was the kind of man to whom people brought their disputes for arbitration, and he seems to have had the same sceptical humour as we find highly developed in his famous son. He refused to take sides in public or private quarrels. 'If a man insisted on telling him his side of the story he would listen patiently to the end and say: "From what you say, I can see that you are entirely in the wrong. Now I shall have to hear the other side; perhaps you are in the right after all."' There was of course plenty of litigation in Motol, as in all *Shtetlach*; Sholom Aleichem and Mendelle and Peretz give us some idea of the bitterness and meanness of the disputes, and if Ozer Weizmann had not been a reluctant as well as a fair-minded arbitrator he would have been swamped by this ungrateful avocation. But it is clear that the Rabbinical dictum of *Torah im Detekh-Eretz*, scholarship and worldly wisdom side by side, was deeply implanted in Ozer Weizmann; it appears again strongly in his son. It is unlikely that if Chaim Weizmann had chosen a non-scientific career he would have been less systematic and practical in his approach to personal and public problems. As it was, he brought to his scientific work the kind of application which we associated with the best Jewish tradition. He understood the power of the tradition. Of Jewish scientific achievements he writes: 'Our great men were always a product of the symbiosis between the ancient, traditional Talmudical learning in which our ancestors were steeped in the Polish or Rumanian ghettos or even in Spain, and the modern Western universities with which their children came in contact. There is as often as not a long list of Talmudic scholars and Rabbis in the pedigrees of modern scientists!'

It is possible to draw a not too fanciful parallel between some of Chaim's childhood experiences and his mature responses to problems. He himself draws one. As a boy in Pinsk he used to take part during the Purim holiday in the money-box collections for Palestine: 'Purim always came in the midst of the March thaw, and hour after hour I would go tramping through the mud of Pinsk, from end to end of the town. I remember that my mother was accustomed, for reasons of economy, to make my overcoats too long for me, to allow for growth, so that as I went I repeatedly stumbled over the skirts and sometimes fell headlong into the icy slush of the streets. I worked late into the night, but usually had the satisfaction of bringing in more money than anyone else. Such was my apprenticeship for the activities which, on a rather larger scale, have occupied so many years of my later life.' He may also have served, less consciously, another kind of apprenticeship, watching his father the arbitrator, or hearing him discuss a case, learning from him— to whatever extent one can learn it—the art of weighing personalities and possibilities.

If it was accident that turned Weizmann's attention to chemistry it was not by accident that he acquired a modern and Western education. That was his father's doing. Though 'Motol was situated in one of the darkest and most forlorn corners of the Pale', though 'communication with the outside world was precarious and intermittent', though 'there was no post office and no railway, and no metalled road passed within twenty miles', Ozer Weizmann belonged to the world of the *Maskilim*, the enlighteners and modernizers of Jewish life, who were far more apt to be found in the cities than the *Shtetlach*. 'He worried overmuch for his children. A Jew of the lower middle class, he aspired to give them the best education. There were twelve of us ultimately, and with his and each other's help nine of us went through universities—an unheard of achievement in those days.' As we have seen, Chaim Weizmann's education was exclusively Jewish until the age of eleven; such it would have remained if his father had not been modernized. *Shtetl* fathers dreaded the thought of a secular education for their children; they looked on it as the first step towards apostasy. Ozer Weizmann, however, sent the little boy of eleven to Pinsk, some thirty miles away, to enter the Russian high school; a few years later the whole family moved to Pinsk, and one young Weizmann after another was launched on secular studies.

By comparison with Motol, Pinsk was of course a metropolis. It had a population of some thirty thousand, of which two-thirds were Jews. The Jewish community had a long and illustrious history; famous Rabbis and scholars are on its rosters; modern Zionist leaders have come from Pinsk. In Weizmann's days it was one of the centres of Zionist agitation. Hebrew periodicals were obtainable there; Smolenskin and Pinsker and Ahad Ha'am, the pre-Herzlian Zionist thinkers and writers were studied; the Yiddish work of Mendelle, Peretz and Sholom Aleichem was read. If we want to schematize Weizmann's childhood-to-manhood years we may divide them into four periods: from his first year to his eleventh, in Motol, he imbibed, on the conscious and sub-conscious levels, his folk-Jewishness; from his eleventh to his eighteenth year Pinsk gave him his first training in Zionist work, and his first exercise in the adjustment of his Jewish to his scientific passions; in Berlin, from his twenty-first to his twenty-fourth year, he 'crystallized' his Zionist ideology and his life's purposes; in Geneva he was already a force in Zionism and a scientist of promise. His departure for England in 1904, at the age of thirty, was his 'withdrawal'—he went to Manchester, he himself says, 'reculer pour mieux sauter'. After Manchester he was in effect, though not officially, the central figure of world Zionism.

Something more should be said about the Pinsk period. It was there that Weizmann made his first sustained contact with the non-Jewish world. With a number of other Jewish boys he went through the high school course. The vast majority of students—and all the teachers—were Russian; the atmosphere in the school was patriotic, tinged with Russian mysticism, and the mystique was not without its attractiveness. There was, in fact, 'a wide assimilatory fringe in Jewish life' in Pinsk. 'For that matter,' Weizmann adds, 'we, the Zionists, did not remain indifferent to Russian civilization and culture. I think I may say that we spoke the language better, were more intimately acquainted with its literature, than most Russians. But we were rooted heart and soul in our own culture and it did not occur to us to give it up in deference to another.' In other words, there was no inner struggle, no temptation, no tug of contrary identities or loyalties. Weizmann showed early his capacity for absorbing cultural values from the non-Jewish world without disturbing effect on the integrity of his Jewishness—integrity in the etymological sense of oneness, wholeness. We are inclined to credit this capacity to the *Shtetl* childhood and education, but again this is a statistical and not an individual explanation. Eight of Weizmann's brothers and sisters, we have seen, ultimately settled in Palestine, but three did not, and one brother was a Russian revolutionary. Among Weizmann's Russian-assimilating school contemporaries there must have been other children of the *Shtetl*. It is a great pity that *Trial and Error* dwells so briefly on the early years, and mentions only the Zionists who came from Jewish Pinsk; we would like to know what happened to some of the assimilating Jewish students, and what roles they played in the later history of Russia and Russian Jewry.

The integrity of Weizmann's Jewishness, so thoroughly established in his boyhood, helps us to sympathize with his feeling of shock when he first encountered German-Jewish assimilationism. On graduating from high school he left Russia for Darmstadt, Germany, to continue his education; he supported himself by teaching in an orthodox Jewish boarding school in nearby Pfungstadt, and this was his 'intro-

duction to one of the queerest chapters in Jewish history'—the
chapter of the deluded 'Germans of the Mosaic persuasion', who
looked on German anti-Semitism as a trivial and evanescent 'misunderstanding' and thought of themselves as descendants of the
Cerusci. The phenomenon baffled the young Weizmann; he found
no channel of communication between himself and his colleagues;
the Jewish orthodoxy of the school was utterly wild to him—it had
none of the folk warmth of Motol; the teachers, and the headmaster
in particular, were the victims of that superiority-inferiority-complex
in which the Jew is all sterling gold and his Jewishness a sort of
private irrelevance. It was a traumatic but useful experience for
Weizmann; he was going to have much to do with assimilationist
Jews in later years.

He endured Pfungstadt for two terms and returned to Pinsk, in
part because of homesickness, in part because things were going badly
at home, and his help was needed. For another year he lived in the
midst of the Jewishness and Zionism of the Pale. When he left for
Berlin, Motol and Pinsk had prepared him for the next stage of his
development.

It was by no means his last contact with the *Shtetl* and the Pale.
Throughout his student years in Berlin and Freiburg, and later when
he taught at the University of Geneva, he invariably spent the
summer vacations in Russia, carrying the Zionist message to ever
widening areas, beginning with the area about Pinsk and extending
his activities till they covered a considerable section of the country.
There was no world Zionist Organization until Herzl created it in
1897; there were only groups of the *Choveve Zion* under the direction
of the Odessa Committee. Weizmann urged the formation of local
groups of the *Choveve Zion* and participated in the modest fund-
raising of those days. Later he agitated for support of the Zionist Congresses. 'From the tiny communities of the marshlands I graduated
to Vilna in the north, to Kiev and even Kharkov, with their large
groups of student bodies, in the south.'

What Weizmann acquired during these summer activities was a
deep knowledge of Russian Jewry, its potentialities and its weaknesses. He was at the heart of that great mass of Jewry which was to
play the dominant role in the building of the Jewish homeland,
giving it a character it still largely retains. Of the four periods into
which I have somewhat artificially divided Weizmann's pre-
Manchester life the last two, Germany and Switzerland, witnessed
his growth into leadership. The first two help us to see more clearly
the nature of the struggle which arose between Herzl and Weizmann,

and the growth and meaning of the 'Democratic Faction', which was ultimately to become the main body of the Zionist movement.

It was a clash between West-European and East-European Zionism; it was also a clash between two powerful representative personalities. From one point of view Herzl and Weizmann had in common an over-riding characteristic and an over-riding objective which should havè kept them united. They were both supremely men of form; they wanted to bring order out of the chaos of Jewry and Zionism; they wanted to overcome the psychological handicaps of life in exile. But the differences of approach and method and experience made harmonious co-operation impossible.

Herzl did not grow into Zionism; Zionism struck him like a thunderbolt. The concept of the Jewish state flashed into him and changed his life, but did not change the effects of his life-experience. He saw the Jewish State in its completeness—army and working hours, flag and clergy, duels and marriage-bonuses. The intermediary steps were conceived in the spirit of a state-in-being. In *Der Judenstaat* he presented this picture to the world, and the Zionist Congress was the anticipation of the Jewish state: therefore the Zionist Congress had to have fitting form and dignity (the delegates had to come in formal attire). Emperors, Sultans, Grand Dukes, Chancellors were at the outset part of the general decor, and the Jewish masses were the central theme.

Weizmann began with the masses. His sense of form did not come to him from immersion in the Western world. Wherever it came from, he felt it as a reaction against the wretched disorder of the *Shtetl* and the Pale. Herzl thought of form as an instrument; for Weizmann it meant a transformation of Jewish life. We may even say that for Weizmann it was a more serious business than for Herzl— for which reason his attitude toward it was more elastic. He was not as solemn about it. He could share the *Shtetl's* derision of it. But while pomp and circumstances as *Narrishkeit* were one thing, form as the craftsmanship of life, in science, politics, social relations, physical surroundings, aesthetics, manners, was a very different thing. It was what the Jewish people had to acquire *inwardly*, and Weizmann was its teacher in personal example and public life. It needed a *Shtetl* man, flesh of its flesh, bone of its bone, a *Shtetl* man who had made the transformation in himself—it needed such a man to initiate the transformation in the people. He had to draw from the *Shtetl* the power to overcome, against the inertia of centuries, the *Shtetl's* ingrained disdain of order and system, which it had come to regard as an essential ingredient of Jewishness. To the *Shtetl* form was a *goyische sach*, a Gentile business; it had to do with uniforms, governments, *olam hazeh* generally. But *olam hazeh*, this world, was the heart of the issue; the Jewish faith is not centred on *olam haba*, the next world, though the Jewish way of life in *Golus* was. Weizmann was a successful teacher and leader in this respect because he knew when form became choreography—necessary choreography, undoubtedly, since such is the language of the world, yet still only choreography as far as the inner man is concerned. He too could therefore be amused by the decorative fallals which belonged to 'impressiveness'; the sardonic *Shtetl* Jew was embedded in the dignified statesman, and the two were on friendly terms.

An illustrative incident occurred at one of the early Congresses. Herzl had proposed that a Vice-Presidency of the Congress be given to Sir Francis Montefiore of England, the nephew of the great Sir Moses Montefiore. 'We did not want Sir Francis as a Vice-President of the Congress,' writes Weizmann. 'He was a very nice old English gentleman, but rather footling. He spoke in and out of season, and in a sepulchral voice, of "*mein seliger Oheim*—my sainted uncle". . . . We did not mind him as a show-piece but we were rather fed up with his sainted uncle and we wanted that particular Vice-Presidency to go to some real personality. . . . When Herzl pressed his point on me I said, "But Dr Herzl, the man's a fool." To which Herzl replied, with immense solemnity: "*Er öffnet mir königliche Pforten*—he opens the portals of royalty to me." I could not help grinning at this stately remark, and Herzl turned white.'

Weizmann regarded Herzl's approach to Zionism as '*simpliste* and doomed to failure'. He had no faith in the rich Jews Herzl was courting, and none in the high negotiations he was conducting with the mighty. There was also, Weizmann remarks, 'a touch of Byzantinism in his manner. Almost from the outset a kind of court sprang up about him, of worshippers who pretended to guard him from the mob. I am compelled to say that certain elements in his bearing invited such an attitude.'

Even when, disillusioned with the rich Jews, Herzl turned to the masses, it was with a technique poles apart from Weizmann's. Herzl's was the magnificent gesture of a Congress, a calling up of the Jewish people; Weizmann's was the laborious tending of little groups, the winning over the student youth, the holding of conferences preceded by preliminary conferences—patient organic construction of a national will that paralleled his idea of patient organic construction of a homeland. In the forlorn Jewish communities of his early missionary work 'it was not a question of preaching Zionism as much as of awakening them to action.' Among the students of the West it was both propaganda and organizational preparation for action. From

Trial and Error, but much more from Weizmann's enormous corres-'
pondence preserved in the Weizmann Archives, we obtain a picture
of relentless activity. While Herzl was breaking his heart trying to get
the grand 'Charter' for a Jewish state by diplomatic negotiations
with statesmen (at the same time holding down his job on the *Neue
Freie Presse*) Weizmann was breaking his back among the little
people (at the same time pursuing his scientific studies); and not a
little of Herzl's heartache was caused by the intransigent 'Young
Turks' of the Zionist movement at a time when he was negotiating
with the slippery Old Turks of the Sublime Porte.

It came to open rebellion—at least Herzl saw it as such in 1901,
when the Weizmann group organized a Conference of the Youth at
Munich; it was the clear intention of this group to 'take over', and to
conduct the Zionist movement according to its special concepts. Herzl
demanded that the conference be called off; he had 'weighty reasons
of state' which he could not disclose; a Zionist Congress was due; he
needed the unanimous backing of the organization; Weizmann and
the other wild youngsters (actually Weizmann was only fourteen
years younger than Herzl) were queering his pitch vis à vis 'the
powers'. And we must remember that Herzl lived at times in a state
of what must have seemed to Weizmann and seems to us now to be
semi-hallucination: he was expecting the 'Charter' at any moment.
He went on expecting it for years—until his death in 1904; his
capacity to survive disappointment was almost inhuman. No wonder
he wrote in his *Diaries*: 'The most wonderful thing is when a man
never gives up.'

But the remarkable feature of that struggle in Zionism at the turn
of the century was its historically co-operative character, and this on
two levels. On one we may see Herzl as the myth, Weizmann as the
demiurge; on the other the two protagonists play identical roles!
Weizmann may have classed the response to Herzl's 'impracticality',
his grand gesticulations, with the *Shtetl's* typical helplessness: all this
talk of Sultan and Emperor was just so much rubbish. But the fact
was—and Weizmann knew it later—that Herzl was startlingly practical. Herzl was avatar on the first level, statesman on the other. 'The
effect produced by *The Jewish State*', writes Weizmann, 'was profound.' Yet 'not the ideas, but the personality which stood behind
them appealed to us. Here was daring, clarity and energy.... If
Herzl had contented himself with the mere publication of the booklet
... his name would be remembered today as one of the oddities of
Jewish history. What has given greatness to his name is Herzl's
rôle as a man of action, as the founder of the Zionist Congress, and
as an example of daring and devotion.'

It was Herzl's irreplaceable function to give form to the overall Zionist movement. He had the daring to present it to the world as the Jewish state on the march; this was more than daring, it was a kind of madness. Weizmann, in *Trial and Error*,[1] written almost half a century after the struggle, is not altogether clear as to his final evaluation of his predecessor in leadership. 'I first saw Herzl at the Second Congress in 1898, and though he was impressive, I cannot pretend that he swept me off my feet. . . . It seemed to me almost from the beginning that he was undertaking a task of gigantic magnitude without adequate preparation.' But that was the very point! Had Herzl waited for 'adequate preparation'—but we hardly know what that means in the circumstances!—he would not have been the tremendous force he was; he would have died before achieving anything. But pursuing the *fata morgana* of the Charter he created the Zionist Congress; and without the Zionist Congress, a supreme creation of form, Weizmann would have found his own task doubly difficult. In the extended explanations Weizmann offers of his opposition to Herzl we feel a certain uneasiness; he does not want to be misunderstood. Herzl was a great man, but the struggle was necessary, inevitable and wholesome.

Perhaps a touch of rivalry remains for the first place in the history of Zionism. These were 'men of destiny'. Herzl knew it explicitly of himself after the 'road to Damascus' illumination of *The Jewish State*. How explicitly Weizmann knew it of himself it is harder to say; he would have considered it naïve to admit it; but the carefulness with which he kept records bespeaks at least a sense of responsibility to history. Often his private correspondence—with his wife, particularly—consists of reports of meetings and interviews, of plans, hopes, disappointments related to the movement. He confided to his letters what Herzl confided to his *Diaries*, but there is this difference: Herzl made it clear that he was writing for posterity; Weizmann, more subtle, would have had it that he was writing for his intimates and collaborators.

With two men so different in their endowments and historic functions we should be wasting our time debating who was 'the greater man'; but, debate aside, there is some interest in comparing Herzl and Weizmann as diplomatists. Elsewhere in this volume, T. R. Fyvel quotes Sir Charles Webster, the distinguished British historian, as saying that Weizmann's achievements in obtaining the Balfour Declaration was the greatest of all feats of diplomacy he had ever

[1] *Trial and Error*, by Chaim Weizmann (London, Hamish Hamilton, 1949, New York, Harper & Bros., 1954).

known. Sir Charles was intimately acquainted with Weizmann and his work; his knowledge of Herzl was at second hand. Who of the two men did more to bring the Zionist claim to the favourable attention of statesmen and the public cannot even be discussed; we can only compare the differences in personalities and historic contexts.

The personalities fitted the contexts. Herzl had nothing to work with but an inspiration. There was no international political situation for him to edge into; there was next to no colonization in Palestine for him to point to. As diplomatist he had to operate with fantasy, and for this he was superbly fitted. His ability to rise above realism was his indispensable asset in the era when there were no realities to hand. When Weizmann entered the international scene things were in flux; there was a 'situation'; also there was something to show in Palestine, at least on a model scale. Weizmann had realities to handle, and for this *he* was superbly fitted. These are striking instances of the congruence between men of achievement and their time.

We may say that Herzl had the imaginative gift of the artistic dreamer, Weizmann the imaginative gift of the artistic scientist. Herzl day-dreamed of the perfected Jewish state, hence the touch of Messianism about him, for Messianism is a kind of compulsive and panicky day-dreaming of perfection; but what saved Herzl from being a false Messiah was that he did more than dream. A powerful realistic impulse drove him in the setting up of the Zionist Congress; the same impulse bade him confide his Messianist side to his secret *Diaries*, in which he frankly notes that if they were made public prematurely he would be considered a lunatic. Weizmann's imagination, not less brilliant than Herzl's, was deployed among the empirical data of the laboratory, literally and figuratively; what is more, he had himself insisted on the setting up of the modest Zionist 'laboratory' in Palestine—or we may call it the pilot plant which would help him to 'sell' his idea to the world.

We associate some of Herzl's diplomatic skill with his experience as political correspondent; for years he watched and reported the debates in the French Chamber of Deputies; there he also acquired some of his flair for political organization. But where did Weizmann find neophyte practice for his—according to Webster—incomparable diplomatic capacities? Where shall we look for the first evidence of his subtle, prehensile grasp of possibilities and characters? The material in *Trial and Error* is scanty until we reach the time of the Balfour Declaration, and by then we have passed beyond our question. His letters are more helpful; but on the whole we must resort to speculation.

Weizmann's own view, as we have seen, is that by 1898, when he

left Berlin, the adult pattern of his life was set. 'Of course I learned
a great deal in later years; but no fundamental change took place.'
Weizmann may have been mistaken in this self-evaluation; there may
have taken place between 1904, when he withdrew to Manchester,
and 1917, when he went to London, an unforeseeable and fateful
maturation; but it is unlikely that such a change can have come over
him between his thirtieth and his forty-third years. He may therefore
be wrong to this extent: the Geneva period (in which I include the
preceding two years in neighbouring Freiburg, where he took his
doctorate in science) represented in his growth more than he realized,
and it was there that his diplomatic gifts were first manifested.

This was the period of the programmatic founding of the Democratic Faction; it was also the period in which the lines of the battle
between Russian revolutionaries and Zionists for the possession of the
Jewish student youth were clearly drawn. Lenin, Plekhanov and
Trotsky were in and out of Switzerland in those days; their political
philosophy had no room for a Jewish nationalist movement; for them
the Jewish problem was peripheral, its solution a corollary. They
resented a Jewish movement which had this problem at its centre.
The Zionist youth was not anti-revolutionary, but the revolutionaries
were anti-Zionist; again, the majority of Jewish students was not
anti-Zionist, but it was overawed by the authority—and the authoritarian attitude—of the revolutionary leaders. 'Thus the mass of
Russian-Jewish students in Switzerland had been bullied into an
artificial denial of their own personality.'

And thus Weizmann, the leading figure in those circles, directed
two struggles in which there was a considerable element of diplomacy. He fought Herzl the Zionist leader while seeking to strengthen
the movement; he fought the revolutionaries while refusing to place
himself and his fellow Zionist in the anti-revolutionary ranks. As he
notes, 'the struggle was not of our choosing . . . our sympathies were
with the revolutionaries.' His antagonists were bound to picture him,
in both instances, as giving aid and comfort to 'the enemy', and
while no one would accuse him of anti-Zionism, he was labelled by
the revolutionaries as a reactionary.

We may call the problem here one of intellectual diplomacy, but
when we think of the details we see the need for person to person
diplomacy, in which evaluation of personalities plays a crucial part.
Which were the serious men and which the windbags? Who had to
be won over, whom could one ignore? Where should one yield, where
insist? Timing is an essential element in action, and intuition comes
into play as well as calculation. All this is part of the diplomacy of
leadership.

Early Life

1 Chaim Weizmann aged 8 in Motol

2 The family house in Motol where he was born

3 Weizmann and Berthold Feiwel, 1900

4 Weizmann (*centre*) in Geneva in 1901 with (*left to right*) Ephraim Lilien, Leo Motzkin, (*sitting*) Feiwel and Martin Buber

5 Weizmann's family in Pinsk, 1911

6 Weizmann's house in Manchester

7 Weizmann and some of the Faculty of Manchester University, 1912

The extent of Weizmann's Zionist activities during that period is hardly reflected in his memoirs; it is from the letters that we gather how much time and nervous energy were taken up by the movement, and we are astonished that anything was left over for his scientific pursuits. He obviously had an appalling capacity for work, and a will that overcame exhaustion. Nor must we forget that he was already learning the bitter taste of leadership; the wheel was turning and when it came full circle Weizmann was to know how Herzl suffered under internal opposition. The Democratic Faction had its own faction from the beginning, and Nachman Syrkin's passionate socialism-without-Zionism was a thorn in Weizmann's side. In the mellow pages of *Trial and Error* Weizmann speaks with warmth and unaffected admiration of Syrkin; but at the time of the struggle his descriptions of Syrkin are far from generous. This we see in his private correspondence; how he expressed himself in public we do not know.

The complications in Weizmann's position at this time invite a larger study than can be given them here. It cannot be denied that Herzl was in an important sense a reactionary figure. His diplomacy belonged to the eighteenth century. He represented the Jewish people and had little acquaintance with it. He worked for its salvation from above, a king negotiating with kings. Neither Herzl nor Weizmann was conventionally religious, but in their respect for religion there was a revealing divergence. Herzl, says Weizmann correctly, 'had excessive respect for the Jewish clergy, born not out of intimacy but of distance'. Weizmann was a democratic figure in this sense among others: he saw that the Jewish people had to be the chief instrument in its own liberation; he worked for salvation from within; and on the whole Weizmann (like his deeply religious father) was anti-clerical. Herzl was painfully anxious to demonstrate that the Zionist movement was not socialist and revolutionary; Weizmann, not a socialist or revolutionary, could not ask the Jewish masses to disguise their hatred of autocracy—Russian autocracy in particular. Herzl was asking the Jewish people to let him manage its affairs; Weizmann wanted it to manage them itself. There was much of the classical *Shtatlan* in Herzl, with this difference: the *Shtatlan* was usually a rich Jew who undertook to represent the Jewish people for the benefit of his class, while Herzl was thinking only of his people. Weizmann, however, conceived of Zionism as the antithesis of *Shtatlanut* in any sense.

All this had become clear to Weizmann in his Berlin period, but it was in the Geneva period that he entered seriously on the practical applications. He was never blind to the unique significance of Herzl, and he was never reconciled to his technique; here is another facet of the need for intellectual diplomacy. But towards the close of the Geneva period Weizmann had already begun the exercise of diplomacy in its ordinary sense. When the struggle over the British offer of Uganda to the Zionists was at its height he made a visit to England and interviewed Lord Percy, then in charge of African affairs, Sir Harry Johnston, the famous explorer, an authority on Uganda, and Sir William Evans Gordon, the father of the Aliens Bill which had sharply cut down Jewish immigration into England. (He does not tell us how, ignorant of English as he then was, he communicated with them.) His interviews confirmed his deep-rooted belief that the Uganda idea was utterly impracticable—this apart from his equally deep-rooted views as to its 'ideological and moral shortcomings'—and the report he wrote contributed not a little, he felt, to the defeat of the Uganda proposal. Relevant at this point is the early evidence of Weizmann's propensity to negotiate, to seek out the right people, to get at the realities and to act on them. That at thirty, an obscure foreigner, ignorant of English, he obtained what seem to have been solid and detailed explanations from these three important men is even more striking evidence of the power to impress and charm which became his mightiest asset.

Without knowing how he came by this personality and these gifts, we see plainly, I believe, that their expression and exercise were closely related to his *Shtetl* and Pale upbringing. He had a special appeal for the Jewishly moulded masses, and was therefore eminently fitted to help them help themselves. They loved him because they knew that he knew them 'inside out' and shared their ambivalence; he loved them without illusion. There was also something piquant in his rise to Jewish world leadership; it was peculiarly pleasing to them that a 'Yiddel from Motolle' should have made the grade, that the world should accept him rather than some distinguished semi-assimilated Westerner. There was a 'knowing' relationship between Weizmann and the Yiddish-speaking masses; they had, as it were, a private wink for each other. It detracted somewhat from the mystique of leadership, but it made the mutual attraction stronger.

Weizmann carried with him the weight of the Jewish masses—as Herzl did not—and the weight of Jewish history. He remained of the *Shtetl* while he transcended it. He was respected by non-Jews for both aspects. He was completely at ease among non-Jews, he felt no discomfort and occasioned none. He did not—as consciously assimilating Jews often do—put his hosts under a strain, practising and tacitly requesting evasion of Jewish subjects. One of his favourite phrases was: '*C'est à laisser ou à prendre*, take it or leave it,' not in a chip-on-shoulder spirit, but naturally and good-humouredly.

The massive relationship between Weizmann's *Shtetl* identity and his effect on the world dominated the public tribute to his memory when he died on 9 November 1952. His tremendous qualities were linked with his *Shtetl* upbringing. 'It is well that we try to understand the elements of native ability, environment and character that made the man and his career.' '. . . a great humanitarian, a man of the moral stature to stand beside the patriarchs and judges of the long, proud past of the Jewish people.' 'Like the industrialist tycoon who likes to call himself a simple country boy, Weizmann would introduce himself as a humble Jew from Motol. He was far more complex . . . he moved about banquet halls, diplomatic conferences, and secret meetings with the aplomb of a great lord . . . yet Motol was never far off. Though Chaim Weizmann was fluent in seven languages, it was in Yiddish that he felt most at home. His humour, too, was peculiarly Yiddish. . . .' 'He belongs to a generation that has seen changes greater than in any similar span of history. Yet within it there can be few men whose end was so markedly removed from their beginning, yet so markedly linked to it by a chain of spirit and purpose.'

This aspect of Weizmann's relationship to his people is of more than biographical or historical interest; it has some bearing on the future of Israel and of world Jewry. The effective part of world Jewry today consists of two groups; those sons of the *Shtetl* and the Pale who have been largely responsible in Israel for making Israel what it is; and those who constitute the majority of the Western Diaspora. With the passing of Weizmann there disappeared the unifying personal symbol of Israel and the Diaspora; he was the last *world*-Jewish leader. The times are such that his greatness in that rôle is not understood—and this lack of understanding is, precisely, the symptom of our present difficulty. World Jewry is engaged in a double task with a single ultimate purpose. The consolidating of Israel as an independent nation and the promotion of a Jewish renaissance in the Diaspora should mesh in the movement towards world Jewish unity; they mesh imperfectly because of conflicting claims for priority in action; and out of this conflict another has arisen over priority *in significance*. A tactical question has been blown up into a vast strategical decision, and we have not, at the moment, a man of Weizmann's moral authority to restate the situation in perspective; nor are we willing at the moment, to recognize that the answer is represented in the heritage of Weizmann's personality.

The conflict is not new. It began with the Zionist movement itself. Shall (or can) Jewry remain a world people with a Jewish state in Palestine, or shall the Jewish state represent the be-all and the end-all? Weizmann, like his teacher Ahad Ha'am, saw in this question a false antithesis. Weizmann *loved* Diaspora Jewry because he was of it; he was the architect of the Jewish state (and so obviously that there was simply no question as to who should be its first President) because he knew the need for it, both in itself and for the sake of a continuing Diaspora Jewry. Beyond all his remarkable gifts it was this unity in duality that lifted him to the position of the most representative Jew of the twentieth century, and made him the symbol of the Jewish future. The distractions of a transitional era obscure the perspective, but it will stand out clearly when the total purpose of a Jewish state will be fulfilled.

Mr Maurice Samuel, author and lecturer, is an authority on Jewish folkways and Yiddish literature. He has translated Sholem Aleichem, J. L. Peretz and Sholem Asch, among others, into English.

1904—1914

CHAPTER THREE

THE MANCHESTER PERIOD

ISRAEL M. SIEFF

WEIZMANN'S DECISION to leave the Continent and settle down in England, certainly one of the most momentous of his life, was in a way a form of retreat. It was, curiously enough, to some extent a result of the great Uganda controversy.

Herzl had been inflamed by the British offer of Uganda primarily because of his concern with the fate of Eastern European Jewry. Yet it was, ironically, among Russian Jews, victims of the Kishinev pogrom of 1903, that the most unyielding opposition to the Uganda proposal arose. Herzl had been successful in rallying the 6th Zionist Congress to the support of Uganda, but although 295 delegates voted in its favour, there were 175 against it, and about a hundred abstentions. The upshot was that the opposition to Uganda could not be stifled; it compelled Herzl to relieve it of responsibility for maintaining the 'unit' rule, marched out of the Congress, and produced the first split in the Zionist movement.

But in spite of Herzl's technical victory the Uganda offer withered on the vine. It was definitely rejected by the 7th Congress, in 1905, a year after Herzl's death, and from then on the Zionist movement, after the secession of the pro-Uganda faction, led by Israel Zangwill, remained undistracted, at least by territorial questions. The resolution of the Uganda controversy was to leave the Zionist movement unshakeably fixed in its concentration on Palestine, and on no other country, as the object of its territorial aspirations.

After Herzl's technical victory, however, Weizmann found himself in a curious position. He had never been able to accept Herzl's stand on the Uganda question, but at the same time he was in no position to challenge it successfully against the tremendous authority and self-confidence still reflected by Herzl and his closest colleagues. With no faith in Herzl's policy on Uganda, and still without an effective following for any other course, what, in fact, could he do but retire, like Muhammad, and wait with patience?

This was how it seemed to him at one point during the aftermath of the Uganda compromise. But there were other factors. The world around him was breaking up. Assailants and defenders were taking up positions. Britain and France, for long rivals in Africa and in the Levant, were drawing together into an *Entente Cordiale*, in order to resist the advances of the Kaiser, a rival newcomer. Even more significant, was the news from Russia. The Tsarist Empire was reeling into defeat at the hands of the Japanese. Russia was losing one decisive battle after another.

It was against this general background of turmoil that Weizmann packed his bags to leave the Continent. In later years, he was never precise or consistent when he came to explain the reasons for his departure from Geneva, and especially his choice of Manchester. In his frame of mind during those critical months, he passed through many changing moods of hope, frustration, disappointment and determination. Sometimes his reasons were personal, as when he was afraid that he was becoming a political *luftmensch*; more often it was political, and linked to his ever-mounting despair over Zionist policy. He could see no way out in the Geneva milieu in which he moved. 'I perceived', he wrote later, 'the utter inadequacy of the Zionist movement, as then constituted, in relation to the tragedy of the Jewish people.'

Herzl's death merely served to underline this inadequacy. Weizmann's departure at that moment, not for the funeral in Vienna, but for provincial Manchester, was perhaps the strongest symbolic act of his career. It was the first public demonstration (to himself if to no one else) of the iron that was in his soul. He recognized that his travail over Zionism had for the time being led him into a *cul-de-sac*, or possibly a parting of the ways. He had to choose one road or the other; there could be no compromise.

His choice of Manchester, though he was directed there by his scientific inclinations and recommendations, was probably accidental. But there can be little doubt that once he decided to leave Geneva, he wanted to go to England more than to any other country. He had great—almost touching—faith in England and in the English. It was a faith that went back to his school days in Motol, and that was to stay with him to the end, despite the many disappointments it caused him. And so Weizmann came to England, settled in Manchester, married his fiancée Vera and maintained his resolve to withdraw from active Zionism—but not for long.

How could he turn his back on the extraordinary changes that were taking place, which demanded a Zionist reassessment? As he settled to his work, the Russian defeat at the hands of the Japanese touched off the uprising in St Petersburg and in Warsaw. Revolution was followed by large-scale mutiny. The foundations of the old world —largely inhabited by 'his' Jews—were beginning to rock. In Britain, too, the Conservative Balfour Administration was entering on its eclipse.

Weizmann's sojourn in Manchester coincided with the last supposedly 'peaceful decade' that preceded the first World War, though it was nothing of the kind. All his life he had been a most sensitive political seismograph, and he could not fail to register the upheaval that had begun, with its implications for Zionist aspirations in Palestine, as well as the Jewish need for a haven somewhere in the world.

The Manchester decade of 1904–1914 gave Weizmann the time to make a reappraisal of Zionist policy and methods, as well as an opportunity to prepare his mind to cope with the changing international scene. With his scientific mind he was always careful to prepare his approach to a problem. He had an ideal objective, which he tried to define as clearly as he could. His struggles with David Wolffsohn, Leopold Greenberg and Max Nordau had not weakened his faith in his methodical approach, but strengthened it. His discussions, speeches and debates helped to crystallize his central idea, the synthesis of practical and political Zionism. Whilst naturally critical of those who opposed him, he was also prepared at all times to put his own ideas and theories to a critical analysis.

My account of the Manchester period is bound to be strongly subjective. My relations with Weizmann were based upon mutual affection and trust. To those who loved him he disclosed the endless treasures of his spirit, and to me, in my youth, he seemed both prophet and statesman—a synthesis of the prophets of the Bible and of the vigorous thinkers of the nineteenth century.

Our intimacy enabled Weizmann to explain to me, without reserve, his motives for many of the ideas and actions that seemed at the time incomprehensible in some ways and too visionary, but that, in perspective I now see as always having led towards the goal of the independent State of Israel.

I had the good fortune, along with my wife and brother-in-law Simon Marks, to have been continuously in Chaim Weizmann's company, from 1913 to 1921, sharing many of his experiences and discussions and also, his often eloquent silences. We spoke endlessly about the future of the Jewish people in terms of the fluid international situation and, after 1917, in terms of the vision conjured up by the Balfour Declaration. Nothing was impossible. The Jewish state was 'just around the corner'. He spoke to us countless times of his hopes and his frustrations, his likes and his dislikes, his visions and his disappointments, his philosophy of life and of science, his love of the Jewish people and his burning faith in the Jews' will to become an independent people and to create a state that would not only be materially prosperous, but that would establish a society reigned over by the ethics of the Bible. He believed that, out of the turmoil of world conflict, the Jews would eventually emerge as the bearers of the Messianic message depicted in Isaiah—especially the words in Chapter 2, Verse IV: 'And they shall beat their swords into plow-shares and their spears into pruning hooks; nation shall not lift up sword against nation; neither shall they learn war any more.'

Weizmann and I had first met at a dinner given by a kinsman of mine in Manchester during the summer of 1913. During the evening, Dr Weizmann explained to the guests the working of the Keren Kayemeth, emphasizing that it was the 'pennies of the people' that would finally redeem the Land of Israel for the House of Israel. The word 'pennies' struck me as a petty unit for such a grand goal; I asked why it was not possible to collect pounds. I added that, for the Manchester Jewish Hospital, we had, one week before our meeting that evening, collected £28,000 from the Manchester Jewish community. Could we not do the same for the Keren Kayemeth? With a boastful gesture, I added that I would be prepared to go to the next Actions Committee to show its members how to do it. Dr Weizmann then invited me to attend the next meeting, which was to be held in Berlin in August 1914. Next morning, our host telephoned me to say that Dr Weizmann considered me 'a foolish fellow'; he was probably right. I telephone Dr Weizmann to say that I wanted to meet him again as soon as possible, to prove to him that my foolishness had been a temporary aberration. He agreed to see me—and so our friendship began.

Looking back now, it is easy to over-simplify the influences that played upon Weizmann during the Manchester years. He never forgot his first talk with Balfour in 1906, and he never deviated from the ideas expressed by him in the letter he wrote in 1885 to his old teacher in Motol, in which he expressed his abiding faith that, unlike all other nations, 'England will have mercy on us.'

His connection with the Manchester Society was a curious one. He liked to talk to the members but never got close to them. There was no intimacy of contact, no real warmth of affection. Of course there were some Zionists to whom he was delighted to talk. But once the conversation was finished he would escape to his laboratories or to his home and there find relief from the discussion on Zionist plans, the majority of which, as it seemed to us then, had little hope of being implemented.

Manchester Jewry was a pleasant society. Numbering about thirty thousand, it was composed, in the main, of Jews from Eastern Europe. Not many Jews from Germany remained within the community; most of them had become assimilated, and indeed, converted to Christianity. There was a small proportion of Sephardi Jews, but they did not play an important rôle in the life of the community. It was, on the whole, a homogeneous group, though there were, to be sure, different levels of prosperity. But there was less snobbery than existed, say, in Germany, between the German Jew and those whom they described as 'Ost-Juden'. There was a certain freedom of association and tolerance between the 'old settlers' and the new immigrants. They were 'landsleute'. The synagogues were the centre; there a pure democracy reigned. They were a charitable community, led by men like Nathan Laski, Charles Dreyfus and others. As in all Jewish communities, the family counted for a great deal. The Zionists were, as yet, a small group.

The arts were dominated by the famous Halle Orchestra, conducted by Sir Charles Halle, and, after his death, by Hans Richter. Besides, Manchester University was an institution of higher learning that housed scientists like Ernest Rutherford and William Henry Perkins, philosophers like Samuel Alexander and historians like Tout.

Manchester was also the centre of a growing chemical industry, the home of Brunner Mond (later the Imperial Chemical Industries) and of Aniline Dyes, of which Charles Dreyfus, at one time a leader of the Manchester Zionist Association, was the Chairman. There existed, therefore, in Manchester, all the elements, in the community and in its cultural life, through which Weizmann could find a sympathetic response to his intellectual and scientific ideas.

I once asked him why he chose to live in England. It was remote from the centre of Zionist activity and at that time he did not know English very well. He replied that he believed England would give him freedom to carry on his scientific work, and, above all, that his Zionist activities would find sympathy and understanding among the people.

In his admiration for England, and in his conviction that its people would somehow understand and even support the Zionist aims and aspirations, he was the spiritual heir of Herzl who, at a meeting in London in 1898 had said, 'From the first moment I entered the movement, my eyes were directed towards England because I saw that, by reason of the general situation of things there, it was the Archimedean point where the lever could be applied.'

It was a similar sentiment that motivated Weizmann when he too looked to England. At the 1903 Zionist Congress on the Uganda project, he said—'If the British Government and the British people are what I think they are, they will make us a better offer' (ie than Uganda). And in 1911, at a Conference of the English Zionist Federation in Manchester, he said: 'The English Gentiles are the best Gentiles in the world. England has helped small nations to gain their independence. We should try and get Gentile support for Zionism.'

Weizmann was thirty years old when he came to England. He had been to London earlier as 'a delegate from Pinsk for the 4th Zionist Congress. At that time he was not a Zionist leader, he was just an ordinary delegate who had yet to win his spurs in the movement. He had no friends in this country, but he was anxious to find Jews with whom he could discuss his visions. It was on the success or failure of his ideas and policies that he judged himself. He was his own self-appointed critic; he needed no other. It was for this reason that he was impatient of outside criticism; he thought much of it was petty and irrelevant.

His first two years in England were not happy. Because of his opposition to the Uganda scheme (in this he was uncompromising) he was cold-shouldered by the Zionists; he felt friendless. But his withdrawal from the organizational centre of the Zionist movement at that time took him out of the main stream of Zionism; it gave him the time and freedom to think through his Zionist principles once again.

How true was it that Weizmann came to England in order to withdraw from Zionism?

It is a fact that he was troubled by the state of Zionism after the 1903 Congress and, more particularly, by the Uganda conflict.

On the other hand, it proved difficult for him to abstain from his interest in the way the Zionist movement was developing. The struggle with the 'politicals' in some measure compelled him to resume his Zionist activities. He began to visit the Manchester Zionist Society and took part in its discussions.

In 1905, he was elected the Manchester Zionist Society's delegate to the English Zionist Federation Conference, and in July of that year, he spoke at a London Mass Meeting on Shekel Day. He was also appointed the Manchester Zionist Society's delegate to the 7th Zionist Congress to be held in Basle in July of that year. Thus he was increasingly drawn into the Zionist movement in this country, although at first he had the utmost difficulty in finding a common language with Anglo-Jews.

One of the outstanding events of 'the Manchester Decade' was, of course, Weizmann's meeting with Balfour, which took place in the Queens Hotel in that city in January 1906. The interview had been arranged by Charles Dreyfus, who was Chairman of the Manchester Conservative Party at that time, as well as Chairman of the Manchester Zionist Society and an ardent 'Ugandist'. Balfour had said that he would be interested in meeting an anti-Ugandist, and Dreyfus thought Balfour would convince Weizmann in favour of Uganda.

But it was the other way round. Balfour asked Weizmann why he was against Uganda, adding that it was a practical project and that the British Government wanted to be helpful. Weizmann replied that Zionism was a spiritual idea that had to be implemented in the Holy Land to keep the movement alive; deflection from Palestine would be idolatry. Uganda, he knew, was a well-meant offer, but the Jewish people would never give their money or their energy to settle a huge wasteland unless it was one with which they had historical and emotional ties. The Holy Land had a magic appeal that would act as an inspiration and a stimulus. Then came the famous conversation that is part of Jewish history, when Balfour was asked by Weizmann if he would change London for Paris. Balfour replied, 'No, but London is the capital of my country.' Weizmann answered, 'Jerusalem was the capital of our country when London was a marsh.' Later in the conversation, still referring to the attitude towards Uganda, Balfour said, 'It is curious—the Jews I meet are quite different,' and Weizmann replied, 'Mr Balfour, you meet the wrong kind of Jews.'

Balfour always said afterwards that it was his first meeting with Weizmann that made him a Zionist.

The interview with Balfour taught Weizmann two things—firstly, that in spite of Zionist propaganda, a leading and distinguished statesman like Balfour had only the most rudimentary and, indeed, naïve conception of what it stood for. Secondly, he felt that if there had been a group in England who could have presented the case for the Jewish National Home to the British authorities effectively and convincingly, it might not have been difficult to enlist their sympathetic, and perhaps active support.

How far the conversation with Balfour made Weizmann see the need for a thorough change in the character of the Zionist movement it is difficult to say, but there is no question of the fact that he felt that the time was ripe for such a change to take place. He had unmistakably passed beyond the Uganda dead point, and felt he must resume his Zionist activities.

His 'Manchester period', and his partial and temporary withdrawal from the Zionist movement, reinforced his desire to take up scientific research again. He liked Manchester University and wanted to become part of it. After a short period in the Research Laboratory, Professor Perkin permitted him to give a weekly lecture on Fermentation Chemistry, and promised to nominate him for a Research Scholarship to start at the beginning of the following year. In 1905 he gave his first scientific lecture in the English language; he recalled that he reached the lecture room with a rapidly beating heart, for he was much more affected by the challenge awaiting him in this lecture room than he had been by any of his important Zionist speeches. Some students stayed behind and asked questions, and he was sure that they were satisfied by his replies. He felt, as he put it, 'triumphant', and from that time on felt much closer to the students.

In spite of the satisfaction he drew from his scientific work, there still existed within him a basic conflict as the result of the continuing partial repression of his Zionist activities. He constantly felt that the future of Zionism demanded his attention. Gradually his mind was building up the main line of strategy to be followed as soon as he was able to take a more active part in the movement.

During this time, many of his Zionist friends (including Shmarya Levin) had been urging him to give up his work at the university and to go to Berlin to head one of the departments of the Zionist Organization there. This offer seemed tempting, since he was disappointed at not having received a full professorship at the university as he had expected after having taken his Master of Science degree. In 1913 he had been appointed Reader in Biological Chemistry; he felt that this might have entitled him to a full professorship, since there was a vacancy at Manchester University in this subject. He was convinced that he had sufficient ability as a teacher and that this, in addition to his good relations with his students, would be rewarded.

Thus the opportunity to go to Berlin and to take up the proposed post with the Zionist movement came at a time when he had to make a decision about a path of his future activities. His sharp sense of pique about the Manchester professorship led him to consider the Berlin proposal, but fortunately for the future of the Zionist movement his wife, Vera, was entirely opposed to the idea. She disliked Germany. In point of fact, Weizmann himself disliked that country when he had first gone there as a 19-year-old student; even at that time he had become aware of assimilated German Jewry—'exerting itself frantically', as he wrote later, 'to efface its own identity'.

It was not only in regard to the Berlin idea that his wife played such an important part in influencing Weizmann's decision. This is not the place for a résumé of Vera Weizmann's activities and her own contribution to the Zionist movement, ever since she came to Manchester in 1906. But what a vital part of those days she was!

She shared in all our discussions, our disappointments, our joys. Her own powerful spirit was an ever-present and indispensable supplement to his faith and courage. Without her his life would have been infinitely more burdensome, particularly in those times of repeated trial and bitter crisis. Vera herself has told me of the nostalgia she has often felt for what she describes as 'the most wonderful epoch of our lives'; in this she includes that first decade of her and Chaim's life in England.

It was, as it happens, through one of the many organizations in which his wife was interested—The Manchester School for Mothers —that Weizmann was first to meet C. P. Scott, the famous editor of the *Manchester Guardian* who was destined to figure so prominently in later events. Describing this initial encounter (which took place at a private home in Manchester in the latter half of 1914, at a party in support of this School for Mothers) Weizmann recalls that Scott invited him to his home a few days later. Weizmann then spoke to him of Jewish hopes and aspirations for Palestine; Scott listened with the utmost attention and, at the end of the conversation that day, said he would like to put Weizmann in touch with Lloyd George (then Chancellor of the Exchequer).

That interview with Lloyd George, which Scott arranged, took place in December 1914. In addition to Weizmann, Lloyd George and C. P. Scott, Herbert Samuel (then a member of the Asquith Government) and Josiah Wedgwood were also present. In the course of the discussion Herbert Samuel announced that he was preparing a Memorandum, for presentation to the Prime Minister, on the subject of a Jewish state in Palestine. This utterly astonished Weizmann, who had (mistakenly, as he confessed later) assumed Samuel to be the type of Jew who, by his very nature, would be opposed to Zionist aspirations.

The interview with Lloyd George was very satisfactory; it led to a further meeting with Balfour, and may have marked the starting point of the road leading to the Balfour Declaration. From the beginning not only Scott but the entire editorial staff of the *Guardian* became staunch adherents of the Zionist cause. Harry Sacher, who was then on the *Guardian* staff, also introduced Weizmann to Herbert Sidebotham, the *Guardian's* principal political writer, who later was to become an unfailing supporter of Zionism.

Weizmann meanwhile continued his work at Manchester University, and so, between 1906 and 1914, his two lives ran side by side, and, during this period, he enjoyed his work as a research scientist more than at any other time. He finally obtained his Doctorate of Science and published a great many scientific papers.

The Uganda split and the continuing struggle between the 'practical' and the 'political' Zionists led to a period of sterile dissension. This was reflected in Zionism at large as well as in the English Zionist Federation. Added to this, there was discord in Great Britain between the Zionist Federation and the Order of Ancient Maccabeans, a friendly society, the head of which was a member of a well-known Anglo-Jewish family—Herbert Bentwich.

Weizmann took an uncompromisingly radical view on the questions that were relevant to these diverse quarrels, whether it was Mount Zion or Uganda, the type of colonies to be established in Palestine, the use of Hebrew in the schools or the establishment of a Hebrew University.

In a lecture given in Manchester in 1905, Weizmann drew attention to the difference between the two attitudes of mind in Zionism, between East and West. The former regarded Zionism as a national necessity, to which the persecution of the Jews had no special relevance. The latter considered it no more than a philanthropic movement directed towards the alleviation of the harmful conditions under which Jews lived in some countries in the Diaspora. This comparison so dominated his mind in those days that he appeared almost to have a contempt for rich Jews who gave so much for charitable purposes. He threw the weight of his sympathy on the side of the Russian Jews who were doing something concrete in Palestine. He made much of the idea that the rich Jews regarded the settlement of the Jews in Palestine as 'not practical' whereas to Weizmann the word 'practical' carried an entirely different meaning. He therefore saw the Uganda project as a form of philanthropic deviationism that would result in a dissipation of the effort of the Jewish masses. But it must be said in justice to the supporters of the Uganda plan that they had been driven to desperation by the pogroms in Russia and their effect on East European Jewry. As Israel Zangwill, the leading British spokesman for the Uganda solution, put it in a speech made in Manchester in 1905: Palestine was closed; 'we do not know for how long. It is not a case of waiting seven years for Rachel and meeting Leah (Uganda). It is a case of Leah or nothing'. Zangwill ended his speech by saying that Palestine in one jump would be too great an effort for the Jews; he added, 'it was too much even for Moses'.

At this period, nearly all British Zionists were supporters of Uganda; Weizmann recalled that it was regarded as a betrayal of Zionist ideals to criticize the project. Of the Jewish leaders in England at that time, only Moses Gaster stood with him as a 'Nein-Sager'—an opponent of the Uganda project.

Weizmann also had to suffer the opposition of *The Jewish*

Chronicle and its editor, Leopold Greenberg, who became very hostile to his ideas and tried to bar Weizmann from the English Zionist movement. The *Chronicle* resented Weizmann's oft-repeated assertion that when he first arrived in England, Zionism was in a state of stagnation, limited to clichés and clap-trap.

However, in June of 1905 the Zionist Federation, at its half-yearly meeting, agreed that it was the unalterable decision of the Zionists to secure the establishment of a publicly recognized and legally secured home for the Jewish people in Palestine. The meeting pledged itself to reject any alteration to the Basle programme or the substitution of any place but Palestine as its goal. Thus, at last, Weizmann's policy triumphed; the Ugandists had been routed.

It was then that Zangwill left the Zionist movement and formed the Jewish Territorial Organization, which Weizmann considered had the advantage of isolating its followers and thus of 'purifying' Zionism. The victory brought him into friendlier contact with the English Zionists, and he was no longer regarded as a 'revolutionary outsider'.

The struggle between the 'political' and the 'practical' Zionists, which had led to Herzl's acceptance of the Uganda offer, was rooted in the idea that there was no point in starting practical work in Palestine unless the 'political charter' had been achieved. The 'practicals', on the other hand, held that nothing could be stable or permanent unless the land had been acquired, colonies established, and large numbers of immigrants settled in Palestine, to evolve as Jews both economically and culturally.

It is, I think, true to say that Weizmann was conscious of two meanings of the word 'practical'. For him, practical work in Palestine was something based on faith; it might very well be impractical in terms of sheer business sense. This contrast in meanings he brought out in a speech in Manchester in 1906, when he said: 'rich and semi-rich Jews might be practical men, but when has the liberation of a people been carried out by practical means? It is the "impractical" Russian Jews who are doing something'.

The discussions that took place on how to utilize a sum of £300,000, which was the capital of the Jewish Colonial Trust (the financial instrument of the Zionist movement at that time) brought out the differing views of the opposing outlooks of the movement. The 'politicals' wanted the capital to be left intact, so that more could be added as time went on, leading to the millions that would be necessary for the eventful right to establish a home in Palestine, which was then Turkish territory.

the foundation of agricultural and industrial enterprises in Palestine was treated with scant respect by the then President of the Zionist Organization, David Wolffsohn, and his colleagues. Weizmann was accused by his opponents of irresponsibility for wanting to use such large sums of money for 'visionary schemes', but Weizmann retorted by saying that 'should the money be lost, the chief thing is that the idea will remain'. He had faith that the Jewish people would be prepared to find the money required if they saw real, constructive work being carried on in Palestine.

Weizmann had imagined that after the defeat of the 'politicals', the Zionist leadership might agree to a policy of gradual peaceful penetration of Palestine, and a full practical programme. He used his time in England to attempt to convert the English Zionist Federation to his views; he thought he would use them as a 'ginger group' to move the Zionist Organization. In this he was disappointed. At the Ninth Zionist Congress, which met in Hamburg in 1909, Weizmann, whilst President of the Permanent Steering Committee, made a vigorous attempt to have Wolffsohn removed and a Presidential Committee of 'practical Zionists' set up in his place. He criticized the Inner Actions Committee, made up of 'practical Zionists', for not being sufficiently active. Wolffsohn first defended the Inner Actions Committee and then offered his resignation 'on grounds of health'.

Weizmann's motion for a Presidential Committee was not voted upon, as the majority of those who were proposed as members refused to stand. The conference ended with Wolffsohn proposing that the status quo be maintained and that the present officers remain in office until the next Zionist Congress.

Thus the battle between the 'practicals' and the 'politicals' continued to be waged until 1911, when Wolffsohn was replaced as President of the Zionist Organization by a Presidential Committee of 'practical' Zionists, under the chairmanship of Professor Otto Warburg, a German Jew of great culture and personal charm. Weizmann took a leading part in the discussions that finally effected these changes, though he did not as yet hold a high office in the Zionist movement Executive. However, as Chairman of the Congress's Permanent Steering Committee, he exercised considerable influence, both in the discussions and in the decisions.

Gradually, new Zionist activities in Palestine were decided upon and instituted. Official sanction was given for a study of the whole country from Dan to Aqaba. Plans were formulated to promote agriculture and industry on democratic principles. Education, schools and cultural development centres were to be promoted to the utmost.

New intellectual forces were to be encouraged to settle in Palestine, to plan and lay down a blue print of effective 'colonization'. There was a determination to reject any activity that was petty and purely philanthropic.

At last, at the 1911 Zionist Congress, Weizmann succeeded in effecting a change. Wolffsohn had decided to retire whatever the Congress might decide. The *Jewish World* correspondent reported that 'all eyes were on Weizmann as, in a voice full of emotion, he gave the names of the future leaders of the movement'. They were Otto Warburg, Arthur Hantke, Schmarya Levin, Victor Jacobson and Nahum Sokolow. Warburg was elected Chairman of the Board, and Weizmann was appointed to the Greater Actions Committee.

The leadership had now passed into the hands of the 'practicals' and Weizmann proceeded to plan for definite constructive work. He believed that the Jewish public would support the schemes 'not out of love of Zionism but because all other projects for dealing with the Jewish question have broken down'.

The new phase did not bring Weizmann any respite from attacks by European and English Zionists. Joseph Cowen of the English Zionist Federation Executive, Leopold Greenberg of the *Jewish Chronicle* and others continued to accuse him of destroying political and diplomatic activity by his plans for colonization and settlement in Palestine.

Writing in *Trial and Error* about his re-entry into the Zionist movement after the defeat of the Uganda project, Weizmann says: 'Manchester became a centre of Zionist thought destined to spread its influence through the surrounding towns and to leave its impression upon English Zionism'. He also refers to a 'strong group of Zionists which had formed in Manchester, including Harry Sacher, Simon Marks and Israel Sieff—young men of great ability and a sense of social responsibility'. Earlier there had been others, such as Joseph Massell, M. Sortman, Nahum Adler and I. Wassilevsky, to mention only a very few of the Manchester Zionists of those days. The other side of the picture, of course, was that during this decade the Manchester Zionist Society had not made much impact on the Jewish community. Its members, fired by Herzl's *Alt Neuland*, were mostly 'politicals'.

With the outbreak of the war in August 1914, Weizmann, who had a remarkable ability to re-assess new situations, quickly came to the conviction that the time had come to concentrate on political contacts. His first objective was to renew his acquaintance with Balfour, and, on the basis of their discussion in 1906, extend its scope to the new possibilities.

As a diplomatist, Weizmann brought to political strategy the orderly mind of a scientific research worker. He understood that with the coming of the war, all nations—even neutrals—would be in the political melting pot, and that from this situation an independent Jewish state might emerge.

He worked out his strategy in Manchester. Britain held the key to the gate of Jewish independence. He felt that the moment of decision was not far off. It might be in his generation. The man who had fought relentlessly against the 'politicals' was to become the model leader of Zionist political planning.

Weizmann made his first journey to Palestine in 1907, after the Eighth Zionist Congress, held at The Hague. He recalls that, during the voyage, 'The Zionist and the chemist were at war within me. I was so anxious to be detached and objective that I denied myself the value of my emotions'. He reports his feelings at setting foot on the land that had been such an integral part of his thoughts since childhood: when he at last found himself face to face with reality the encounter was 'neither as good nor as bad as he had anticipated'.

At that time, the Jewish population of the country, then under Turkish rule, totalled about eighty thousand; there were some twenty-five colonies on the land. 'The dead hand of Halukah', Weizmann wrote, 'lay on more than half of the Jewish population and, in an age which was to witness the reconstruction of the Jewish homeland, they were a useless, and even retarding element.' Even the Bilu pioneers, motivated though they had been by devotion and the highest ideals, had fallen into the habit of relying on charity. The few colonies were detached and scattered: there was no real scientific study of soil conditions nor anything pertaining to it; there was no system for training and absorbing new immigrants. On the other hand, in a few places, such as Merchavia, Ben Shemen and Hulda, there was reassuring evidence of the real type of Zionist enterprise that had always been envisaged. The Gymnasium (or High School) had been established in Jaffa, and the Bezalel School in Jerusalem.

After his tour, Weizmann determined that, on his return to England, he would re-emphasize, in spite of all opposition, the need for immediate practical work in Palestine. But more than anything, he was wedded now to the idea of a Hebrew University in Jerusalem. It was an uphill struggle; it took years to produce any results. However, in 1913, at the Eleventh Zionist Congress in Vienna, Weizmann was able to report progress. He told his audience that 'prominent Jewish scholars, neglected because of their race, suffering material and moral humiliations, would find a place where they could devote themselves to study as well as to their people. The Hebrew University would attract new forces to the country and contribution to its cultivation and exploration. It would be our spiritual dreadnought and we could achieve with it greater successes than other peoples with their armies and navies. The only dignified reply to our being barred from other universities is the foundation of our own university.'

Baron Edmond de Rothschild's support for the idea of a Hebrew University was promised—one of the conditions being that Weizmann should get Professor Paul Ehrlich, then at the height of his scientific career in Germany and reputedly quite detached from Jewish matters, to head the committee. Eventually an interview was arranged and when he was finally able to steer the conversation in the direction he wanted, Weizmann spoke of the university. He gradually won the interest of Ehrlich, who after a while remarked that he had given Weizmann an hour of his time, while the corridors of his laboratory were filled with Counts, Princes and Ministers who would be grateful if he gave them only ten minutes. Weizmann replied: 'Yes, Professor, but the difference between me and your other visitors is that they came to receive an injection from you. I came here to give you one.'

The outcome of the interview was that Ehrlich agreed to join the University Committee. The first meeting was arranged to take place in Paris on 4 August 1914, but the outbreak of the first World War decreed otherwise.

The months before the outbreak of war also witnessed a bitter struggle between the German Jews and other Zionists, about the language of instruction at the Haifa Technicon, which had been established in 1913. After much conflict, the Hilfsverein der Deutschen Juden—who had insisted on the use of German, withdrew its support from the schools; the Zionist Organization took over. This was to be the beginning of the Hebrew school system in Palestine.

During the summer of 1914 there came the prologue to what might be called 'The Acetone Story'. In August of that year, Weizmann (who had just returned to Manchester from Switzerland) was among the many scientists asked by the War Office for information about any of their work that might have some military value. Weizmann immediately offered to put the details of his fermentation process at the disposal of the authorities. Shortly afterwards, the Chief Research Chemist of Nobel's (the explosive manufacturers) called at his laboratory, together with other senior representatives of that organization. They offered to acquire Weizmann's process on very favourable terms for him; a contract was negotiated. Unfortunately, an explosion at the Nobel factory made it impossible for them to carry the project further and Weizmann released them from their contract. Later Nobel brought his process to the notice of the British Government. This eventually led to Weizmann's interview with Winston Churchill (then First Lord of the Admiralty) who asked him if he could produce thirty thousand tons of acetone, urgently needed for the war effort. The story of Weizmann's response to that appeal is well known. Indeed, it has become almost a legend, so much so that it has often been assumed that the Balfour Declaration was granted almost automatically to Weizmann because of this service he had rendered. The myth was dispelled by Weizmann himself. In *Trial and Error* he writes, 'Actually, Lloyd George's advocacy of the Jewish homeland long predated his accession to the Premiership, and we had several meetings in the intervening years, as will be seen below.'

In looking back on the 1904–1914 decade, it is interesting to recall the relationships that existed between Weizmann and some of the other outstanding Zionist personalities of that day.

Ahad Ha'am, whom he first met during his student days in Berlin, had, from the beginning, been an inspiration to him. His own views on the false and illusory hopes of the assimilated Western Jews (and those of Germany in particular) were given added conviction by an essay written by Ahad Ha'am at that time, entitled 'Slavery in the Midst of Freedom'.

The association continued spasmodically (Ahad Ha'am was Weizmann's senior by twenty years) and it was not really until 1905–6, when Ahad Ha'am came to live in London, that a warm friendship developed between the two men. Weizmann has recalled that although—for economic reasons—it was not easy for him to travel often from Manchester to London, he did so whenever he could. In Ahad Ha'am's company, he found comfort and solace from his own difficulties; he regarded him as friend, comrade, teacher and adviser.

Shmarya Levin, too, had made a profound impression upon him. Later this developed into a deep affection and almost unbounded admiration—a somewhat rare reaction in Weizmann, who was usually given to moderate and temperate assessment of people.

These two personalities originally met at the Second and Third Zionist Congress, and subsequently visited the United States together on several occasions on Zionist propaganda meetings. Indeed, Weizmann records that these journeys together meant so much to him that when he had to go to the States after Levin's death 'he felt orphaned'. The style of Levin's oratory, with its brilliant application of biblical themes to current problems, his devastating wit (particularly in Yiddish) made a great appeal to Weizmann, who often quoted, with obvious pleasure and affection, some of the retorts Levin was famous for. In some ways, his own style of oratory, rich in Jewish parable, was similar to Levin's; he described him as a 'great teacher and dazzling personality, as well as a sterling collaborator and warm-hearted friend'.

Perhaps somewhat more complex was his relationship with Jabotinsky. I think it should be said that there has often been mis-understanding of Weizmann's attitude. However vehemently the two great personalities may—especially in later years—have disagreed in many issues, Weizmann had tremendous respect for Jabotinsky's sin-cerity and integrity, and a genuine sympathy for him in the dis-appointments that were to become such a tragic aspect of his Zionist life. The two men became close friends (a fact of which many of Weizmann's Zionist colleagues disapproved) and, indeed, for a time (during the early days of the first World War) shared rooms in a house in Chelsea. Weizmann then pleaded with Jabotinsky to under-take Zionist propaganda work, saying that it was in this field that his real genius would manifest itself. The suggestion met with a pained reaction; Jabotinsky was convinced that political work was his forte.

So far as Ussishkin was concerned, while Weizmann had the highest respect for him, and though, on the whole, the relationship between the two men was amicable, they never quite attained the warm intimacy that developed with Levin and Ahad Ha'am. The same may also be said with regard to Nahum Sokolow, although, since the latter lived in England, and he and Weizmann worked together during those fateful years, they had more opportunity of developing an appreciation and understanding of each other's personality.

Looking back now on Weizmann's emergence as the outstanding Zionist leader, we can see what extraordinary part in this develop-ment was played by the fact that he was able to stay, so to speak, on the sidelines in Manchester during the fateful decade that ended with the first World War. Without losing his intimate contact with the movement, his sojourn in Manchester enabled him to assess the changing world in better perspective than he could have done either in Berlin or Geneva. In Manchester, above all else, he had an oppor-tunity to withdraw and reflect. He was not constantly engaged as he had been when he left Geneva.

But for this he had to pay a price. Weizmann was never—certainly not during his Manchester period—what we would now call an 'organization man'. He was not the sort of man who could cultivate friendships for the sake of political benefits. He was no flatterer, and his intellectual preoccupations, his quick mind, and his intensely

Jewish wit, often gave the impression of either aloofness or intellectual arrogance. This was not so noticeable in his own milieu, but in Manchester it was liable to be observed. He was, moreover, not a man who sought friends. Friendships came naturally or not at all. He had his intimate circle among the Manchester Zionists, and he had his scientific friends. But outside their ranks he was respected and feared rather than loved. Like many other men of his calibre, he did not suffer fools, either gladly or silently. With men like Ahad Ha'am and Shmarya Levin he was at home and happy, and even with Jabotinsky, despite political differences, he found a common language. But the same was not true of dour men like Ussishkin or intellectuals like Sokolow.

Nor, as his stature rose to become the foremost Zionist spokesman in England, was he lightly accepted by the Zionist leadership in Berlin. When in 1912, on Weizmann's insistence that talks should begin with British political personalities, it was decided to do so, it was not Weizmann who was entrusted with the mission, but Nahum Sokolow. And those who were with Weizmann at the Vienna Congress of 1913 well remember his lonely eminence.

The first World War changed the lives of all mankind; it also flung the destinies of the Jewish people into a new channel. At a crucial moment Weizmann's scientific work and political activity fused with great brilliance and unprecedented historical appropriateness. Their product, the Belfour Declaration, gave Jewish history an unforgettable landmark. And it was Weizmann's sojourn in Manchester that may be considered its incubating-chamber.

Mr Israel M. Sieff is prominent in British public life and the business world. He was one of Dr Weizmann's early associates after the latter settled in England. Secretary of the First Zionist Commission to Palestine in 1918. He is now Honorary President of the Zionist Federation of Great Britain and Ireland.

WEIZMANN AND SCIENCE

CHAPTER FOUR

CHAIM WEIZMANN AS BACTERIOLOGIST

SELMAN A. WAKSMAN

AS A BACTERIOLOGIST, Weizmann is known mainly for his work on the anaerobic fermentation of certain carbohydrates to give acetone and butyl alcohol. Although it was Pasteur who first demonstrated that butyl alcohol was a direct product of carbohydrate fermentation by specific butyric acid bacteria, Weizmann not only established the practicality of this process but also demonstrated that some of these bacteria produced acetone in addition to butyl alcohol. The idea of producing synthetic rubber by the polymerization of isoprene, a chemical substance that could be formed from isoamyl alcohol, which could be produced by direct bacterial fermentation, appealed strongly to certain chemists and bacteriologists. A British firm, Strange and Graham, Ltd, was led to engage in a comprehensive programme in this direction. A large group of eminent workers in the fields of chemistry and bacteriology was assembled to attack this problem. In addition to Weizmann, Perkin, Fernbach, and various others participated. The group did not hold together long. Weizmann left it in 1912 and engaged in his own research. He soon succeeded in isolating a starch-decomposing anaerobic organism, named *Clostridium acetobutylicum* Weizmann. This organism had the capacity to form both acetone and butanol, both important industrial solvents. At first acetone received most of the attention, as indicated above. But when the first World War came to an end, the need for *n*-butanol was greatly increased as a result of the growing automobile industry.

The manufacture of acetone by the Weizmann process from corn and horse chestnuts was first described by Nathan in 1919. I can tell this story best by quoting Kelly[1], who described this process in detail, especially the part played in its discovery by Dr Weizmann.

[1] F. C. Kelly, *The Growth of An Industry* (Houghton Mifflin Co, New York, 1939).

While an instructor at the University of Manchester, Weizmann had for several years been trying to produce a synthetic rubber. To do that on a practical scale he must have an adequate supply of certain ingredients, particularly a kind of alcohol called butanol, not then available commercially. This led him to experimenting on means for obtaining butanol by fermenting starch and sugar. To produce the fermentation he tried various kinds of bacteria. Weizmann did not have to look far to find bacteria for his experiments, inasmuch as they are contained in every clod of earth, in the air we breathe, in the water we drink, and in every plant that grows—though visible, of course, only under a strong microscope. It is estimated that under average conditions a pound of good soil contains from one hundred to two hundred and fifty billion bacteria. Under the microscope many of these bacteria look much alike even to a scientist; but scientists know that however much they may look alike, there are great differences in what they will do. After experimenting with many kinds, Weizmann found, on an ear of corn, bacteria having tastes and inclinations that did not occur in others. These came to have the scientific name of *Clostridium acetobutylicum* Weizmann, though they commonly go by the nickname of B-Y (the B for bacteria, and the Y for Weizmann). Clostridium means spindle-shaped; these bacteria have a habit of forming spindle-shaped clusters.

After long, tedious tests, Weizmann discovered that when bacteria of this particular kind were turned loose and left to their own devices in a kind of soup, or mash, of cooked corn, they caused it to ferment rapidly and changed it into a solution containing—besides water—butanol, acetone, and a little ethyl alcohol. There was three times as much acetone as alcohol and twice as much butanol as acetone. These three solvents could then be separated from one another in pure form by fairly simple distilling operations.

Weizmann could not obtain butanol by this bacterial means without also getting acetone and ethyl alcohol. His interest was only in butanol as a necessary raw material for his synthetic-rubber experiments. The British Government, on the other hand, was not concerned about butanol, nor about ethyl alcohol; but they did have a crying need for acetone, and they set to work to make use of Weizmann's new bacterial fermentation process. The Ministry of Munitions adapted six distilleries in England to this purpose. Two of these were operating satisfactorily when it became evident that a shortage of grain would make it impossible to carry on in England alone on a scale large enough to meet all requirements. The British then decided to install plants in India and Canada. The Indian factory was not completed until after the Armistice and was later sold to the Bombay Government for conversion into an ordinary alcohol distillery. In Toronto, Canada, however, a plant for making acetone by the Weizmann method was in successful operation for about two years before the war was ended.

After the United States enlisted in the war, the British War Mission bought the plant of the Commercial Distillery at Terre Haute, Indiana, and remodelled it for use in making acetone by the Weizmann process. A little later, the United States Government bought the Majestic Distillery and the Allied War Board incorporated ownership of these two plants under the name of the Commercial Solvents Corporation of New York.

What the above story fails to tell is that the 'Weizmann process' was one of the first bacterial processes utilized on a large scale for the production of an industrially important product. It is true that lactic acid, acetic acid, ethyl alcohol, citric acid, and certain other microbiological processes were known and actually utilized on a large industrial scale, but none had served to revolutionize a whole industry as had that of Weizmann. It is one of the few important processes developed during the first World War that have resulted in great benefit to mankind.

The work of Dr Weizmann on acetone and butyl alcohol fermentation was immediately taken up by a number of different investigators. It is sufficient to mention the work of Dr H. B. Speakman in Canada (1919), of Dr G. C. Robinson (1922), and especially the extensive studies of the University of Wisconsin group headed by Professor E. B. Fred (McCoy et al., 1926; Peterson and Fred, 1932). In 1927, for example, Weyer and Rettger made a comprehensive study of six different strains of *Cl. acetobutylicum*. Storage of the spores for a period of six months apparently decreased the power of the culture to produce solvents. Rejuvenation of the cultures, by alternate pasteurization and sub-culturing, and destruction of the vegetative forms and the weaker spores by pasteurization yielded vigorous strains for fermentation among the most active spore-formers. In this respect, Weyer and Rettger fully confirmed and enlarged upon the ideas of Weizmann, who had previously advocated heat for treating the spores of a bacterial culture 100 to 150 times to improve its fermenting ability.

The actual part played by Dr Weizmann in the development of the butyl fermentation industry has been summarized, at my request, by Dr Fred of the University of Wisconsin. Dr Fred had an ideal opportunity to know Dr Weizmann intimately, since it was he who, early in 1921, accepted the offer of the Commercial Solvents Company to help them in the development of the particular fermentation process (an offer I had once unwisely declined!) Dr Fred writes:

There is no doubt whatsoever that Dr Weizmann's discovery of the butylclostridium, now called *Clostridium acetobutylicum*, was the foundation on which was built the whole industrial exploitation of the butyl alcohol fermentation. Others had known for nearly fifty years that certain clostridia could produce butyl alcohol but no commercially feasible process had been developed in spite of considerable effort in the few years preceding the Weizmann discovery. The Fernbach[1] process, although findings had seemed encouraging, had not been commercially successfully in a plant in England. And so the way was open to trial of a new organism; also the drastic need for acetone by the British in the first World War worked in favour of the Weizmann process, which was capable of 'large yields' of the solvents from a 'simple' mash of corn meal and water. Fortunately, the Weizmann organism was a naturally vigorous clostridium, able to grow in the plain corn mash because of its own proteolytic system and acid tolerance in the range of acids naturally produced in the fermentation. Hence it carried through the fermentation of corn 'unaided'. Dr Weizmann also, perhaps by chance, discovered the technic of heat shock to 90° C 100° C for one or two minutes at each subculture from the spore state. Probably there are several advantages in this procedure, such as driving out dissolved oxygen from the medium, killing the weaker non-sporulating strains in the population, etc. But it is very interesting that recent work has shown heat shock to be actually capable of inducing spore germination.

Thus Dr Weizmann, in his heat shock process, had the key to: (a) growth of his anaerobe in an open vessel with protection from air at the surface of the medium; (b) avoidance of degeneration, which is serious with clostridia; and (c) controlled initiation of growth, which is so essential in handling commercial starter cultures. One can only marvel that Dr Weizmann, the pioneer in butyl fermentation, should have hit upon so much of the technique

[1] In 1924, when I visited Dr Fernbach at the Pasteur Institute, he told me the details of the two processes. He could never forgive Dr Weizmann for succeeding where he himself had failed. This was the main reason for Dr Fernbach's refusal to become interested in Zionism, as he told me then.

needed to make the commercial fermentation successful, as it certainly was.

Professor Fred spoke in glowing terms of Weizmann the man:

My association with Dr Weizmann (began) in Terre Haute during 1920–1921, working for Commercial Solvents . . . those were very busy days; often we worked all day and all night trying to find out what was wrong with the fermentation. We had a terrible time trying to overcome contamination and sluggish fermentation. When you go from the test tube to a 60,000-gallon fermenter, you run into many problems—as you well know.

He paid a number of visits to Terre Haute, but never remained for more than a day or so. As you perhaps know, he was a fine specimen—physically tall, handsome, and a very able speaker. While in Terre Haute, he kept all of us busy trying to protect him from the endless number of people . . . who all wanted to see him and have him give a lecture.

Aside from some cursory correspondence, I met Dr Weizmann personally only on one occasion, but it was a memorable one. Early in 1938 I received several letters from Professor Adolf Reifenberg, of the Hebrew University, and from Dr Yehiel Thone, head of the Palestine Land Development Company, inviting me to come to the Holy Land and make a survey of the Huleh peat bog, to be followed by a study of the peat itself. I was at that time engaged in a detailed study of various types of humus, and had had considerable experience with the nature of different peats throughout the world. I therefore welcomed the opportunity to examine the peat areas of the ancient bog in Palestine, known in biblical times as the Springs of Meron.

My visit to the Huleh resulted not only in the gain of considerable information on the depth and nature of the peat, but also in the creation of a desire for a more detailed study of the agricultural utilization of the peat. Subsequently, a large quantity of the peat was collected and sent to my laboratory in New Brunswick, where I completed my studies on it early in 1942. When I submitted my report to Dr Thone, however, I was asked not to publish anything about it until further consideration.

Dr E. D. Bergmann, a close associate of Dr Weizmann, came to see me in 1944 to discuss the nature and utilization of the Huleh peat. He also brought me an invitation from Dr Weizmann, who was at that time visiting New York, to come to see him in order to discuss an important problem.

On the appointed day, Dr Weizmann received me very cordially and invited me to have tea with him. After certain introductory remarks, notably pertaining to the utilization of the Huleh peat, he asked me rather bluntly: 'Would you be willing, when the land of Israel becomes a reality, to leave the USA and come to Israel to become a Director of the Experiment Station at Rehovoth?'

With all my desire to help in the development of a 'homeland' for my people, I could not even consider this invitation for two important reasons: 1 Although I studied in an agricultural institution and was connected for nearly three decades with an agricultural experiment station, I was concerned but little with practical agricultural problems, my work being entirely theoretical (soil, water, industrial microbiology) in nature. How could I attempt to direct an organization that would require the ultimate in a knowledge of practical agriculture? 2 My studies of antibiotics were reaching their zenith at that time; streptomycin recently had been isolated in my laboratory, several other antibiotics were waiting to be studied; all this required my undivided attention. At that time I could hardly leave this work, which was the culminating point of my career, and go off into a new field of endeavour, especially one in which I had only limited knowledge.

I told all this and much more to Dr Weizmann. He smiled and said: 'Well, how about microbiology? Don't you think this is a science that should be developed in our new country? Both you and I have had much interest in this field. You should come to help develop this field. In a land so devoid of natural resources, this field would offer new resources.' To this I replied that, although I was in full agreement with him concerning the potentialities in microbiology, we had better wait until the whole level of science and industry in Israel had been raised before we began to think and plan for a centre or at least for a group of workers devoted to this particular science. Weizmann agreed to this and added: 'In that case, do you promise me that when the times comes, you will come to Israel and help us in establishing such a centre or organize a group of young microbiologists?' This I promised.

Several years passed before another opportunity to talk with Dr Weizmann presented itself. I went to Israel again in 1952. Unfortunately, as we came to Dr Weizmann's home in Rehovoth, we found him on his sick bed, from which he was never to rise again. Then, I was not yet ready to fulfil my promise to Dr Weizmann, for I had come only to participate in a discussion of the need for an Antibiotic Centre in Israel. But perhaps this might have been the beginning of a real microbiological centre. How much I missed Dr

Weizmann's counsel and support! I still live in the hope that I may help in some way to bring this about so that my promise to him may finally be fulfilled.

Professor Selman Waksman is Professor Emeritus (Microbiology) at Rutgers State University, in New Brunswick, N.J., USA. He is a Nobel Laureate in Physiology and Medicine (1952).

CHAPTER FIVE

THE SECRET OF LIFE

RITCHIE CALDER

IN THE simple religion of the jungle Dyaks of Borneo there is no 'Hereafter'. There is, however, a touching belief which can be translated as 'To be remembered'. In his last hours, the mortal must have around him his kinsmen and his friends. He bequeaths his last breath to them and as long as they remember him he will live on.

Chaim Weizmann has many titles to immortality but one of the highest is that which, like the Persian Emperor Darius, he might have conferred upon himself—'Friend of my Friends'. In his last years when, in the fickleness and jealousies of politics, there were those who grudged him even his place in history, those friends gathered around him and encircled him with the enduring proofs of their friendship.

He could look out from his study window and see their personal devotion taking shape as the buildings of the Weizmann Institute. It is given to few men to read, in their life-time, such a magnificent and affectionate obituary written in stone.

Like a dying Dyak, Weizmann bequeathed his last breath to his friends, because by their foresight he was able to breathe into that masonry a living purpose. He whispered to it the Secret of Life.

It has been suggested that the Institute was 'Weizmann's philosophy embodied in stone'. That sounds fine but it is not true, because it implies too much and too little. It suggests that the Institute has spelled out something which he had clearly in mind but, as he would have been the first to protest, this is an over-simplification. Moreover, it diminishes the devotion of friends and followers who, with an extraordinary insight, have given effect to his inspiration in ways he could never have predicted.

The over-simplification is excusable because it is easy, by hindsight, to make everything fit into a consistent pattern. (I know, because I had to have such a pattern for *The Hand of Life*, the account of the first ten years at the Institute.) Nevertheless, while his influence still pervades the Institute and while the purpose and guide-lines he provided are evident, it has, like a child growing from infancy, through adolescence, into adulthood, assumed its own character.

This would have pleased Weizmann. He once said, 'I am a chemist. I am not an authority on evolution but I imagine that evolution means a compromise between something which is rigid and static and something which is flexible and dynamic.' He might have (and his friends would have respected his wishes) decided the pattern, rigid and static, embodying his own direct scientific interests. He did not; he left it to the dynamics of evolution to grow, organically in the climate of twentieth-century science. There is no rubric, no scientific liturgy, which one can quote and say 'Weizmann said it shall be so'. There have been times in the still-short history of the Institute when a posthumous 'Weizmann veto' has been invoked but the evolutionary principle has prevailed in the spirit, not the letter, of his intentions.

The Weizmann Institute might have embodied Weizmann as the chemist. Instead it is fulfilling him as a scientist.

Much that it has become, or is becoming, he himself could not have foreseen, because science is developing quickly, and in directions which were not self-evident when he died in 1952. Yet the latest developments are a mutation of his own career-interests, as an organic chemist and as a microbiologist—as the man who put microorganisms to work as industrial chemists. The Institute, through its own process of evolution, is moving into the chemistry of evolution itself—into the 'life sciences' through molecular biology. This is the quest for the chemical and physical secret of life itself.

As in so many circumstances in Weizmann's life, there was, in the beginning of the Institute, a sense of destiny. It began with tragedy. A young student died, the son of Israel and Rebecca Sieff and the nephew of Simon, now Lord Marks. In their hour of grief, his family turned to one whom they had always found to be a source of comfort and of wisdom. They had known him when he was a lecturer at Manchester, where he had combined his researches and his teaching with his intensive activities for the Jewish people. And there had grown up between them a mutual friendship which was unstinting and exacting.

Typically, Weizmann, when they turned to him for consolation, took them for a walk among the trees of Hyde Park. They talked of death but around them life was burgeoning. They discussed the boy and what he had hoped to become. He had been interested in science and had wanted to make it his career. With the vision and sensitivity that was Weizmann's enduring quality, he made a suggestion: The Nazi persecutions had already begun—persecutions that were to reach the climax of horror ten years later. Eminent Jewish scientists were being hounded out of their laboratories and Weizmann proposed that in Daniel Sieff's memory a science institute should be set up in Palestine. Weizmann saw, in such an institute, a sanctuary for many of the scientific refugees. But he also foresaw a research centre which would serve the needs of the country and at the same time form part of the world community of science. He had ideas, too, about the ways in which such an institute could help to break down the walls which fenced off one section of knowledge from another.

He did not offer his friends just words of comfort; he gave them a purpose to serve: In memorializing Daniel Sieff they would serve science as the boy had hoped to serve it; they would offer hope to the despairing; and they would benefit the Jewish Homeland.

They endowed the Daniel Sieff Institute and, in 1934, it was built in the sandy wastes, then called the 'Gateway to the Negev', the desert of the South. Weizmann chose the site, and it seemed a strange choice, for this was desolation, a landscape without a tree or a blade of grass. Some suggested that Weizmann was being perverse and that the Institute should have joined the Hebrew University on Mount Scopus at Jerusalem.

Weizmann, however, was never capricious. He had two justifications for suggesting this site: one was historical, the other was immediate and practical. In AD 70, when the Romans were besieging Jerusalem and the destruction of the Temple and the dispersal of the Jews were imminent, Rabbi Yohanan persuaded the Roman commander to withdraw from the Judaean Hills to the coastal plains and to establish a school of learning at Yavne. For 2,000 years the Jews in their wanderings had cried, 'Give us Yavne and its sages.' The site at Rehovoth adjoined Yavne. The other reason was that the Agricultural Research Station already existed there. In a country where not only food but industrial prosperity would have to be wrested from the neglected and reluctant soil, Weizmann saw a partnership, between the fundamental research the Institute might carry out and the practical needs of the farmers. He foresaw the chemists' being able to derive, from agriculture, the chemical materials for the industries Palestine still lacked.

The Sieff Institute was opened on 3 April 1934 by Richard Willstatter, the pioneering chemist who was so great a personality and warm-hearted a man. Over the gates of the Institute were written 'Work for this country. Work for Science. Work for Humanity'. And it is worth recalling Willstatter's advice to the scientists on that occasion: 'Seek not to multiply your work, nor to write many papers. *Non multa—multum*. I ask the people of this country: have faith in this Institute; do not expect showy or speedy results. The members of this Institute must work as free researchers, furnished with fully adequate means, in an atmosphere of absolute confidence.' That might have been Weizmann himself speaking but then again, of course, these are the sentiments of any thoughtful scientist.

The Daniel Sieff Institute provided Weizmann himself with research facilities so that he could transfer some of his scientific work to the Jewish Homeland. There he could have his laboratory and there he planned to have his home. In 1934 he and his wife lived in a little rented bungalow and he used to go every morning to the Institute, extending his own researches and following the work of his colleagues, some of whom, as he had intended, were first-class scientists from Germany. This scientific idyll was interrupted when he was re-elected President of the World Zionist Organization and the Jewish Agency in 1935. From then on it became his retreat, where he could find respite from his arduous missions as the Ambassador of Zionism in the chancelleries and cabinet rooms of the great Powers.

This ambivalence of statesman—and—scientist, had, of course, characterized Weizmann's whole life. His reputation as a scientist was indestructible. He was not only a university scientist, but an industrial innovator. His discovery, in Manchester before the first World War, of a bacterium that could convert sugar and starch into acetone and butyl alcohol profoundly affected our industrial civilization. He proved not only that 'bugs are cheaper than B.Sc's' in laboratory experiments but that a bacterium could be used as a machine tool in the large-scale production of industrial chemicals. Indeed it was more fundamental than that because it provided a way of extracting chemicals from the sun: the growing plant absorbs the energy of the sun and uses it to convert the elements of the air, water and soil into carbohydrates—the sugars and starches. Weizmann's bacterial methods recovered that energy (in the case of acetone) as an explosive force.

His discovery was of critical importance during the first World War when Britain's munitions shortage was threatening defeat. His process made it possible to produce the acetone necessary for smokeless gunpowder. His bacteria could digest grain or chestnuts and yield acetone for the guns of Flanders. Similarly, in the second World War, he made an important contribution to the American war effort because his fermentation processes made butyl alcohol available as a source-material of synthetic rubber.

These interventions were historic but his work affected many other fields as well. Less well known, at least to the public, was the rôle he played, through 'Blitz Broth', in helping to feed the shelter-population in the air raids on Britain. There was a shortage of pro-tein, which is necessary to build and maintain the tissues of the body and which in food-affluent societies can be provided by milk, meat or eggs. In that case the vegetable proteins—since all nutriment derives initially from plants—have been pre-digested and converted by the intermediate animals. Much vegetable matter goes to waste because the human digestive system and the chemistry of the body cannot effectively break down the vegetable matter and make constituent chemicals available for body-building. Weizmann discovered an agent that could provide this intermediate stage: it was a yeast cell. Yeast, a micro-organism, could feed on the vegetable matter and then could be 'plasmolysed'—'milked' of the liquid contents of its cells. This provided a substitute for meat. A soup, reinforced by Weizmann's yeast protein, was produced for the people in the shelters, many of whom came back hungry from work to their refuges and left them to face another day's work. 'Blitz Broth', with a hunk of brown bread, could sustain them. When the paratroopers were dropped for the liberation of Europe, their iron ration was this same 'Blitz Broth'.

It is easy to romanticize, as Lloyd George himself did, the part that Weizmann's notable scientific achievements played in the realization of his Zionist aims and of the creation of the Jewish Homeland in Palestine. With a tidiness that is never true in history, one might say that acetone in the first World War won the Balfour Declaration and that butyl alcohol, in the second World War, ensured the US recognition of the State of Israel. Weizmann himself, knowing the laborious years, the betrayals, and the cruel disappointments in the political struggles for Zionism, resented this strip-cartoon version of history. Once, when with journalist glibness I described Israel as 'a state founded on science', he demurred. 'It can be', he said, 'but it was not.'

Nevertheless (metaphorically) with his diplomatic top hat, he wore the white overall of the scientist. His credentials as a chemist were the visiting-card which opened many, and some unexpected doors to him. Reading his own, and others' accounts, one sees how the two personalities, the burning zealot and the cool chemist, were com-pounded to produce enduring impressions on those he met.

Men who make history like to take liberties with it. They are impresarios who accommodate dates and events, and even the *dramatis personnae* to scenes of their own setting. Lloyd George was

such a one and Weizmann had wry comments to make on the colourful description (in the *War Memoirs* of Lloyd George) of how 'Dr
Weizmann with his discovery not only helped us to win the war, but
made a permanent mark upon the map of the world'.

Weizmann has corrected this record. 'His narrative', wrote Weizmann in *Trial and Error*, 'makes it appear that the Balfour Declaration was a reward given me by the Government, when Lloyd George
became Prime Minister, for my services to England. I almost wish
that it had been as simple as that and that I had never known the
heartbreaks, the drudgery and the uncertainties which preceded the
Declaration. But history does not deal in Aladdin's lamps.'

Similarly the glamourized versions of the chemist's influence on the
political attitudes of the United States, were discounted by Weizmann. Nevertheless it was his scientific work, as he admitted, which
gave him his first access to President Roosevelt. It was his butyl
alcohol process which appealed to Mr Henry A. Wallace, the vice-
president who was in the throes of a distasteful and indeed disreput-
able struggle with the oil interests that controlled the source material
of synthetic rubber. Wallace later wrote 'The world will never know
what a significant contribution Weizmann made towards the success
of the synthetic rubber programme at a time when it was badly
bogged down and going too slowly.'

The truth is that the statesman and the scientist were the two
strands in the thread of one personality and that they had both been
woven into the fabric of history.

At a fateful meeting at which, with his forceful arguments, Weizmann had voiced the claims of his people, Lloyd George said in an
aside to Herbert Samuel, 'When you and I are forgotten, this man
will have a monument to him in Palestine.' When this was repeated
to Weizmann his comment was, 'Should anyone ever take a fancy to
put up a monument to me, I hope he will be told that Palestine is the
only place where I should like to have it.'

In his own lifetime, Weizmann saw that monument taking at least
one shape in the Weizmann Institute of Science.

It all began in anticipation of his 70th birthday, 27 November 1944.
The war was still on. The State of Israel, as events were to prove,
had still to be born in blood and sacrifice. But 'The Chief' was going
to have a birthday, a Psalmist's three-score years and ten, and some
of his multitude of friends decided that he should have a gift worthy
of the occasion. They tried to find out what he would want and, in
the same self-abnegation of his reply to Lloyd George about a king's
honour, he said, 'For myself, I need and want nothing, but if you

wish you may do something for the expansion of the Sieff Institute.'

The Sieff Institute had already established for itself a sober reputation in the scientific world. It had attracted able scientists and its researches and published works commanded respect. It had not become, as it might have, Weizmann's private laboratory, dominated by his special interests. These were wide enough because they had taken him from classical organic chemistry into microbiology and the experimental and industrial use of bacteria; into physical chemistry and the study of how elemental atoms are bound together by electrical forces to form molecules; into polymer chemistry, which is the linking of molecules into complex structures such as proteins or plastics; and into bio-chemistry which is the subtle synthesis of chemical in the living 'factory' of the plant or human body. All these had been reflected in the work of the Institute but their range had been extended by independent and diversified fields of scientific inquiry by his colleagues at the Daniel Sieff Institute.

They had also demonstrated, as he had intended that they should, that research had a relevance to the needs of Palestine. During the war, the isolation of the Middle East from supplies of pharmaceuticals had set the Sieff scientists looking for source materials in the indigenous plants of Palestine so that (when it came) the State of Israel had a vigorous pharmaceutical industry. And a great deal of fundamental work had been done, with promising avenues to be further explored.

Perhaps this was what Weizmann had in mind when he suggested the expansion of the Sieff Institute—an increase in facilities so that good work could be done better and advances encouraged. But his American friends, who were the initiators of the idea of a birthday gift, once they knew that 'The Chief' had opted for science, had more ambitious intentions. They had an original target of a million dollars and they wanted an institute which would be identified, by name, with Weizmann. This raised a delicate question: after all, the Daniel Sieff Institute had been endowed by the British Marks-Sieff family, although it had had active supporters in the United States. Meyer Weisgal was given the job of sounding out the family. He approached Israel Sieff to get his reactions to the new proposition, in which the Sieff Institute would become a unit in the Weizmann Institute. There was no argument about that; Israel Sieff had only one criticism—'A million? Why not five?' And the thinking and generosity has been on that scale ever since.

To say that the friends who accepted this scientific mandate from 'The Chief' knew nothing about science is not derogatory. The American Committee formed to further the interests of the Institute consisted of men of affairs, many of whom had been interested in the Sieff Institute. They called in Meyer Weisgal to organize the appeal. A devoted friend of Weizmann in all his Zionist struggles, he was a journalist, turned impresario; science to him (at that point in any case) was a spectacular that he was prepared to stage as he had once done *The Eternal Road*. They could recruit, as they did, a Planning Committee of distinguished scientists but their function, in the first instance, was to house Weizmann's wishes.

A research institute is not just an architect's drawing, nor the flow-sheet, nor the blue-print, of a business enterprise. The Weizmann Institute was unique in its origins, inspired in its conception, and, itself, provides a laboratory study of the nature and growth of research. One might say that it expresses the personality of Weizmann rather than his philosophy—because 'philosophy' suggests definitions and clear intentions. In the Weizmann Institute these were never really defined and would, indeed, be undefinable.

On the white Galilean marble of the amphitheatre, which adjoins his grave on the hilltop overlooking the Institute, the article of his scientific faith is inscribed:

I feel sure that science will bring to this land both peace and a renewal of its youth, creating here the springs of a new spiritual and material life. I speak of science for its own sake and applied science.

Weizmann believed in 'pure' science, in the sense of academic research, curiosity and the quest for knowledge uninhibited by any immediate compulsions to produce practical results. In this sense science is like the unpredictable rains that replenish the springs. As Weizmann demonstrated in his own career as a chemist this does not mean that 'pure' science is an end in itself; the springs provide the wells from which human needs are met. But science to him was something more than gadgets or products; it was the environment modern culture must grow in. He wanted a scientific sanctuary in which research workers could think and work and experiment without pressures; but he did not want them, or the Institute, to be completely withdrawn from the lives of the people.

The conflict between 'pure' and 'applied' science has persisted for a very long time. It goes back to Plato and his attitude to Exodus and Archytas, when by experiments and recourse to instruments, they solved problems which the theorists considered insoluble. Plutarch described that quarrel:

. . . Plato inveighed against them with great indignation, as having corrupted and debased the excellence of geometry, by causing her to descend from incorporeal and intellectual to sensible things, and obliging her to make use of matter, which requires much manual labour, and is the object of servile trades; then mechanics were separated from geometry . . . being a long time despised by the philosopher . . .

'For a long time' meant over 2,000 years, during which Plato's enthronement of theory over practice continued to tyrannize Western thinking.

When, as has happened periodically, there are debates as to whether the Weizmann Institute should undertake teaching or should turn to researches that show practical possibilities, to commercial purposes, Weizmann can be invoked both for and against. He did remove the Institute, in its origins, from proximity to the Hebrew University of which, as a teaching institution, he had laid the cornerstone on Mount Scopus, but he put it next door to the Agricultural Research Institute so that scientists would not forget that there were practical applications as well. These debates have been resolved with the pragmatism he himself would have applied.

He insisted that it must, as an institute of true science, be truly international, and he recognized that because of its remoteness, geographically, from kindred institutions, it had to be scientifically viable while keeping open its lines of communication with the rest of science throughout the world.

Between its conception in 1944 and its birth in 1949, another factor profoundly influenced the character of the Institute; this was the creation of the State of Israel. From being an outpost of experimental science in the Middle East it became a research centre in a new state, and the change carried with it new responsibilities. In an embattled country struggling to survive, basic research—the indulgence of scientific curiosity—would, in the short term, be regarded as a luxury and an irrelevance. There are wholly understandable pressures, both direct and indirect, to put the priorities of the country before the international aspects of science. There are the sanctions of public opinion, which distrusts scientific hedonism, but there is also a feeling among some of the scientists that in the country's time of difficulties they ought to be out digging ditches. This conflict of loyalties—to Israel or to the Commonwealth of science—can never be fully resolved but the people of Israel and the patriotic scientist must realize that in the long term the status of the Weizmann's Institute as a world centre of science, will be one of the country's greatest assets. It will make the difference between science as a flourishing plant with roots and borrowed know-how, which is like a cut flower, which withers.

Weizmann never concealed his disappointment that the Daniel Sieff Institute had failed to provide a refuge, as he had hoped it would, for the eminent victims of Nazism like the Nobel Prize winners Fritz Haber and Willstatter. The first was responsible for one of the greatest technical successes of the age, or of any age—the conversion of nitrogen of the air into ammonia and nitric acid. These two chemicals are necessary for the making of explosives and also for artificial fertilizers—that inevitable contradiction of science, to destroy or to benefit mankind. He had become a Christian but it did not save him from Nazi persecution. He was stripped of his academic position, of his fortune and his honours. Weizmann offered him the sanctuary of the Sieff—'The climate will be good for you. You will find a modern laboratory and able assistants. You will work in peace and with honour. It will be a return home for you—your journey's end.' He agreed and set out for Palestine but was taken ill at Basle and died there. But he bequeathed his library to the Sieff Institute. Willstatter presided at the opening of the Institute but resisted all the entreaties that he should become its director. Instead, he stayed on to suffer humiliations in Germany until war broke out in 1939. Then he was expelled and he found two rooms in which to live in Switzerland where he died toward the end of the war. Weizmann also failed to persuade Albert Einstein, James Franck, Hermann Weyd, Placzek, Wiegener and many other famous refugees. They chose the West rather than Palestine.

(In their defence, there is the argument that the scientist is a citizen of the world. When Peter Kapitza, the Russian scientist who was one of Lord Rutherford's most brilliant and favoured associates at Cambridge, went back to the USSR on holiday and was 'retained', Rutherford swallowed his bitterness. He said, 'A scientist can work anywhere if he has the means,' and shipped to Moscow the equipment of the laboratory he had had specially built for Kapitza.)

Some may have hoped to turn the Weizmann Institute into a living Pantheon for the already famous and to attract to it the great Jewish scientists and Nobel Prize winners. Efforts were undoubtedly made but, as in Weizmann's experience of the 1930's, while many were prepared to identify themselves with it they would not go there to live and to work. Weizmann may have been disappointed but he did not repine. Instead he took a large part in selecting the scientific heirs to his ideas and he opted for youth. The Institute attracted a remarkable group of young scientists, both native-born and from abroad. History will prove its good fortune in not becoming a retreat for venerable scientists. It has made and is making its own reputation on the reputations of the young.

The Institute has developed quite unpredictably. It has grown around, but also away from the Daniel Sieff Institute. The 'something' that might have expanded the Sieff Institute might have been, like the scientific workshop that makes the Institute largely self-sufficient, merely an elaboration of scientific services. Weizmann's own research interests demanded spectroscopy, X-ray crystallography, radio isotopes, biochemical and biological assay, mathematical physics, and other modern refinements. But these, at Rehovoth, from being services, have become fundamental researches —disciplines in their own right. The Sieff Institute was concerned with the chemicals that produce cancer as well as with those that might stop it, but the international distinction of the Weizmann Institute lies in its basic studies of the nature of cancer itself. Weizmann used his yeast cells to break down proteins into amino-acids, but his successors have taken a world-lead in artificially creating amino-acids. He saw, and rightly, that plastics could provide the industrial materials which Israel lacked. These polymers are familiar as teacups and table-tops, as nylons and handbags, as pipes or as the gear wheels of industry. The Institute which bears his name, however, pioneered the fundamental research into quite different polymers, which can change desert sand into soil, take salt out of water or explain the subtle processes of the living body. A laboratory of nuclear science might not have been in Weizmann's birthday prospectus but the work which has been done there has commanded the attention of nuclear physicists throughout the world.

Even in the 1930's, Weizmann had established the principle of coming-and-going. He insisted that the research workers at the Sieff Institute should not feel themselves isolated; that they should move about the world and that distinguished scientists should be encouraged to visit and reinvigorate research at Rehovoth. This principle is even more important today because an institute for which Weizmann recruited youth must remain perennially young. There has to be replenishment by new youthful talent and by new ideas. A research institute of this kind therefore must be a kind of cistern with talent flowing in and out and this has been made possible by enabling the Weizmann scientists to travel, to act as visiting professors in overseas institutions and to carry on their work in other laboratories. These are Francis Bacon's 'Merchants of Light' who (in *New Atlantis*) maintained a trade 'not for gold, silver or jewels, nor for silks, nor for spices, nor for any other commodity of matter; but only for God's first creature, which was light; to have light of the growth of all parts of the world....' And so the Weizmann Institute has become an *entrepôt* of science in the Middle East.

Weizmann provided for his Institute, therefore, not a blue-print but an inspiration. He gave it not a tradition, but a lack of inhibition. He did not try to create its science in his own image but left it to grow by its own mutations. He bequeathed his breath and those friends who remembered him took the intangible and, with instinct and generosity, made it real.

There is a sense of his fulfilment in the new developments of the Institute, in the setting up of the Institute of Life Sciences in which many disciplines, including his own of organic chemistry, are combining to plumb the living processes and to discover, in physical and chemical terms, The Secret of Life.

Professor Peter Ritchie Calder is Montague Burton Professor of International Relations at Edinburgh University. He has written many works on science and history, including the best-selling The Inheritors (*US title* After the Seventh Day).

CHAPTER SIX

VISION VERSUS FANTASY

AHARON KATZIR-KATCHALSKY

IN HIS BOOK, *The Aims of Education*, Whitehead says: 'In training a child to activity of thought, above all things we must beware of what I call "inert ideas"—that is to say ideas that one merely received into the mind without being utilised, or tested, or thrown into fresh combinations.'

The importance of training on the basis of a living example is well known from everyday life. It is clear that mere logical understanding and intellectual conviction do not give the student an executive capacity. Nobody can learn to play the piano by mastering the logical principles of composition or harmony. It is the operational method that leads the student to an acquisition of the technique of music.

The teaching of moral behaviour belongs to the same class. Decent human behaviour is not acquired by learning the principles of sociology or by studying the moral systems of different societies. Only through the practice of a certain set of moral rules, as demonstrated by living examples, do we acquire our moral behaviour. In this field a few chosen people whose life-work sets a standard for human behaviour can serve as a prototype for the education of the young. These people do not deal only with pure philosophical ideas, the riddles of the universe, or the harmonious structures of being, but encompass the whole pattern of human life, the innumerable human relations in the complicated ensemble of interactions between one social group and another.

The subject matter with which such men deal is so complicated, it requires such a fine intuitive orientation in an undefined and unknown world, that their emergence is very rare, and their imprint on the development of society is generally profound and enduring. What these people create is not just a philosophical structure based on a logical sequence of ideas; it is their life-work itself, the sequence of their actions that is summed up in the form of an operational philosophy.

Weizmann was such a spiritual leader. His life-work is a prototype from which one can learn today and whose value is becoming clearer with the passage of time.

He himself recognized the educational significance of a man's life-work. In his lecture at the Tribune Forum on 21 October 1947, he said the following: '... The Jewish contribution to human values, wherever the Jew has been true to his character, has issued from 'being.' Among Jews the notion of a philosopher who taught one system and lived according to another, who divorced himself from his theories, has always been unthinkable. A man was not considered a teacher merely because he was clever. If what he said was not in keeping with the way he lived, and if the two together did not constitute an example, he could not be a teacher. For, it was argued, if he cannot teach himself, how can he teach others?'

Spiritual leaders who become ideal prototypes of human behaviour are typically mature personalities. They overcome the narcistic tendency of creating for themselves an infantile closed world in which their fantasy is allowed full play. They fulfil the basic requirement of maturity; they forego the pleasures of children's dreams and are ready to grapple with reality directly. They recognize the limitations of the real world and the restrictions of human life. They do not rely on miracles but try to make the best of the possibilities presented by a real world. Weizmann, who was a scientist to the marrow, clearly recognized that the lawfulness of the universe and human life is a set of restrictions. He knew, however, that it is only within the limits of restriction that freedom becomes meaningful. It is not the attempt to forget the limitations imposed by natural order that makes men free, but the other way round—the recognition of law is the basis of free and purposeful human action.

This mature view of freedom made Weizmann the typical man of *vision*. While the man of fantasy builds castles in the air that satisfy his inner wishes but bear no relation to reality, the activity of the visionary is an expression of a creative imagination based on the recognition of the limitations imposed by nature or society and on the intuitive perception of the dynamic forces bringing about future developments.

While the immature person given to fantasy is subject to moods of depression whenever his petty constructions encounter the impact of external facts and his infantile ideas fail to materialize, the visionary whose actions are based on reality is not generally subject to fits of pessimism and usually has an optimistic outlook on life. It was the mature optimism of Weizmann's vision, the intelligent, balanced appreciation of the social reality of the twentieth century, and the free imaginative choice within the limitations of constructive evolution that made him the leader of the Jewish people and the outstanding model for the education of the present generation.

The legacy of great spiritual leaders is subject to a crucial experimental test—the test of historical survival. Only those whose life-work and example express the profound experience of mankind and whose vision represents the fundamental needs and urges of numerous people are remembered by history.

On a historical scale the ten years that have passed since Weizmann's death are a very short period. However, in view of the breakneck pace of modern social and technological change, ten years may be regarded as a relatively long historical era. During these ten years the amount of human knowledge has doubled, the technical changes in industry and agriculture have revolutionized the economic and social structure, and modern means of communication have brought the world into every home. Man slowly begins to feel himself not only a citizen of the globe but an inhabitant of the solar system as a whole. The flood of information is so overwhelming that events which only a short time ago made headlines have been entirely erased from our memory. Politicians who only yesterday 'made history' have fallen into oblivion, and it is only the handful that have influenced the more profound layers of the human soul whose imprint continues to be felt today.

Weizmann's life-philosophy has left such a strong and permanent impression on the Jewish people and the State of Israel, its reflection in the international mind is still so strong, that even now, ten years after his death, letters continue to be addressed to the late President of the State and he is still accused by his opponents for many activities of the State. Weizmann's permanent living legacy invites a painstaking analysis. Such analysis, however, faces the great difficulty that Weizmann's heritage does not consist of books or articles summarizing a clear-cut philosophy. It is not only that more pressing obligations prevented him from devoting enough time for leisurely contemplation, but as a man of science he always resented a dogmatic *Weltanschau* that would distort his direct contact with reality.

If one can speak at all about Weizmann's philosophy, it was by and large an operational method, using an open-minded approach, always capable of change in the light of current critical experience. A closer inspection, however, of his speeches and extempore writings reveals that, behind the matter-of-fact discussion of concrete situations, there is an underlying set of fundamental principles that guided his judgment. In Weizmann's life-work these principles played a rôle similar to that of the fundamental methodology of science, which organizes fragmentary knowledge into an harmonious, self-consistent unity. Some ideas of Weizmann that constituted his permanent legacy will be the subject of the following discussion.

The dilemmas facing a modern scientist were forced on young Weizmann quite early. Decades before scientists became conscious of the heavy social responsibility resting on those who created technological weapons, Weizmann was called on to make some of the weightiest decisions of his life. His problem was not dictated by the recognition of the danger involved in the transfer of the results of scientific research into the hands of an irresponsible group. He did not need the challenge of the atomic war to realize that the clash between the 'two cultures' might lead to the doom of mankind and that scientists were obliged to apply their humanizing contribution in order to save mankind from potential extermination. Thirty years before Russell and Einstein summoned scientists to participate actively in social affairs, many years before Niels Bohr realized that a total change in the attitude of modern man was imperative and that the scientific outlook could provide the basis for a renaissance of international morals, Weizmann made his decision.

From many points of view·Weizmann's road to social responsibility was simpler than that of the Western scientists who, for many years, regarded humanism as an expression of Aristotelian teleology and sterile scholasticism. As a young Jew in a small community within the 'Pale of Settlement', as the son of a struggling, oppressed and persecuted nation, he absorbed from early childhood the elements of Zionism, and of its Messianic hopes, and a readiness to take part in a movement for the liberation of his people. In his impoverished little village Motol he became imbued with feelings of social responsibility for those whose life is always precarious. This responsibility, however, became a difficult burden when he discovered that he could make an excellent scientific career. Getting out of the Pale of Settlement, acquiring Western culture and science, made it very easy to forget the moral responsibilities acquired in childhood.

However, a scientific career did not blind him to the realities. In his letter to Mrs (later Lady) Schuster in 1912, he says:

> Even as a boy of fourteen I had to fight my own battles; I had to struggle for every inch of my long way in Russia as a poor Jew coming of poor Jewish parents; at the Universities of Berlin and

Geneva I had to work my way by doing analytical work in the night, teaching work and all sorts of jobs.

Nine years ago I thought I found a place of rest: I became a university lecturer. I did some good research work and could look confidently into the future. But my chief retired and all his assistants had to leave. The only place where I could find work was England. Neither in Germany nor in France had I the slightest chance as a Jew to get on. I landed in this country with eighteen shillings in my pocket and plenty of good intentions. Perkin was awfully good to me. I worked hard and he did all he could for me. Slowly I worked my way up.

But all this time, Mrs Schuster, my ambition was centred on one cardinal point: to accumulate as much experience as possible and to work myself up to a senior head position and to go away to Palestine. *In the hardest moments of my life this ideal is the guiding star. It is the dream of my life.*

As early as 1912 his candidature for a full professorship was well under way; at the same time his scientific friends were pressing to have the high distinction of membership in the Royal Society bestowed upon him. He was immediately successful in his scientific research, an excellent teacher, and a welcome member of the scientific group in England. It was rather easy to forget his brethren in far-off Russia and to devote himself to a private career. None of the horrors of modern scientific technology weighed on his conscience. Science still seemed to be the 'road of progress', the road of emancipation and liberation of oppressed people, and one could easily justify scientific activity with agreeably liberal reasons.

Weizmann, however, did not take this easy road. Even as a young man of twenty-eight he had looked squarely at his own private responsibility and made his decision. It was Weizmann's conviction that the liberation of the Jewish people was not a matter of a materialistic renaissance, not the establishment of another Levantine state, but that it could only come about by building a centre for the renaissance of the Jewish spirit. The vehicles of this renaissance, in his opinion, must be institutes of higher learning, and at that time his primary concern was with the establishment of the Hebrew University. But he did not feel that his task was finished by writing a pamphlet and making some luke-warm propaganda for the University.

In a touching letter to his fiancée, later his wife, he writes the following: 'I stand before two alternatives. If the project for the University progresses it will be unimaginable for me to be occupied in chemical work simultaneously. . . . You know very well what chemistry is to me, what is the laboratory, its joys and sorrows. But you know at the same time, my dearest, that the thought of the University is no less dear to my heart. Chemistry is my private occupation. It is this activity in which I rest from my social tasks. Forgetting now about all material calculations, I would like to pose the problem to you from a purely moral angle: the alternative is difficult, horribly difficult.'

His original decision was to abandon scientific activity and devote himself to the institution that seemed to him to contain the kernel of the Jewish national home. Later, however, he came to the conclusion that he ought not to give up his scientific activity but must look for a new synthesis, a synthesis in which his scientific creation would merge harmoniously with his Zionist leadership. He was very much aware of the difficulties; in 1914 he wrote his friend Julius Simon:

> I know very well that you are devoting to the Zionist case the same amount of time as I do and that you are as tired as I am. There is, however, a certain difference, which makes my problem more difficult than yours. Under the conditions of my life during the last one and a half years it has been personally impossible to create scientifically. After every trip I am torn apart, thrown out from the conceptual framework of science, and before I have the possibility of getting back to my science, I have to travel again. Not talking about the daily letters and the little troubles, it is the constant tension which makes it impossible to concentrate on scientific problems.
>
> On the other hand, it is unimaginable for me to give up the things here. First, because I have in the laboratory numerous interesting problems which will endow me with a good name in science, and secondly, because for Zionism itself, I should not give up what I have reached hitherto. Nevertheless, serving two gods is extremely difficult.

Weizmann's attempt to reach a synthesis was based on a profound recognition of the nature of modern science and the recognition that within science itself the attitudes had changed. Science was no longer the materialistic 'anti-humanistic' movement of the nineteenth century. Though reluctant to speak about his attitude to science as a basis for a new humanistic outlook, he made clear his attitude in a remark during the Nineteenth Zionist Congress in 1935:

> I am not a Marxist, I do not know whether I am a bourgeois, but I am surely not a capitalist. However, my non-Marxism has a

different meaning from that used in the present-day attacks on Marxism. I am a chemist and I have had the possibility to follow the development of the sciences during the last few years.

I believe that the scientific materialism which started with Hegel and Darwin and has developed recently to the outlook of Einstein, Eddington and Jeans shows that the basis of historical materialism does not hold today as solidly as it did, say twenty years ago. I do not intend to present a dissertation on materialism, but I would like to say only this: in a world in which the line of demarcation between matter and energy has disappeared, in a world in which Newton's teaching of gravitation has been undermined to a greater extent than the programme of the parties of the Jewish State, in a world in which the scientific and economic bases are suffering a deep crisis, it would be unwise for a man with partial scientific discipline to adopt the one or the other possible form of society.

Today so-called historical materialism looks to me as a piece of ingenuous one-sidedness. However, the economic fundamentals of this materialism contain something which brings to light the spirit of Jewish prophetical teaching. Only when this is realized can we understand how it has been possible for our workers in the Emek, brought up as they were on Judaism and on Marxism, to achieve the synthesis of ideals that they have achieved.

Weizmann was one of the first to grasp the humanistic implications of Einstein's theory that matter and energy are different aspects of a profound unity that cannot be expressed in tangible forms. In spite of his social responsibilites he had sufficient time to ponder on and recognize the revolutionary change in the scientific attitude brought about by the discovery of the duality of particle and wave forms of matter and light, and he saw clearly that this new non-materialistic science was much closer to humanism. In the world of modern science, where logic has become a highly practical science and physics a highly theoretical doctrine, where the rôle of the observer cannot be divorced from the objective results of experiment, the long-standing barrier between the subjective human spirit and the objective world seems to crumble. Science is consciously becoming an integral part of human culture, another expression of the determination of the human intellect to understand both itself and the world.

Within this outlook the social responsibility of a scientist is not dictated by practical reasons only, or by the fact that the scientist is indispensable for guidance in a maze of technicalities that only he can master. For Weizmann, the social responsibility of science was intrinsic to the very fact that science was an integral part of a great human effort, and could not be dissociated from the culture of his time. The scientist is neither a superman nor an outcast unconcerned with ordinary human needs. He is a citizen carrying out an important task and producing cultural values that must be integrated within the general framework of cultural development.

In one of his last speeches, at the first session of the Knesset in Jerusalem in February 1949, Dr Weizmann said:

> First let us strive to strengthen our constructive resources of science and research, which are the basis of human achievement. Yet, for all the decisive importance of science, it is not by science alone that we shall win through.
>
> Let us build a new bridge between science and the spirit of man. "Where there is no vision the people perish." We have seen what science leads to when it is not inspired by moral vision—the atomic bomb threatening to destroy the entire planet.
>
> All my life I have tried to make science and research the basis of our national endeavour, but I have always known fully well that there are values higher than science. The only values that offer healing for the ills of humanity are the supreme values of justice and righteousness, peace and love.
>
> Zion will be redeemed with judgment, and her converts with righteousness.

Weizmann's philosophy on the relation of science and humanism was deeply influenced by the teaching of the great Jewish philosopher who was Weizmann's intellectual guide and teacher, Ahad Ha'am.

Ahad Ha'am was the first philosopher who recognized that Judaism was a culture characterized by the survival value of any profound culture that encompasses numerous aspects of human life. He maintained that what preserved the Jewish nation during the 2,000 years of the Diaspora and enabled the Jewish people to retain a unity which transcends geographical, political and economic diversity, was the unity of its cultural heritage. According to him, the power of cultures was discovered early by the sages before the destruction of the Second Temple. They realized that the survival of the Jewish people, which could not be based on military power, on economic strength or political influence, could be placed on a cultural foundation. Their culture could carry the Jews through all the vicissitudes of a hostile and changing world.

Rabbi Yochanan Ben-Zakai had realized, during the Roman siege óf Jerusalem in the year AD 70, that cultural values need not be the product of an unconscious historical development, but could be fostered consciously and purposefully.

In a short article published in 1891, Ahad Ha'am wrote:

> While the Romans besieged Jerusalem, while outside the walls the sword prevailed and inside the walls hunger ruled, the youth of Israel made final efforts, with no hope for victory, to fight their people's foes. At the same time the elder sages were sitting in Yavne and dealing with the regulations governing purity and impurity. The warriors were embittered with the Pharisees who were concerned with eternal life while their brethren were being exterminated by sword and imprisoned.
>
> But we know now that the Pharisees were right, and that while the Jewish heroes who sacrificed themselves for momentary life died a righteous death, their war did not save their nation from extermination. Those quiet Pharisees saw the future development from the beginning and realized there was no hope to build their national life on the basis of momentary achievement. They devoted themselves to eternal life in order to build a new world for the future generations who were to live scattered in the Diaspora.

Ahad Ha'am felt that a Messianic Zionism like Herzl's, a Zionism that envisaged its aim in the reconstruction of a material Jewish national home, did not meet the needs of the Jewish people nor meet the problem of the Jewish nation in the twentieth century. He recognized that it was not only the physical persecution of the Jews which underlay the urge for a national solution in the form of a national home, but that the growth of nationalism during the nineteenth and twentieth centuries, the upsurge of chauvinism and of a sterile assimilation endangered not only the Jews themselves, but Judaism as a culture. His conclusion was that the primary task of Zionism was the revival of Judaism, of a creative and developing Judaism, and not only the establishment of a physical asylum in the land of Israel.

In a penetrating analysis based on the direct observation of what was going on in the Palestine of the beginning of the century, Ahad Ha'am wrote openly and sharply that the prospects of developing a little Balkanic country surrounded by enemies were very limited. Only if the State of Israel were to fulfil a spiritual mission, if it were to become the centre of a cultural renaissance, if it were to play a rôle in the life of every Jew in the world by providing new cultural values, traditions of learning and moral attitudes, only then would the State of Israel perform its task, gain international justification and be able to survive the potential hostilities foreseen by Ahad Ha'am some fifty years before the establishment of the State.

Weizmann, following Ahad Ha'am's reasoning, and being imbued with the idea that science was an integral part of modern life, reasoned further that if a centre was to be established in Israel that would justify its existence both from the Jewish and international point of view, it had to be one in which science would merge with human values and would help in translating classical Jewish traditions, outlook and modes of life into contemporary acceptable language. As early as 1903 he published, together with Martin Buber, a famous pamphlet in which he pointed out that the translation of cultural Zionism into practical terms meant the establishment of a Hebrew University. In 1918 he took the first steps to realize this objective. While British guns were still roaring on the outskirts of Jerusalem, while Turkish troops were still seen on the horizon, Weizmann laid the foundations of the Hebrew University on Mount Scopus. At the ceremony he said:

> It seems at first sight paradoxical that in a land with so sparse a population, in a land where everything still remains to be done, in a land crying out for such simplicities as ploughs and roads, we should begin by creating a centre of spiritual and intellectual development. But we Jews know that when the mind is given fullest play, that when we have a centre for the development of Jewish consciousness, it will coincide with the fulfilment of our material needs. In the darkest ages of our existence we found protection and shelter within the walls of our schools and colleges and the tormented body of the Jew found relief and consolation in a devoted study of Jewish science.
>
> Amidst all the sordidness and squalor of the ghetto there stood the greatest of schools of learning where numbers of young Jews sat with our Rabbis and great teachers. These schools and colleges served as great reservoirs that during the long ages of persecution stored up an intellectual and spiritual energy which, on the one hand, helped to maintain our national existence and, on the other hand, blossomed forth for the benefit of mankind once the walls of the ghetto had fallen.

It was clear to Weizmann that the establishment of a Hebrew University did not mean the creation of an ivory tower, of a closed group living a monastic life in the temples of science. To him science was a social function that had to keep in constant contact with the life and interests of the people. In 1918 he said:

The Hebrew University, while trying to maintain the highest scientific level, must at the same time be rendered accessible to all classes of the people. The Jewish workman and farm labourer must be enabled to find there a possibility of continuing and completing his education in his free hours. The doors of our libraries, lecture rooms and laboratories must be wide open to them all. Thus the University will exercise its beneficial influence on the nation as a whole.

Earlier, in his speech at the Eleventh Zionist Congress, he said:

It is a fact that the Jew possesses a strong intellect. If we understand well the tasks of a colonizer, if we reckon not only the manual strength but also the psychology of our colonizers, we cannot ignore these intellectual gifts. We shall, on the contrary, try to use them even for economic purposes. Although we have at present an ardent desire to see our people plough the fields and to make it faithful to its soil, we know that we are and shall always be the People of the Book. Our strongest weapon is the spirit, and it is our duty to cultivate this spirit, to sharpen the weapon with which we must fight for a better existence. The University will be our spiritual dreadnought; it will be of greater value to us than armies and navies are to other nations.

How close to his heart was the spiritual and scientific renaissance of the Jewish people one can learn from his speech at the Congress in Basle in 1946. This was the first Congress after the second World War, when news about the extermination of the Jews in Germany became known and the Zionist movement tried to sum up the terrible losses sustained at the hands of the Nazi forces. Several speakers in different languages tried to express the feeling of despair, of desolation, and horror. Only Weizmann, however, speaking in plain Yiddish, succeeded in putting the feelings of the Congress in simple words. When he spoke, the Congress rose to its feet and listened with tearful eyes to the simple words of its great leader.

Weizmann did not so much grieve over the material losses; he was mostly concerned with the terrible blow the Nazi assassins had inflicted on Judaism by the destruction of its centres of learning. He said:

Everything that we have lost in this generation in learning, in wisdom, in good deeds and moral, are things that one cannot weigh on a balance or measure with a yardstick, things that have the highest importance and that the enemy has destroyed. All this can be rebuilt only very slowly in the future generations. Because of this, for us every Jew who studies, every school and every synagogue that is opened, is a real national treasure. It may be that, in the course of many centuries, we shall be able to fill the deep losses we suffered in the communities of Warsaw, of Odessa, Kishinev, and Vilna. It is both our obligation and our privilege.

The obligation to build a scientific centre in Israel, to carry on the legacy of the Jewish tradition, was always in the back of Weizmann's mind. In *Trial and Error* he says:

> Our great men were always a product of symbiosis between the ancient, traditional Talmudic learning in which our ancestors were steeped in the Polish and Galician ghettos or even in Spain, and the modern Western universities with which their children came in contact. There is, as often as not, a long list of Talmudic scholars and Rabbis in the pedigrees of our modern scientists. In many cases they themselves have come from Talmudic schools, breaking away in their twenties and struggling through to Paris or Zurich or Princeton. It is this extraordinary phenomenon—a great tradition of learning fructified by modern methods—which has given us both first-class scientists and competent men in every branch of academic activity, out of all relation to our numbers.

From Weizmann's operational point of view the value of science and the meaning of culture were not only a matter of a passive aspect of timelessness: culture is a dynamic factor that changes mankind. Two generations before modern economy fell under the sway of technology, many decades before automation began to enter industry and agriculture, Weizmann saw clearly the potentialities dormant in applied scientific research. Moreover, he understood that science provided a great opportunity to help small nations to develop and to strengthen themselves without expanding or enslaving their neighbours. Beyond topographical or geographical dimensions Weizmann saw very clearly the new and powerful dimension of science. While the Nazi psychopaths were preaching an expansionist policy to give the German people more *Lebensraum*, Weizmann was indoctrinating his people with the idea that one could create an enormous *Lebensraum* by peaceful means through the creative activity of the scientist. Instead of the conquest of foreign natural resources, instead of the brutal struggle for mineral wealth, for God-given *richesse*, he preached the fostering of the human spirit and the encouragement of ingenuity and resourcefulness. In the final analysis these will prove to be the best means of overcoming poverty and suffering throughout the world.

He once said: 'Our sages used to say, If there is no flour there is no Torah. But,' he went on, 'more important is the reverse statement: If there is no Torah there is no flour.' Today learning is the basis of all practical things, and Torah and application are joined together.

Since any industrial activity is based on the utilization of adequate sources of energy, Weizmann's primary concern was with problems connected with energy resources. He realized quite clearly that Israel, in spite of its proximity to the rich oilfields of Arabia, had practically no sources of local fuel, neither oil or coal nor wood, and this made him look to the inexhaustible source of solar energy, which could provide tremendous amounts of motive power, especially to the poorer parts of the globe. Available estimates tell us that the amount of solar energy pouring on the globe in three days is equivalent to all of the sources of uranium which could be used for atomic energy. The difficulty with solar energy, however, is the mode of its utilization. It is a very diffuse form of energy, which for the time being no one has succeeded in harnessing satisfactorily.

Weizmann felt that one of the best ways to make use of solar energy was through the plant world. The photosynthetic apparatus of green plants is one of the best devices for storing solar energy in the form of energy-rich organic materials. It may be said that all of Weizmann's scientific life-work was devoted to the utilization of plant materials as a basis of industry. Thus, even in his early work, which led to the discovery of the acetone-butanol fermentation process, Weizmann advanced a revolutionary idea that proved of tremendous value in our modern industrial development—that biological agents, bacteria, yeast and fungi, could be used as industrial materials in the conversion of plant material into chemical raw materials. As early as 1911 he was active in synthesizing rubber from chemical raw materials based on vegetable sources; later, in the second World War, he showed how some of the basic materials of modern organic industry, such as synthetic rubbers and plastics, could be obtained by biological means from plants, which are merely stored solar energy.

In his struggle to provide Israel with a scientific foundation Weizmann never lost sight of the inherent dangers. With his sharp analytical vision of the development of mankind, he recognized the latent tendencies dormant in a technological society. These may lead to the dominion of machine-like technocrats whose only aspiration is higher efficiency; they are essentially the priests of a new system of idolatry in which the gods of Automation and Mass Production determine the course of human life. Weizmann saw clearly the disruptive and degrading effect that this modern technicalization process could have, especially on smaller, underdeveloped countries that lack a well-established tradition and a cultural background sufficiently strong to withstand the impact of an automatized society.

In a society dominated by automated industry, where the economic structure as a whole is too complicated to be grasped by the citizen, in a world in which international relations are too involved to be understood by the ordinary man, democracy loses much of its meaning. The decisions made by the masses are not dictated by logical conviction or by an understanding of the intricacies of the factors ruling human life. That is why an increasing number of the people are escaping from social life into the domain of their petty private interests, the so-called 'privatism' in which the great humane ideals of justice and peace, international understanding, and human love are replaced by the ideal of owning a car, a television set, a refrigerator, and a private home.

Many modern psychologists believe that for life to become meaningful and rich, a pioneering purposefulness must exist in the activity of the State. Young people should realize that they must carry on the ideals of previous generations; the older generation should be imbued with a vision that far transcends their private interests. It was a similar recognition of these social goals by Weizmann that made him close in spirit to the pioneering movement of Israel. He once said at a Zionist Congress:

> The Histadruth, with which, I am happy to say, I have the friendliest relations, has a very special harmonious synthesis of learning and of socialism, a synthesis that is not in a vacuum, but that has become a reality in the thankless Land of Palestine. It is this reality that gives modern Israel its special interest. It is this that attracts the interest of the world to Israel.
>
> Do you believe that the world is interested in a million orange boxes? Oranges grow elsewhere too. The world is longing for something new and pure, for a new form that will help it extricate itself from present-day confusion. The elements for this new form have been created through the work of the present-day generation in Israel.

It is in this spirit that Weizmann looked for the synthesis of science and humanism, for technological development and pioneering spirit. There is no better phrase with which to close this article than that used by Weizmann himself:

The prophetic vision that out of Zion will come forth the word of the Lord is not only a legacy of the past, but is the commandment of the present and the hope of the future.

Professor Aharon Katzir-Katchalsky, Professor of Polymer Science at the Weizmann Institute, is President of the Israel Academy of Sciences and Humanities.

1914–1919

CHAPTER SEVEN

WEIZMANN AND THE BALFOUR
DECLARATION

T. R. FYVEL

THE FIRST Zionist Congress, the Balfour Declaration, the proclamation of the State of Israel: each of these three milestones, these three historic occasions in modern Jewish history demanded special qualities from the Jewish leader concerned. Among other qualities, the calling of the first Congress required—dare one say it?—the touch of Herzl's far-soaring journalistic flair. The proclamation of the State called for the courage which Ben-Gurion had in plenty. But as for the feat in persuasion which in 1917 made the Balfour Declaration possible, it could be said that this was the most decisive achievement of all, and what it also demanded from Weizmann was that rarest of gifts—supreme political artistry.

After all, this Declaration in which the British Government—at a grimly undecided stage of the first World War—undertook to facilitate a Jewish national home in Palestine, has in retrospect an improbable look when one considers the forces opposed to it.

The Jewish bankers and capitalists of the West were with a few notable exceptions hostile to Zionism; so were most of the British military and officials in the Middle East; so was the French Government, and the Vatican. In 'persuading' the British Government, against this opposition, the Zionists with their empty coffers and scanty organization, and their individually important yet isolated well-wishers, could only pit the existence of the Yishuv, the Jewish community in Palestine, the faith of their followers, and, above all, the political skill of Weizmann and his unique access to the British Government. As General Smuts said about the British War Cabinet: 'We were persuaded—but remember that it was Dr Weizmann who persuaded us.'

What therefore would have happened, if Weizmann, when in 1904 he decided to concentrate on his scientific career, had chosen to go not to Manchester University, to England, but to some other country, as he might so easily have done? The question has its fascination, for one can surely say that in that case the history of Zionism might have been very different, and much else besides. But if we deal with history as it happened, this remains speculation, for it was Manchester which Weizmann chose; but since he later called this an inspired decision, it is interesting to see what it involved.

The start was inauspicious and gave no hint of the drawn-out love affair between Weizmann and Britain which was to ensue. (Like many a love affair, it had its melancholy ending, but this was only many, many years later.) In Switzerland, Weizmann had seemed to live at the centre of a continuous European and Jewish debate: there were the arguments with Jewish Assimilationists of the Right and Left, and the internal politics of Actions Committees and Congresses, the exhausting battle against Herzl over the Uganda offer. But when Weizmann in 1904—now aged thirty—crossed the Channel, it was as if he had left not only the Continent but the sounds of this whole great international debate behind him. English life at the outset seemed to him foreign and strange. In Manchester, he worked at first on a budget of £3 a week in a tiny basement laboratory provided by his sponsor, Professor Perkin. In this basement (as he later put it), the thick Manchester fogs weighed as heavily on his soul as on his lungs. He felt lonely, cut off from his fiancée and friends; the English Zionists seemed provincial beyond belief. Even when in 1906 he married and was joined by his attractive and talented wife Vera, their material circumstances were at first depressing. Vera had already qualified as a doctor on the Continent, but while she studied for her English degree, the couple lived in dismal lodgings. To pay off the instalments on new furniture, Weizmann had to work overtime. He sat up night after night, often with his infant son Benjamin on his lap, marking Oxford and Cambridge examination papers at an average rate of two shillings per piece. Writing later about these early years in England, Weizmann marvelled at the youthful stamina which had enabled him to endure.

Yet however hard the start, every page of Weizmann's recollections also shows that precisely with his move to England something new, a decisive change, took place in his life. For his *Wanderjahre* were over; from the start he struck roots in Manchester, in the life of England; he felt an attraction to which he responded. Step by step, since Weizmann did not lack talent in any direction, his situation improved. He found financial backing for his research work from his friend, Charles Dreyfus. The lectures to which Professor Perkin called him at the university proved eminently successful; he took his

Doctorate of Science; in 1910 Vera qualified as a doctor and became a Medical Health Officer of the Municipality of Manchester. With both the Weizmanns working, their financial situation was much improved. Indeed, it was soon comfortable. They had a pleasant Manchester home and a growing circle of friends.

But Manchester also offered something more. Weizmann's life was always in essence a Zionist life; and, as soon became apparent, he grew aware of a new confidence, new ideas, through his contact with liberal England where, as he put it, 'freedom of thought and speech were as taken for granted as the air one breathed'. It was in this free English atmosphere that Weizmann in 1906 felt able to return to continuous Zionist activity. And now we come to his special and personal relationship with England, the unique personal position in England that he created for himself and which was already very important in his early Manchester days.

It is clear that just as Weizmann took to England, so the English took to him, and in a particular and unique way. On Weizmann's part, what always attracted him in English life was its upper-class tradition: the practical, not over-intellectual English outlook towards political affairs, the easy informality of English social and academic life, even the conversational flippancy which could cover serious purpose. To all these traits, he adapted himself quickly, but his assimilation was always one with a difference. He never for a moment suggested that he was anything but a Russian Jew, who in spite of his own privileges remained completely identified with the Jewish masses of Eastern Europe, and so was their spokesman. And from all that has been written about Weizmann by his non-Jewish friends, one thing emerges. It was this, his natural gift for blending his full and distinguished English life and his Zionist faith, which impressed his non-Jewish friends and acquaintances. One could say, indeed, that it was through this balance in his own personality that many of them caught their first glimpse of the profundity of Zionism and of what was involved in the Jewish problem.

This special gift was already evident during Weizmann's early Manchester days. In 1906, when he had been in England for only two years, a Parliamentary by-election brought that aristocratic and sceptical British politician, Arthur Balfour, to Manchester. Weizmann talked to him for half an hour about the problems of the Russian Jews and about Zionism. Balfour soon forgot the name of this casually-met Russian-Jewish lecturer in chemistry, but never the impact of Weizmann's personality, nor the picture of the Russian Jews Weizmann had drawn.

From this standpoint, that of the propagation of Zionism in the years before 1914, one can also see what fortunate assets Weizmann's choice to settle in Manchester yielded him. In academic Manchester, he was in a city which was still the vital centre of the British liberal tradition. Among men accustomed to think internationally, he could find a ready response to the concept of Zionism; and in the light of the far-flung nature of British imperial politics, he himself could see Zionism and Palestine in a new perspective. Secondly, Manchester gave him access to one of the world's great universities, where he moved among, and talked to, men like Sir Arthur Schuster, a philosopher like Prof. Samuel Alexander, physicists like Ernest (later Lord) Rutherford, Nils Bohr and others—men who many years later were still to be in close contact with Weizmann as active supporters of the Jerusalem University. Thirdly, Manchester gave Weizmann a vital access to one of the world's great newspapers, the *Manchester Guardian*, whose political interests spanned the globe and whose famous editor, C. P. Scott, moved as an equal among statesmen. For example, it was C. P. Scott, by then won over by Weizmann, who told him casually in London in 1914 that they should drop in on Lloyd George, so that Weizmann might talk to him about Palestine —it was as easy as that, or at least for Weizmann.

But this is jumping ahead. By and large, the years 1904–1914 were for Weizmann an extremely busy period of preparation. He was well established as a lecturer in Manchester; he gradually extended his parallel private research work into the fields of biochemistry and bacteriology, which involved visits to the Pasteur Institute in Paris. Zionism also involved constant travel. Weizmann and his wife attended Congresses and other Zionist occasions on the Continent. In 1907, for the first time, he visited Palestine, where he met men like Ruppin and Chankin, noted the new spirit introduced into the Yishuv by the Halutzim, and returned confirmed in his belief in the absolute need for uninterrupted 'practical work' in Palestine, however small in scale. At the Congress of that year, he characteristically coined the phrase of 'synthetic Zionism': the political and diplomatic propaganda for a Charter, and practical colonization in Palestine, on however small a scale, were not opposed alternatives for the Zionist movement but had to be carried out in conjunction. He also worked indefatigably for his favourite project, the idea of a Jewish university in Jerusalem. While in those days it could be no more than an idea, there was something characteristic of Weizmann in the blend of steadfast vision and sober practicality with which he lost no opportunity of enlisting support for the idea in all the academic circles in which he moved.

In England, though he held no official position in the Zionist

Federation, he took part in the work of the English Zionists, gathering round him a circle of younger followers, such as Simon Marks and Israel Sieff in Manchester and Harry Sacher and Leon Simon in London. During these years it was also an asset to Weizmann that the most eminent Zionist resident in England should have been Ahad Ha'am, whose liberal and pragmatic concept of Zionism matched Weizmann's own outlook. In 1913 came a chance which almost might have had fateful consequences. In one of his few setbacks in England, he was passed over for a full professorship at Manchester University, and at the same time received a tempting offer to transfer his scientific work to Berlin. Fortunately Vera and he decided against a move. And then, in August 1914, came the thunderclap of the first World War. In July 1914, he and Vera were in Berlin; the outbreak of war found them in Switzerland. Through an anxious Paris, where Weizmann consulted Baron Rothschild, Weizmann hastened back to England to see what he could do for his adopted country and also for Zionism, by this time parallel themes in his life. As he recalled, it was a gloomy and frightening homecoming. And yet, the war with all its terror—academic work seemed at a temporary standstill, Zionist international contacts were shattered—had in fact also opened up new possibilities and hopes; indeed, quite wild hopes as Turkey entered the war against Britain. Just as a further British imperial advance into the Middle East to safeguard oil supplies and imperial communications had long been expected, so had the idea of a Jewish settlement in Palestine under British auspices been brought up from time to time, as a possible part of such a British expansion; but in the years before 1914 only romantically, just as a notion. Now, suddenly, as the guns thundered on the Western front and British Middle East forces moved into action against the Turks, the notion had become a concrete post-war possibility. And for Weizmann, this transformation meant that it was also *his* hour. As he wrote: 'Thus hope begets action and justifies itself. . . . It was a time of uncertainty; and I went about with my hopes, waiting for my chance.'

In fact, he created his opportunity to transfer the centre of Zionism. In November 1914, after consultation with friends, he wrote his historic letter to C. P. Scott, quoted in *Trial and Error*:

Don't you think that the chance for the Jewish people is now within the limits of discussion at least? I realize, of course, that we cannot 'claim' anything, we are much too atomized for it; but we can reasonably say that should Palestine fall within the British sphere of influence, and should Britain encourage a Jewish settlement there, as a British dependency, we could have in twenty to thirty years a million Jews out there, perhaps more; they would develop the country, bring back civilization to it and form a very effective guard for the Suez Canal.

One could say, perhaps, that with this letter a new period of Zionist history began, the dual phase of Weizmann's leadership and Anglo-Zionist involvement. For now Weizmann's British contacts also bore fruit. The story of his career as a scientist and as a Zionist during the next three years—years of grim war—reads like one of romantic success. On 3 December 1914, when he met C. P. Scott early in the morning just off the train in London, as he often did, Scott said: 'We're going to have breakfast with Mr Lloyd George.' So for Weizmann it was breakfast with the Chancellor in Downing Street. There, Weizmann also found Herbert Samuel among the guests. To the 'surprise of his life' (Weizmann's own words) he discovered that Samuel was not, like most prominent Anglo-Jews, an anti-Zionist. Far from it, Samuel was a supporter of the cause, and on his own had submitted a memorandum to the Prime Minister, Asquith, about the Jewish state in Palestine. An invaluable contact!

Lloyd George, meanwhile, had listened patiently, promised to give Weizmann's views serious thought, and suggested that Weizmann should also see Balfour at the Admiralty. Weizmann asked his friend Professor Alexander to introduce him, but again the contact came without effort. Balfour sent Alexander a postcard: 'Dear Sam; Weizmann needs no introduction. I still remember our meeting in 1906.' This time, the conversation between Weizmann and Balfour lasted for several hours and in spite of its general philosophical nature was to be politically crucial. Balfour had, on the Jewish question, been strongly influenced by the Cosima Wagner circle in Germany, and had his reservation about the rôle of rich Jews in Europe. Weizmann swept these irrelevancies about isolated rich Jews out of the way. He talked instead about the intolerable situation of the Jewish masses and about the only solution of a definite status for the Jewish people, in a Jewish homeland in Palestine, and under normal conditions of life. In the end, Balfour said: 'You work for a great cause. You must come again and again.'

Before long came further vital contacts. British war industry in 1916 suffered from a shortage of acetone, a substance important as a solvent in the making of high explosive for naval guns. Weizmann's special process of producing acetone by fermentation attracted attention. In March 1916 he found himself again at the Admiralty, this time in the presence of Winston Churchill, who greeted him: 'Dr Weizmann, we need 30,000 tons of acetone. Can you make it?' Given official position and wide powers and resources, Weizmann was pre-occupied with this task in the British war effort for the next year. And this meant many things. First, a move to London: the new house he and Vera took at 67 Addison Road in Kensington (where his second son Michael was born) became a Zionist centre for years. It meant possibilities for Zionist work on a new level. Now Weizmann could work from London, and with new status, from his own position in the British war machine which, as he said, brought him into touch with 'all sorts of personalities, high and low, in the British Government'.

Through the upheaval of 1916 it had also become—fortunately for Weizmann—a new Government. Lloyd George was Premier, Balfour at the Foreign Office, both already interested in Zionism. Among the men in key positions whom Weizmann met, talked to and inspired with sympathy for Zionist aims—as he said, the task during 1916–17 involved him in 2,000 interviews—one can only mention a few. They were largely men of imaginative outlook: Lord Milner, a liberal imperialist and a member of the War Cabinet; Balfour's Under-Secretary at the Foreign Office, Robert Cecil, another man of ideas and ideals, to gain fame as one of the architects of the League of Nations; Sir Charles Webster and Colonel Meinertzhagen in the Intelligence Directorate of the War Office, through whom Weizmann had an invaluable contact with General Macdonogh—soon another supporter—and the General Staff; influential journalists like Wickham Steed, foreign editor of *The Times*, and Herbert Side-botham of the *Manchester Guardian*; and finally Sir Mark Sykes, Chief Secretary to the War Cabinet and entrusted with special responsibility for Middle East affairs—in Weizmann's words 'one of our greatest finds'.

All in all, quite an array of men who understood Zionism and were sympathizers to varying degrees. Of course, Weizmann had not been working alone. Herbert Samuel, though after 1916 no longer in the Government, was of considerable help; so were members of the Rothschild family. From 1916, Weizmann's hand was also strengthened because he had with him in England Nahum Sokolow, who was a leading member of the Zionist Executive and enjoyed intimate diplomatic contacts especially in France and other Latin countries. Weizmann and he worked closely with leading English Zionists such as Dr Gaster, Joseph Cowen, and Herbert Bentwich. To assist Weizmann, a special political office had also been opened in Piccadilly, run by Weizmann's young disciple Simon (today Lord) Marks; among those associated with this office were Ahad Ha'am, Harry Sacher, and Israel Sieff. Out of all these efforts, so Weizmann said, a Zionist Political Committee gradually and inevitably emerged. It was, in fact, constituted at a meeting with the English Zionist Federation late in 1916. It was quite an unofficial body—the only member of the Zionist Executive on it was Sokolow. But by now Weizmann was ready for further action. As the war was proceeding on its grim course; as the possibility of America's entry into the war on the Allies' side came a step nearer; as a British offensive against the Turkish forces in Palestine was being prepared, it was decided by Weizmann and his friends to advance from general propaganda to political action—to press the British Government for a definite declaration of policy in favour of a Zionist Palestine. And so, at the beginning of January 1917, the Political Committee drew up the famous memorandum, 'Outline of a Programme for the Jewish Re-settlement of Palestine', which was with all its imperfections a first draft of a Zionist Charter. Towards the end of January 1917, after several conversations with Sykes, Weizmann handed him the memorandum for submission to the War Cabinet. And with this move, as he said, the battle was joined. He and his friends 'had stepped into the world arena; we had taken the plunge into international politics . . .'

What followed between January and November 1917 was the struggle for the Balfour Declaration, whose stages Mr Leonard Stein has now so excellently documented. But in a personal study about Weizmann one must, I think, here pause to consider a number of facts which illuminate the real magnitude of his achievement.

First, he had become the effective representative of world Zionism without holding any official position, until for convenience's sake he was made President of the English Zionist Federation some time in 1917. He was not on the Zionist Executive, nor even an inner member of the Actions Committee. At what precise moment it was that Weizmann realized that Herzl's mantle of world Zionist leadership had descended on him is not easy to say. Perhaps one could say simply that through the sheer stature of his personality he took on this rôle and so moved Zionism from its Central European into its British phase.

One must also recall that this move required boldness. When the war in 1914 shattered Zionist ranks, the Zionist Actions Committee —as it seemed, quite logically—had established a bureau on neutral soil in Copenhagen, to try to maintain international links. As a British citizen, and because he staked everything on the British con-nection, Weizmann would have none of this. Without hesitation, he cut himself off from this bureau, an action noted by the British authorities. This required a faith in British victory which many other

Zionists of Continental origin did not share. But Weizmann never wavered in his belief in his own superior insight into British strength. The move to link Zionist fortunes so definitely with Britain also required the highest diplomatic skill, because Russia was Britain's ally, and in Zionist eyes the Tsarist regime was after all the traditional persecutor of the Jews. At various times, as many East European Jews received the advancing Germans as liberators, as anti-Russian feelings rose high among the masses of American Jews, Weizmann found himself in difficult situations; he was assailed by his fellow Zionists. (Russian Zionists like Tschlenow and Ussischkin, in particular, saw Zionist prospects very differently.) Solving these constant problems demanded on Weizmann's part the highest diplomatic skill and patience—the skill and patience of an artist—as well as steadfast faith in his ability to steer an Anglo-Zionist course.

These qualities were soon to be taxed to the full, because the whole direct Zionist approach to the British Government was at any time in 1917 fundamentally a gamble. Zionist historians, writing with the hindsight of the achievement of the Balfour Declaration, have mostly underestimated how frail was Weizmann's whole exercise in persuasion in the corridors of the British Government. He might have been fortunate, in the outlook of the men he found there. But, as Sir Charles Webster has written,[1] these same men

> were labouring under an immense burden in this, for Britain, most critical year of the war, when the submarine losses reached new heights, the French mutinies threw on Britain the main burden of defence in the West, the United States was not yet ready to take part in the conflict, and the Russians were about to make a separate peace with the Central Powers.

In such a situation, the difference between general sympathy for Zionist aims and concrete political action was always immense. Lloyd George and his colleagues had other things to think about than Dr Weizmann; they had constantly to consider other allies and forces—France, the Arabs, the United States, whose policies often ran counter to Zionism. Indeed, this difference between theory and action was at once brought home to Weizmann and his friends with a shock.

Weizmann, together with Sokolow, Herbert Samuel, Lord Rothschild, Dr Gaster, Harry Sacher and others, met Sir Mark Sykes in his personal capacity at Dr Gaster's house, for a full-dress discussion on 7 February 1917. To their unpleasant surprise, now that it came to the point of discussing British political action, they found Sykes

[1] Sir Charles Webster, *The Art and Practice of Diplomacy* (Chatto and Windus, London, 1961).

hedging about the whole idea of a post-war Jewish Palestine under British rule, which he had on previous occasions quite warmly discussed. There was the difficulty of Britain's commitments to the Arabs, he said, though he thought there could be an arrangement about this if the Zionists helped the Arabs elsewhere in the Middle East. However, there were also the awkward different views of Britain's allies, above all the French. He suggested the Zionists might therefore do well to try out their ideas in Paris. He also casually threw out an alternative: that the Zionists might aim at a much more limited Charter, allowing them to develop areas in Palestine they had already settled. And so on.

To Weizmann and his friends, Sykes's changed attitude was bewildering. Had they known it, there was an explanation for it. At this particular time, Britain's hands were tied by the secret Sykes-Picot Agreement with France. France and Britain throughout the war were sharp rivals in a race to expand their post-war influence in the Turkish Middle East. When Sir Henry MacMahon in 1915 promised British support to the Arab movement of independence, the French energetically staked their own claim. In the eventual secret agreement on respective Anglo-French spheres between Sykes and the French representative, Picot, it had been agreed that in return for French concessions elsewhere, Palestine was to be divided by a line running from Acre to Tiberias. The area north of the line was to fall to a greater Syria under French aegis; that south of it to be placed under Anglo-French condominium.

The terms of this Sykes-Picot Agreement, of course, cut right across the idea of Palestine as a Jewish National Home. The jolt was, therefore, all the greater when in April 1917 (through C. P. Scott) the terms became known. Now the Zionists had to think again; it was a shock to realize that the re-thinking might have to be fundamental. As Weizmann put it, the preoccupation was now 'not with recognition for the Zionist ideal but with fitting its application into the web of realities'.

Fortunately, the situation was not as disastrous as it appeared at first, for the British Government, including Lloyd George himself with his activist views about a British Middle East, also pretty clearly did not like the terms of 'Sykes-Picot'. Indeed, the key figure here was Sykes himself. An amateur in politics, a romantic Conservative, who had flung himself with enthusiasm into his imperial task, he had his own idea of what he wanted to see, and this included a Jewish Palestine as part of an Arab Middle East under British auspices. In this sense, all international Zionist pressure for a British protectorate over Palestine was to him a useful lever against French claims. So the concept of the National Home under British protectorate was still there, though the real obstacles to Zionist aims were now also apparent. Weizmann in April pursued them further in discussion with Robert Cecil, the Foreign Under-Secretary. Cecil listened sympathetically and suggested that it would help if the Jews of the world expressed themselves in favour of a British protectorate over Palestine—above all, influential American Jews. This was, in fact, already being done. Weizmann was fortunate in that at this time the head of the Zionist movement in America was that remarkable personality, Judge Brandeis, with whom he kept in close touch. When Balfour in April visited the United States, Brandeis took the opportunity to assure him that not just a few Jewish capitalists but the mass of ordinary American Jews stood behind the aim of a Jewish Home in Palestine under British protection, an assurance from a man in President Wilson's entourage which Balfour noted. So the situation in April– May 1917 was at least fluid—though no more than that—for there had been another setback for Weizmann. The British spring offensive against the Turks, which the Government had hoped would carry General Allenby to Jerusalem, so that Britain could discuss the future of Palestine as the power in physical occupation, had faltered badly and was about to collapse. Together with the tense war situation on greater fronts, this was decisive. We have the testimony of Mr Leonard Stein that by May 1917, the War Cabinet had apparently lost interest in an immediate declaration about a Jewish National Home.

Casting about for new moves, Weizmann told Robert Cecil that he might visit the British-occupied area of Palestine. Instead, he found himself off on a brief wild-goose chase, which he has entertainingly described in his memoirs. The US was now in the war; the British Foreign Office received news that Henry Morgenthau, the former US Ambassador to Turkey, was travelling to the Near East as personal envoy of President Wilson in an attempt to detach Turkey from the Central Powers on a promise of lenient treatment. The puzzled Foreign Office had heard that Morgenthau thought the Zionists could be helpful in this enterprise. Equally puzzled, Weizmann saw Balfour who to his complete astonishment proposed that Weizmann should go to meet Morgenthau as an official British representative, in order to talk him out of his attempt at amateur mediation. Attended by a picturesque British intelligence officer, Weizmann promptly obtained leave from the Admiralty, and travelled by train through France and Spain to Gibraltar where he met the Morgenthau delegation; only to find it 'embarrassingly apparent' that Morgenthau had no clear-cut ideas at all whether the

Turks were genuinely ready to detach themselves from Germany, and under what terms they might do so. Weizmann, by now schooled in the harsh realities of the war and power politics, quickly recognized the amateurishness of the enterprise. However, as he said in *Trial and Error*:

> We talked in this vacuum for two whole days. It was mid-summer, and very hot. We had been given one of the casements in the Rock for our sessions and the windows were kept open. As Mr Morgenthau did not speak French, and Colonel Weyl did not speak English, we had to fall back on German. And the Tommies on guard marched up and down outside, no doubt convinced that we were a pack of spies who had been lured into a trap, to be court-martialled the next morning and shot out of hand. I must confess that I did not find it easy to make an intelligible report to Sir Ronald Graham.

A brief interlude, a waste of time. At once, Weizmann was plunged back into action. As the shape of the war changed dramatically in the later half of 1917, the real test in the see-saw struggle for the Balfour Declaration had arrived. And if we look back on Weizmann's rôle, we see that for him it was a ceaseless struggle on three levels. There was the level of big-power politics, fluctuating with the cataclysm of war, in which Weizmann knew that his access to the great was valuable, but still, just access. On a second level he had simultaneously to fight an impassioned battle against anti-Zionists within British Jewry; and as if this were not enough, there were also bitter and constant inter-Zionist dissensions, which twice brought him to the point of angry resignation. All this within the space of a few months. Yet in the end he pulled through; he kept all the threads together.

As for the great stage of world politics, here the changes came thick and fast. With America's entry into the war and President Wilson's own proclaimed aim of 'no annexations, no secret treaties', the Sykes-Picot treaty faded out: that was a clear gain. Against that, with the US in the war, the American Jews were in British eyes no longer so directly important. But against that, again, President Wilson was the new star on the scene: and in view of his 'no annexations' policy, a Jewish National Home in Palestine could again be a factor favouring British plans in the Middle East; and this became more important as the renewed British offensive in Palestine could be confidently expected to bring the whole country under British occupation.

Meanwhile, on the other side of Europe, the Tsarist regime had fallen and the Russian Provisional Government had abolished the disabilities of the Russian Jews. The argument that only Palestine was the answer to Jewish oppression in Eastern Europe therefore, inevitably lost some force. True, Weizmann's philosophy and, indeed, all Zionist aspiration went much deeper, and the number of organized Russian Zionists in fact soared; but it was no longer so simple to put the argument across to British politicians: Weizmann's powers of inspired persuasion were again fully extended.

How Weizmann arranged to adjust Zionist tactics to this flood-tide of events would take too long to tell here: the fact is that he succeeded. But here we come to something referred to before in this chapter, namely Weizmann's parallel struggle with the anti-Zionist leaders of British Jewry—self-appointed, but still 'leaders'—which in the end had its impact on the wording of the Balfour Declaration.

One thing has here to be noted for an understanding of Weizmann's whole position. In view of the Jewish-Arab conflict which later ensued, it is pertinent to recall that it was not so much this conflict which preoccupied attention in the months before the Balfour Declaration. To Lloyd George, Balfour, Milner and Sykes, as they thought of further British imperial expansion, the picture of a large Arab Middle East under British auspices with a small corner in Palestine set aside for a Jewish National Home seemed at the time perfectly feasible, as it did to Weizmann himself a little later in his talks to the Emir Feisal. No, the final climax in the campaign for the Balfour Declaration has to be seen as very much an inter-Jewish struggle between Weizmann and a group of Anglo-Jewish leaders, in which the members of the British War Cabinet were in effect asked to judge between two rival philosophic views of the Jewish predicament.

To understand this particular conflict, one has also to see it in its historic context, especially as in later years it simply faded out. British Jewry at the time of the first World War consisted of a majority of new immigrants—there was plenty of enthusiasm for Zionism in Whitechapel—and a smaller number of well-to-do established Anglo-Jewish families. Some of these were passionate opponents of Zionism. This emotion, again, has to be seen as based not only on the usual assimilational outlook, but affected also by insecurity. The first World War years were a time when important British Jews could still open *The Times* or the *Morning Post* to find veiled or even open anti-Semitic attacks. For example, when Edwin Montagu in June 1917 was made Secretary of State for India, he was attacked in the *Morning Post* as a 'politico-financial Jew' who as a Jew must have dual allegiance! Against this background, with their emotions sharpened by fear, it is not surprising that the assimilationist English

Jews should have seen a danger to their status in the Zionist concept of 'Jewish nationhood', and should have reacted accordingly.

The counter-campaign, urging the British Government to reject Zionism outright and to press instead for full citizen rights for Jews everywhere, was waged through the 'Conjoint Committee' (representing the Anglo-Jewish Association and the Board of Deputies). Its President was Claude Montefiore, whom Weizmann credited (with a touch of irony) with being 'a high-minded man who considered nationalism beneath the religious level of Jews—except in their capacity as Englishmen'. Its secretary was Lucien Wolf, in Weizmann's eyes a gifted but embittered man, who simply could not understand how he had been outflanked. *Trial and Error* reads:

> It was hard for Wolf, who knew how to handle the Foreign Office, to look on while Zionists came along and established connections in his preserve; the more so as Zionism was in his view a purely East European movement, with a certain following in the East End of London, and beneath the notice of respectable British Jews. It was still harder, in fact impossible, for him to understand that English non-Jews did not look upon his anti-Zionism as the hallmark of a superior loyalty. It was never borne in on him that men like Balfour, Churchill, Lloyd George, were deeply religious, and believed in the Bible, that to them the return of the Jewish people to Palestine was a reality, so that we Zionists represented to them a great tradition for which they had enormous respect.

In retrospect, I think the matter was more complex. It was just because Lucien Wolf and English Jews like him had a haunting fear that even their anti-Zionism did *not*, in fact, assure their complete Englishness, that their opposition grew so bitter. At any rate, Lucien Wolf as spokesman of the Conjoint Committee in 1915 rejected all co-operation with the Zionists on the grounds that the 'national postulate' of Zionism and even the demand for special privileges in Palestine, was 'dangerous and provoked anti-Semitism'. For the next two years, Wolf and his friends engaged in a continuous campaign, by way of meetings, pamphlets and letters to the press, in which they denounced Zionism as an aberration conceived by 'foreign Jews'. One's impression is that for long they had not realized the full measure of Weizmann's contacts with the War Cabinet. It was when they did so in 1917 that their campaign assumed a touch of hysteria.

On 24 May 1917 the two heads of the Conjoint Committee, Alexander and Montefiore, published a long statement in *The Times*, violently repudiating the Zionist position on behalf of British Jewry and urging the Government not to accede to Weizmann's demands.

The battle was joined. True, *The Times* replied in a remarkable leading article, written by Wickham Steed himself: 'Only an imaginative nervousness suggests that the realization of territorial Zionism, in some form, would cause Christendom to turn round and say: "Now you have a land of your own, go to it." ' The ranks of British Jewry were also shown to be divided. The Chief Rabbi and the Sephardi Haham both repudiated the attack. But the battle was on, and if the hostile Anglo-Jewish leaders spoke for a small Jewish community, they held important positions. Now, also, a new figure entered the scene, among Weizmann's opponents perhaps the only man of real stature, Edwin Montagu.

Edwin Montagu, a member of an old Anglo-Jewish family, was a sensitive, complex, self-centred man—able and imaginative, as the reforms associated with his name in India showed. As Secretary of State for India from mid-summer 1917 onwards, he had risen to a position of unique distinction for a British Jew. From his whole attitude it was clear that he was a passionate Assimilationist—just as Weizmann identified himself completely with Zionism, so in Montagu's mind the Jewish cause was associated with assimilation and with his own status and career as a leading British Jew. When appointed to the Government, he was personally in a difficult position. The Asquith faction in the Liberal Party had taken it badly amiss that he had gone over to Lloyd George. He had also been sharply wounded by hostile anti-Semitic attacks against his appointment in such papers as the *Morning Post*. It was at this unpleasant juncture that he found—as he saw it, to his horror—that the Government was considering a pro-Zionist Declaration which recognized the concept of Jewish nationality, of a Jewish 'national identity'. From his whole reaction, it is evident that this situation threw Montagu right off his intellectual balance. In his preoccupied mind, the impending British recognition of Zionism became magnified into a mortal danger to his status as a British Minister of the Crown, and to that of all other English Jews—even after the Balfour Declaration was issued and he was on his way to India he kept talking bitterly about a stab in the back from his Ministerial colleagues. However, if Montagu's counter-attack again Weizmann had a touch of hysteria, as a member of the Government he could also provide highly effective opposition from within. As soon as Montagu was appointed, Weizmann was, indeed, warned of this danger, and so it turned out.

On 18 July 1917 the Zionist Political Committee submitted to the Government its draft form for the Declaration which, as Weizmann said, had been carefully worded to stay within the limits of the general British Government attitude as elicited by him, and which

Lord Rothschild handed to Balfour. The operative passage in the draft read:

> His Majesty's Government, after considering the aims of the Zionist Organization, accept the principle of recognizing Palestine as the National Home of the Jewish people and the right of the Jewish people to build up its national life in Palestine under a protection to be established at the conclusion of peace, following upon the successful issue of the war.

On 17 August Weizmann cabled optimistically to Felix Frankfurter in the United States that the draft had met with the approval of the Foreign Office and of Lloyd George. It remained, of course, to be officially approved by the War Cabinet, but from his preparatory talks Weizmann felt confident that this would quickly be done. But the next stage was unexpected delay—the British anti-Zionists were straining every nerve—and on 3 September Weizmann learned that the Declaration had, as accident would have it, been discussed at a Cabinet meeting which Lloyd George and Balfour did not attend. In their absence, an impassioned intervention from Edwin Montagu had caused the withdrawal of the item from the agenda, to be temporarily shelved. The way out was a British cable to President Wilson to sound him out, for which Weizmann was unprepared. Wilson, on the advice of Colonel House, replied that the Declaration seemed to him untimely, and that was that.

Here was an unexpected and (as it looked to some) perhaps even a crucial disaster. As Lord Rothschild wrote pessimistically to Weizmann:[1] 'Do you remember I said to you in London, as soon as I saw the announcement in the paper of Montagu's appointment, that we were done?'

What of Weizmann? He said he 'did not feel as desperate, but the situation was unpleasant'. Here, at any rate, was the crisis. Now Weizmann and his friends had to act, and inspired action was needed.

One can perhaps also say that this crisis month of September, more than any other period, illuminated the special nature of Weizmann's personality, his strength, his weaknesses, for during this same time he was also emotionally involved within his third constant battle, that within the Zionist ranks themselves. The conflict of the moment had arisen over Vladimir Jabotinsky's plan to raise a special Jewish unit of Russian and other Jews (eventually to be organized as the Zion Mule Corps) to fight with the British forces in Palestine against the Turks. Weizmann had given the proposal his backing, for once

[1] Leonard Stein, *The Balfour Declaration*. Valentine Mitchell, London, 1961.

against the advice of some of his close colleagues. Jabotinsky, another dramatic artist in politics, had clearly exerted a personal spell over him. However, Jabotinsky's whole idea of a special Jewish military force was opposed not only by anti-Zionists but by many leading Zionists as utterly needless and only harmful at a time when so many Jews were already serving in the Allied forces as citizens of their countries. A storm of criticism, therefore, blew up. Even Weizmann's friend and mentor Ahad Ha'am dismissed the special force as an 'empty demonstration'. Weizmann, however, remained curiously obstinate in supporting Jabotinsky, and as the storm broke both the strong and the weak spots in his political leadership were revealed. As a political artist, he had the enormous asset of his vision and of the self-confidence it gave him; but by the same token he could not brook personal opposition to his ideas among those near him. By the mere fact of such personal criticism, his entire vision, his entire self-confidence, could be suddenly shattered—suddenly everything could seem no longer worthwhile. And so, over this relatively minor argument about the special Jewish force, Weizmann in the initial months of August and September 1917 twice offered his resignation from the Chairmanship of the English Zionist Federation and the Political Committee. The rather stilted letters of resignation he sent to Sokolow had an air of intense wounded dignity. How far the confusion in Zionist circles had gone is shown by a letter from one of Weizmann's intimate friends, quoted by Mr Stein: 'In general I agree that this Declaration business is of no very great importance, and I do my best within my own little circle to keep the sense of proportion. . . . I'm inclined to think that Weizmann has outlived his usefulness as a Zionist leader. He has got to break with Jabotinsky or with us. . . .' In the outcome, Weizmann succeeded in doing neither. But had he really meant to go through with his resignation, or did his attitude merely mark one of those spells of utter exhaustion and pessimism which were to recur in his later political life? It is hard to know. Fortunately, Weizmann's dismayed friends—Scott, Ahad Ha'am, many others—prevailed upon him not to go: but the incident reveals the emotional reserves on which he had to draw at this crucial stage of his great battle.

The task was this. With his passionate anti-Zionism, Edwin Montagu inside the Government represented a new and dangerous obstacle to Weizmann's entire plan. To overcome this, Weizmann had once again to use his ultimate asset—his personal access to the statesmen who were shaping the destiny of the war, and his ability to convince them of the truth of his larger view of the Jewish situation: the plight of the Jewish masses, the real meaning of the Zionist hope. Once he embarked on this task, Weizmann's counter-offensive was massive. He maintained close contact with Mark Sykes, who was fighting his own parallel battle for the Declaration in the British interest. During September Weizmann saw Balfour, who assured him that his views were unchanged; he cabled Brandeis and Frankfurter, who were able to obtain greater support for the Declaration from Wilson; he saw Smuts; at the end of the month he saw the Prime Minister, Lloyd George, who promised that the Declaration would be put back on the agenda of the next Cabinet meeting. Before this happened, on 3 October, Weizmann also submitted a memorandum, signed by Rothschild and himself, to the Foreign Office, in which he said:[1]

> We cannot ignore rumours which seem to foreshadow that the anti-Zionist view will be urged at the meeting of the War Cabinet by a prominent Englishman of the Jewish faith who does not belong to the War Cabinet.... We must respectfully point out that in submitting our resolution, we entrusted our national and Zionist destiny to the Foreign Office and the Imperial War Cabinet in the hope that the problem would be considered in the light of Imperial interests and the principles for which the Entente stands. We are reluctant to believe that the War Cabinet would allow the divergence of views on Zionism existing in Jewry to be presented to them in a strikingly one-sided manner.... We have submitted the text of the Declaration on behalf of an organization which claims to represent the will of a great and ancient, though scattered people. We have submitted it after three years of negotiations and conversations with prominent representatives of the British nation. We, therefore, humbly pray that this Declaration may be granted to us. This would enable us still further to counteract the demoralising influence which the enemy press is endeavouring to exercise by holding out vague promises to the Jews, and finally to make the necessary preparations for the constructive work which would have to begin as soon as Palestine is liberated.

The next day, 4 October, the British War Cabinet met, this time with Lloyd George and Balfour present, and the debate was restaged. Once again too—and in this way history was made—the decision turned on the view the Cabinet was to take of the world Jewish situation and Jewish aspirations. Montagu would not budge. He argued his anti-Zionist case even more emotionally. To Lloyd George he had written a few days before: 'Judge of my consterna-

[1] *The Balfour Declaration, op. cit.*

tion. . . . If you make this statement about Palestine as the National Home for Jews, every anti-Semitic organization and newspaper will ask what right a Jewish Englishman, with at best the status of a nationalized foreigner, has to take a foremost part in the Government of the British Empire?' At the Cabinet session Montagu in addition brought in the hazard of his prospective mission to India. 'How', he asked, 'would he negotiate with the people of India on behalf of His Majesty's Government if the world had just been told that His Majesty's Government regarded his national home as being in Turkish territory?' Montagu's whole harangue was the passionate *cri de coeur* of a British Jew of 1917, who, on this one vulnerable point of his Jewishness, had lost all sense of perspective. The reply in favour of the Declaration was given to the Cabinet by Arthur Balfour. It is pertinent to the Weizmann story to see how realistically Balfour by now saw the Jewish situation and the likely way in which it would develop. The Zionist movement, Balfour said,[1]

> though opposed by a number of wealthy Jews in this country, had behind it the support of a majority of Jews, at all events in Russia and America, and probably in other countries. He saw nothing inconsistent between the establishment of a Jewish national focus in Palestine and the complete assimilation and absorption of Jews into the nationality of other countries. . . . What was at the back of the Zionist Movement was the intense national consciousness held (sic) by certain members of the Jewish race. They regarded themselves as one of the great historic races of the world, whose original home was Palestine, and these Jews had a passionate longing to regain once more this ancient national home. . . .

Balfour concluded by stating that he understood President Wilson was favourably disposed towards the Declaration, but that the German Government for its part was now also trying to capture Zionist sympathies; two facts which both made a British Declaration timely.

On this basic principle, Montagu saw that by now Lloyd George, Balfour and Milner were immovable. It was his exit. He was in any case about to leave for India, to vanish forever from this Jewish debate, and to incur no damage to his career. Yet the despairing, neurotic violence of his final protest once again had an effect. It caused the Cabinet, in the way such collective bodies react, to agree to another brief delay, to perhaps another piece of re-drafting to meet objections. This hesitation—by such frail threads do decisions hang—also provided time for the intervention of an entirely new figure, George Curzon (later Marquis Curzon) In his lofty aristocratic

[1] *The Balfour Declaration, op. cit.*

way, Curzon was uninterested in arguments as between Zionist and anti-Zionist Jews, but he was easily the foremost Middle East authority in the Cabinet. It was from the standpoint of this haughty expertise, though he was not strongly partisan, that he now found the Declaration to be too ambitious for the limited possibilities of Jewish colonization offered by Palestine; and he, therefore, also proposed some further postponement and reconsideration.

And so on. To Weizmann, who had been anxiously waiting not far away, this lack of a firm Cabinet decision on 4 October brought yet another disappointment, all the more disturbing because unexpected. The War Cabinet, he was told, had in the end decided to obtain some further clarification. A new draft of the Declaration would be forthwith submitted to leading Zionist and anti-Zionist British Jews for their comment. It would also be submitted again to Washington, to elicit President Wilson's opinion.

Now Weizmann was angered. Crucial days were passing. In Russia, the Provisional Government was tottering; who knew what would happen? On 9 October he sent a strong letter to Philip Kerr (later Lord Lothian), personal secretary to Lloyd George, in which he again denied the right of the wealthy Anglo-Jewish anti-Zionists to speak for 'British Jewry', let alone Jews elsewhere:[1]

> Zionism is not meant for these people, who have cut themselves adrift from Jewry; it is meant for those masses who have a will to live a life of their own, and these masses have a right to claim the recognition of Palestine as a Jewish National Home. The second category of British Jews, I believe, will fall into line quickly enough when this declaration is given to us. I still expect a time, and I do so not without apprehension, when they will even claim to be Zionists themselves.

To emphasize this point, the utmost Zionist support was mobilized. Within a few days, some three hundred Zionist and other Jewish bodies in Britain sent in resolutions to the Foreign Office in favour of Palestine as the Jewish National Home. Not only that: so alarmed was Weizmann about this last-minute hitch that he sounded out Herbert Samuel about the possibility of some understanding with the more moderate British non-Zionists, to end what he called this 'humiliating fight', which to him affronted Jewish dignity.

As it happened, such a move was not needed. The British Government was, in fact, no longer questioning the principle of the Declaration, but its limits and wording. But in this respect, the delay had already sufficed for some cautious second thoughts. The new draft

[1] *Trial and Error, op. cit.*

submitted by the Government to the Jews and President Wilson was not Balfour's formula, but Milner's, re-drafted by Leopold (later Lord) Amery, to meet not only Jewish but now also possible Arab objections, for in the meantime highly critical messages had also been coming in from British General Headquarters in Cairo. The new formula read:

His Majesty's Government views with favour the establishment in Palestine of a national home for the Jewish race and will use its best endeavours to facilitate the achievement of this object, it being clearly understood that nothing shall be done which may prejudice the civil and religious rights of existing non-Jewish communities in Palestine, or the rights and political status enjoyed in any other country by such Jews who are fully contented with their existing nationality.

For Weizmann and his friends the new wording yet again provided an unpleasant surprise as if to underline for them the fluidity of all wartime politics. The difference between the new text and that passed earlier by Balfour appeared far-reaching. Whereas the first text had defined Palestine as 'the national home of the Jews', the second only spoke of 'a national home in Palestine'. Weizmann was not interested in the addition concerning the rights of Jews elsewhere, put in to satisfy Montagu and his supporters. What he thought worrying was the wording of the proviso that the rights of the existing population should not be prejudiced. As he noted, the new phrasing seemed both to impute oppressive Zionist intentions, and could be interpreted to justify a decisive limitation of Zionist efforts.

However, this and no other was the draft Declaration now offered by the British Government. Weizmann and his colleagues, and since in the end it depended on himself, Weizmann, had now to make a swift decision. That the anti-Zionists would endeavour to object, to temporize and to delay, was clear. Should the Zionists for their part also reject the Declaration in its ambiguous new wording? Weizmann came to his decision. After all, to court further postponement was in the climate of the time a leap into the unknown. Weizmann could also see the whole historic situation in its proper momentous perspective. After three years of endlessly patient pressure on the British Government, after his own two thousand interviews, he now had obtained that Jewish Charter which had for so long eluded Herzl. As he put it in *Trial and Error*:

It goes without saying that this second formula, emasculated as it was, represented a tremendous event in exilic Jewish history—and that it was as bitter a pill to swallow for the Jewish assimilationists as the recession from the original, more forthright formula was for us.

And so, acceptance it was, and now events moved forward again. On 16 October, President Wilson, advised by Brandeis, sent the British Government his approval of the Declaration, though asking that for the moment this be kept confidential. On 24 October, the Foreign Office, prodded by Weizmann, sent a note to its Chief, Balfour, pressing him for a fixed date of publication. There was to be still one further delay. George Curzon, the very last of leading British statesmen to intervene, announced his wish to circulate yet one further memorandum, which he did on 26 October. In this memorandum, described by Leonard Stein as 'magisterial', Curzon reiterated his view that Palestine, as a small and impoverished country, already inhabited by half a million Arabs, offered few chances for Jewish colonization. Any extravagant Declaration could, therefore, only disappoint Jewish hopes. Yet, having had his say, Curzon was also ready not to press his objections too far and to recognize that the Declaration in other ways had its diplomatic advantages for Britain, above all to forestall the possible 'sinister designs' of the Germans to make such a declaration first. With this, the last obstacle was out of the way. On 31 October, the War Cabinet approved the draft (Edwin Montagu was by now far on his way to India) and on 2 November, Balfour wrote as follows to Lord Rothschild—for various reasons Weizmann had decided the Declaration should not be addressed to himself but to the bearer of one of the most potent Jewish names:

Dear Lord Rothschild,

I have much pleasure in conveying to you, on behalf of His Majesty's Government, the following declaration of sympathy with Jewish Zionist aspiration which has been submitted to, and approved by, the Cabinet.

'His Majesty's Government view with favour the establishment in Palestine of a national home for the Jewish people, and will use their best endeavours to facilitate the achievement of this object, it being clearly understood that nothing shall be done which may prejudice the civil rights of existing non-Jewish communities in Palestine, or the rights and political status enjoyed by Jews in any other country.'

I should be grateful if you would bring this declaration to the knowledge of the Zionist Federation.

It was eleven years after Weizmann's first interview with Balfour at the Manchester by-election. Now he noted:

While the Cabinet was in session, approving the final text, I was waiting outside, this time within call. Sykes brought the document out to me, with the exclamation: 'Dr Weizmann, it's a boy!'

Well—I did not like the boy at first. He was not the one I had expected. But I knew that this was a great event. I telephoned my wife, and went to see Ahad Ha'am.

A new chapter had opened for us.[1]

Weizmann was now forty-three; in his middle years an outstanding figure, a man of compelling charm, happily married, surrounded by devoted friends. The day of the Declaration was a high point of his life. Without official position—he was not to be elected President of the World Zionist Organization until 1920—he had made Jewish history through being simply himself, Chaim Weizmann, and as such unique. By reason of his intuitive sympathy for Britain, he had set himself to move the centre of Zionism from Middle Europe to Britain, and had succeeded. He had set himself to obtain the Jewish Charter through linking Zionism with British policy, and had succeeded. The new chapter, that of the Anglo-Zionist connexion, could now begin. At the same time, almost effortlessly, he had become a well-known figure in the British political scene and simultaneously had risen to an eminent place in theoretical and applied science, with a significant contribution to the British war effort to his credit.

Perhaps there was never again to be quite an equal moment of success in Weizmann's life. For the next Jewish chapter, that of the Anglo-Zionist phase, lasted for thirty years, from 1917 to 1947. Without it, the entire development leading to the State of Israel could not have taken place: of this there can hardly be any doubt. But the new chapter was also to be a frustrating and often bitter experience. Hardly was the ink dry on the Balfour Declaration, when Weizmann was made aware of a new enemy, the conservative hierarchy of the British military and officials in the Middle East, who spoke for what they thought Anglo-Arab interests and whose counter-offensive against Zionism was to continue for thirty years.

This fact also prompts some concluding reflections on Weizmann and the Balfour Declaration and the particular moment in history at which it was achieved. First, Weizmann was perfectly right to accept the re-drafted Declaration rather than to risk delay. What mattered in the ensuing power struggle was not so much the wording of the Balfour Declaration. It was always the only Charter the Jews had. What mattered simply was that it existed, that it was there. How the

[1] *Trial and Error, op. cit.*

Zionists clung to it and kept it in the forefront is a matter of history. What stands out, too, is how supremely important was Weizmann's timing. Mr Richard Crossman, in particular, has brought out how the Declaration came just in time. For only four days after Balfour's letter to Rothschild, Lenin and Trotsky seized power in Russia: history changed. Simultaneously with the Bolshevik Revolution, there came the increasing impact on world politics of the United States, itself an anti-colonial force. In 1917, one could say, the end of empire was already visible; with Lenin's and Wilson's proclamations, there began that vast popular upheaval which led to Asian and African independence, and of which Arab nationalism formed a part. This is not to say that Weizmann was just in time in achieving the Declaration against the still inadequately heard claims of the Palestine Arabs. As has been said, in the hopeful climate of 1917, Lloyd George, Balfour, Milner and Sykes as much as Weizmann believed that under British auspices, accommodation between a large self-governing Arab Middle East and a small Jewish Palestine was perfectly feasible. But what could have affected British policy decisively already in 1918 was that new imperial trend of seeking to flatter and contain Arab nationalism within a British mould. A delusion, no doubt, but one which might already in 1918 have provided a major and perhaps fatal obstacle to Weizmann's ambitions. Indeed, events showed more and more that Weizmann in 1917 seized a moment of opportunity which might never have returned.

Even brief mention of such obstacles, too, brings one back to the question: how did Weizmann achieve his aim? For if one looks back at it, at the motives which swayed the members of the British Cabinet at a time when the British army in France was reeling from the shock of Passchendaele and the war was far from decided, one comes up against the heart of the matter. All the factors usually adduced for the Cabinet's support of a Zionist Palestine—the idea of winning over the Russian Jews, the American Jews, the rivalry with France, the idea of justifying British occupation of Palestine—all these motives do not appear adequate to explain how a group of leading British statesmen were for a time supporters of Zionism, some indeed ardently so. For any convincing explanation, one has to come back to the additional factor of Weizmann as an individual and to his inspired years: to the way in which out of his own life as a Zionist, as a scientist and as a British citizen, he built up his Anglo-Zionist concept and set out to persuade those who could put it into effect. Sir Charles Webster, the eminent British historian, who first encountered Weizmann at the War Office in 1917, has put it as follows:[1]

[1] *The Art and Practice of Diplomacy, op. cit.*

With unerring skill he adapted his arguments to the special circumstances of each statesman. To the British and Americans he
could use biblical language and awake a deep emotional under-
tone; to other nationalities he more often talked in terms of
interest. Mr Lloyd George was told that Palestine was a little
mountainous country not unlike Wales; with Lord Balfour the
philosophical background of Zionism could be surveyed; for Lord
Cecil the problem was placed in the setting of a new world
organization; while to Lord Milner the extension of imperial
power could be vividly portrayed. To me who dealt with these
matters as a junior officer of the General Staff, he brought from
many sources all the evidence that could be obtained of the
importance of a Jewish National Home to the strategical position
of the British Empire, but he always indicated by a hundred
shades and inflexions of the voice that he believed that I could
also appreciate better than my superiors other more subtle and
recondite arguments. This skilful presentation of facts would, however, have been useless, unless he had convinced all with whom
he came into contact of the probity of his conduct and the reality
of his trust in the will and strength of Britain.

It is for these reasons that Sir Charles Webster considered Weizmann's achievement the greatest of all feats of diplomacy he had
known. Yet writing from a Jewish viewpoint, in retrospect, one can
perhaps go still closer to the heart of the matter. Weizmann saw not
only the possible ideals but also the defects of the men he talked to,
as he only too clearly saw those of his fellow-Jews. One has to view
his essay in persuasion in the context of the prevailing mood of the
age, including its particular streak of anti-Semitism. As has been
shown, this was a cruder time when a Jewish political figure, such as
Montagu, could still be openly attacked in the British press, simply
because he was a Jew. Mr Leonard Stein has from documentation
interestingly brought out how the main authors of the Balfour
Declaration all had their specific anti-Jewish feelings. Lloyd George
could express them vulgarly, Arthur Balfour philosophically, Smuts
and Milner uneasily, Mark Sykes, at least in his earlier days, romantically. All had their reservations not only about East End immigrants and rich Jewish financiers, but even about English gentlemen
of the Jewish faith, and therefore, besides support, just a touch of
antagonism also entered into the Balfour Declaration. But this is
detail: what Weizmann achieved was that for a magic moment—
under the spell of his eloquence—these British statesmen looked at
the problems of Jewish Diaspora through Zionist eyes, through Weiz-

mann's eyes. The moment was brief (brief for them collectively) but it sufficed; for what came of it was a new phase of Jewish history.

Mr T. R. Fyvel, author and political writer, has been a keen student of Zionist affairs since his youth. His father, Berthold Feiwel, was one of Dr Weizmann's intimates from the nineties onwards, and a leading figure in the Zionist movement.

1919–1929

CHAPTER EIGHT

THE FABIAN DECADE

ROBERT WELTSCH

BEFORE THE tribunal of history Chaim Weizmann will be regarded as the architect of the Jewish National Home in Palestine that later turned into the State of Israel. Yet his leadership was constantly challenged by the movement he served.

He realized a long-cherished dream of his people. But destiny had so wrought that he had to act alone and on his own responsibility during the convulsions of a world war, and when he encountered the masses of the Zionist movement again, when hostilities were ended and while the world was still shattered by unrest, the reunion was clouded by misunderstanding. Coming from quite different surroundings amidst a rapidly changing world, his fellow Zionists knew little of his own struggles and heart-breaking vexations, nor had they any knowledge of the political climate he had to work in. From the very beginning there was a kind of tension between the new leader of Zionism and the others who believed he needed their guidance and claimed the right to supervise his fidelity to his people. Without taking note of the peculiarities of the outside world they dealt with, they wanted an unbroken continuity of tradition. They brought to the unknown West notions of government and nationalism that prevailed in Russia and that often were irrelevant outside. Seen from within, the whole decade from 1919 to 1929, as well as the rest of Weizmann's life, was characterized by an antagonism between himself and large parts of the movement. It was ever present, and it became manifest in the bitter open struggles of the Zionist Congresses. To be sure, before referring to the underlying causes and intricacies of the objective situation, it must be stressed that Weizmann also had faithful friends who stood by him with unselfish devotion, from whose loyalty he drew much encouragement. In spite of all attacks, his personality was to dominate the Zionist scene internally and externally.

During the first World War Weizmann was not, in a formal sense, the elected leader—or president—of the Zionist movement. The last

pre-war Congress, held in Vienna in 1913, did not envisage the shifting of the Zionist centre of gravity to England, nor did it expect
revolutionary changes in world politics. That Congress retained the
usual character of a party convention, mainly occupied with
squabbles between the old group of 'political' Zionists under Wolffsohn and Nordau, and the ascending 'practical' Zionists to whom
Weizmann belonged. The main object of controversy was the administration of financial institutions like the Jewish Colonial Trust,
which the Wolffsohn group did not want to entrust to the Zionist
Executive lest it fail to observe businesslike principles and risk money
entrusted them by shareholders and depositors in questionable 'practical' experiments in Palestine. In any case the scope of colonization
in Palestine under Turkish rule was limited. Some time at the Congress was also devoted to the discussion of the idea of a Hebrew
University—rather remote at that time, yet a matter that Weizmann
was much involved in. The Vienna Congress elected a Zionist Executive with the seat in Berlin, which was advisable because of its
geographical position between East and West, and because a headquarters in Russia was out of the question. German Zionism was
comparatively strong both organizationally and intellectually. Nobody suspected that in a year the world would be submerged in a
European war.

It is very remarkable that fundamental Zionist unity could be upheld in spite of the division caused by the war. Totalitarian thinking
in State affairs was not yet as firmly established as it is today. It was
clear, however, that all political efforts for the sake of Zionist aims
had to be made separately by Zionists within the two camps, to a
large extent on their own authority and responsibility and without
much regard to the bodies elected on quite different assumptions
The Zionists in the area of the Central Powers, allied with Turkey,
were allotted the task of preserving the existing Yishuv in Palestine.
On the other hand, as time went on it became clear even to Central
European Zionists that the ultimate fate of Palestine would be
decided by the Western Powers and especially by Great Britain.

The spokesmen for Zionism in England had to a large extent to be
self-appointed, although some links with 'legality' were established
when Dr Tchlenov and later Sokolow reached England. The story
of how Weizmann emerged as the main figure of political activities
has recently been told again by Leonard Stein in his comprehensive
and brilliant book *The Balfour Declaration*. From the point of view
of overall Zionist politics in the world crisis it is especially interesting
to learn how both sides in the war tended to attract Jewish sympathies by various degrees of support for Zionism. A rather mystical

belief in the might of Jewry may partially explain the amazing fact that Weizmann, alone or together with some members of the Zionist Political Committee, succeeded in persuading British Ministers that he represented a Power. He was recognized as diplomat of a people that had no political status whatsoever and no territorial consistency, in the face of the opposition of almost all the Jews who until then had counted. He became the *de facto* leader of Zionism, at the most important spot. Yet, with the exception of the East End of London and some parts of American Jewry hitherto not too well organized for political action, he was isolated and cut off from the traditional centres of the Zionist movement.

Thus it was natural, after the war, for a certain estrangement to have taken place between the single parts of the movement. Weizmann's indefatigable efforts and his astounding success were, of course, well known the world over. They had been enthusiastically welcomed by Zionists everywhere. But after a short time they were taken for granted. People were disappointed when they found out that the results did not exactly conform with what Zionist speakers had read into them. It must be recalled that the Jewish masses in Eastern Europe who formed the bulk of the Zionist movement had undergone an extraordinary (though child's play compared with the second World War) ordeal of oppressions and expulsions, of changing regimes and military occupation, of deprivation and revolutions. They had buoyed themselves up by Messianic hopes of some kind of redemption from outside. The young generation, largely uprooted and imbued with nationalist and socialist ideals, proclaimed its willingness to sacrifice itself for the idea of Jewish rebirth. They were far away from political realism and economic necessities as understood in the West. By the time the Zionist Conference met in London, in July 1920, the scene was set for a grievous clash.

Many of the delegates floated in the clouds, but Weizmann was well-grounded, since he had undergone the most enlightening though alarming experience before the Conference met. He had been the head of an official Zionist Commission that went to Palestine in March 1918. The British had accorded him the appropriate status, and he had had an opportunity to learn on the spot the immense obstacles to a swift transformation of the country. On his arrival Weizmann had established good relations with the Commander-in-Chief, Lord Allenby, but he also noticed the hostility and obstruction of the military administration at the top and in the lower ranks. The Balfour Declaration had not been promulgated in Palestine at the time of Allenby's entry into Jerusalem, and both Jews and Arabs had got the impression that the administration did not take it seriously.

The Jewish population in Palestine, the Yishuv, was flabbergasted, since it could not understand the cleavage between the declarations in London and the actual state of affairs in Palestine. They were not always diplomatic in the presentation of their grievances; Weizmann, too, had to learn that the Yishuv was not easy to handle. The Political Report to the XII Zionist Congress (1921), apparently written or inspired by Jabotinsky, gives a vivid description of the paradoxes of the situation Weizmann was confronted with, and in *Trial and Error* Weizmann devotes three full chapters to this great episode. First the 'negative side'—all the trouble with the military rulers that nevertheless culminated in the great speech Weizmann made in his farewell interview with Allenby. Weizmann calls it a 'tirade', but actually it was a product of his finest art in finding an unforgettable wording for a historical situation:

> You have conquered a great part of Palestine, and you can measure your conquest by one of two yardsticks: either in square kilometres—and in that sense your victory, though great, is not unique: the Germans have overrun vaster areas—or else by the yardstick of history. If this conquest of yours be measured by the centuries of hallowed tradition which attach to every square kilometre of its ground, then yours is one of the greatest victories in history. And the traditions which make it so are largely bound up with the history of my people. The day may come when we shall make good your victory, so that it may remain graven in something more enduring than rock—in the lives of men and nations. It would be a great pity if anything were done now—for instance by a few officials or administrators—to mar the victory.

The 'positive side' was marked by two spectacular events, one political, one spiritual: the agreement reached with Emir Feisal, the then outstanding figure of the Arab world, and the laying of the corner-stone of the Hebrew University. Weizmann's own narration of that historical meeting with Feisal on the Transjordanian plateau near Akaba stirs the imagination but makes pathetic reading today, now that the glorious hopes of an Arab-Jewish understanding, a fruitful and harmonious co-operation have gone with the wind, at least for the time being. It was, however, a good beginning and it was continued in Paris at the Peace Conference later, when Feisal wrote his famous letter to Frankfurter. At all these functions Colonel T. E. Lawrence lent a helping hand. The laying of the corner-stone of the University in July 1918 was a modest ceremony compared with the actual opening in 1925, where Balfour gave the key address and Herbert Samuel said 'Shehecheyonu'. But it was moving and memorable as a tribute to the spirit while the guns of the war still boomed. It was of symbolic value to Weizmann, who never lost sight of the fact that without a great spiritual revival the National Home would be meaningless. A house of learning was to him the most important need as it was for Yohanan ben Zakkai. Although professionally a man of 'science', he never lost sight of the importance of the 'humanities'. He was deeply convinced that science was the most important factor in the development of the country, in its preparation for productivity and for mass settlement on a thin and arid soil. But not less passionate was his desire that the new Judaea should become a source of human enlightenment, of ethical progress, a centre of which could be said in truth and not in the conventional easy-going manner, that the Word would go forth from Zion. This was to him the essence of Zionism; it was more essential than political forms, which necessarily are of a transient nature.

When the Zionist Commission returned to London, the war had come to an end. A decisive and busy time began for the Zionist leadership. They had to defend what they had obtained in war time, and to turn it into solid foundations. Great preparations had to be made for the Peace Conference, and finally the Jewish Delegation, led by Weizmann but including also anti-Zionists like Sylvain Levy (representing French Jewry) was received by the Council of Ten in Paris on 23 February 1919.

In London the Zionist Actions Committee was in session. That was the first meeting of Weizmann and the British Zionists with some of the leading Continental and American Zionists, good friends of the past, with whom, however, they had fallen out of pace completely owing to the different circumstances under which they had been living during the war. Weizmann was struck by their misinterpretation of the Balfour Declaration. Some of them, he says in *Trial and Error*, had already brought with them a list of Cabinet members for the first Cabinet of the Jewish State! Seen against the background of political reality it must have appeared to Weizmann like a scene from a novel by Mendelle Mocher S'forim or by Sholem Aleichem, both of whom have so brilliantly and warmheartedly satirized the native sense of unreality that dominated the minds of secluded Eastern Jews.

The happenings before the Peace Conference, with the treachery of Sylvain Levy and the 'miraculous intervention' of Lansing, which gave Weizmann the opportunity of a rejoinder, were communicated to the Zionist gathering in London in a Report that has become famous. In his second speech to the Ten, Weizmann had used the striking formula that Palestine was to become 'as Jewish as England

English', which later gave rise to misunderstanding, since hostile propaganda interpreted it as meaning that the Arabs should be eliminated, although in his speech Weizmann had explicitly included the recognition of the rights of the non-Jewish population.

In the following months of 1919–20 Weizmann went to Palestine twice. Gradually the pattern evolved that was to pervade his life until the struggle was over: Jerusalem—London—New York were the focal points he had to move between. The situation in Palestine gave sufficient cause for worry, but there was one outstanding feat that set in motion the practical work and determined the whole course of Zionist work during the next decade—the purchase of 80,000 dunams in the Emek Yezre'el. This transaction, in the face of strong opposition from Zionist leaders, including the Americans, was due primarily to Ussishkin, whom Weizmann had supported in this matter. From that moment 'Emek' became a battle cry, a flag for the Jewish youth in Europe, a moral concept, connected with an idealistic, austere, pioneering life that appeared as the highest manifestation of national devotion and romance. It gave impetus and content to Zionism, and decided the victory of so-called 'Labour Zionism'—a child of the Russian Revolution of 1905, inspired by A. D. Gordon's ideal of tilling the soil with one's own hands and thereby changing human nature—over the more rational ideas of the promoters of privately owned businesses, supported by the Americans and large numbers of Continental, primarily Polish, Zionists. Weizmann, though not underestimating the importance of private initiative, sided wholeheartedly with the enthusiastic youth, and remained firmly allied to Labour, at least until 1939, when the second World War created entirely new conditions also within the Zionist movement. What was most important to him was that Halutzim had already started pouring into Palestine by 1920, without waiting for personal safeguards, while colonization by business interests would have taken much more time and in any case would have been on a small scale. The other side of the medal was, of course, the urgent necessity of providing funds for this penniless mass immigration. As the deficits grew this became the first priority. It turned the President of the Zionist Organization into a sort of King of Shnorrers (to use the title of a famous Zangwill novel)—a task he did not regard as a degradation. Nobody had a right to scorn him—the blame lies on the movement that filled its mouth with nationalist phrases but was unable to secure the most primitive financial foundation. It was the President himself, and no one else, who had to head the canvassers who knocked at the doors of complacent Jews the world over to remind them of their duty towards the National Home.

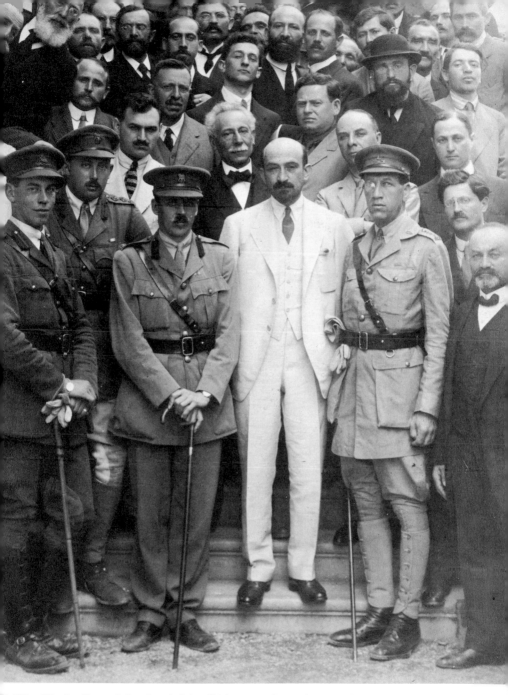

3 The Zionist Commission headed by Weizmann, Jerusalem, 1918. (*Left to right*) Edwin Samuel, son of the first High Commissioner to Palestine; Major the Hon W. G. A. Ormsby Gore (now Lord Harlech); Major James de Rothschild and Joseph Sprinzak (later the first Speaker of the Israel Knesset). (*In the background*) Mordechai Ben-Hillel Hacohen; Eliahu Berlin; Israel M. Sieff; Dr M. D. Eder; Dr Sylvain Levy; Sir Leon Simon; Dr Ben-Zion Mossinsohn and Aaron Aaronson

*In the
Middle East*

9 Weizmann and Emir Feisal, later the first King of
Iraq, at Ma'an, Jordan, 1918

10 Laying the corner stone for the Faculty of Physics at the Hebrew
University of Jerusalem, 1925. (*Left to right*) Lord Balfour, Sir Herbert
(later Lord) Samuel, Judah L. Magnes, Weizmann, and George Shuster

11 Weizmann with Chief Rabbi Jacob Meir, Shlomo Meyuhas and
community leaders in Jerusalem, 1925

America

12 Albert Einstein and Weizmann
in America, 1921

13 Weizmann in Chicago, 1933. The reception committee included Meyer W. Weisgal,
Louis Lipsky, Judge Harry M. Fisher and Governor Horner

Contrary to expectations, no secure and stable position had been created in the Middle East by 1920. The war had left a legacy of chaos. The Great Powers quarrelled with each other, giving the impression that nothing was definitely settled and thus encouraging malcontents. The clash between the French and (British-protected) Feisal in Syria disturbed the whole area. Because of these disorders Jewry had to deplore the loss of one of the most valiant groups of its defenders: Joseph Trumpeldor, with five comrades, was killed at Tel Hai on the Syrian border. In Jerusalem, too, the situation was deteriorating; while Weizmann was celebrating Passover with his mother in Haifa, the first Arab assault on Jews occurred in Jerusalem. That was a terrible reminder of the unsatisfactory state of affairs and a grave shock to Weizmann. In the ensuing trials not only the Mufti and other instigators, but also the organizer of Jewish self-defence, Jabotinsky, were sentenced to fifteen years' imprisonment (later quashed). Immediately after these depressing experiences Weizmann had the satisfaction that the San Remo Conference in April 1920, which definitely settled the political differences between the Powers, also confirmed the British Mandate over Palestine with all the clauses relating to the Jewish National Home, and that Herbert Samuel, who had himself contributed so much to the Balfour Declaration, was appointed first British High Commissioner— a Jew as British Proconsul in the land of the Jewish National Home.

It was under the impact of this hectic course of events that the Zionist Conference of 1920 met. Zionist delegates the world over had been debating the advent of the Jewish State in all its imaginative details, and they were strongly influenced by world events, especially by the slogans of Wilsonism and Leninism. They arrived full of praise and gratitude for the man who had led Zionism to victory. No one doubted that Weizmann had emerged as the leader; his actual election was a mere formality. But many Zionists felt chilled, if not to say deceived, when they discovered that Weizmann was not the Messiah. There was, as Weizmann used to say later on, no royal road to Palestine. Instead of a performer of miracles who could attain everything by sheer will-power or by quoting resolutions of Zionist assemblies, they found a worried man who knew he had committed himself to an enormous task he had neither the means nor the power to carry out. It was not a clash of 'East' and 'West', but of emotionalism versus realism, between the social and psychological upheaval of a disintegrating and revolutionary Eastern Europe and the comparative stability of the Western world. The personal tragedy of

Weizmann was that he himself knew only too well the state of mind
of his people, as he, too, had come from Motol and Pinsk, while at
the same time he realized the futility of pure emotionalism in the
fight with very hard political and physical facts. Gradually, the persistent criticism that he had not achieved a still greater miracle, or
that he had accepted a too restricted Charter for Palestine, grew into
mutual resentment and rancour. The dialectics of this malaise became manifest when Weizmann concluded the survey of his activities
with the outcry: 'That is what we have done. Jewish people, what
have you done?'

It was, of course, a nonsensical and unjust reproach. To whom was
it addressed? Who was the 'Jewish people'? What could it have
done? It existed only in a very vague impersonation. The first World
War and the Russian Revolution had undermined and thrown into
confusion the old solid positions of the Jewish people in Eastern
Europe, and American Jewry had only just begun, during the war,
to tackle all-Jewish responsibilities. At that time it was hardly more
than the conglomeration of two incoherent groups: on the one hand
the small group of 'notables', customary representatives of the upper
strata of Jewish society, wealthy families mainly of German origin,
who functioned as representatives because, thanks to their social
standing, they could exert some influence in public life according to
the old system of *Shtadlanut*; on the other hand, masses of immigrants
from Eastern Europe who had arrived after 1882 and just begun to
make their first advance on the social ladder, largely thanks to the
rapid development during the first World War. They included the
large and influential camp of Labour organizations with more or less
socialist leanings, imported ideologies of the *Bund* and to a lesser
extent of the Poale Zion.

Yet Weizmann's remark is very illuminating. It shows the full
depth of his grudge in face of the criticism voiced, not by 'the Jewish
people', but by the vastly increased camp of the spokesmen of
Zionist parties. Weizmann knew well that he had somehow 'bluffed'
the British Government and other Powers by claiming to be the
representative, while not of a Great Power, yet of an imponderable
great power that backed his demands. In a deeper sense, as harbinger
of a historical process, he was right; but in terms of tangible facts he
had at his command not only no national body of unified purpose
but also no material means or tools capable of carrying out his programme even in a limited way. Protected by the clouds of war time,
when the most fantastic ideas could tentatively be adopted if one
thought they might serve some purpose, Weizmann had been able,
thanks to the magic of his personality, to convince the statesmen of

the world that the establishment of a Jewish State in Palestine by that unknown quantity, the Jewish people, was a practical proposition. The time had now come when all such nebulous projects would be more thoroughly scrutinized, and it could be assumed that much of the stock of war-time talk and promise would be discarded. It was of the utmost importance to demonstrate immediately that the Jewish national desire was no joke and no fake, nor a pseudo-messianic and unreal dream, but a well-considered and well-planned enterprise that could be set in motion if the authorities co-operated.

Weizmann knew that time was pressing; he often quoted the words Lloyd George said to him at the Peace Conference: 'You have to take your chance now, because the political world is in the state of the Baltic Sea before it freezes. As soon as it is frozen, nothing can be moved, and one has to wait a long time until a second opportunity arises.' Weizmann had called to London many of his old friends and experts and instructed them to evolve an economic plan. Most of the Zionist leaders who came to London from Russia offered their (un-wanted) advice on political matters but could not help in the practical work. It suddenly became obvious that colonizing a country could not be accomplished by mere Zionist conviction but demanded expert knowledge of a very elaborate technical nature. People who were able propagandists and debaters at Zionist Congresses or in fighting anti-Zionists still did not know how to make barren soil fertile or how to move masses and organize labour for the building of roads. Within the very narrow limits of the pre-1914 practical work, at that time mainly conducted by the so-called Odessa Committee (founded in 1890 by the Hoveve-Zion) in a backward Turkish Palestine, some devoted men and good Zionists had played a leading rôle. Work at that time had been mainly based on propaganda and on collecting modest funds from Russian Zionists, also on establishing small com-panies that more often than not went bankrupt after a short time, and on negotiations with Turkish officials of the old school. Modern methods were unknown, and the dimensions of the work were small and undaring. Nobody—certainly not Weizmann—would underrate the achievements of this period. But it was a misunderstanding to assume that one could continue in the same way under a British administration. This created a delicate situation, apt to hurt the susceptibilities of a great number of good and loyal men who for many years had been Weizmann's comrades in the fight for Zionism. Many of these people did not see their own limitations and firmly believed that the old Zionist veterans were the right men to give advice and to stand at the helm. Weizmann painfully sensed the shortcomings of his crew, and he was always looking round to find more suitable men for the practical jobs, mainly in the Western world, even if the people in question had not been Zionists before and did not know all the subtleties of Zionist philosophy. At one stage Weizmann persuaded Angelo Levi-Bianchini, a first-class man of great abilities and experience who had filled important appointments as an Italian Navy officer and diplomat, to become the head of the Zionist Immigration Department. Disastrously, Levi-Bianchini (forgotten today) was killed in Deraa in Transjordan in August 1920 in an Arab attack on a diplomatic train. But I still remember Weizmann exclaiming in despair: 'I can have Levi-Bianchini, and they want to force me to take Sheinkin!' (a veteran Russian Zionist).

Of the men assembled at that time in London, only Bertold Feiwel and Julius Simon had some understanding of practical requirements. Julius Simon prepared a detailed colonization plan, assisted by an ingenious mystery man, Abraham Sonne. But the more such plans were composed in theory, the more the difficulties became apparent. A system of financing the work could only be found with the abundant participation of American Jewry, and perhaps through the co-operation of a class of wealthy Jews in Western Europe, though these had been opponents of Zionism (with a few notable exceptions such as Baron Edmond de Rothschild). But when the Conference assembled in 1920, it slowly became clear that no concerted plan of practical value would come out of it. It was an absurdity at that juncture: masses of delegates from revolution-stricken Eastern Europe came to London under completely false illusions, expecting that here in London there would be offered a ready-to-wear Jewish State to which one could address one's wishes and demands, most of them activist and socialist. On the other hand there was the American faction, a *mixtum compositum* from the two groups indicated above, but under a strong leadership and a unifying whip. Seen from Weizmann's angle, these people came mainly to criticize the only man who actually *had* performed a spectacular feat. His outburst: 'Jewish people, what have *you* done?' struck a note that dominated the scene for many years to come.

The two great issues that emerged after 1920 and that in some respect are interrelated, are (a) the political situation and the so-called Arab problem, and (b) the mobilization of Jewish forces for the building up of the National Home by enlisting the co-operation of non-Zionist Jews who were to be made to share the responsibility by joining the Jewish Agency set up in Article 4 of the Palestine Mandate.

Both these matters were the central points on which the battles within the Zionist Organization and at the Congresses had to be fought. They practically filled the whole inner history of the Zionist movement until 1929, when both reached a climax: one a successful conclusion in a glorious setting, the other a tragic explosion that brought about a turn for the worse.

If we decide to regard the Zionist Congress as a 'parliament', Weizmann had no steady majority there. His election as President and leader was unavoidable because he *was* the movement; without him everything would have collapsed the next day. But in order to bring this election about all sorts of parliamentary manœuvres had to be executed, and in controversial matters a compromise formula often had to be found that could be interpreted in a way only just acceptable to Weizmann, though not in the sense originally intended. Sometimes, he left the Congress in despair while the factions were still horse-trading in committees, and without awaiting his actual election.

Weizmann could rely only on a section of the General Zionists, primarily British, American and Central European, and on the Labour camp, which vitally depended on fund-raising for the continuation of its activities in Palestine. The decisive stage of Zionist activity during the 'twenties was, quite consistently, the immediate settlement of large tracts of land, which could be reclaimed partly from big Arab landowners and partly from the Government and had to be made fit for colonization by sanitation, drainage, irrigation, etc, and at the same time the provision of work for immigrants. The Halutzim were in fact the best human element available for Palestine, if not the only one. Palestine had no attraction for the capitalist eager for profit, nor could the Jewish—even Zionist—middle class do much, except buy plantations or set up shops, all important but not fundamental.

Palestine was a pioneer country. The would-be settlers, preferring communal work and imbued with socialist ideas, trusted that some public authority, the Government or the Zionist Commission, would provide them with all that was necessary: sustenance, land and tools. This task the Zionist Organization claimed for itself; it never occurred to it to concede that authority to the Mandatory Government. But when it came to actual fulfilment it was revealed that the Organization had no money, not even for the most restricted programme of acquisition of land and settlement. Weizmann knew that the provision of this money was also the supreme political necessity, and that defection would not only be a setback to the Halutz on whose idealism the movement depended, but also teach the Mandatory Government that Zionism need not be taken seriously. The

Government itself, in the vice of an economy campaign after the war, was not prepared to spend money for purely Jewish purposes.

The Labour parties, organizers of the early waves of immigration, were well aware that their work could not exist without large public funds, and that Weizmann was the only leader capable of raising them. So they were bound to him and stood by him at the Congresses, though not always in a gracious way. Often they felt obliged to make all sorts of declarations and reservations lest they be regarded as less nationalistic or extremist in their aims than the Opposition, or in order to save their 'socialist' souls while co-operating with 'bourgeois'. In the end, Labour was always part of the parliamentary majority required for the continuance of the Weizmann regime; the religious party of Mizrachi could in most cases be conditioned by their own Halutz section, and/or by some 'bribe' in the form of seats in the Executive or allocations in the budget. So Weizmann always formally had a majority until 1931, even though the Opposition dominated the Congresses. A large part of his supporters were, in fact, a sort of opposition *manqué*.

By the 1920 Conference Weizmann already knew that the most urgent action was a popular appeal for money, which under the circumstances had to be addressed primarily to American Jewry. He was persuaded by leading Russian Zionists like Naidich and Zlatopolsky that the best way would be an appeal for large sums in analogy to the old Biblical principle of *Maasser*: one-tenth of everybody's private income should be given as voluntary taxation for the purpose of the National Home. This was, of course, a futile idea to which not only the Brandeis group but also other sober minds who preferred realistic thinking were reluctant to agree. Finally, the rhetorical inclination of some Americans, even Dr Silver, kept the upper hand; one did not hesitate to proclaim a target of £25,000,000 sterling for which not the slightest prospect existed. The Keren Hayesod was born. Most clauses of its charter were equally unreal and never took effect. Weizmann did not care for the details of the scheme. The main point was that immediate funds should be forthcoming. So he plunged into this project, brushed aside all objections that interfered with the immediate raising of 'national', ie public—as distinct from private—funds, and later embarked upon his pilgrimage to the Jewish masses in America in the hope of finding support there also, at least among some of the wealthier Jews. That had to have priority over attempts to attract private means for investment, since private business also presupposed some general adjustments that could not yield profits, such as the preparation of the soil and of the men, institutions for health and education, and so on, which had to be made out of public funds, à fond perdu.

Weizmann had come to the 1920 Conference with the idea of enlarging the circle of interested people, especially businessmen, who could be useful both as the bearers of private initiative and for inspiring confidence as to the solidity of economic policy. But at the Conference he had to overcome the one-sided views of those who wanted to put all the stakes on private initiative, although he knew that some of their views were sound. This was the background to the unfortunate conflict with Louis Brandeis, which was one of the most fateful results of the Conference.

There was, perhaps, a psychological predicament that contributed to the split. Weizmann became irritated when other men, among them those whom he for one reason or another regarded as his antagonists, expressed views that were in fact similar to his own, but that he himself could not easily put forth because he saw also the other side of the matter, which the others ignored. He also thoroughly disliked the puritan type of American Jew, which was humourless and moralizing and often seemed self-righteous. So he was alienated from two men with whom he had many views in common but with whom he was unable to co-operate: Louis Brandeis and Judah Magnes. They were in some way representative of the two main objectives of Zionism: Brandeis in the quest for new men outside the Zionist Organization and for an economic programme, Magnes in the field of Arab policy. Much of the period 1919–1929 was embittered by Weizmann's resentment against these men.

The events of the Annual Conference of 1920 were a riddle to many who could not see what was going on behind the scenes and in the irrational sphere of personal susceptibilities and rivalries. Brandeis came to London, after his visit to Palestine, convinced—as indeed was Weizmann—that the new era with its completely new tasks demanded a thorough overhaul of the Zionist apparatus, from both the personal and the organizational side. He also stressed that the settlements, and indeed the Yishuv, should become self-supporting as quickly as possible. Businesslike management was a conditio sine qua non, otherwise colonization would become a bottomless barrel. Nothing was more obvious to Weizmann himself. Brandeis, like Weizmann, wished to acquire the services of men of stature in economic life, who were accustomed to bear great financial responsibility and understood the necessity to balance a budget. There were certain obvious candidates for the purpose, although nobody knew whether they would be prepared to answer the call. It was clear that no conditions of ideological identification could be put to such men. They would have to be recruited as experts, as partners in a fascinating enterprise of building a new society to which they would be attracted because of their Jewish feeling of solidarity. Weizmann himself conducted negotiations with men like Lord Reading, Sir Alfred Mond, Sir Robert Waley-Cohen, all first-rank businessmen in the City of London. They were prepared to collaborate as non-Zionists although, as shown later, only to a certain extent. It is, however, difficult to decide whether at that early stage it would have been possible to get them more fully committed, and engaged in economic planning and execution, if the response from the Zionist side had been more encouraging. Brandeis wanted to transform the Zionist Organization so that these people could become members. As a matter of fact, it quickly became clear that the Zionist movement was not in a mood to invite non-Zionists to collaborate. Most Zionists at that time still regarded the struggle of ideas within the Jewish camp as their main task. After recognition by the British Government they felt that victory had been theirs. They were not prepared to share this glory with their distrusted enemies of yesterday. Moreover, a new era of democracy had dawned in all human affairs; the messages of America and Moscow were moulding a new world. It seemed obvious to most of the Zionists, especially those from Eastern Europe, that they could not possibly now give an honoured standing to the 'notables' who had hitherto rejected Jewish nationalism and ruled the Jewish institutions in an autocratic way. The first hints of Weizmann in this direction aroused anger and suspicion in the ranks. Brandeis proclaimed, certainly erroneously, that with the achievement of the Balfour Declaration—analogous to Herzl's 'Charter'— the political era of Zionism had come to an end, and what was needed now was expert work according to strict business principles. This oversimplification angered Weizmann, who knew that the Balfour Declaration was not the end of the struggle, and that its preservation would be at least as difficult to secure as its proclamation had been in war time. Brandeis incurred the wrath of other delegations when his Reform Plan was understood to imply the dissolution of time-honoured institutions dear to their hearts. Brandeis deeply resented Weizmann's separatist negotiations which were directed toward the establishment of an Economic Council without jurisdiction in Zionist political affairs. He also naturally declined a suggestion that he should resign his office as a Justice of the US Supreme Court to become a professional Zionist leader. The views of Brandeis and Weizmann were so divergent that a split in the movement was inevitable.

No real reform resulted from the Conference, and once again Weizmann had to lean heavily on Yiddish-speaking East Side Americans. A compromise was reached for the composition of the London Executive to which Julius Simon and Nehemia de Lieme were elected for the outspoken purpose of carrying out the necessary reorganization in Palestine. Despite Brandeis' objections Ussishkin was elected as head of the Palestine Executive. Later, when the Report of the Simon–de Lieme Reorganization Commission appeared, it was met with fierce hostility in Palestine by the people with vested interests, and sabotaged throughout. It had, in fact, to be abandoned, and Weizmann had to part from such old friends as Julius Simon and to ally himself with men of the more popular Zionist tradition and with extremists like Jabotinsky—an unnatural alliance that could not last.

In America the split seemed at one moment to have brought a fatal disruption into the movement. But with the Convention of the Zionist Organization of America that took place in Cleveland in 1921 the leadership passed to Louis Lipsky. Himself American-born, and completely at home in the English-speaking tradition, he rallied to himself both the Yiddish-speaking segment of the movement and a considerable part of the 'Americanized' elements in a repudiation of the Brandeis concept of Zionist development. For more than two decades, Lipsky was to remain Weizmann's key supporter in America. For a considerable period men like Stephen Wise, Julian Mack and Abba Hillel Silver held out against the popular will, but ultimately their opposition faded, and Wise and Silver especially went on to become influential leaders of American Zionism.

It was only logical that in the period following the 1921 Zionist Congress Weizmann became a 'Brandeis' to many of the men who had supported him at an earlier stage and now found him lacking in what they understood as democracy and radicalism. Like Brandeis, he was considered to be undermining the Movement's nationalist foundations. The Congress majority had forced him to accept a scheme envisaging the enlargement of the Agency by 'democratic' procedures instead of including self-appointed notables who were not democratically elected. For this purpose it was proposed to call a World Congress freely elected by Jews the world over--a sort of duplication of the Zionist Congress, especially as the franchise was to be linked to all kinds of basic nationalist creeds. Weizmann was sceptical. He knew that such a Congress would be opposed by all who feared the anti-Semites' insinuation of Jewish international conspiracy. If it were possible at all, it would not yield a genuine reinforcement of Zionist strength. It would bring in, under a different name, the same kind of men who were already Zionists.

When it became clear that Weizmann was determined to proceed with his Jewish Agency plan and had already started negotiations in America and elsewhere, two of the Congress 'parties', Revisionists under Jabotinsky and Lichtheim, and Radicals under Izhak Grunbaum and Nahum Goldmann, declared war on him. It came to tumultuous scenes at the Congresses and finally to the resignation of Jabotinsky, Lichtheim and Soloveichik. The Revisionist party was formed in 1925 under the leadership of Jabotinsky mainly for the purpose of conducting an activist policy, a 'political offensive' against the Mandatory Power, to obtain the right to form a Jewish Legion (a military force) and what they called a 'Colonization Regime'. They argued that these extremist nationalist aims could be attained only by a radically nationalist leadership, and that for this reason Weizmann's scheme of including non-Zionists in the Jewish Agency had to be rejected. It may be assumed that Weizmann in his innermost feelings even had some sympathy with some of the Revisionists' political grievances. He often had to wrangle with the British more bitterly than any of his colleagues. But he knew from his own experience how absurdly futile it was to expect an improvement of the position by a political offensive of the sort the Revisionists had in mind. He also knew that it was hopeless to get, for such a militant programme, Jewish backing substantial enough to impress the British Government. Times had changed; there were no war-time conditions; the Zionist movement alone was weak and in permanent danger of financial collapse. No, this was not the way; one had to look for other means.

Before the Agency was constituted the Zionist forces were strengthened by the co-operation of prominent Jews and Jewish bodies within the 'neutral' organization of the Keren Hayesod, which had assumed a special standing under its own Board of Directors, with its own branches in all countries, and played a very important rôle during the 'twenties. It even developed its own philosophy. Kurt Blumenfeld, one of its most successful leaders in Germany, himself an uncompromising Zionist and staunch Weizmannist, developed the idea that the Keren Hayesod was a meeting-ground for Zionists and non-Zionists for practical and unpolitical purposes while each of them retained the freedom of his own views and political action outside the Keren Hayesod, especially in local Jewish life. He called it *Bündnispolitik*—a policy of alliance. So the way was paved for collaboration within the Agency. It is arguable that the independent fund-raising instructions created an organizational confusion, but that was partly the result of the fact that in many respects the Zionist Congress, with its ever-growing party strife, proved unworkable.

The resistance to the enlargement of the Jewish Agency was only one side of the overestimation of Zionist power and potentialities after the Balfour Declaration. The other side, much more momentous, was the misunderstanding of political realities. In face of the general trend of proclaiming the self-determination and liberation of countries and peoples *en masse*, the exaggerated propaganda in conjunction with the Balfour Declaration had created a fantastic notion that the Jews, with their aspiration to long-withheld national existence, were on the same level as the Czechs, Poles, Croats, Lithuanians and heaven knows what else. All these had achieved the transfer of power in their own territory, where they had lived under foreign rule for centuries. It goes without saying that the case of the Jews was completely different. Moreover, not even the majority of Jewish nationalists, let alone of the Jews in general, were agreed that Palestine should be their National Home in a literal sense. They interpreted their nationalism in terms of 'national autonomy' in the territories where they lived, especially in the new East European states. For some short time it even seemed that there would be a democratic Russia, in any case a democratic Ukraine, where a huge Jewish national Congress was held before the Bolshevik victory put an end to these dreams.

It remains a matter for speculation how the emergence of a democratic Russia—in accordance with the hopes attached to the revolutionary government of the liberal Kadets, of Prince Lvov and Kerensky—would have influenced Jewish destiny. With its immense material and intellectual potentialities, freely and fully developing, it would possibly have attracted the best forces of the Jewish people and have promoted both assimilation (in the old sense) and Jewish nationalism, perhaps a blossoming of Jewish (and Hebrew) culture whose centres, even under Tsarist oppression, had always been in Odessa, Vilna and Warsaw. It would also have made possible the active participation of Russian Jews, with all their tradition of *Hibbat Zion*, in the building up of Palestine. One may assume that Russian Jews would have become rich (some of them were before 1917) and would have contributed materially as much as American Jewry or more. Undoubtedly they would have provided an inexhaustible army of pioneers in all walks of life, perhaps more than they did anyhow when Russian Halutzim came to the shores of Palestine as fugitives from the Bolsheviks. Such speculations, not foreign to Weizmann's mind, are, alas, futile.

As it was, however, under the impact of the nationalist and socialist upheaval in Eastern Europe, the Jewish masses regarded Palestine as their state, to whose dominion they were entitled like the Poles in Poland. It is true that the British Government had promised a National Home, identified with a state not only in the Jewish mind but in the mind of many highly placed statesmen, with some vagueness. But there were almost no Jews in Palestine, and there was an Arab population. And even in 1920 not many Jews except the refugees from Russia and the Zionist pioneer (Halutz) movements were prepared to transfer their own domicile to an unknown and backward land. In any case, the settlement of a new population was a slow and painful process, with political, economic, financial and psychological implications. All these factors, political as well as financial, could, by their failure, halt the whole development at any moment. What could be done to prevent that? What power was in the hands of the Jews?

Faced with the grumbling crowd of Zionist critics who blamed their leader for the failure of reality to come up to their dreams, Weizmann was aware that his only weapon was the appeal to the goodwill of the British and the invocation of their solemn pledge. This pledge could be regarded as legally binding, in so far as it was legalized, under British pressure, by the Peace Conference, later by the San Remo Conference and finally by the confirmation of the Mandate by the League of Nations. Then as now not too much reliance could be placed on so-called international law. Apart from the fact that it was subject to interpretation and could be whittled away (as the National Home idea actually was at a later stage), the whole concept of international law was doubtful. There was always a chance to claim a change of circumstances or physical inability to fulfil a pledge. International relations are kept by the balance of power and not by juridical clauses, except where these conform with the interests and goodwill of the power concerned.

Weizmann knew he had to convince the British, daily, that the implementation of the Balfour Declaration was both in the British interest and a moral necessity. But he had to grapple with almost insurmountable odds. True, Britain was interested in keeping Palestine against the French, and she could not abandon the chief pretext for the occupation of the country. But the unexpected vehemence of Arab nationalism created an entirely new situation, and it was no secret that many prominent British men—and women—played a leading part in encouraging that nationalism. Still more were impressed by it. In the first period of military occupation in 1918,

Zionism was regarded as complete nonsense by the generals. With a few exceptions, like Colonel Meinertzhagen and Wyndham Deedes, they treated it as non-existent. They saw primarily the inhabitants of the country, with whom they had come to terms as all military rulers must when they have to replace the conquered authority. Most officials were hostile or indifferent. The Moslem-Christian Committee in Palestine represented the great majority of the population, and the Arabs invoked the pledges of the Allies who had promised freedom and self-determination to the population as late as on 8 November 1918. Moreover, the transition from war to peace was not as smooth as expected. There was turmoil in Central Europe, disunity among the Allies, conflicting nationalist claims everywhere (symbolized by the case of Fiume). The construction of Arab kingdoms went awry, all plans had to be reshuffled again and again, local tribes rose not only against British rule, but also against the sort of Arab regime the British had in mind.

At that time, the British public was war-weary and not prepared to continue the fight for unwanted British rule in distant places. A powerful agitation at home demanded the liquidation of all British commitments in the Middle East. British newspapers shouted daily that Britain should not make additional sacrifices but clear out of the Middle East 'bag and baggage'. The resurrection of the Turkish nation in 1922 and its spectacular victory over the British-backed Greeks changed the whole outlook in that region. In spite of his anti-religious attitude, Kemal Ataturk's campaign aroused the admiration of Moslems, the more so when he proclaimed that he had no intention of restoring the Ottoman Empire or of dominating other peoples. The British had to abandon the Greeks despite the promises given them by Lloyd George, who himself had to resign over this issue. And he had been the head of the Cabinet that had given another pledge, the Balfour Declaration! Balfour's chair was now that of Lord Curzon, a quite different character, not at all too fond of the Zionist experiment.

The international constellation was ignored by those who attacked Dr Weizmann. He alone knew better than anyone else how delicate it was. He was haunted by apprehensions lest more active opposition on the side of the Arabs lead to a similar treatment of the Zionists as the Greeks suffered in 1922 and the Armenians had suffered before, namely, that under changed circumstances pledges could not be implemented. This had to be avoided at all costs. Only a moderate policy, which though sticking to fundamental rights did not push the British into an impasse, could hope to keep British goodwill and understanding. There was no prospect of a steady addition of political rights; the maximum that could be hoped for was to prevent a turn for the worse.

That is what Weizmann, after the most severe crisis Zionism had to overcome, said at the Karlsbad Zionist Congress in 1923:—'I am not ashamed to say: I have no successes to produce. After the Mandate there will be no political successes for years. Those political successes which you want you will have to gain by your own work in the Emek, in the marshes and on the hills, not in the offices of Downing Street. It is sufficient if your diplomatic representative (if you insist on this description) can hold the position. On political offensives at least my own humble person will not embark, even at the risk of being regarded by some of you as a coward.'

The years following the Annual Conference of 1920 were in fact a time of 'crisis in permanence'. There was a double crisis, political and economic. We shall deal with each in brief separately.

The *political* crisis dragged on because the confirmation of the Mandate by the League of Nations was postponed for three years, and in the meantime all kinds of attacks were made against it in order to prevent its legalisation, not only by the Arabs who submitted petitions and even proceeded to threats, but also by other interested parties (some as mighty as the Vatican). While at home vociferous protests in press and Parliament were raised against the waste of 'the taxpayer's money' on troublesome adventures in the Middle East— the Government expenditure in Palestine alone amounted in the fiscal year 1920–21 to £8,000,000—the situation in the Arab countries remained confused. In March 1921 Colonial Secretary Winston Churchill summoned his Eastern experts to Cairo, and they decided to enthrone Feisal in Iraq and establish a separate state in Transjordan under his brother Abdulla. The Pesach holiday in Palestine, which had caused disturbances in 1920, passed without incident in 1921, but on 1 May, a Jewish May Day demonstration, which was misunderstood or intentionally misinterpreted by the Arabs, was the signal for a well-prepared Arab assault. The Jewish immigration centre in Jaffa was stormed and many Jews killed, among them the writer J. Ch. Brenner, who had always advocated peaceful relations with the Arabs. Other acts of violence followed in several colonies, and the Jewish population of Jaffa fled to Tel Aviv. It was clear that the police had not done a proper job against the attacking mob and that a great deal of responsibility fell upon the Government. The indignation of the Jewish public was justified. When, in order to appease the Arabs, Sir Herbert Samuel on 3 June (the King's birthday) made a speech in which he interpreted the Balfour Declaration in a very restrictive sense and proclaimed a temporary stopping of immigration, the Zionist world was in uproar—and against Weizmann, too. Yet in retrospect it remains a fact that after the reassuring explanation to the Arabs there was no further outbreak in the country until 1929, and Jewish colonization could calmly proceed as far as its own financial resources permitted.

The Royal Commission of Inquiry appointed by the British Government under the chairmanship of Chief Justice Thomas Haycraft, condemned Arab violence, blamed the attitude of the police and criticized the Palestine administration. At the same time it set the pattern for all following Commissions of Inquiry by analysing the underlying causes of the outbreak. It hinted that the misgivings of the Arabs may not have been entirely groundless, and it recommended a policy of safeguards to the Arabs in order to dispel their understandable fear of being displaced by the newcomers. After that the British Government had constantly to defend the Mandate against a hostile public opinion by pointing out that it did not imply a displacement of the Arab population nor special privileges to Jews (a negation of the very meaning it had in the eyes of Zionists) and that the Jews would not have a share in the government of the country. The summary of this campaign was embodied in the White Paper (Cmd 1700) on 22 June 1922, which contained the Correspondence of the Government with the Arab Executive and with the Zionist Organization as well as the so-called Churchill Statement (which was actually drafted by Samuel). It was perhaps a personal rebuff to Weizmann (which he bore with dignity) that his remark at the Peace Conference that Palestine should be as Jewish as England English, widely publicized by Zionist propaganda, was explicitly refuted. The Statement made it clear that the Jews would have no right to impose their nationality on the non-Jewish inhabitants of the country, nor would they have any governmental functions except in the management of their own communal affairs. The Jews must know, however, that they were in Palestine 'as of right and not on sufferance'. Neither the Jews nor the Arabs should think they depended on sufferance by the other side. Both communities should be entitled to develop their national and cultural life without interference, and they should live peacefully side by side, while all affairs concerning the country as a whole were administered by the Mandatory Power. The 'Statement' as it stood was not a 'Zionist victory'. It did not underwrite extremist Zionist aspirations, it did not conform with messianic hopes. But it was an attempt to give as fair a chance to both sides as could be done. This was intended to satisfy the sense of justice which the liberal world—on which the

Jews had to rely—applied to a problem that was not a contest between right and wrong but between right and right. The Arabs rejected it. They could afford non-co-operation as they were sitting on the spot and needed no change; in any case they enjoyed much better conditions than under Turkish rule. Moreover, their wish to introduce 'democracy'—majority rule—was in accord with the general trend of opinion created by Wilsonism; they had never had democracy before. As to the Zionists, they had no choice but to accept the British declaration. It obscured their image of the goal, at least for the time being, but it did not close the door to immigration and settlement. Its limitation to 'economic capacity' seemed reasonable unless it was interpreted in too static terms. The Zionists themselves were not interested in exceeding the economic capacity and in creating a crisis for themselves that would result in something Arab opposition alone could not achieve, namely the stoppage of further immigration for mere economic reasons.

Doubtless grinding their teeth, the Zionist Executive agreed to the Statement as a basis for practical policy, though probably with a mental reservation as to the ultimate aim. All members of the Executive signed the document, including Jabotinsky. Later Jabotinsky explained that he had signed under pressure, believing that otherwise the Mandate would not be confirmed. But his colleagues whom he condemned, had been in the same position! In this whole desperate struggle for salvaging the war-time achievements, whose burden lay primarily on Weizmann, the motive for concessions was always to choose the lesser evil. Revisionists and others afterwards demanded the withdrawal of the Executive's agreement to the Churchill Statement. That was easy demagogy for those in opposition. Weizmann, bearing the responsibility for the survival of Zionism, could not afford it.

The Mandatory Government continued its efforts to win the Arabs over for some sort of toleration of the Mandate and of Zionism. They offered them concessions intended to improve their standing and remove their feeling of inferiority. One such proposal was the formation of an 'Arab Agency', corresponding to the 'Jewish Agency'—a logical misconception, of course, since the Jewish Agency represented an international and not a local factor. But if that would satisfy the Arabs and create a workable parallelism for the sake of positive co-operation of both peoples, it would have been practical. Weizmann was inclined to a flexible policy if it brought some progress. The Arabs rejected it; they were not prepared to accept anything short of full democracy.

So the political crisis continued unabated. The Arabs won influential friends the world over, especially in London, and the Zionist Executive had to be continuously on guard.

It is only natural that Weizmann considered everything that could bring some kind of *modus vivendi* with the Arabs. It was difficult because the Arabs themselves were split, the situation in Arab countries was chaotic, and there was no authorized Arab leadership. One man seemed to be both representative and reasonable: Emir Abdullah. He was a shrewd politician, not blinded by illusions, though naturally an Arab patriot, and he saw the advantages that could accrue to the Arab cause by coming to an arrangement with the Zionists and also promoting the swift building up of such backward Arab regions as Transjordan. He had a modern concept of federation and autonomy, based on the unity of the Fertile Crescent. At one moment it seemed as though there were a possibility of an Abdullah-Weizmann axis, a continuation of the Weizmann-Feisal accord of 1918–19. It would have implied some modification of the conception of an isolated Jewish state, of course; but it would have opened the road to an entirely different development of the Middle East and to an incomparable expansion of Jewish activity and immigration. It was an idea worthy of statesmen of the greatest stature. But it came to nothing after silly press reports unleashed premature rumours. There was also some suspicion that the British did not like this form of rapprochement, which would have made them superfluous. Anyhow, this 'red herring' gave rise to another explosion of indignation in the ranks of Zionists who were persuaded that Weizmann wanted to 'give up' something of the pure national ideal.

Perhaps the most important and most enlightening speech of the whole period was made by Dr Weizmann at the Twenty-sixth Annual Convention of the Zionist Organization of America on 17 June 1923, in Baltimore. At this decisive conference Weizmann's policy had been under strong attack, but was finally approved with a big majority. After the vote Weizmann took the floor at 2 AM. He started by repeating his own famous saying of 1920: 'Jewish people, what have you done?' He explained the position in Palestine where 'starving Halutzim and unpaid teachers are destroying the Mandate' and that it would be foolish to believe that against this situation we could appeal to British bayonets. He said that former non-Zionists were converted to Zionism not by the Balfour Declaration, but by the idealism and sacrifices of 30,000 Halutzim. Finally, he answered the critics who had accused him of selling out Zionism to the Arabs. He said:

For years we have drafted political resolutions that we Jews want to live in peace with the Arabs. We have passed resolutions which have the character of a pledge. But as soon as it comes to taking decisive and effective steps to carry out those resolutions, because the realization of all these problems is a question of life or death of our work in Palestine, one is attacked from all sides. A clamour is raised that one sells out to the Arabs or to someone else all that is sacred to Zionism. It should be clear to our great politicians that one cannot put off the Arabs with empty talk. For years we have made decisions, and whatever the Jewish National Home will ultimately become, even if it absorbs millions of Jews and if, as I hope, there will be a Jewish majority in Palestine, it will nevertheless remain an island in the Arab sea. We have to come to an understanding with this people which is akin to us and with which we have lived in concord in the past. Naturally it would be better if Palestine and the neighbouring countries were unpopulated. It would be better still if the Nile flowed there instead of the Jordan, better still if Moses had led us to America instead of Palestine, better still if we had to deal with Englishmen and not with Jews. But we have to deal with Jews, and in Eretz Israel there is the Jordan, and there is a people which resists our coming and which holds Palestine encircled from north and south, east and west, and with it we have to arrange ourselves in a serious way. This can be done by reason and by faith of political honesty; for these are the strongest weapons a single man possesses.

Actually, the silver lining on the horizon of Arab-Jewish relations quickly faded away. The attempt to find some common ground with leading Arabs, mainly supported by a group of old-established Jewish pre-war settlers whose co-operation Weizmann at that time thought useful, yielded no positive result. Neither did the negotiations that Colonel Kisch in Palestine and sometimes also the London Executive conducted with so-called moderate Arabs. All of them rejected the Balfour Declaration. The extremists, under the leadership of the Mufti, got the upper hand. Some Zionists, especially of the Socialist wing, put forth the theory that one could not negotiate with the reactionary effendi class because they feared the progressive influence of Zionism, which might undermine their social standing. As a matter of fact, the old Arab guard, whose authority was rapidly waning, was more susceptible to argument and more interested in peaceful development than the younger generation with its modern views of democracy. As soon as the radical nationalism and anti-colonialism which seized all Asian (and in our days African) peoples after the first World War, began preoccupying the Arabs too, the prospects of an understanding dwindled away. Arab policy became increasingly intransigent. It will never be possible to determine whether there were genuine chances of an Arab-Jewish accord in the early 'twenties. Weizmann regarded it as his duty to explore all lanes in this direction, but, as stated above, he was not supported by the majority of Zionists, who had been brought up in the philosophy of exclusive nationalism; and at least in later years, Arab intransigence, often encouraged by Western influences, made a *rapprochement* unfeasible.

Apart from the political troubles, the period was dominated by the permanent *economic* crisis. It is difficult to imagine the conditions of workers in the 'twenties, when today (1962) even the slightest hint of a possible freezing of over-inflated wages in Israel gives rise to complaints and bitterness. Unemployment was a regular feature, workers lived on an appalling minimum, often on the dole, which was a heavy unproductive drain on the Zionist Exchequer. There was genuine starvation in the communal settlements and elsewhere, Zionist money-chests were empty, officials and teachers did not get their salaries and were finally paid by some paper-bills issued by institutions or even by private persons; debts accumulated everywhere. The first waves of immigration were followed by stagnation and even emigration (1923)—not for political reasons. The Executive had again and again to adopt emergency measures in order to prevent a complete breakdown, and no serious projects could be initiated for development and extension of settlement.

The unfavourable trend was temporarily relieved in 1924–25, when a large number of middle-class immigrants arrived, primarily from Poland, where the new financial laws of Grabski had resulted in a heavy deterioration of the situation of Jewish traders. This so-called 'Fourth Aliyah' led to violent intra-Zionist disputes, since Labour circles feared they would lose their monopoly and privileged position. They charged the new immigrants with simply transferring the small shops of the Polish Jewish *Shtetl* into Palestine, thus imperilling the ideal of a social as well as national renewal of the Jewish people through the creation of a new type of Jew, the working man living on his own soil. The influx of a middle-class element with private means also had one undesirable side-effect: the spreading of land speculation. Unfortunately, there were some dishonest agents who sold to would-be immigrants in Poland at exorbitant prices in advance plots of land that on the spot turned out to be quite different from what the buyer had been promised. Though perhaps only a few people were involved in such activities, it created a bad reputation for the Fourth Aliyah.

Weizmann was strongly attacked by the exponents of the Fourth

Aliyah because he allegedly had spoken contemptuously of 'Dzika and Nalevki'[1] instead of realizing that it was only this element—typical of the Jewish masses of Poland—that could transform Palestine into a densely populated area. Weizmann left no doubt that he could see no real prospect for a population consisting mainly of shopkeepers in overcrowded cities for whose existence there was no reasonable basis unless they went over to productive work in industry and agriculture (as some of them actually did).

Those doubts were justified. After 1925 many of the people of the Fourth Aliyah were disappointed and went back to Poland. But nobody was more prepared than Weizmann to acknowledge the lasting contribution that they, too, had made to the building up of the country. After the debacle of the Fourth Aliyah a new crisis developed. The labour settlements were affected and emigration reached a new peak in 1928 because there was no solid economic absorptive reservoir. In 1927, the Congress was confronted by the necessity of taking drastic steps to consolidate the settlements and make them self-supporting. This had to have priority over the launching of new enterprises and new deficits.

It is impossible to describe in detail the vacillations of immigration and the financial crises during this whole period. It is relevant here only in so far as it affected Weizmann's activities; it was one of the main factors that forced him to occupy himself with the question of money. Circumstances in Palestine were not apt to change his view that all depended on solving the problem of finances; he saw this longed-for possibility first of all in the broadening of the top circle that bore the responsibility; in other words, in the enlargement of the Jewish Agency.

Perhaps, in anticipation of later events, it may be allowed to say that the enlargement itself, when achieved in 1929, actually had more 'moral' than material importance. It symbolized the rallying behind the programme of the National Home of Jewish forces hitherto outside the Zionist movement. It did not stop the financial crises, which actually dragged on until two unexpected events, set in motion by deplorable causes, changed the situation fundamentally: in 1933 the advent of German Jewish refugees with immense funds, private and public, and in 1940 the stationing in Palestine of the British Army with its unprecedented spending, from which all local earners profited.

The paramount task, after the ratification of the Mandate, in addition to committing the Jewish people as a whole to active personal

[1] Famous overcrowded streets in the pre-Hitler Jewish quarter of Warsaw.

and material participation in building the National Home, was the adaptation of practical work to the existing realities of Palestine. Innumerable times Weizmann explained his approach: 'I am a scientist, I know there are physical laws and facts which cannot be abolished by persuasion or by resolutions. One has to try to work with them and to use them to one's purpose. Their negation can only end in failure.'

What were the realities of Palestine? Weizmann had said it at Baltimore with bitter irony. Palestine has a certain climate and a certain geographical position, it has stony ground and deserts, and it has an Arab population. We have not created the desert and we have not invented the Arabs. They are there. So we have to try to turn the desert into fertile country, and to live with the Arabs. We have also to reckon with the character of the Jews. It would be easier to colonize a country with Englishmen or with Danes. I still remember a scene in Weizmann's room in Great Russell Street in 1924, when he had a discussion with Professor Mead, a famous American agricultural expert from California who had been invited to study conditions in Palestine and to submit a plan for agricultural colonization. After describing all the difficulties and the requirements for making the land suitable for settlement, Mead finally came to the human factor and explained how important it would be to have settlers with an old peasant tradition, who had learned from childhood how to till the soil. He said: 'It would be much better for your enterprise if you would employ Danish peasants instead of urban Jews.' Yet Zionism was an enterprise for the rehabilitation of a people and not for the colonization of a country!

The majority of Zionists did not take notice of the presence of the Arabs. From the beginning, this had baffled such thinkers as Yizhak Epstein, Ahad Ha'am and others. In Zionist councils any mention of the Arabs aroused fury. The only faction that took the problem seriously were the Revisionists, but they saw the solution in military action. This seemed a fantastic proposition in 1922, and even if a Jewish Legion, which Jabotinsky described as the 'Alpha and Omega of Zionism', would have been victorious there would still have been a vacuum in Palestine, since no viable Jewish settlement existed.

Weizmann knew that an attempt at military conquest could only result in a total defeat of Zionism. In addition, however, it contradicted his own moral feeling to establish a Jewish state, even if it had been possible, at the expense of another people. He respected the natural attachment of the Arab inhabitants to the soil of their fathers and to their homeland. Palestine was an underpopulated country and there should be room for the newcomers side by side with the existing population, if proper measures were taken for the economic and technical development of the country. For 400 years of Turkish rule all modern progress had been neglected. Irrigation, sanitation, electrification, the construction of roads and ports, modern agricultural methods, evolution of industries, all these were the primary requirements. They were more important than political declarations which would be empty phrases as long as they remained unrelated to any living realities. In the meantime, pending the accomplishment of all these enterprises, for which immense capital, brains and toil were necessary, Weizmann knew that one has to be very cautious in political demands and should not provoke rebuffs that could only strengthen the opposite side. The existing political arrangements, including the position of the Jewish Agency, should suffice to enable the Jews to carry out their work, and the British administration, a modern Western administration, gave it a far better chance than they had had before, perhaps even better than an inexperienced Jewish administration could do.

Jabotinsky believed that the political and general situation permitted, indeed required, the formation of a Jewish Legion for the conquest of the country. Weizmann had been one of the supporters of the Legion in 1917 (he even risked a serious estrangement from his master Ahad Ha'am on this account); this was during the first World War when consideration of neutrality, and concern for the position of Jews in enemy countries, i.e. Germany and Austria, was the main reason for opposing it. The situation in 1925 was quite different. At the 1925 Congress Weizmann said that he had originally sympathized with the Legion idea, but now considered it harmful. The key to the situation, he said, lay on a quite different level, '. . . in genuine friendship and co-operation with the Arabs to open the Near East for Jewish initiative . . . Palestine must be built up without violating the legitimate interests of the Arabs—not a hair on their heads shall be touched. The Zionist Congress must not confine itself to platonic formulae. It has to learn the truth that Palestine is not Rhodesia[1] and that 600,000 Arabs live there, who before the sense of justice of the world have exactly the same right to their homes in Palestine as we have to our National Home. As long as this thought has not penetrated into our flesh and blood, you will always have to look for artificial narcotics, but you will see the future in a false perspective.'

---

[1] The allusion to Rhodesia may appear curious to many readers in 1962, but forty years ago Rhodesia with her vast under-populated reserves of land was considered an empty country that only awaited colonization by immigrants from outside who would invest money and develop it according to plan, as Cecil Rhodes himself had envisaged at the beginning of the century.

It was a fateful constellation but perhaps not entirely accidental that the realization of Zionism coincided with the emergence of Arab nationalism in a much more dynamic form than it had had before. True, there existed an Arab national movement almost ever since nationalism had undergone its spectacular nineteenth-century growth in the Balkans and in Central Europe among peoples under foreign rule. It got a special impetus after the 1908 revolution of the Young Turks. But it was not until the first World War that it evolved into a semi-popular movement in which Moslems and Christians took part, to the extent that the formerly hostile (and certainly not fully reconciled) two religious groups joined hands in demanding political independence. It is unnecessary to repeat the familiar story of the British connexion with the Sherifian family of the Hashemites in Mecca and the stirring up of nationalist hopes, and of the impact of the Russian Revolution and President Wilson's doctrine of self-determination. There is no doubt that this whole ideological upheaval, which gave an unprecedented and unexpected push to Jewish nationalism, for the first time penetrated, together with other modern European concepts, into colonial regions as well. Having grown up in Europe in close touch with European freedom movements, relying on a large literature and on the ferment of the age-old religious longing for Zion, Jewish nationalism was naturally far more advanced than Oriental and especially Arab nationalism. But the fact remains that in the decisive hour of Zionism it was confronted by an Arab nationalism that though immature in many respects already contained the essential ingredients of a struggle for political self-rule. Certainly it distrusted the influx of foreign elements that aspired to become masters of the country.

Zionists were not prepared for this encounter. Taking their metaphysical right to the possession of Palestine for granted they regarded with moral misgivings any forces contesting this thesis. Thus the Arabs who did not consent to hand their country over to the Zionists appeared not only as political adversaries but as criminals, later to be called 'gangsters and murderers' when they opposed the Jews actively. The existence of the Arabs had never played a rôle in Zionist consciousness, and to many Zionists it appeared that some sinister force, possibly anti-Semitic, had invented the Arabs in order to make difficulties for the Jews. The British themselves were especially suspect: they used the Arabs as an excuse to check or prevent the implementation of Jewish rights. A clash of interests had to manifest itself, and when it came the Zionist world at every juncture accused the Mandatory Power of treachery. More often than not it included its own leader in the condemnation.

During the whole decade Weizmann had to cope with this absurd attitude that made him the scapegoat for an objective historical situation. He had steadily to conduct negotiations with the Mandatory Power and to invoke the pledges given to him during the war and incorporated in the basic Constitution of the country, namely the Mandate. But he could not shut his eyes to the fact that Palestine, apart from being the land of the Balfour Declaration and of Jewish colonization, was also a country with an existing population that the administering Government had to serve. This population enjoyed a kind of preference simply, through being on the spot, with all its immediate needs. For Britain there existed from the very beginning a duality of tasks, and it was almost certain, according to all human logic, that in the case of open conflict between the two objects it was the actual population and not the expected—and at that time dubious—would-be newcomers who would 'win'. We have only to consider that in terms of 1960 and of the present doctrines of the United Nations in Africa in order to understand the delicate situation in which Zionism found itself as soon as the first World War was over and the world settled down to stability.

It was Weizmann's greatest achievement that he mastered this situation during this decade by his prudent and cautious understanding.

At the Congress of 1925 Weizmann had the satisfaction of being able to point out that Palestine was at that time the quietest part of the Middle East. This was a vindication of his own moderate and cautious approach and also of the wise and far-sighted policy of Sir Herbert Samuel, who had also been violently attacked by the Congress although on the termination of his office many were equally indignant that the British Government did not renew his appointment. In 1925, the Arabs and Druses of Syria staged a revolt against French rule, which led to the deplorable bombardment of Damascus by the French Army. In the Arab Peninsula Ibn Saud had just expelled King Hussein from the Hedjaz and occupied Mecca and Medina. In Iraq there had been violent demonstrations. And there was no Zionism in all these countries. In Palestine, there seemed to be hope of peaceful development, especially as Lord Plumer, the new High Commissioner, made it clear that he would not tolerate violence. Zionism seemed to have a chance to come to some arrangement with the Arabs although the Arab nationalists had not given up their opposition. Weizmann told the Zionist Congress that two things would have to be done: 'First of all, the Arabs would have to be convinced that we are serious in our will to build up the National Home, and second that the spirit in which we carry out this building

up is a spirit of freedom, tolerance and brotherliness for all'—
the implication being that the masses of the Zionists were deficient
in both accounts: they neither cared enough to let Zionism appear as
a serious enterprise, by immigration, investment, the purchase and
improvement of land, the building of villages and towns, nor did
they show, in their practical behaviour and in the language they used
in speeches and propaganda, the spirit Weizmann had spoken of.
Shortly before, the Mandate Commission of the League of Nations
in Geneva had for the first time paid more attention to what their
lawyers and experts called 'the dualism of the Mandate'. The re-
tiring High Commissioner, Sir Herbert Samuel, had had to face a
barrage of heart-searching questions before the Geneva Commission.
One of the principal speakers at that Congress, Dr Chaim Arlosoroff,
rightly pointed out that Sir Herbert had discharged his task with
great dignity and countered the attacks on the National Home with
firm conviction. In any case, the proceedings in Geneva were a cold
shower to the vociferous politicians who had demanded that the
Zionist Executive should accuse the Mandatory Power before the
forum of the League of Nations. That was another illusion—Weizmann told the Congress—that his critics would have to abandon. But
what about those matters that are in the power of the Jewish people
itself? One of the most important warrants the Zionist Organization
had obtained from the Government, the Rutenberg concession, had
been left unexploited because for four years the money was not forthcoming. This vast enterprise would have opened great opportunities;
electrification would have meant power for industry, irrigation,
facilities for new settlements and absorption of immigrants, transformation and modernization of the country. Weizmann felt he was
powerless also vis-à-vis the Government if the Jewish people refused
to provide the money and the brains for this kind of work.

It was easy for delegates at congresses to revolt against Weizmann
and to adopt radical resolutions. It was much more difficult to convey these resolutions to a British Government that seemed to be
growing weary of the Zionist enterprise. Weizmann challenged the
British with great tactical skill. But sometimes his reluctance to
oppose every British suggestion was dictated not only by tactical con-
siderations, but by political and moral judgment. In connexion with
General Arthur Wauchope's plan of a Legislative Council for Palestine—a plan that Weizmann felt democratically minded Jews could
not reject a limine—he says in his Autobiography: 'I was called not
merely an appeaser, but a British agent—and this accusation was
periodically revived whenever I clashed with the extremists of the
movement. It is no doubt still current.' But such an accusation

was 'current' also before that time, from the very beginning of Weizmann's leadership. Weizmann says he had 'to preach the hard doctrine that the Balfour Declaration was no more than a framework, which had to be filled in by our own efforts'. He knows that 'the arguments which I conceived to be so reasonable must have sounded like bitter mockery of their cherished hopes'.

The 'dualism' of the Mandate ultimately led to the finding by the Peel Commission that the Mandate was unworkable and that partition was the only solution conceivable. But up to 1937 the Zionist Organization had to do everything in order to prevent the conclusion that the Mandate was unworkable, for without the Mandate the whole Zionist enterprise was in jeopardy. It was, therefore, very unwise, from the Zionist point of view, to exert any pressure that would have had this undesirable result. Political slogans that seemed to imply Zionist domination and disregard of Arab rights had, therefore, to be dismissed as the verbal excesses of 'extremists' that were not endorsed by official Zionism. That task of shielding Zionism by political moderation had to be performed by Weizmann. Steering the Zionist ship through this rough sea was Weizmann's great achievement, and it was for this that he had to pay the penalty of being besmirched as a 'British agent'.

More restrained opponents, who did not doubt his honesty, accused him of 'minimalism' or defeatism. Once a speaker at a Congress derisively called him a 'cunctator'. Indeed, he could be compared to Fabius Cunctator, of whom the Roman poet said:

Unus homo nobis cunctando restituit rem.

He knew precisely what was essential and what was not, and he successfully applied his 'Fabian' tactics to avoid hopeless battles with forces superior to his own. Under the prevailing circumstances and in the political climate of the 'twenties, the maximum to be hoped for was freedom of practical work, as far as the Jews were ready and able to perform it. But in order to pursue this policy, Weizmann had to bare his own chest to the arrows of Zionist criticism, while at the same time he was an untiring and most effective advocate of Jewish demands in the British chancelleries and elsewhere.

As a matter of fact, his accusations of the British Government were most emphatic; there were few, if any, Zionists who could have dared to use similar language. He was not subservient. Sometimes, his unrelenting argument seems imbued with grief and indignation at what he regarded as a personal betrayal. Branding Weizmann as a defeatist or minimalist was a distortion. He knew exactly how far he could go without bringing the relationship with Britain to the breaking-point. He did not condone the obstacles placed in the way of Zionism by the Administration, but in order to argue he had to grasp their point of view. The opposition of the British Occupation Army and later of Colonial administrators to introducing such an explosive element into a country whose order they were responsible for was not wholly mischievous, as Zionist complaints often suggested. There were also many benevolent people among them who were, however, startled by the boldness of the Zionist idea and shocked by the ignorance of local conditions often exhibited by the Zionists. In 1918, when the Zionist Commission under Weizmann's leadership arrived in Cairo on their way to Palestine, Sir Reginald Wingate, British High Commissioner in Egypt, wrote to Lord Hardinge that he found them 'reasonable but woefully uninformed as to conditions in Arab countries'. He therefore 'recommended them to feel their way carefully and do all in their power to show sympathy and goodwill to the Arab and Moslem peoples with whom their future must lie. . . . I also warned them to be very careful in regard to their discussions on the acquisition of land. . . '[1] It was perhaps a tragedy that the Zionists, preoccupied not only with plans for the future (which always had been made without any thought for the Arabs), but also with internal quarrels, failed to heed this warning. Most of them regarded it as a disguised attempt at curbing Zionist activity and thereby condemning it to failure from the very beginning.

One of the psychological facts with which Weizmann had to contend in his relations with the Zionist public was the Jewish inclination to regard all history and all world events as though some conspiracy against the Jews were involved. Pre-Zionist Jewish historiography was mainly laments over persecution and suffered injustice. This was, of course, justified to a certain extent, but other factors and motives had to be appreciated as well. The age-old distrust against the *goy*, the inheritance of generations of oppressed Ghetto Jews, and the experience of Russian Jews since 1882, was not absent in Weizmann himself; but in his close contact with the liberal Western world he had learned to look at things more objectively. As political leader he could not share the popular prejudice that the Jew must always be right and the *goy* always wicked. On the other hand, he knew his Russian Jews very well, he was one of them after all, and he was aware of the difficulties that would inevitably arise from the impossibility of finding a common language between this type of Jew and the British administrators. This anxiety was the source of Weizmann's conflict with Menahem Ussishkin, the declared

[1] Sir Ronald Wingate. *Wingate of the Sudan* (London, Murray, 1955, p. 225. New York, Transatlantic, 1957).

leader of Russian Zionists and President of the 'Odessa Committee', who, after his emergence from Bolshevik Russia, assumed as a matter of course that he would be the only one eligible to stand at the helm of the building up of the National Home. Ussishkin was regarded as the very incarnation of uncompromising nationalism and Zionist will-power. Did he not represent the veterans who had, under most difficult circumstances, built Jewish colonies and acquired land in Palestine in the face of an unfavourable Turkish administration? Without the colonies, whose existence was due not to the official Zionist Organization but to the Odessa Committee and Baron Edmond Rothschild, any Zionist demands during the first World War would have had no basis. Ussishkin was considered the 'man of iron' of Zionism; his slogan was 'nothing can withstand will'. Unconcerned with objective facts, ignorant of the Western world and distrustful of its methods, he came to London in 1920 with a maximalist programme, which seemed to be fantasy to the men of realist outlook merely from a financial point of view, let alone politically. Ussishkin compelled the 1920 Conference to agree to a Colonization budget of four million pounds, and he had little understanding of political complications. After a short time, it became evident that the budget had to be ignominiously cut, not to a half or so, but to ten per cent, and even this money was not available. The years after the Annual Conference of 1920 were marred for Weizmann not only by the unfortunate struggle against Brandeis, but also by the fight against Ussishkin, which in some respects was more difficult because Ussishkin enjoyed a mystical reputation as a stubborn nationalist and a man of the people. Weizmann had to conduct a war on two fronts within the Organization. When at the Conference Brandeis wanted to oust Ussishkin, it proved impossible and Weizmann had to agree to Ussishkin's appointment. Actually, it was clear to Weizmann that Ussishkin was not the man for the job. In 1923, he had to be removed from the chairmanship of the Palestine Executive to the presidency of the Keren Kayemeth land-buying agency. As political representative Weizmann replaced him by Colonel Frederick Kisch, an experienced British soldier and diplomat who had served in India. A man hitherto completely unknown to the Zionist ranks elected to the most delicate office of the movement! It was a bitter pill for the Zionist public to swallow, but ultimately they yielded to Weizmann's pressure as they had to do in other matters, too. Kisch proved to be a good choice and became an ardent Zionist.

The great D-Day of the Jewish Agency came in August 1929. It was the triumph of Chaim Weizmann. 'Seven years of my life or more were consumed by it,' he said. The Great Assembly did not fail to stir the imagination even of the sceptics, a whole galaxy of non-Zionist Jews famous in the world at large, all identifying themselves with what was actually the purpose of Zionism, and expressing solidarity with the Jewish people, was without precedent or parallel, surpassing even the first Zionist Congresses, which had been boycotted by the Jewish 'Establishment' of Western Europe and the United States. Menahem Ussishkin had the greatness to 'acknowledge defeat': he extolled Weizmann as the creator of a new and glorious epoch in Jewish life.

The climax was reached at the Constituent Assembly after the Fifteenth Zionist Congress in Zurich to be followed, alas, immediately by an anticlimax when on 23 August the riots broke out in Palestine that changed the whole scene fundamentally. A still heavier blow was in the offing. The Black Thursday (24 October 1929) at the New York Stock Exchange started an economic catastrophe in America and the world and ruined the hopes of raising more funds for Palestine in the United States. It made the whole edifice collapse like a house of cards and ended in bitter disappointment. A new turn in Zionist history came about only in 1933, when after the advent of Hitler thousands of German Jews fled to Palestine, bringing with them vast capital and enthusiastic—though often ill-conceived and illusionary—initiative to a country on the verge of bankruptcy.

The Jewish Agency was born under an inauspicious star. Shortly after the Zurich Congress it suffered an irreparable blow when the man who was intended to be one of its pillars and its protagonist on the most exposed and important front, Louis Marshall, died on 11 September. He was soon to be followed by another of the key Americans, Lee Frankel. Moreover, the Palestine disturbances and the worldwide economic crash hamstrung the Agency almost from its inception.

It has sometimes been suggested that there was a causal connexion between the setting up of the Agency and the Arab revolt. The convocation of so impressive and potent public figures appeared to the Arabs as a definite threat. They feared that the Zionists, strengthened morally and materially, would step up their offensive for the conquest of Palestine, and they wanted to prejudge such a development by swift action. They were to show the British Mandatory power as well as the Jewish world that the Arabs would not sit idle while their country was being swamped.

It is just possible that such thoughts occurred to the shrewder and more advanced Arab leaders like the Mufti, Hajj Amin el-Husseini and his lieutenants. But the precipitation of the outbreak was perhaps not as premeditated as it seemed. The immediate cause was a Jewish (Revisionist) demonstration at the Wailing Wall, which was construed by the Arabs as an attempt to storm the Aqsa Mosque. It was unwise to follow the Mufti into the trap of religious controversy. This Weizmann had always tried to avoid but he had lost control over events in Palestine. (Unfortunately, Lord Plumer had resigned the High Commissionership in 1928 owing to ill-health.)

The question whether the outbreak of 1929, which at first took the form of ugly murder and, indiscriminate cruel bloodshed against the most peaceful and helpless section of the Jewish community, was the beginning of an Arab 'revolt' or whether it was only as most of the official Zionist commentators and Palestinian pressmen contended, the work of 'robbers and murderers' incited by criminal conspirators, is now of minor historical interest. It may be said that at that time Arab nationalism was not yet fully developed in the European sense, and the collective xenophobia still had a predominantly religious character. Religious and nationalist issues were always confounded in the East. Looking back in 1962, after all we have witnessed in the formerly colonial world, we can hardly doubt that such outbreaks as the 1929 Arab atrocities had a definite political aspect. Indeed, it may be said that relations with the Arabs were now to become the over-riding problem of the Zionist movement. Before the State of Israel was established the Arab problem was also the chief source of paralysis in British Government policy, and today, with the State of Israel surrounded by Arab states, the outlook remains enigmatic.

Nevertheless, seen in historical perspective, Zurich was the crowning of Weizmann's endeavour. It was the last international Jewish gathering of undisturbed splendour and grandeur. It was the work of one man, Chaim Weizmann. He had fought against terrible odds and maintained his faith in spite of furious and obstinate opposition within his own camp. Now he had been blessed in staging an event unique in modern Jewish history, which left its mark on the consciousness of the generation.

Mr Robert Weltsch, journalist and political writer, who now lives in London, was a leader of the German Zionist movement and edited its principal organ. He has written extensively on Israel and on Zionist issues.

CHAPTER NINE

A PORTRAIT IN ACTION

LOUIS LIPSKY

IT IS curious to recall that when Weizmann first appeared on the American scene in 1921 he was preceded by his reputation as a purely cultural, non-political Zionist—an 'Ahad Ha'amist'. He was known as a young man who had contradicted Herzl and had, indeed, crossed swords with him dramatically. His characteristic contribution to Zionism, the development of synthetic 'organic' Zionism, realistically involved in living processes and hence superior to the abstractions that debilitated so much of Zionist oratory, was not as yet well known in the United States.

Weizmann had, to be sure, long since acquired international stature. He had become a distinguished chemist, well known in Great Britain and France, whose work had made an important contribution to the Allied victory in the first World War. A by-product, and a vital by-product, of his scientific work had been financial, and hence to a large extent political independence. The Weizmanns could maintain a luxurious home in London and extend hospitality to many celebrated personalities in the world of politics and science.

Because of his success in scientific and technological work he could once more immerse himself completely in Zionist affairs, in which I had first seen him functioning in 1913, at the Vienna Congress. At that time he had given an impression of studied indifference to what was going on around him. He looked easily bored. In 1913 he was still the promising young man who had debated with Theodor Herzl and the followers of David Wolffsohn at the first Congresses.

At the Vienna Congress he was the chairman of a Congress sub-committee and was called upon to settle internal disputes and to bring in a list of various nominations. As a member of that committee I saw him operating close up. Weizmann's rulings were a study in temperament. He was impatient with *pilpul* and sharp in procedure; he had a mordant sense of humour. He was scheduled to address the

Congress on the Hebrew University, but the imperious Ussishkin took the initiative away from him and announced the beginnings of a fund. Weizmann's *referat* became a matter of no more than academic interest. The older men dominated the caucuses, and Weizmann stood in the rear of the hall, his eyes half closed, listless. He was a ready debater and liked to speak; but in Vienna he lacked drive. He seemed to be listening and waiting. There were few intimations of the coming war. The burden of all speeches was: Get along with the work in Palestine as best you can. The last I remember of the Vienna Congress was Weizmann's look of fatigue as he reported the nominations at the end of the Congress.

By 1921 all that had changed. Weizmann was no longer the apparently listless young man I remembered from the Congress in 1913. He was conscious of standing on a high platform; he had banished the trivial, and spoke as though he were being used by the Jewish cause as its medium.

His leadership had been confirmed at an international conference held in London in 1920. This conference had not only revived the democratic structure of the organization, but thoroughly revised it. This had been of crucial significance. Not only were the main survivors of the war in attendance, including many disoriented Russian Zionists, but a delegation of some forty Americans, led by Louis D. Brandeis, had made its appearance. It was the most substantial American group that had appeared in the international Zionist movement.

England had shown her willingness to accept the Mandate over Palestine, but the actual building of the Jewish National Home was to be the responsibility of the Movement. The miracle of propaganda was to be followed by the even greater miracle of securing the manpower and gathering the material resources for the task of creating the National Home. The funds of the Jewish Colonial Trust could not be used for hazardous enterprises. The meagre resources of the Jewish National Fund were limited to the redemption of the land. There were no reserves.

It was in London that the Keren Hayesod was founded and an appeal issued to world Jewry. The level of giving was raised and an era of large-scale fund-raising set in. A tremendous wave of popular excitement passed over all Jewish communities. The funds raised, however, were always inadequate. There were chronic deficits and strange book-keeping procedures. Weizmann had to devote himself to the continuous grind of collecting funds in every part of the world. He became the most effective of all Zionist propagandists.

The London Conference of 1920, the first conference where a

really massive American delegation played any rôle, revealed a basic divergence of view that had long been ripening beneath the surface of Zionist life in America. There was a dispute at the Conference between European and American Jews, which concentrated on the programme of colonization and how the budget was to be financed. Involved, also, was the question of leadership. The Europeans insisted on the Americans' sharing in the leadership, provided, however, that Brandeis would participate personally in the activities of the administration.

In essence this dispute involved the profoundest issue in the Zionist movement and possibly in Jewish life as a whole. Put most broadly, it involved the question of allegiance and responsibility.

The American movement was at this time under Brandeis's almost unquestioned leadership, and Brandeis, for all his devotion to the Zionist cause, refused to serve it by doing anything that might lay him open to a charge of disloyalty vis-à-vis the United States. He felt it impossible for himself to undertake any obligation whatever to Zionism as a world movement that might in any way infringe on his prior loyalty to the United States. His attitude was, in fact, an early forerunner of a point of view that has beset the Zionist movement since its inception—concern with the question of so-called 'dual loyalty'.

Brandeis's unbending determination not to involve himself in any international enterprise was duplicated on the domestic scene by his distaste for the work of persuasion, harangue and propaganda inherent in any democratic movement. He did not wish to be confined in his behaviour by the necessity of manipulating his own followers in democratic combat, still less of submitting to the influence and control of Jewish representatives outside the United States.

Thus, at the London Conference that proclaimed the Keren Hayesod, when Brandeis categorically refused to accept a responsible position in the joint Zionist campaign aimed at the implementation of the new programme, a breach with the world Zionist movement seemed inevitable.

The issue was joined when Shmarya Levin decided to launch a campaign on behalf of the Keren Hayesod without the approval of the American leadership under Brandeis, who believed that by holding the purse-strings of the largest Jewish community in the world—which he thought he could control—his views should be taken into account regardless of votes at congresses or conferences.

But the masses of American Jews were not controlled by such views. In fact, they were prepared to meet Dr Weizmann as the victor in a movement that had brought recognition of the age-long

Jewish hope. He had helped to make the dream of Herzl a political
reality. They gathered at the Battery and awaited the moment when
he touched American soil. They cheered him on his way to his hotel,
lingering in the lobby for hours for him to appear. The largest mass
demonstration ever held in New York greeted him when he was
given a public reception by a national committee. These audiences
were not impressed by the debate. They were impressed by the
historic facts Dr Weizmann symbolized; to them he was the image
of the national Jewish hope.

The Cleveland Convention of 1921 wrested from Brandeis and his
followers the leadership they had held for seven years. It was developed entirely by the forces of American Zionism; there was no
carpet-bagging influence. Its leadership was American, the methods
adopted were those of American democracy, its publications and
parliamentary tactics had an American authorship. Weizmann would
have preferred to have Brandeis in London, but not Brandeis giving
orders to people in London while he stayed on in the United States.

When Weizmann entered New York Bay in the spring of 1921 to
launch the Keren Hayesod, by an intensification of the campaign
already begun by Shmarya Levin, he found the controversy within
the ranks of American Zionism fully ablaze.

Zionist opinion in the United States was divided in its support of
the Keren Hayesod, which the Jewish Agency depended on for the
initiation of the new tasks imposed on the Zionist movement by the
Mandate.

It was of course impossible for any Zionist agency to operate
without funds, and Weizmann had no reserves. Hence the American
conflict blocked the entire future of the movement. Weizmann, called
upon to carry this whole issue to the Jews of the United States for
settlement in public discussion, assumed a gargantuan task, whose
performance may legitimately be considered a *sine qua non* of the
whole subsequent development of Palestine.

Essentially a man of peace, Weizmann would surely have found it
most compatible with his temperament to accept compromise and let
time settle the issues. But Palestine could not wait. The Americans
wanted to negotiate and Weizmann felt he had no authority to
negotiate. He was dealing with a challenge to the organization maintained intact from Herzl's day as the corporate responsibility of the
Zionist movement. To have departed from that line would have
created two Zionist centres, two Zionist authorities, two Zionist funds
(or more). It would have made the task of the Jewish Agency
impossible.

There were peacemakers who sought to adjust differences. There were turbulent conferences. At times it looked as if Dr Weizmann was about to yield, but his resistance was stiffened by pressures from London and Jerusalem and by his colleagues in New York. His adversary, Brandeis, was a man who had great qualities of endurance, who had fought a powerful railroad group with amazing tenacity, who had evolved his own idea of how Palestine should be rebuilt, and who would not easily be deflected from his course. Brandeis seemed unable to appreciate what the democracy of the Zionist movement meant in terms of economic resources. He seemed to have in mind a planned economy for a people not yet organized, for whom a land had to be prepared, who did not have to be consulted as to what kind of a home should be built for them. His hand was not being forced by time and need.

In the last analysis, American Zionists abandoned Brandeis, or rather, he in effect abandoned American Zionism. By an overwhelming majority American Zionists repudiated the position taken by Brandeis and his friends; they elected a new leadership. Following an un-American tradition, the defeated party retired from the organization, abandoned the struggle and awaited the time when their cause would be vindicated. It never was.

Weizmann gradually won over the Jews of America. He cut deep into the minds of those who had come to the United States from foreign lands, and restored them to the Jewish traditions that American life had been shaking them loose from. More and more they were influenced by ideals that were born in far-off places.

By the time the enlarged Jewish Agency was agreed to in Zurich in 1929, Weizmann had succeeded in bringing together all elements of Jewry—neutrals, sympathizers, and partisans. It may be said that when the extended Jewish Agency was established, with the co-operation of Louis Marshall, Warburg, Léon Blum, Herbert Samuel, Oscar Wasserman and others, Weizmann was at the height of his service to the Zionist movement.

From the very beginning the technique of fund-raising in America that Weizmann adopted was to exalt the vision of Jews to high achievement in all directions. Generally speaking, he depended on individual initiative and on nurturing confidence in the future; he believed in tackling objectives with faith in the sacrifices that Jews were prepared to make, and in raising their hopes for the conquest of the land. He had faith in the dedication and the endurance of Jews during periods of financial difficulty; deficits were to be overcome by the organization of the people.

American oratory has its own standards, which foreigners seldom appreciate. It stems from the rough and ready West. Its dependence upon sound suggests the open spaces. Weizmann did not qualify as an American orator. His voice was not resonant. He had few gestures. He used no grouping introductions or exalted perorations. He hated the impersonation of emotion. He had no ear for the rhythmic phrase. He had acquired the English gift for understatement. He did not propagandize himself as a person. He was not made for stage effects.

In spite of these limitations, no Jewish speaker ever made the same deep and lasting impression—even in the United States. Dr Weizmann spoke as if his words were the issue of suffering. He made the impression of a murky flame that had to be fanned to give heat. Shmarya Levin had burning passion; Sokolow was a master of brilliant narrative and analysis and of sly humour; Ussishkin took his audience by storm with sledge-hammer blows; Bialik spun exciting ideas and fascinated his listeners with figures of speech that did not require form to make them live. Weizmann had none of these qualities. He established an identification of himself with what his words were trying to convey. He seemed to be able to capture the wisdom of Jewish life. He drew his thoughts out of an invisible responsibility. There was prophetic significance in his phrases—a mystery striving to explain itself. There was a stateliness in his speech that was unique. He seemed to speak ex-cathedra for the silent Jewish people. He was their interpreter and advocate. A cause had found a voice for a people emerging from the clouded past and demanding justice from the modern world.

Weizmann had the extraordinary ability to speak to Jews in terms of their ancient heritage, and to summon them to the realization of their immense latent powers. He had the greatest pride in the Jewish heritage, and immense confidence in the positive qualities of the Jews, though he was sometimes agonizingly aware of the many Jewish shortcomings he regarded it as the business of Zionism to eliminate. Though he used curiously few Yiddish expressions when he spoke in public, he seemed somehow to derive his strength from a vast reservoir of Yiddish. He made the impression on his Jewish audiences of a seer, telling them what they could and must do in order to realize their innate powers.

He grew with his responsibilities. His personality acquired stature. It was formed by his intimacy with Jews the world over, as well as by his adjustments to the non-Jewish world. He sensed difficulties before they appeared. He was over-cautious. He never took refuge in formulas or programmes. He coined many formulas but threw them away with great unconcern.

When he spoke to American Jews he saw before him not a fractional part of Jewish life but a microcosm of all Jewries. He saw more Jews from his home town than he had ever seen in Motol or Pinsk. These were the relatives of the Jews of Vilna, of Warsaw, of Bucharest, of Krakow and of Vienna. They were waiting for him to speak and they would·rise and greet the historic opportunity he would describe. They were thirsting for his words. A leadership that could not speak to them in the language they understood, that persisted in going its own way without considering their feelings, prejudices and ideals, would not be able to lead them in the great period of building. These Jews declined to raise any barriers between Zionists in America and Zionists in Europe. They were not aware of any double loyalties. They had become Zionists through the passion of their leaders in Russia, in Poland and in Rumania. They had not been separated from other Jews by time and distance. They were not the lost tribes of Israel. They were kinsmen who had wandered from home and who had found freedom in a new land, but they remembered their origins.

In the course of years, with great patience and skill, Weizmann led some of the dissidents of 1921 back to active Zionist service. But his aim was the winning of the philanthropists and assimilationists. Brandeis had won a number of such converts, but they were not in the leadership of Jewish communal life. The American Jews could be reached only through their responsible organizations, which were growing in influence and resources. Their leaders, however, maintained the traditional opposition of the Reform movement. The implications of Zionist ideology alarmed them. However, when President Wilson gave his approval of the Balfour Declaration and a joint resolution of the American Congress accepted it, the same desire to be loyal to the United States led them to greet the Declaration and to approve of Palestine as the Jewish National Home. Tremendous popular excitement prevailed. There were parades and mass meetings. The Balfour Declaration was regarded as a great historical event. The prejudices of the past—especially against Zionism—were softened, but the Zionists were by-passed. The ideal was ignored but the fact was accepted. The armour of the many non-Zionist reform rabbis was pierced and their hearts were touched. They now became friends of the Land. The philanthropist, Nathan Straus, was interested in several Palestine projects. Samuel Untermeyer, the corporation lawyer, became the head of the American Keren Hayesod. The ageing Jacob H. Schiff, the militant, outspoken opponent of Zionism, publicly reversed himself and expressed his faith in Palestine as a Holy Land, the centre of the Jewish religion.

The new trend toward Palestine gave Weizmann the opportunity to push forward his proposal for an enlarged Jewish Agency. He found a powerful friend in a man of strong convictions who was regarded as the leader of the non-Zionist group. Louis Marshall was a distinguished American but unlike Brandeis, was deeply involved in Jewish communal affairs. He was the chairman of the American Jewish Committee and an officer of the Jewish Theological Seminary. He was stubborn and had strong prejudices; but he could be persuaded by reason. He was greatly influenced by his contact with Jewish leaders when he went to Paris as a member of the American delegation to the Versailles Peace Conference.

Weizmann found in him a loyal friend and stubborn supporter, without whose influence and aid he could not have succeeded in winning non-Zionist co-operation for the Jewish Agency.

Weizmann brought the non-Zionist delegates to Zurich in 1929, when the extended Jewish Agency was formally established. That was a scene without parallel in Jewish history. The leaders of the Jewries of the world were present on its platform. It aroused intense interest throughout the world. With difficulty, the Zionist Congress ratified the constitution of the Agency. Then the non-Zionists followed suit; the American non-Zionists uniting with non-Zionist groups from all parts of the world. Finally, both sections met, and with impressive ceremonies all agreements were sealed.

Thus the Jewish Agency contained two new types of Zionists—whole-hearted Zionists, and practical Zionists who were theoretically non- or even anti-Zionists. In a way it was really a forerunner of the present situation within world Jewry since the triumphant emergence of the State of Israel; world Jewry is almost unanimously pro-Israel without having become Zionist. The edifice of the enlarged Jewish Agency was sturdy enough to withstand the redoubtable shocks that rained down on it from almost the moment it was formed—the death of Louis Marshall, the Passfield-MacDonald White Paper, the Arab riots and the general political attack on the Zionist movement that ensued. The dense interaction between the Jewish Agency and the World Zionist Organization created the mould that eventually gave shape to the eruption of the Jewish State in 1948.

Thus, with the vital and indeed indispensable support of American Jewry, in the form that was assured by the Cleveland Convention of 1921, Weizmann set his stamp on the World Zionist movement and on the state that emerged from it. Despite all Weizmann's political setbacks later on, the institutions of modern Israel are unthinkable without that stamp.

Mr Louis Lipsky of New York City, man of letters, organizer and orator, has been prominent in world Zionism since before the turn of the century. He has served as President of the Zionist Organization of America and member of the World Zionist Executive among other high offices.

1929–1939

CHAPTER TEN

TOWARDS THE PRECIPICE

JULIAN LOUIS MELTZER

THE FOUNDING of the Jewish Agency in August 1929 was certainly the major achievement of Weizmann's middle career. It was a great peak, toward which Weizmann had been striving ever since the Balfour Declaration, and which, with all its shortcomings, dominated the Jewish scene throughout the following decade.

While it is true that its invigorating effect was to be somewhat neutralized by the Arab riots of 1929 and by the worldwide financial crisis caused by the American stock market crash in October that year, nevertheless the establishment of the Agency was one of the major political acts of Weizmann's life.

Many varied and disparate elements of Jewry had been brought together, for the first time in a millennial history, inspired by the single objective of furthering the building up of the National Home. Of the great and famous in Zionism and among the Jewish people, who was not there? Each of the five daily sessions, which lasted until 14 August, had its star orators. Louis Marshall, who, with Weizmann, was one of the chief architects of the extended Agency, and Léon Blum, French Socialist leader; O. E. D'Avigdor Goldsmid, prominent among the Anglo-Jewish 'Brahmins', and Sholem Asch, the Yiddish writer and playwright; the American leaders Louis Lipsky and Rabbi Stephen S. Wise; Hermann Struck, the artist; the venerable Rabbi Ezekiel Lipshitz, President of the Union of Rabbis in Poland, and Dr Lee K. Frankel, the American economist, handsome and silver-haired; Dr Cyrus Adler, of Philadelphia, and Chaim Arlosoroff, of Jerusalem; David Ben-Gurion, David Remez, and Menahem Ussishkin, that Gibraltar of Zionism; Nahum Goldmann, and Rabbi Ben-Zion Uziel, of Tel Aviv (later to become Chief Rabbi of Palestine): hallowed names in Zionist and Jewish history.

For Weizmann, the occasion represented the consummation of seven years of continuous and arduous effort, ever since the League of Nations had in July 1922 awarded Great Britain the Mandate over Palestine. He ended his inaugural address on a hopeful note:

> We have established the extended Jewish Agency in the conviction that we meet as free and equal men and that our partnership rests on mutual respect. The question of convictions cannot be regulated by articles of constitution, but what we can and wish to regulate here is the system of practical work.

As he concluded he was greeted with a standing ovation lasting several minutes.

The scene was the main hall of the picturesque *Tonhalle* of Zurich; the time was mid-afternoon of Sunday, 11 August 1929; and the occasion was the momentous first meeting of the council of the enlarged Jewish Agency. His appearance in the large chamber, accompanied by Louis Marshall, Lord Melchett, Felix Warburg, Herbert Samuel, Albert Einstein, and the bankers Max Warburg and Oscar Wassermann, had evoked a stirring reception. As one newspaper correspondent present described it, jubilant scenes were witnessed 'as the powerful emissaries of world Jewry appeared together on one platform at a gathering which was to lead to the signing of the historic compact between Zionists and non-Zionists, uniting the Jewish people'.

Speaker after speaker, following Weizmann, dwelt on the same high note of hope and promise. In a cordial message read out to the eminent assembly Sir Eric Drummond (later the Earl of Perth), Secretary-General of the League of Nations, declared in part:

> The Palestine Mandate recognizes the principle of the establishment of the Jewish National Home in the country.... It seems evident that the steps now being taken to put the Agency and thereby the efforts to carry out the ideals of Zionism on a larger basis cannot but be favourable to the accomplishment of the aims laid down in the Mandate.... Today's event will always be regarded as a happy one in the interests of both Palestine and the Jewish people in all parts of the world.

Yet, for all the grandeur of the event and the general elation of mood, Weizmann was under no false illusions as to the attitude of the non-Zionists towards the ideological content and purport of Zionism. With his masterly flair for understatement, he had made this clear in the inaugural address. In touching upon the difficulty of regulating convictions by statutes and official formulas, he indicated subtly how he felt about the chances for success during the initial phases of the Zionist and non-Zionist partnership. He knew full well the

character of those convictions; over the years, his close contacts with
the non-Zionist leaders, especially those in the United States and
Germany, had given him an intimate insight into their thoughts and
feelings about a Jewish state.

But he was an óptimist, too; his sanguine outlook was as evident
as his realistic assessment of the prospects. Earlier in his opening
address he had said, 'I earnestly trust that the labours of the Council
will redound to the lasting advantage of the Jewish people and to
the honour of the Jewish name.'

Although the signing of the document that formally set up the
Agency was a foregone conclusion, the discussion of the text, as well
as the form and methods of operation, took up most of the five
sessions. The final ceremony, however, made up for all the hours upon
hours of argument and debate. Following Weizmann and Nahum
Sokolow, who signed for the World Zionist Organization, the representatives of Jewish communities in twenty countries including
Palestine appended their signatures. It read like a roll-call of celebri-
ties. Then, according to the *New Palestine* (New York, 25 August
1929) an unusual scene took place:

> After Weizmann and Marshall had signed, these two Jewish
> leaders, the first a chemist of high standing, a dignified leader of a
> great movement, and the other a distinguished constitutional
> lawyer, a man of 73 years, noted for his calm logic, threw aside all
> pretence of unemotionality and embraced and kissed each other
> with unashamed tears in their eyes. Other delegates could be seen
> doing the same. Zionists and non-Zionists indiscriminately cele-
> brated the historic occasion with a lavish display of affection.

One of the mementos of the occasion, now among the Weizmann
Archives at Rehovoth, is a message which Einstein scribbled to Weiz-
mann on the spur of an obviously thrilling moment. Using the Dolder
Hotel notepaper, Einstein wrote:

*An diesem Tage ist die Saat Herzls und Weizmanns in wunder-
barer Weise gereift. Keiner von den Anwesenden blieb unbewegt.*
                              A. Einstein. 11. VIII. 29.

Weizmann's opening address at the founding conference of the
Jewish Agency Council and his subsequent contributions to the discussion were no mere rhetorical flourishes, but the delineation of a
definite goal and purpose. This was evident from what had happened
during the preceding two weeks. The Sixteenth Zionist Congress had
opened in the *Stadttheater* at the Zurich lakeside on Sunday afternoon, 28 July, in the presence of hundreds of delegates and guests,

'with a pomp and solemnity such as no previous Congress witnessed', according to the *New Palestine*. One Hebrew writer observed at the time, 'A sense of destiny pervades this gathering; we are in the ante-chamber of history.'

During the stormy proceedings Weizmann had fought tooth and nail for the adoption of the Agency constitution against opponents and critics who were still dubious about the proposed alliance with the non-Zionists. For all his disappointment and grief in later years at the way in which the non-Zionists manipulated their partnership in the Jewish Agency, he never lost faith in the original motives underlying its creation. He remained inflexibly dedicated to the ideal of Jewish unity in the building up of the National Home; and, in line with his credo of 'political acts backed by practical facts', his oft-proclaimed synthesis of Zionism, he was prepared to endure much that was unpalatable for the sake of fostering the material aspects of the undertaking.

Weizmann's attendance at the Sixteenth Congress was his first appearance at an official Zionist gathering after practically six months in retirement due to severe illness. He had been under constant medical treatment since the end of 1928. He had then returned to London from the second of two onerous fund-raising tours and political negotiations with the non-Zionists in the United States that year. The cumulative toll of his activities had brought him to the verge of physical collapse in December, and he remained bedridden for many weeks. Even his hurried trip to Palestine in April 1929 had been undertaken against doctors' orders. He had wanted to be in the country at the same time as the bankers Felix Warburg and his brother Max, who had decided to pay a visit at Passover, so as to ensure that they came away with the proper impressions. He was apprehensive about the possibility of friction between the Yishuv leaders and the non-Zionist visitors.

In the event, there was no need for him to have worried. Their visit produced excellent results, both for the Yishuv and themselves; their morale remained unimpaired; for himself, fortunately there were no untoward effects upon his health. On the contrary, he benefited enormously from his ten-day visit. To some, 'the air of Eretz Israel maketh wise', as the Jewish sages had it; to him, it was a case of 'the air of Eretz Israel maketh well'.

Weizmann's greatly improved condition by the time of the Congress at the end of July was a great relief to his friends and adherents. The first session, at which he gave the opening address, was devoted to the twenty-fifth anniversary of Herzl's death; he delivered a glowing tribute to his memory. He then surveyed the progress made in

Zionist work in the previous two years 'to convert the neglected soil into the fruitful and blossoming land which is to become the home of the Jewish people', and went on to speak of 'the negotiations with the American non-Zionists (which) have created the basis upon which the structure of the enlarged Jewish Agency can be erected'.

He said:

We Zionists were always convinced that after the attainment of our political goal our functions would have to be changed. The Jewish National Home, which already exists, is no longer merely a Zionist affair; it is a Jewish affair. It is a centripetal force which attracts Jewish energies from all parts of the world by its mere existence. Through the fact of its existence alone it brings about a union and association of Jews for the purpose of a common cause. It has been a source of gratification to us to be able to observe this wonder-working power of Palestine.

Congress ran its customary polemical length; the usual—some called it 'inescapably traditional'—late-night sessions lasting into the small hours of the morning were part of the experience. Debater after debater entered the lists, among them Vladimir Jabotinsky. Weizmann intervened during the seventh session on Wednesday evening, 31 July, and—according to a contemporary report—'at its close he received an ovation that lasted for ten minutes'. Clause by clause, the draft Agency statutes were hostly contested after the discussion of them began on 7 August. This went on throughout the fourteenth session, which lasted a record fourteen hours and ended only at 2:40 AM Friday morning, 9 August, with a vote of 230 against 30 for the slightly modified draft. The sixteenth and final session of Congress closed in the early hours of Sunday, and that same afternoon the delegates repaired to the *Tonhalle* for the first Agency Council session.

Weizmann left Zurich with his wife for a holiday at the mountain resort of Wengen, in the Bernese Oberland, nine days after the Council meetings had ended. Weizmann was still exhilarated by a sense of achievement. As he described it in *Trial and Error* many years later: 'I felt free from care, I anticipated confidently a future which would witness a great acceleration in the building up of the National Home.'

The date of their journey to Wengen was a fateful one, 23 August 1929, the very Friday of the Arab outbreaks in Jerusalem, from which the violence later spread to other parts of the country.

With the Jewish state now a living and concrete reality, independently governed by its own democratic institutions and represented on international councils, one cannot help being struck by the utter improbability of it all. It seems incredible, looking over the record of events in the ten years after the Zurich gathering, that anything short of total failure could have awaited the Zionist cause, let alone the Yishuv's metamorphosis into sovereign nationhood.

Certainly the Arab attacks upon the Yishuv, more especially the pre-1914 pious communities, launched a few days after the delegates left Zurich, could have spelled the doom of Jewish national hopes, so lately soaring. The outbreaks originated through religious incitement. Some weeks earlier the ,Supreme Moslem Council, of which the president was the Mufti of Jerusalem, Hajj Mohammed Amin el-Husseini, had begun cutting a new door from the Aqsa Mosque directly into the enclosure of the *Kotel Maaravi*—the Western Wall —behind it. These building works were an infringement of the *status quo* regulations at the Western Wall; they were intended to give Moslem worshippers direct access from the Mosque area into the approach to the Jewish shrine. Much to general Jewish indignation, the Palestine Administration took no effective steps to halt the breach of the standing regulations, and of the wall, and tension began to mount.

The Agency Council had ended its sittings at Zurich on Wednesday. That same evening was Erev Tisha b'Ab, the eve of Lamentations commemorating the destruction of the Temple in Jerusalem in 70 CE; throughout that night thousands of pious Jews made the pilgrimage through the walled Old City to the *Kotel Maaravi*. The next day, the 9th of Ab, a protest parade of some two thousand Jewish youths marched to the Wall as a demonstration against the supine attitude of the authorities towards the Moslem building works. It was followed on Friday by an incursion of hundreds of inflamed Moslems from the Mosque area into the Wall enclosure, where they damaged and destroyed prayer-books and ritual articles and wounded the Jewish beadle and another Jewish bystander.

Passions mounted in Jerusalem throughout the ensuing week, and the climax came with the attacks by armed Arab townsmen and peasants, nine days after Tisha b'Ab, on 23 August. It was the signal for the massacres that took place among the Jewish communities at Hebron and Safad, and the assaults on Jewish settlements elsewhere. Before the violence was quelled, 133 Jews were killed and 339 injured; and 116 Arabs were killed and 232 wounded, mainly in fighting British police and troops. Property and livestock damage ran into hundreds of thousands of pounds.

The after-effects were considerable and far-reaching. Weizmann received the news of the initial attacks in Jerusalem as though 'struck by a thunderbolt', as he wrote in his autobiography. He and Mrs

Weizmann returned hurriedly to London, where he started on his futile round of calls and attempted interviews with leading members of the Government. He tried to see the Prime Minister, Ramsay MacDonald, but his efforts were fruitless. The Colonial Secretary, Lord Passfield (formerly Sidney Webb), no friend of the Zionist cause at the best of times, similarly avoided seeing Weizmann for some time; when he called at Passfield's home with Colonel Josiah Wedgwood, they were received only by Lady Passfield (Beatrice Webb). In their conversation she showed little sympathy for what had happened; Dr Weizmann quoted her remarkable comment: 'I can't understand why the Jews make such a fuss over a few dozen of their people killed in Palestine. As many are killed every week in London in traffic accidents, and no one pays any attention.'

The trend of impending developments became obvious to the Zionist President before long. As he wrote, 'When at last I managed to see Passfield and his friends in the Colonial Office I realized at once that they would use this opportunity to curtail Jewish immigration into Palestine. . . . The machinery was set in motion for the political attack on our position in Palestine.' From then on it was a long, hard and painful struggle against the Socialist Government and the entrenched bureaucracy at the Colonial Office: the Foreign Office was not to enter the arena against Zionism until almost two decades later: and Weizmann fought it, both in and out of presidential office, with vigour and determination.

One document of that period that makes interesting reading now, thirty-three years later, was a memorandum drawn up at a conference of prominent Jewish personalities at Marienbad, in Czechoslovakia. The conference, summoned on 28 August 1929, five days after the Jerusalem outbreak of rioting, framed ten specific demands that Dr Weizmann was asked to present on behalf of Palestine Jewry to the British Government. The memorandum began by urging Whitehall 'to issue a statement in clear and unmistakable terms that the recent disturbances in Palestine on the part of the Arabs have in no way affected its policy regarding the establishment of the Jewish National Home as enunciated in the Balfour Declaration and laid down in the terms of the Mandate for Palestine'.

The other demands set out in the memorandum pertained to the remedying of salient shortcomings in British policy, more particularly in the spheres of immigration and defence and in regard to the status of the Western Wall. The signatories were Chaim Nachman Bialik, who presided, Meyer Dizengoff, David Yellin, Dr Benzion Mossinsohn, Dr Moshe Glickson, Morris Rothenberg, Meyer W. Weisgal, Dr F. Rottenstreich, Dr Nahum Goldmann, Nathan D. Kaplan, and

Joseph Weiss. Meyer Weisgal, then Secretary of the Zionist Organization of America, was requested to proceed forthwith to London and hand the document to Dr Weizmann.

While the shock of the August disturbances still reverberated through the Jewish world, a second blow stunned it at this time. Louis Marshall, who had been elected Chairman of the Agency Council with Lord Melchett as co-Chairman, passed away after a grave illness which had stricken him following the Council sessions. He was the stalwart among the non-Zionist supporters of the extended Agency plan and the prime mover in the efforts to bring the group into the partnership. His death at this critical juncture was regarded as of near-calamitous proportions.

Had Marshall lived a few more years, the glittering promise of those days of awe and noble purpose ushered in at the founding of the extended Agency might have been promoted by the non-Zionist elements with somewhat less reluctance than they began to evince. His broad vision and dynamism had swept along those of his associates who had started to be somewhat timorous in their evaluation of a programme of combined Jewish action for national redemption. The level of thinking and planning among the group dropped appreciably after Marshall's passing. The attitude towards the Jewish State idea became so inimical as, in one notable instance in later years, to evoke a terrific blast from Weizmann against one of the American members of the Agency Executive representing the non-Zionists. His letter was a masterpiece of polite and restrained vituperation.

Instead of the American and other non-Zionist leaders coming out to settle in Jerusalem to share in the direction of affairs, professional executives were sent. Although efficient and useful, they were no substitute for top leadership. Rifts and divisions set in over petty issues, and discord extended into a wider area of ideology and methodology. The deterioration of relations with the British Government from the end of 1929 on was hardly calculated to make things easier for Weizmann and his Zionist colleagues; indeed, one dark suspicion that lurked in Zionist minds at the time was that the Whitehall policy-makers hoped the experiment of the enlarged Jewish Agency would fail, thus lending more force to the process of whittling down or ignoring the commitments under the Balfour Declaration that, as one cynic remarked, began on 3 November 1917.

Lamentably the days of awe and noble purposes were tempered by a creeping sense of disappointment. Yet Weizmann's faith in the ultimate establishment of the State and his optimistic appraisal of the less remote future were unimpaired. Critics accused him of lulling the credulous into a sense of false security by these statements, but it was a stable trait of his Zionism. In December 1929, he addressed the Anglo-Palestine Club in London in these terms:

> The late events have proved that not a single Jew in Palestine has been shaken. The Jews in London and New York are more frightened than the Jews of Jerusalem. . . . No amount of pogroms will frighten us, no amount of hot air let loose even by our own Zionists will deter us from our purpose. We will work with the Arabs to build up Palestine as the country in which two peoples will live in respect and friendship. . . . We are in Palestine and we shall stay.

Privately Weizmann coined an apophthegm that Lord Samuel was to quote to Mrs Weizmann many years later, after her husband's death. He said: 'Difficulties take a long time to solve; the impossible always takes a little longer.'

One of the initial steps taken by the British Government in the wake of the 1929 disturbances was to suspend negotiations for a Legislative Council, for which in any event neither the Jews nor Arabs were eager; another was to appoint a commission of inquiry under Sir Walter Shaw, which came out two months later. It was the first in a long and wearisome procession of inquiries, collective and individual, which filled the shelves with reports between 1929 and 1947.

A principal by-product of the Shaw Commission's report was the decision to send Sir John Hope Simpson to conduct a spot investigation of the so-called development potential. In his findings he made much of the concept of 'absorptive capacity' first bruited in the Churchill White Paper of 1922. Thus was the basis laid for the British Government's new policy of restricting immigration and suspending Jewish land purchases from Arabs: the Passfield White Paper of 21 October 1930.

Reaction was immediate, outraged and worldwide. Weizmann resigned the presidency of the Jewish Agency: Lord Melchett and Felix Warburg resigned as Chairman of the Council and Chairman of the Administrative Committee of the Agency respectively. The Government was very much taken aback by the unpopular vote at the division after the famous House of Commons debate on 17 November and by the widespread sympathy expressed for the Zionist cause. Private talks went on with a special Cabinet committee headed by Mr Arthur Henderson, and less than four months after it had been announced the Passfield policy was discreetly yet none the less effectively reversed. Ramsay MacDonald's letter to Weizmann dated 13 February 1931, whilst not an explicit withdrawal of the White

Paper, none the less led in due course to a significant change in the official attitude.

It was Weizmann's view that, irrespective of its form as a document, 'the letter rectified the situation'. Under its terms the Palestine Administration changed from cold to lukewarm towards the Jewish national affair, especially after Sir Arthur Wauchope succeeded Sir John Chancellor in 1932 as High Commissioner. Immigration rose to 40,000 in 1934 and to 62,000 the following year. Weizmann emphasized a salutary contrast: 'Jabotinsky, the extremist, testifying before the Shaw Commission, had set 30,000 a year as a satisfactory figure.'

Throughout his career the pattern of Weizmann's activities fell broadly into three well-defined divisions: the external political struggle, the internal political struggle, and his intermittent return to science. In his political guise he was active on two fronts: the one, vis-à-vis the statesmen, politicians and government officials of Great Britain, the United States, and other countries; the other, vis-à-vis the politicos, party members and sectarians of the Zionist movement and its fringe bodies, whether on the extreme right or the extreme left, both inside and outside the Zionist Organization. From the clamour and tumult of these battles, from the dust and din of many a Congress fracas, from the hurts caused by 'the slings and arrows of outrageous fortune', he often turned with relief to his beloved laboratory; there are many indications to show his olfactory preference for the smell of chemicals to the smell of Zionist party strife.

Detached though he was in habit of mind and thought, and scornful of petty intrigues and bickering, he was not insusceptible to the barbs of internal criticism; indeed, he sometimes displayed an undue sensitivity to them. An illustration of this facet of his character can be seen in his reply to critics at the Seventeenth Congress at Basle in July 1931.

It was at the evening session on Tuesday, 7 July. He began by saying that as 'at all previous Congresses, it has again been my fate to listen for hours on end to criticism and attacks against myself—this time perhaps to a greater extent than ever before.' To his mind, the moment was too grave for them to indulge in polemics; it was a difficult time for Zionism, and the gravity of the hour imposed upon all of them the utmost degree of responsibility for their utterances.

He vigorously defended the Executive's handling of the 'Mac-Donald Letter' issue. It was perfectly plain from the terms of the letter itself, he said, that where a conflict existed, it was the letter and not the (Passfield) White Paper that must prevail. Such was the opinion of authoritative legal and political circles in England. Then, in one of his famous mordant broadsides: 'I have been unfortunately unable to descry in the speeches of the Opposition any hint as to how the existing discrepancy between the possible and the desirable is to be removed.' The concluding part of his address reads today like a litany of faith. He said:

> We Jews have always had to suffer from being misunderstood. Zionism and its realization in Palestine is an attempt to remove this misunderstanding. It is perhaps one of the greatest of our difficulties, and it would be naïve to believe that ten years of work suffice to overcome such obstacles. I do not believe that Palestine can be attained through a short-cut. What I believe is that we shall attain our National Home through hard tedious and deep suffering. We are all bound up together in strong faith in the Zionist idea and its realization. But deep faith in a cause is not manifested through heroic phrases but through the patience with which daily difficulties are met. In this spirit we must continue on our way without hesitation. . . .

According to the Congress protocol, there was loud and prolonged applause at the end of his reply. But the mood of majority was inexorable; and on a roll-call ballot, they passed a resolution of non-confidence in his policy. Thus was he voted out of office.

It was a bitter moment and a bitter pill to swallow. The memory of it was to linger for many years, until the end of his life. Yet at that juncture, as he recorded later, he fought against brooding over the event or allowing his emotions to overpower his judgment. Although troubled by some misgivings about his age and the rapid advances made by chemistry since he had left it, he decided to open a laboratory in London. He was now in his fifty-eighth year and had not been inside a laboratory, except for a casual visit, for some thirteen years, since 1918. It was a daring step to take; he felt as if he were starting out in science all over again.

One might interpolate at this point, as an illustration of the dichotomy which had developed in his life, the reminiscence of a conversation Mrs Weizmann had with him in 1917. As she recalled it many years later, he had finished his work on acetone, and he said to her, 'I cannot serve two mistresses, politics and science. I must choose between one of them. Which shall I give up?' She went on: 'This wise man, who was extraordinarily naïve in some respects, added, "If I give up science, it won't be for long. Jews need the Land, Eastern European Jews need the country. American Jews have the money. It is simple: Jews will give the money, we shall transport the people to Palestine, the problem will be settled, and I shall go back to my beloved science." '

As Mrs Weizmann commented, it was not to be; he was taken away from science. And one cannot help but speculate that, at the back of his mind, he always felt he had made the wrong choice.

But in spite of the drawbacks of a long absence from research, Dr Weizmann embarked with some success on new ventures in organic and biochemistry. After the Daniel Sieff Research Institute began to function in 1934, his scientific publications poured out in steady succession until 1951; and they form a substantial number of the seventy-seven papers he contributed, during his scientific periods, to leading professional journals.

Like Cincinnatus, Weizmann was not permitted to remain in retirement without interruption. But it took the Zionists much less time to importune him with requests and saddle him with tasks than the nineteen years before the Romans in their day sought out their leader on his farm.

That Weizmann was not entirely averse from entertaining these offers may be judged from his remarks: 'I found it impossible, in those years of crisis ... to abstract myself even temporarily from Jewish life.' But, this time unlike Cincinnatus, he was not offered dictatorship over his people; Zionist procedures were far too democratic for that.

Thus there came about that period in Weizmann's life when, in spite of his devotion to laboratory routines, he found himself 'loaded with outside obligations'. It was an indeterminate kind of existence; he was not actually in formal office, yet informally he was still part of the Zionist establishment. He was turned to for counsel, advice and active help time without number; and he continued to occupy the presidency of the Jewish Agency and Zionist Organization in all but name: a circumstance that greatly annoyed Nahum Sokolow, the official incumbent.

His 'outside obligations' during the interregnum between 1931 and 1935 included the presidency of the English Zionist Federation and of the Youth Aliya, and the chairmanship of the Central Bureau for the Settlement of German Jews set up by the Jewish Agency when Hitler's menace became potent. He continued his extensive exchange of correspondence with people all over the world, much of it by hand, as evidenced by the holographs in the Rehovoth archives. Some of these letters survive in draft form; they were never mailed. One of his favourite maxims was, 'You never regret the letters you do not send.'

Among other chores Weizmann undertook fund-raising missions overseas. His tour of South African Jewish communities with Mrs Weizmann, and accompanied by Dr Alexander Goldstein, on behalf of Keren Hayesod during the first five months of 1932, was an unqualified moral and financial triumph. Not only did he bring the eagerly awaited word of Zion to scores of small communities, some of them hardly more than a score of families in size, but he achieved a record collection unparalleled in any previous campaign in the Union. There was hardly a city, town or market centre where he did not address a Zionist society, communal organization, club or lodge. Their itinerary quartered the map—Potchefstroom, Krugersdorp, Pretoria, Johannesburg, Germiston, Benoni, to which a capacity audience flocked from many small townships and outlying farms on the *veldt*; Durban, Bloemfontein, Kimberley; Burghersdorp and Queenstown; East London, Grahamstown, Port Elizabeth, Oudtshoorn, and Capetown; the Rhodesias, North and South. These names are taken at random from their travel schedule; these Jewish communities were among the many that increased their contributions to Keren Hayesod by as much as fifty per cent over the 1930 campaign figure: the 'tradition' in South African Jewry has always been biennial drives.

It was not entirely unpleasant to travel around in South African summer, and they had relaxations—including a visit to a huge game reserve, where they saw lions roaming around freely. But it must have been an exacting routine before they embarked on 13 May on the SS *Windsor Castle* from the Cape of England. Weizmann's humour remained pristine; and an amusing incident occurred at one of the final banquets of the tour. The chairman of the evening rose and announced his donation of an equivalent amount in guineas to the Hebrew numerical value of the guest of honour's first name: Chaim—68. Whereupon Weizmann stood up and remarked amid loud laughter and applause, that he had a second name, Azriel, of which the Hebrew letters combined into a total value of 318!

One message which Weizmann left behind, during an address at Bloemfonetein, holds an authentic ring of prophecy that thirty years of history have failed to dim:

With all the difficulties in their way, the Jews demonstrated that Palestine could be built up and that Jews could build it up. They conducted their work by the strength of a great ideal. This ideal moved the earth and a little of heaven. It produced a new breed of men as if by a miracle.

During the four years he remained out of supreme Zionist office, from
the Seventeenth until the Nineteenth Zionist Congress, Dr Weizmann
forsook one aspect of his pattern of activities; of this he wrote in
Trial and Error:

> I took no part in the inner political struggles of the Zionist
> Organization and did not even attend the Eighteenth Congress,
> that of 1933. I was extremely chary of lending colour to any
> accusation that I was 'planning a return', or that I was in any
> way hampering the activities of the Executive then in power.

But he bent his full energies to the two other aspects, the external
political struggle and the creation of the Daniel Sieff Research Institute at Rehovoth. Within the compass of the first, he went on with
his quiet diplomacy in the high quarters where he was *persona grata*,
with the knowledge of members of the Executive, Selig Brodetsky
among them; while as for the second, he felt that in returning to
science he was helping to fashion a new and vital force in the building of the National Home.

Late in December 1932 he paid the last visit of his life to Germany.
He went to Munich to consult with Richard Willstatter on the scientific programme of the Daniel Sieff Institute and to invite him to the
opening ceremony the following spring. Whilst there, at a gathering
in the home of the local Jewish community head, Eli Strauss, a
veteran Zionist and an old friend, he bluntly warned them to clear
out of the country. 'Hitler means every word he said,' Weizmann
cautioned. 'If you cannot get out now, send your money to Palestine.
We don't want it, we won't use it. Keep it there, so that when you
eventually come, you won't be penniless.'

In the event, about eight million pounds sterling in goods and other
media were sent from Germany to Palestine under the *Ha'avara* or
transfer scheme.

It was for the same cause, the rescue of German Jewry, that he
undertook a brief and dramatic visit to the United States early in
July 1933 at the invitation of Meyer Weisgal. He spoke on Jewish
Day at the 'Century of Progress' exposition in Chicago organized by
Weisgal. The vast Soldiers Field with its 131,000 seats was insufficient
to hold the concourse drawn from all over Illinois and other states
by the magic of Weizmann's name. And Weizmann received the fee
of 100,000 dollars which Weisgal promised if he came—a handsome
honorarium for those days, and for these, too!—and which he
utilized, as he said, to open 'a new business'—the fund for German
Jewish refugees. It was while travelling to the United States by ship
on the Saturday that he received word, both from Mrs Weizmann

and Selig Brodetsky, of the murder of Chaim Arlosoroff on the beach in Tel Aviv. Mrs Weizmann, who had been told of the dastardly act over the telephone from London, cabled him from the country home of Lord William Percy where she was a week-end guest, and Brodetsky cabled from London. He at once sent back a message expressing his shock and conveying his condolences.

The Daniel Sieff Research Institute was inaugurated with much éclat on 3 April 1934, on a site adjoining the Jewish Agency's Agricultural Experiment Station at Rehovoth. It was an impressive occasion. The notables of science rubbed shoulders with notables in other walks of life. A new epoch of scientific pioneering in Jewish Palestine was initiated. As Israel M. Sieff put it at a memorial gathering in Rehovoth twenty years later:

> He saw in the Institute the beginning of true scientific research and the acquisition of knowledge and experience which would fructify the life and the spirit of the country. . . . He saw scientific knowledge as a means of breaking down every obstacle which stood in the way of the economic and social progress of the country, as well as a means of accelerating the application and practice of fundamental knowledge to the life of the people.

From then on Weizmann spent a good deal of his time at this beloved centre of research whenever he was in the country; and made use of his study in the Daniel Sieff Institute both for his scientific work and for political meetings and consultations after his resumption of the Zionist presidency. It was more than a *pied-à-terre* in Rehovoth; it was a haven. Science had always been his sheet anchor.

When the Nineteenth Congress met at Lucerne in 1935, Weizmann, not without some justified misgivings, acceded to the pleas of supporters and former adversaries to return to the official leadership. His decision stemmed from a keen recognition of the increasingly critical situation in the Mediterranean area, and he reached it not without a sardonic reflection that he would probably 'again be made the scapegoat for the sins of the British Government'. For he remained loyal to his spiritual affinity with England and to his firm belief that the Zionists must continue to throw in their lot with that country.

Intervening in the general debate on 27 August, he declared:

> Notwithstanding our differences of opinion with the Mandatory Power, the Jewish people must never forget that it is to England that we owe this opportunity of discharging a memorable historic function. It is only to be expected that transitory difficulties will

from time to time arise in our day-to-day contacts, but there will none the less always remain the basic solidarity between ourselves and Great Britain, of which our achievements in Palestine are the outward and visible sign.

And also:

From the great cultural and scientific centre which is now growing up in Palestine, we hope that light and learning may radiate throughout the neighbouring countries, and that their Arab inhabitants may be among the first to benefit. But that will only be possible when we have built up a strong Jewish Palestine, and have thereby assured peaceful co-operation between all elements of the population, both there and in Transjordan.

Again he had to pick up the threads loosened or severed when he had stepped out of office four years later. Once more there were the meetings with Prime Ministers and government officials, the contacts with prominent members of the League of Nations and its Permanent Mandates Commission, and with an eminent trio in particular— William Rappard of Switzerland, Lord Lugard of Great Britain, and Pierre Orts of Belgium. Once more the innumerable talks, the private interviews, the conferences *in camera*, the elucidations and representations.

It was ceaseless, purposeful and patient diplomacy, which drew its sole authority and support from moral principles and the canons of social justice. It had to counter the evasiveness of governments and functionaries who weighed up ethical positions against political expedience, and made no bones about which must be the more compelling. There could hardly have been a world diplomat, whose letters of credence were his own persuasiveness, more experienced than Weizmann in the shifts and stratagems practised by those with whom he had dealings in the capitals of the world.

But he had never been a cynic for the sake of sterile cynicism, nor a defeatist accepting the shabbiness of defeat as an ineluctable alternative; in spite of the interminable frustrations and disappointments with which his mission to the Gentiles was studded, he persevered in what came to be universally recognized as the greatest one-man diplomatic errand in history.

Several months after the close of the Zionist Congress at Lucerne, or, to be precise, at the end of December 1935, the Colonial Office in London for some reason felt the time propitious for the revival of the proposal for a Legislative Council in Palestine. Upon being approached Dr Weizmann and his colleagues on the Agency Executive rejected the plan in the form offered, on the grounds that its intent and implementation would after a while crystallize the Yishuv at permanent minority status. On the other hand, the Arab nationalist leaders appeared inclined to proceed with the talks; although their attitude had always been outright repudiation of the Mandate because it incorporated the Balfour Declaration, and their proclaimed policy was the complete independence of Palestine under Arab majority rule, a slight crack developed in their stone-walled front, and there were signs of an amenable response on their part to Sir Arthur Wauchope's overtures.

They were invited to send a deputation to London representing the five different Arab parties. But under the impact of the familiar clan rivalries they failed to reach agreement on the composition of the delegation, and their collective amenability evaporated. In any event, the Arab rebellion that broke out in the wake of the general Arab strike in Palestine in the spring of 1936 finally scotched the plan altogether. From then until the fateful post-second World War period it was not to be heard of again.

That was the year of Haile Selassie's departure into exile from Ethiopia after vainly resisting Mussolini's invasion; of Hitler's *coup* in the Rhineland; of the widespread strikes in France; of the great Communist purge trials in Russia; and of the Spanish civil war. Across this ominous canvas the Arab rising blasted its fiery path as yet another eruptive element of the doomed latter half of the 'thirties. A perplexed and fearful world read the headlines and wondered what new disaster was on its way.

For the better part of three years, at each end of the Mediterranean, the civil war in Spain and the fighting in Palestine dragged on their parallel bitter courses. In the one country, in the West, intervening by scheming Powers was overt; in the other, in the East, it was covert. By the end of the Palestine rebellion in August 1939, the toll had reached 5,774 casualties, of whom 450 Jews were killed and 1,944 wounded, 140 British killed and 476 wounded, and 2,287 Arabs killed and 1,477 wounded: of the latter, many by their own compatriots for reasons of revenge and blood-feuds, besides those who fell or were injured in clashes with the security forces and Jewish defenders. The property damage in urban and rural areas, and the harm done to the country's economy, were incalculable.

Throughout the beleaguered years the Yishuv pursued a policy of *Havlagah*, or self-restraint, which Weizmann extolled as 'one of the great moral political acts of modern times'. The concept of *Havlagah* contained more than a discipline of non-aggression and refusal to launch physical reprisals, and of self-defence only in the face of direct attack. It provided also a vigorous response to violence through the medium of constructive effort, and it was the spur to the creation of 'political facts by practical acts'. In short, the Arab rebellion of 1936–1939 was matched by a new accession of Zionist land pioneering, the dominant theme of the epoch which witnessed the building of the watch-tower and stockade settlements and of which Hanita, in Upper Galilee, begun in 1936, was the proud symbol.

The cycle of civil commotion and administrative restrictions imposed upon the victims was a heavy burden for the Yishuv to carry. Dr Weizmann was compelled to admit ruefully in later years that 'violence paid political dividends to the Arabs, while Jewish *Havlagah* was expected to be its own reward'. The Palestine Government's report for 1936 to the League Mandates Commission did not even mention the Jewish policy of self-restraint, and in June 1937, after the report was published, Weizmann was provoked into writing from London a letter of stinging rebuke to High Commissioner Wauchope in Jerusalem.

But the carcass of those murdered years hid a trove of honey, as did the carcass of the lion told of in the fourteenth chapter of the Book of Judges; and to the sweetness thereof, as Samson testified in his day, may be likened some of the circumstances that produced the Report of the Palestine Royal Commission.

The Palestine Royal Commission marks a watershed in Zionist history, and, indeed, in the history of the State of Israel, for it was at one of its hearings that the notion of Jewish sovereignty on a specific territory was given concrete expression. For the Zionist movement it was the turning-point in the political struggle for official acceptance of the Jewish people's historic right in Eretz Israel; this was the first time that a body as august as the Royal Commission had given thought and voice to the very idea of such acceptance: and it might well be regarded as the moment of dawning truth for the appraisal of Zionist realities.

The Royal Commission was appointed by the British Government in May 1936, a month or so after the fresh outbreak of Arab violence, 'to investigate the causes of unrest and alleged grievances of Arabs or of Jews' and to submit appropriate recommendations for their solution. It was not until November of that year, however, that the Commission actually went out to Palestine; and by the time it left, two months later, it had heard 113 witnesses at 30 public and 40 private sessions, and on returning to London heard 10 more at one public and 8 private sessions.

Much has been written over the years about the Royal Commission and the high quality of its composition. Writing in *Trial and Error*, Dr Weizmann gave his judgment as follows:

Many of us felt that this was not only an extremely competent body, but that it would prove to be both thorough and impartial. The findings of such a commission, we believed, would go a long way towards solving our problems. For my own part . . . I became deeply convinced that a new and possibly decisive phase in our movement might now be beginning. Knowing something of the records of the members of the commission, I had complete confidence in their fairness and their intellectual honesty.

At first, when the questions were put to him at a private hearing by the Commission, Dr Weizmann thought he was being led into a trap and he was consequently wary in his replies. But then, as he sensed the direction towards which the exchanges were going, he began to realize the significance of the trend developing among the members, although his answers remained equally cautious. It was from that time that he projected his own thinking to encompass the still-vague concept of Partition and of a Jewish State in divided Palestine.

His own first appearance was at a public hearing in Jerusalem on 25 November 1936. He had come up from Rehovoth, where he was busy at his research, in that same laboratory where Lord Peel visited him and asked what he was doing, to be told: 'I am creating absorptive capacity.' The Zionist President, now two days short of his sixty-second birthday, was received with great deference and consideration. He spoke for over two hours, with only one short break, mostly from notes and without a prepared text.

One passage in his address has won an immortal place in history. In dwelling on the position—soon to be the plight—of the Jewish communities of Europe, he declared:

There are in this part of the world six million people doomed to be pent up in places where they are not wanted, and for whom the world is divided into places where they cannot live, and places into which they cannot enter.

The task of the Royal Commission is complex, and it has come at a time when the Jewish position is darker than ever before, even in our history.

It was not until the fifty-first meeting, held privately in Jerusalem on Friday, 8 January 1937, that the subject of partition was first broached to him. No one was with Weizmann at the time; he came alone. Those present at the hearing were the six members of the

Commission—Earl Peel, Sir Horace Rumbold, Sir Laurie Hammond, Sir William Carter, Sir Harold Morris, and Professor Reginald Coupland; the Secretary, Mr John Martin, of the Colonial Office; a representative of the Palestine Administration, Mr P. G. Heathcoat-Amory; and a shorthand-writer.

It was an epochal confrontation, for out of it burgeoned the first practical gropings towards the solid basis of a Jewish State. As Weizmann was to write later:

> I was asked how the idea struck me, and naturally answered that I could not tell on the spur of the moment, nor would I give my own impressions except after consultation with my colleagues. Actually I felt that the suggestion held out great possibilities and hopes. Something new had been born into the Zionist movement, something which had to be handled with great care and tenderness, which should not be permitted to become a matter for crude slogans and angry controversy.

He started out with a brief statement discussing the position in the Arab world and mentioning certain Zionist overtures towards certain influential Arab groups, and made some points about the glaring imbalance of Arab feudal ownership. He was sharply interrogated on these statements by Lord Peel, Sir Laurie Hammond, and Sir Horace Rumbold. He then spoke of the possibility of 'this Commission converting itself at some stage or another into a negotiating Commission' between the parties involved, and added: 'You would find us ready to go a long way towards meeting the situation, say for five years, for ten years.' Until then the Arab leaders had not appeared before the Commission, but had now agreed to do so, and Dr Weizmann thought that their decision 'indicates a certain amount of change of heart and it may be something which, if carefully followed up by the Commission, may lead on to something. The Mufti should not stand in the way of a big thing like peace.'

A few minutes later, about the middle of the hearing, Professor Coupland sprang the surprise. He couched it this way:

> Dr Weizmann, looking ahead and supposing, for the sake of argument, that your hopeful prospect of harmony proves unrealizable in the course of the next five or ten years, what practicable alternative might there be?
>
> With that question in your mind, would you comment on this scheme, which really deserves to be called more than cantonization; it is really partition on a federal basis, as we see it. . . . If after a period of federal partition, the only solution, or *a* solution, seemed to be effective partition, meaning that in due course and

under a treaty system these two blocks of Palestine become Independent States of the type of Egypt and Iraq in treaty relations with Great Britain, that is really the ultimate point on which I want to get your view.

Weizmann was still hesitant about committing himself. He remarked that he would not 'raise the formal point that it is against the Mandate; we are all aware of that point and I do not want to waste your time'. Coupland admitted that 'it implies the termination of the Mandate'. Thereupon Weizmann said that 'this possible solution, perhaps in five or ten years' time, would be an easier thing than the present situation', and he added: 'I think it is based on some erroneous conception that we have large tracts of land today in one block.'

The meeting then began to talk of the areas that would be available for the proposed respective 'blocks of Palestine'. After indicating the total areas in Jewish possession in various parts of the country ('next to nothing from Gaza to Jaffa, and in the coastal plain we have 550,000 dunams out of 3,000,000 dunams, that is, actual land in possession'), Dr Weizmann stated that 'in ten years' time, if we are allowed to work and attend to our work, and work more or less in the plains, then it may be more compact and possibly it may be better'.

He continued to feel his way warily. Answering Sir Morris Carter, he said there was not very much more than the 550,000 dunams in the coastal plain either under contract or on option, while as for the Valley of Jezreel there were 180,000 out of 450,000 dunams.

'Unfortunately, we are not sufficiently strong in any part of Palestine to say that this is a basis wide enough,' he remarked.

'You would be outnumbered?' Sir Laurie Hammond asked.

'Either we shall be outnumbered or we shall have to "dominate" or to rule the people who do not want the colony to be there,' he replied.

Towards the end of the hearing, the following dramatic exchange occurred:

PROFESSOR COUPLAND: If there were no other way out to peace, might it not be a final and peaceful settlement—to terminate the Mandate by agreement and split Palestine into two halves, the plain being an Independent Jewish State, as independent as Belgium, with treaty relations with Great Britain, whatever arrangements you like with us, and the rest of Palestine, plus Trans-Jordania, being an Independent Arab State, as independent as Arabia. That is the ultimate idea.

SIR LAURIE HAMMOND: With a British Entente?
DR WEIZMANN: Yes. I appreciate that. Permit me not to give a definite answer now. Let me think of it.

Finally, when the Chairman thanked him and he was about to withdraw, Dr Weizmann said, 'I have to thank you all for your patience and kindness to me. Perhaps I may have the opportunity of coming back to this problem.'

The opportunity to come back to the problem. . . . One of these occasions was soon presented. On one of the early Saturdays in February 1937, Weizmann and Coupland arranged to meet at Nahalal. He came there from Rehovoth whilst the other was brought to the village by Joshua Gordon, liaison officer of the Jewish Agency, directly from Jerusalem.

It was a drab winter day and they had to be provided with gumboots to wade through the thick mud on the village paths from the cars to the Girls' Agricultural School, where facilities for the secret conference had been arranged. The two of them spent the whole day together indoors. They did not budge from their quarters until the evening. From morning onwards, as the villagers outside speculated over what was going on, they exhaustively discussed partition and its implications.

We have a curious record of Coupland's attitude towards their conversation from Coupland himself, given in a private conversation much later, in November 1946, with Mr Aubrey Eban, who became Israel Ambassador to the United States and is now President of the Weizmann Institute of Science.

When Eban saw Coupland in Oxford in the middle of November the latter was still very firm in his support of partition, which after a lapse of more than nine years still seemed to him the 'only solution compatible with justice and logic—the lesser injustice'.

Coupland admitted to Eban that his conviction about the urgency of partition came to him during this conversation he had with Weizmann in Nahalal. After listening to Weizmann's definition of the conditions necessary for the National Home to flourish, he reached the conclusion that these conditions could never be expected from the British Government in its then strategic situation. He had said to Weizmann: 'There needs to be an operation; no honest doctor will recommend aspirins and a hot-water bottle.' Coupland added that he would not have offered partition as the Commission's proposal but for this talk with Weizmann.

Thus this tête-à-tête in a shabby little Palestinian hut created the germ of what some years later was to become the State of Israel. Weizmann was well aware of the implications of their talk: as they emerged at starlight he said, turning to the group of farmers standing there, 'Hevra, comrades, today we laid the basis for the Jewish State!'

Weizmann was going on to Haifa to spend the night with his mother. He told one of the veteran settlers, Yaaqov Oury, in Yiddish: '*Itzter gei ich onzogen di besoora mein mammen*—I'm going now to tell my mother the news!'

Undoubtedly there was the stuff of drama and history in that encounter at Nahalal. Indeed, the circumstances were such that if, in his *Diaries*, Theodor Herzl were able to declare with justice, 'At Basel, I founded the Jewish State,' then surely Chaim Weizmann was equally warranted in asserting with no less candour exactly four decades later, 'At Nahalal, I brought the Jewish State within our grasp!'

But of course, there was at that time still some very hard slogging ahead. The real struggle might be said to have barely started. The Royal Commission's brilliant report, a unanimous one to which all six members put their signatures, was published by the British Government on 7 July 1937. Part III of that 400-page document, entitled 'The Possibility of a Lasting Settlement', analysed 'the problem of Palestine' which had been created by 'the force of circumstances'. The judgment was a firm one:

'The conflict (between Arabs and Jews) has grown steadily more bitter. It has been marked by a series of five Arab outbreaks, culminating in the rebellion of last year. . . . This intensification of conflict will continue. The estranging force of conditions inside Palestine is growing year by year.'

The proposal for the 'drastic treatment' of the problem came in Chaper XXII on page 380 of the Report (published as Command Paper 5479):

'We feel justified in recommending that Your Majesty's Government should take the appropriate steps for the termination of the present Mandate on the basis of Partition.'

The commissioners added that there were 'three essential features of such a plan':

'It must be practicable. It must conform to our obligations. It must do justice to the Arabs and the Jews.'

What did Weizmann think of the plan?

He made his position crystal-clear in *Trial and Error* some ten years or so later, and his words have a touch of authentic prophecy as we look back over the historic experience of the past more than fourteen years since the State of Israel was established:

> It was my own deep conviction that God had always chosen small countries through which to convey his messages to humanity. It was from Judea and from Greece, not from Carthage or Babylonia, that the great ideas which form the most precious possession of mankind emerged. I believed that a small Jewish State, well organized, living in peace with its neighbours, a State on which would be lavished the love and devotion of Jewish communities throughout the world—such a State would be a great credit to us and an equally great contribution to civilization.

What did the British Government think?

In its White Paper on policy for Palestine accompanying the report, the Government offered a series of interim administrative measures—'while the form of a scheme of partition is being worked out'—which, in effect, would reduce the Jewish National Home to farcical proportions. As Weizmann pointed out, 'These measures were put into effect before Jewish opinion on partition had been tested. They were the first steps towards the nullification of the Balfour Declaration; actual nullification came with the White Paper of 1939. It was the classic technique of the step-by-step sell-out of small nations which the great democracies practised in the appeasement period.'

What did the Zionist Congress of 1937 think?

Weizmann had always held the opinion that a Jewish State, even if located in only part of Palestine, could maintain an eventual population of three million. But the Twentieth Congress at Zurich split over the issue. Passions ran high between the *Ja-sagers* and the *Nein-sagers*, the yeas and the nays; Weizmann stood up staunchly to his critics. In his address on 4 August, he urged that two criteria be applied to the principle of partition—after all, it was only the principle, and not the actual scheme, which Britain accepted:

> Firstly, does it offer a basis for a genuine growth of Jewish life, for the development of the young Palestinian culture, for rearing true men and women, for creating a Jewish agriculture, industry, literature—in short, all that the ideal of Zionism comprises?
>
> Secondly, does the proposal contribute to the solution of the Jewish problem, a problem pregnant with danger to ourselves and to the world?

And so to the vote, which was to adopt the following resolution:

The Congress declares that the scheme of partition put forward by the Royal Commission is unacceptable.

The Congress empowers the Executive to enter into negotiations with a view to ascertaining the precise terms of His Majesty's Government for the proposed establishment of a Jewish State.

In such negotiations the Executive shall not commit either itself or the Zionist Organization, but in the event of the emergence of a definite scheme for the establishment of a Jewish State, such scheme shall be brought before a newly elected Congress for decision.

It is a matter of record that no definite scheme was devised. The Commission under Sir John Woodhead, which arrived in Palestine in April 1938, failed to produce any workable proposals for partition; its report in October that year was negative. The Royal Commission document, which had tackled the Palestine problem in depth and had penetrated to the core of the situation, was buried under the mound of British reports, statements of policy, White Papers and Blue Books, and similar publications of the three decades of British rule in Palestine.

Yet through the zigzags of British policy and the convulsions of the second World War the plan survived, in a state of suspended animation, to be reincarnated a decade later at the United Nations Assembly in 1947. It is true that this time the British Government could scarcely claim any credit for it, but it was this original plan for partition that was applied, in so far as it pertained to the Jewish State, under UN auspices, and was thus an integral part of the organism that became the present State of Israel. 1938 was an inchoate year. The external position remained confused and dangerous, with the Arab rebellion dragging the country down. General Wavell left the country on reappointment, General Haining took his place; and Weizmann found time, in April, to see them both. One bright spot of those years was the close friendship which he and Mrs Weizmann struck up with Orde Wingate, but of course Wingate was at too junior a level to be of great political help.

Internally, the relations within the Agency Executive were none too happy; there was a good deal of friction. But the Political Committee, made up of both Zionist and non-Zionist elements, was a useful body and Weizmann attached great value to its advice and support. He was not overly impressed by certain highly placed non-Zionist members of the Anglo-Jewish community, however; and in a letter to Sir Simon (now Lord) Marks on 14 May 1938 he wrote:

I think we have to recognize frankly that they are people who, for reasons of their own—valid or not, selfish or not—are definitely against a Jewish State. They were equally against the Balfour Declaration, but they have had to acquiesce in it because of the success of our work. . . . They will oppose a Jewish State as long as they can. When it becomes a *fait accompli* they will grind their teeth and acquiesce in it. And when later it is successful, we shall find them climbing on the bandwagon.

The next round in the political struggle came with the St James's Palace round-table conference early in 1939. Jewish and Arab representatives, including those of other Middle East countries, were brought together by the British Government to discuss and produce a settlement. Neville Chamberlain's agreement with Hitler at Munich the previous October had hammered home the lesson that these parleys were, at the most, a forlorn hope and that the policy of appeasement still held sway. Indeed, Weizmann indicated his own sceptical evaluation when, at a meeting of the Palestine Discussions Conference Committee set up by the Jewish Agency and held at Great Russell Street, he observed: 'The actual presiding officer at the (St James's Palace) Conference is not the British Government, but Jamal Husseini (the Palestine Arab leader). Whatever he gives his consent to, goes through; the moment he puts in a *caveat*, the thing is dropped.'

The Prime Minister, Neville Chamberlain, delivered the opening speech at the Conference on 7 February 1939. In replying, Weizmann said:

The hopes and prayers of millions of Jews scattered throughout the world are now centred, with unshaken confidence in British good faith, on these deliberations. We believe that all our work in Palestine has been the result of a grim necessity to face realities, and I would submit that no reality is today more bitter than that which the Jewish people is called upon to face. . . . We have endeavoured through all these difficult years to maintain that co-operation with the British Government which has always been the cornerstone of our policy, and we are approaching our present task in the same spirit.

He was unremitting in his efforts to win some form of Arab understanding. During the London conference he had met and held a friendly chat with one of the leading Egyptian delegates, Aly Maher Pasha; and at the end of March 1939, while en route to Palestine, he stopped over in Cairo, where Maher Pasha arranged for him to meet the Prime Minister, Mohammed Mahmoud Pasha, and other Egyptian statesmen. They received him with cordiality; but, as he observed drily, 'Of course, one had to discount, in these unofficial conversations, both the usual Oriental politeness and the fact that private utterances are somewhat less cautious than official ones.' Nothing came of the overtures.

The White Paper of 17 May 1939 was a negation of even the faint wisps of hope that had existed. It provided a new Procrustean bed for Jewish national aspirations; there was no alternative but to reject it. Weizmann wrote to Leopold Amery in London drawing attention to the gloomier aspects of the situation; he broadcast to the Jewish community of the United States. He was unflagging in his efforts to arouse public opinion.

Although he had intended remaining at Rehovoth for several months, possibly until the 21st Congress at Geneva, his associates urged him to return to address a last-minute personal appeal to Prime Minister Chamberlain, and he flew back to London. The Prime Minister received him, but that was all; his pleading met with no response.

The House of Commons debate on the 1939 White Paper resulted in the familiar line-up of the benchers for and against the Government. Winston Churchill gave one of the great speeches of his career, but it produced no change in the Government's policy, and the sympathetic remarks by pro-Zionist MPs could at the best be only of cold comfort to those who divined the realities of the situation facing the Jews of Europe.

Late in the evening of 24 August 1939, Weizmann bade a moving farewell to the delegates at the Twenty-first Congress at Geneva. The war clouds were gathering thickly. Both he and his auditors were in a hurry to return to their homes before the tocsins sounded. The atmosphere of the final session was charged with the sombre realization of impending destiny! The leave-taking was terribly painful.

Weizmann said in part:

It is with a heavy heart that I take my leave. . . . If, as I hope, we are spared in life and our work continues, who knows—perhaps a new light will shine upon us from the thick black gloom. . . . My heart is overflowing. . . .

We shall meet again [prolonged applause]. We shall meet again in common labour for our land and people. Our people is deathless, our land eternal.

There are some things which cannot fail to come to pass, things

without which the world cannot be imagined. The remnant shall
work on, fight on, live on until the dawn of better days.

Towards that dawn I greet you. May we meet again in peace
[prolonged applause].

(Deep emotion grips the Congress. Dr Weizmann embraces his colleagues on the platform. There are tears in many eyes. Hundreds of
hands are stretched out towards Dr Weizmann as he leaves the hall.
—Protocol of the Twelfth Session of the 21st Zionist Congress,
24 August 1939.)

Few of the European delegates of whom Weizmann took leave in
Geneva that sad evening in the summer of 1939 survived the Nazi
slaughter-houses.

The decade of agony was about to begin.

*Mr Julian L. Meltzer, writer and translator, has lived in Jerusalem
since 1921. For many years he was a working journalist and Palestine correspondent of the* New York Times, *1937-1948.*

1939—1949

CHAPTER ELEVEN

TRAGEDY AND TRIUMPH

ABBA EBAN

'There is darkness all around us and we cannot see through the clouds. . . .'

DR. WEIZMANN.—*Closing address to the 21st Zionist Congress, 24 August 1939*

WEIZMANN STEPPED into his car and sped through Geneva towards the French frontier. The Soviet-Nazi pact had been announced two days ago and Europe now braced itself for the shock of war. The lights were going out and none knew when they would be re-kindled. Mrs Weizmann and Blanche Dugdale, Balfour's niece, accompanied him on his way. His farewell speech had included words of deep pathos for the delegates of Polish Jewry. And the Palestine delegates were high in his thoughts. Mrs Dugdale was to record that night in her diary: 'Chaim embraced Ussishkin and Ben-Gurion as though he would never let them go.'

The imminent war spelt misery for many nations. For the Jewish people it threatened a vast and comprehensive havoc without precedent in recorded history. Nor was there any prospect of shelter from the coming storm. A few months before, the Chamberlain Government had published its White Paper on Palestine which would turn the Jewish National Home into a stunted ghetto with locked doors, living within a pale of settlement under Arab rule. And now the Jewish disaster was merged with the universal tragedy. Weizmann had dreamt of a Jewish people, happy and free, restoring the mainsprings of its vitality in the home where its nationhood was born. He had touched multitudes of people, including the leaders of many nations, with the ardour and beauty of that dream. The hope was now in full eclipse. As the Nazi columns prepared to fall on Europe and tear it limb from limb, an immense and seemingly inexorable danger menaced every Jewish home. Would the old continent ever again sustain a life inspired with those elements of reverence and order without which civilization falls into chaos? And even if victory

came, how many of the Jewish masses—nine million of them from
the Rhine to Eastern Russia—would stand a chance of surviving for
the celebration?

Weizmann was not an orator of heat and passion. His discourse
was usually pitched on a low key and hedged in with scientific doubt.
But he had exaggerated nothing in his last speech to his followers:
'There is darkness all around us and we cannot see through the
clouds . . .'

There flowed into his mind the memories of a previous journey across
Switzerland to London. It had been in 1914 when the war was a few
weeks old. His assets then were very few. He was a lecturer in
chemistry at Manchester University, modest in the hierarchy of a
Zionist movement which was itself no serious force in international
politics. Neither he nor the cause which he served had then enjoyed
the eminence which they now possessed. But there was then a
promise in the air, of new and wonderful opportunities to be
snatched from the changing interests and fortunes of the powers.
History moved in a twilight zone between a world that was dying
and a new order struggling for birth. And Chaim Weizmann was
then young and free, unburdened by history, failure, disillusion or
public office. It was the springtime of his people's hope and it was
good to be alive. He had swiftly gathered a few men around him,
watched and nursed his chances, and then intervened in the central
political arena with such massive authority and sureness of timing as
to change the whole direction of his people's history.

The wave of this victory had borne him high on its crest to a
position of unrivalled leadership in Jewish life. The two decades
that had passed since then had seen much strife and toil, some disillusion and great progress towards the goal. The concrete testimony
of success lay in the 550,000 Jews of Palestine and the busy microcosm of a free society which they had created. If the Jewries of the
world had listened to him more seriously there would by now have
been a larger and stronger base from which to spring. He was desperately aware that time was running out: Arab nationalism, which
had been inert and almost acquiescent in 1917, was now a robust and
growing adversary. British statesmanship was awakening from the
generous impulse of 1917 into a mood in which the space and wealth
of Arab lands loomed larger than the more imponderable values
which Zionism expressed.

Weizmann had suspected that this would happen. The Balfour
Declaration, like all cherished things, was fragile and of transient
lease. Everything depended on whether it could be replaced in time

by a geopolitical reality more substantial than itself. By 1939 this had neither happened, nor completely failed to happen. Palestine Jewry was too real to be entirely ignored, but not so strong a reality as to impose a decisive compulsion on future events. Weizmann, the diplomat, had implored the powerful Jewries to turn their minds away from diplomacy towards the concrete forces which alone gave diplomacy its solid content. He recoiled from ringing utterances about Jewish statehood which some movements in Jewry regarded as a substitute for creating the state itself. The practical toil of settlement was for him not a substitute for political sovereignty, but the prior condition of its attainment. In all his speeches the business of state-building was described in the strong but gentle imagery of organic growth. 'If you root a tree deep in the soil and water it with love and devotion, it will grow and it will flourish and its branches will reach to heaven'!

His own position in the political world already conveyed a premonition of Jewish sovereignty. Heads of state received him with courtesy, ministers and high officials with apprehensive respect. They stood a good chance of being enticed into an unplanned commitment—or exhausted by the tempest of his historic emotion. But they behaved towards him as though he were the President of a sovereign nation equal in status to their own, engaged as his own emissary in a perpetual series of summit conferences. He and they knew that this was not formally true; but something in his presence and in their own historic imagination forbade them to break the spell. The Jewish people had produced a President before it had achieved a State; and somehow this made the claim of statehood seem less far-fetched in many eyes than it would otherwise have been.

From the masses of his own people he was separated by the range and distinction of his contacts, by his taste for elegance, order and sophistication in daily life, and by the broad scope of his cultural experience, extending from Jewish folk tradition across European humanism into the atmosphere and discipline of scientific method. But in style and spirit he was not remote from them. They admired his level-headed, balanced attitude towards his own personal eminence. They knew that he was gripped by a single theme and that his life was commanded exclusively by their own central interests. He refused to dissipate his versatile attainments in varied and scattered fields. The strands of his multiple interests were woven together in a single texture. Felix Frankfurter[1] has remarked on Weizmann's quality of single-mindedness:

[1] Harlan B. Phillips, *Felix Frankfurter Reminisces* (New York, 1960), p. 184.

He was implacable in the pursuit of his object—implacable. Nothing else interested him except the realization of a Jewish Palestine, but he had the kind of insight, understanding and imagination that made him realize that a lot of other things were relevant to that. . . . He didn't care what else happened. He wouldn't read the newspapers about anything else except in so far as his instinct told him that this, somehow or other, was related to Palestine.

For this total consecration to their purposes his followers rewarded him with an awed respect. He was deeply rooted in their memories and origins. To foreign chanceries he might come as a skilled diplomat. To the Jewish masses he was the gifted son of a timber merchant in Pinsk. His language, voice and mannerisms never ceased to convey the rich and solid culture of the Jewish pale. Unlike Herzl, Nordau and Brandeis, he had not come back to 'discover' the Jewish people in his later years. There was nothing external about him. He sprang from the womb of Jewish life. There had been no gaps or interruptions in his career of total Jewish identity. And so his people surrounded him with reverence, affection, loyalty—and simultaneously, as was their custom, harried him at critical times with unbelievable torments of criticism and doubt. Sometimes they would reject him formally, only to fall at once into a passion of repentance and move heaven and earth for his restoration to their midst. Even when he was removed from office Jewish communities refused to recognize anyone else as the paramount envoy of Zionism.

There was no doubt in their minds, or in his, that destiny had linked them together in tireless pursuit of Jewish redemption, and that it was his lifelong vocation to be the spokesman and commander of their highest cause.

On his road from Geneva to London he had seen Paris plunged in gloom. Something was already visible of the disorganized apathy which augured the doom of France.

In London he set up his command post at his apartment in the Dorchester Hotel and in his office at 77 Great Russell Street across the road from the British Museum. This celebrated office was remarkable for its dinginess, discomfort and lack of hygienic provision —but in these respects it did not differ greatly from one of the more aristocratic ministries in Whitehall.

It was a time for long-term plans, not for sudden victories. In 1914 the slate was clean. Now it had been disfigured by the ugly scribblings of the White Paper. This betrayal had been simultaneous with the

Munich settlement and congruous with it in all respects. Indeed, the day after Munich, Jan Masaryk had come to Weizmann's home, after pacing London's streets in a mood of cosmic despair, to predict a whole new series of Munichs. Small peoples were going to be sacrificed one by one in burnt offering to appease the violent tyrannies which were then the favourites of historic fortune.

The future of Palestine was not the major concern of the British people as it went about collecting its gas-masks, recruiting its expeditionary force, evacuating its children from the cities, and casting an anxious eye on its sprawling, vulnerable expanse of empire. Weizmann surveyed the field and defined the first objective. There was clearly no chance for a new and favourable definition of the final political solution. His aim was to put the White Paper into refrigeration and create conditions in which it would appear after the victory as a grotesque and unseemly anachronism. The first goal was to get the Jewish people represented in its own identity amongst the armed forces to be mobilized for Hitler's defeat. Behind the flag consecrated in battle the Jewish people would rally after victory to claim its national rights.

On 29 August, Weizmann addressed the Prime Minister Mr Neville Chamberlain in solemn terms:

> In this hour of supreme crisis, the consciousness that the Jews have a contribution to make to the defence of sacred values impels me to write this letter. I wish to confirm, in the most explicit manner, the declarations which I and my colleagues have made during the last months, and especially in the last week: that the Jews stand by Great Britain and will fight on the side of the Democracies.
>
> Our desire is to give effect to these declarations. . . . The Jewish Agency is ready to enter into immediate arrangements for utilizing Jewish man-power, technical ability, resources, etc.
>
> The Jewish Agency has recently had differences in the political field with the Mandatory Power. We would like these differences to give way before greater and more pressing necessities of the time.

On 5 September he requested a meeting on this theme with Leslie Hore-Belisha, the Secretary of State for War. On the following day he went to see the French Ambassador M. Corbin to offer the recruitment of a Jewish Legion in France. Within the next few weeks he laid down a dense bombardment. Between September and December those who heard him expound his cause included Winston Churchill, Leopold Amery, Malcolm Macdonald, Lord Halifax, Robert

Vansittart, Walter Elliot, Oliver Harvey, Archibald Sinclair, Lord Chatfield; the Labour leaders, Attlee, Bevin, Greenwood and Williams; Walter Monckton, R. A. Butler and the Duke of Devonshire—and every editor or politician who came within his grasp.

It was like 1917 again. His energy cascaded everywhere. His health was resilient rather than robust, but it was sensitively attuned to his mood and spirit. The pace was urgent. From the continent came fearful news of the 'solution' which Hitler was preparing for the Jews of occupied countries. The Jewish Army was a moral necessity for Jewish history as well as the credentials of future nationhood. He knew that political persuasion was a long patient task. In the negotiations for the Balfour Declaration he had conducted two thousand conversations to create a climate in which the idea might burgeon and yield fruit. His gifts of persuasion flourished more in such quiet councils than in the storm of public debate. His method was to trace every thread which led to the formulation of policy and to impress upon it the tension of his own intellectual and moral force. He neglected nothing. He even met the Egyptian Ambassador on 28 September to recall a conversation with the Prime Minister Mohammed Mahmoud Pasha a few years earlier and to arrange, at the Ambassador's suggestion, for further meetings at regular intervals.

There was not only the danger of standing still. It was seriously possible for his cause to fall backward. A group of Ministers, led by Malcolm Macdonald, was bent on pushing the anti-Zionist policy further by enacting legislation under the White Paper limiting Jewish land purchase to an insultingly small area of the country. Palestine would become the second country after Germany in which affiliation to the Jewish faith would be a disqualification for the ownership of the land. Macdonald was inflexible in his hostility. He refused Weizmann's petition for the rescue of 20,000 Jewish children from Poland, and his request for visas to be granted to 169 Zionist leaders who had received permits to enter Palestine before the outbreak of war. Macdonald sanctimoniously told the Jewish Agency delegation that 'he fully realized the tragic consequences of his refusal for those involved'.

In October Weizmann had gone to Switzerland to seek intelligence on the plans of German scientists for the support of Hitler's war. He had interrogated leading refugee scientists and given his impression to Lord Halifax on October 23. The hostility of the Colonial Office was now offset by two developments which some Zionists called 'the beginning of the thaw': Halifax agreed with Weizmann that it would be irresponsible to raise new frictions by enacting the White Paper land restrictions. 'It was impossible to have these things cropping up now.'

More substantively Weizmann had made a dent on the minds of military leaders. On 14 November the Chief of the Imperial General Staff, General Sir Edmund Ironside, had informed him of his resolve to release forty-three young Jews whom the Palestine Government had sentenced to long imprisonment for 'indulging' in military training. 'Fancy' the General said, 'They have condemned one of Wingate's lads to life imprisonment: he ought to have been given the Distinguished Service Order.' When Weizmann said that Macdonald was obstructing the Jewish Army project the General replied: 'Oh, I see. But the Jewish Army will come all the same. Besides, if it is to be a better world after the war, the Jews must get Palestine.'

The better world was far away, and in the meantime the task was heavy. Weizmann now planned a visit to the United States. Britain was showing an apprehensive deference to American opinion. It seemed unlikely that the issues of the war would be resolved without the intervention of American power. As the fighting in Europe became bogged down in deadlock between the Maginot and Siegfried Lines, the apathetic neutralism of American opinion became a serious portent for the anti-Nazi cause. On the Palestine issue, too, the American scene was still dormant. The United States had not committed itself to the White Paper. Indeed Roosevelt had criticized that document strongly in a note to Secretary of State Cordell Hull in May 1939. America remained the strongest of the factors not yet thrown into the balance on which the Jewish fate was poised.

Moreover, Weizmann had begun to explore new directions in applied chemical research with a view to meeting the anticipated shortages in strategic materials. In Britain he was encountering resistance arising partly from bureaucratic habit and partly, perhaps, from the apprehension that Weizmann's successes in chemistry often seemed to have consequences beyond the scientific field.

He was weighed down by many anxieties. In October he had spent a day saying farewell to his younger son Michael an air-force officer reporting for air-combat duty. At Great Russell Street he had effective counsellors at many levels — Locker, Lewis Namier, Blanche Dugdale, Brodetsky: but he had no real deputy. Moshe Sharett's arrival from Jerusalem now strengthened the political department and reinforced the vigour of its deliberations; but his absence from Palestine could not be envisaged for any great length of time. The administration of Sir Harold MacMichael was pressing for further implementation of the White Paper despite the adverse judgment on its legal validity by the Council of the League of Nations on the eve of the war. Weizmann's talk with Ironside had given hope of success in the struggle for the Jewish Army. He could not stay in America for long if the momentum of his effort was not to run down.

There was little direct news of the fate befalling European Jewry. But Weizmann's prognosis was grim. In a letter to Sharett which reached Jerusalem early in October he had written:

> About half of the Jewish population of the world finds itself under the sway of Hitler and Stalin. . . . I have tried to get some idea about the state of the Jewish population in Poland and the extent of the catastrophe which has befallen them. . . . The American Ambassador here can get no information. Our friends in the United States neither. . . . One stands appalled before the dimensions of the disaster which is unfortunately in inverse proportion to our power of sending any assistance.

He placed strong hope in Churchill, the First Lord of the Admiralty, who was straining at Chamberlain's leash, scarcely concealing his impatience with the sluggish policies by which the Government 'prosecuted' the war. Churchill had deputed Brendan Bracken to maintain close contact with the Zionist leaders on his behalf. And on 17 December Weizmann had a clear-cut conversation with him.

The prospect of Churchill's intervention was to accompany Weizmann through many days of doubt and torment in the ensuing years. As a veteran War Minister clearly marked even then for the highest office, Churchill must have known the weight that Weizmann would attach to his words and attitudes. And on that December morning he began to engage himself in a series of friendly expressions which grew progressively in intensity and force across the years of war.

Weizmann's note on the 17 December conversation was dictated for dispatch to Jerusalem a few hours before his departure for New York.

> Mr Churchill was very cordial, and deeply interested in Dr Weizmann's forthcoming visit to America. He made optimistic observations on the progress of the war.
>
> Dr Weizmann thanked Mr Churchill for his unceasing interest in Zionist affairs. He said: 'You stood at the cradle of this enterprise; I hope that you will see it through.' Mr Churchill asked what Dr Weizmann meant by 'seeing it through'. Dr Weizmann replied that after the war the Zionists would wish to have a state of some three or four million Jews in Palestine. Mr Churchill said: 'Yes, indeed, I quite agree with that.'

The
War
Years

14 With Mrs
    Weizmann
    sailing on Lake
    Kinneret, 1944

15 With Mrs
    Weizmann,
    New York, 1943

16 Weizmann speaking at the Biltmore Conference, New York, 1942

17 Visiting 'illegal' immigrants at the detention camp, Athlit, near Haifa with Weisgal, 1945

18 Before the Holocaust, 21st Zionist Congress, Geneva. (*Seated left to right*) Moshe Sharett, David Ben-Gurion, Weizmann, Eliezer Kaplan

19 Speaking at the laying of the corner stone of the Weizmann Institute of Science, Rehovoth, 1946

On 20 December Weizmann set out for the United States, where he remained for ten weeks. He was warmly received by American Jewry, but there was no general framework of American policy within which the Jewish effort could exert its special tension. On 8 February he had his first meeting with President Roosevelt who was friendly in tone but vague in substance. Roosevelt acknowledged Palestine's rôle in receiving refugees from Hitler's Europe, but took Weizmann aback by asking whether other countries 'such as Colombia' might not absorb refugees. The Zionist leader patiently explained the distinction between temporary refuge and permanent settlement. He confessed his fear that the end of the war would find European Jewry shattered; but there would be two or three million left outside the Soviet system and it would be possible and urgent to bring a million of these to Palestine at once. He told Roosevelt that the logic of the Peel Report advocating a Jewish State in Palestine offered the principle and kernel of the solution.

How far the British Government still remained from this principle was now illustrated by the decision to enact the land restrictions in February. The British Ambassador in Washington, Lord Lothian, tried to allay Weizmann's wrath with a detailed letter expressing the 'earnest hope and belief that these facts and arguments will give you an insight into the motives that have impelled his Majesty's Government to make their present decision'.

Equipped with an all too precise insight into 'His Majesty's Government's motives', Weizmann arrived back in London in March 1940 and bitterly informed his colleagues that he would refuse to seek interviews with British Ministers. In April he went to Switzerland to see Professor Willstaeter about an invention which a German refugee chemist had laid before him for converting salt water into fresh. In early May he presided at a meeting with Ben-Gurion's participation to discuss whether a more active resistance to the White Paper should be pursued in Palestine. The difficulty now, as for a few years to come, lay in the agonizing duality of the British rôle. In the specific context of the Palestine problem Britain was the opponent of Jewish hopes. But in the world struggle she was the primary obstacle to a Hitler victory which would mean the strangulation and cremation of all Jews, including those of the National Home itself. How to oppose British policy during the war while simultaneously longing for her victory was a political dilemma more cruel than any other nation had to face.

Across these deliberations now came the thunder of great events. Holland and Belgium were overrun, France brought to her knees,

Chamberlain overthrown—and Churchill, growling with leonine
defiance, advanced towards the 'finest hour'.

The composition of the new government revived Zionist hopes. But
these did not go beyond the frontier of sober realism. In a memorandum drafted on 14 May Ben-Gurion acknowledged that 'three of the
five members of the War Cabinet are friendly to us', and that the
new Colonial Secretary, Lord Lloyd, 'though a known pro-Arab is
nevertheless an honest and sympathetic man'. On the other hand, he
added 'we should beware of over-optimism'. The difficulties in securing the complete and formal reversal of the White Paper policy 'are
practically insuperable'. In these conditions he urged concentration
on short-term objectives—'the development of war industries, supply,
and the immediate training of Jewish cadres for a Jewish division'.
At the same time the Zionist movement should formulate its demand
for a final solution in terms of 'the establishment of a Jewish State
in Palestine'.

Weizmann found these views congenial. The tensions within the
Zionist leadership which had been ominous in April were now dispelled. On May 19 Weizmann and Ben-Gurion paid a call on Lord
Lloyd. It was the former who in a moving tribute to Dutch Jewry said
that 'the birthplace of Spinoza is in Nazi hands'. In a lashing assault
of a kind to which British ministers were not accustomed to listen,
Weizmann added that the British 'were now being punished for not
having realized earlier that when Hitler fought against the Jews, his
real objective was England'.

London was now alive with a sense of peril. The concern of British
statesmen was not with the security of Palestine but with the survival
of Britain in her own islands. In a conversation with Weizmann in a
taxicab late in May Mrs Dugdale conveyed a Cabinet Minister's
opinion that invasion was possible and indeed imminent. She asked
whether Weizmann would consider removing himself to America 'to
preserve himself for the movement'. He heatedly dismissed the suggestion and flung himself into intense diplomacy on a broad front. If
Britain, now exposed to greater danger than any yet confronting
Palestine, was to be engaged in preoccupation with Zionism, all
Weizmann's capacities of penetration would be sorely needed. His
colleagues were now moved to wonder by the access which he
achieved and the attention which he commanded beyond the intrinsic
priority of his cause in British eyes. In a few weeks he had secured
a directive from Churchill to Lord Lloyd to place no obstacle in the
way of the Jewish war effort. Arms searches stopped and increased
use was made of Jewish industrial production.

On 14 June when Italy had entered the war Weizmann pressed imperiously for an increased development of Palestine Jewry's military strength. In a letter to Lord Lloyd he wrote:

We request that the Jews of Palestine be given the fullest opportunity of organizing for Home Defence. Time presses. Things possible today may become impossible tomorrow. Delay may mean the annihilation of the half-million Jews in Palestine, and the destruction of all our work.

We ask His Majesty's Government, whatever they may decide about our offers of help, to allow the Jews of Palestine, under the direction of the Jewish Agency and the Jewish National Council, and under the control of the British Military Authorities, to organise as many military units as they can, and to train their men, as far as possible with the help of the British forces in the country.

Action is required at once. Speed may make all the difference between life and death for us. Before victory is won, Jewish Palestine may be in supreme danger. If we have to go down, we are entitled to go down fighting, and the Mandatory Power is in duty bound to grant us this elementary human right.

He had now secured an official place in the scientific war effort as an honorary chemical adviser to Herbert Morrison, the Minister of Supply. His aim was to develop the catalytic cracking of heavy oils to yield benzine and toluene. He carried out new investigations of various fermentation processes, including the production of isoprene, which later became important for the synthetic manufacture of rubber. At one time he found it difficult to tear himself away from the laboratory in favour of the thankless tasks awaiting him in Great Russell Street.

Churchill and other Ministers were now pressing him to make another visit to the United States in order to stimulate Jewish and general opinion in favour of the anti-Nazi cause, for whose defence Britain now stood alone in the field. The Zionist leader insisted on a definite commitment in favour of a Jewish Army. Patience was running out; indeed that of Ben-Gurion was exhausted, and he exploded into scepticism and dissent.

At last, early in September, the break-through seemed to come. At a luncheon with Churchill, Weizmann received the Prime Minister's formal approval for the establishment of a Jewish fighting force.

On Friday 13 September 1941, a meeting took place at the War Office with Mr Eden, Secretary for War, presiding, and Lord Lloyd and a Foreign Office representative in attendance. Mr Eden com

municated to Weizmann officially that 'the Government had decided
to proceed with the organization of a Jewish Army, on the same basis
as the Czech and Polish Army. Its size, to begin with, would be 10,000
including 4,000 from Palestine. They would be trained and organized
in England and then dispatched to the Middle East.'

Mrs Dugdale wrote in her diary: 'The Walls of Jericho have
fallen, fallen. I looked in at the Dorchester at about 5 pm and found
Chaim just back from the interview elated and solemn. He said, "It
is almost as great a day as the Balfour Declaration." Orde Wingate
was also there, radiant.'

In the following months this achievement was to be corroded by
delays and evasions. Four long years were to pass before a Jewish
Brigade group came into existence. But the break-through of 1941,
at the time of its occurrence, was a significant reassertion of Weizmann's skill and power. He had contrived to win a decision which
went against all the prevailing winds of British policy. His confidence
in his ability to change the current of events was restored at a
moment when his spirits were perilously low. The criticism of some
of his colleagues was provisionally silenced. He felt himself to be re-
gaining command of events. Lord Halifax, the Foreign Secretary,
tells in his memoirs, of encountering Weizmann during a violent air-
raid on London sitting in a shelter serenely reading the Hebrew
Bible. On one occasion a light-hearted feeling impelled him to dis-
card his car and take a ride on top of a London bus—to the astonishment of some Zionists on the way to Golders Green who thought that
they were afflicted with hallucinations.

News now reached Weizmann of a Cabinet meeting on 2 October
at which Churchill had repudiated the White Paper and affirmed
that 'the Jews must have territory'. Two weeks later he was informed
that the War Cabinet had formally ratified the Jewish Army project.
In February 1941 he was put into contact with a senior officer,
General Hawes, who had been appointed to command the Jewish
Division.

All Zionist victories have been followed by the swift repentance of
those who had conceded them. The Balfour Declaration might well
have been shelved if it had come to a decision a month later than
November 1917. In 1947 the retreat from the United Nations partition resolution was to begin on the morrow of its adoption. Weizmann's victory on the Jewish Army was now to be shattered by a
resolute counter-attack from the pro-Arab school of British diplomacy. On 14 February the new Colonial Secretary Lord Moyne
wrote to Weizmann refusing his impassioned appeal for a 'substan-

tial allocation of immigration certificates to be issued immediately to Rumanian Jews'. 'Rumania', wrote Lord Moyne blandly, 'is regarded as enemy occupied territory. The machinery for verification of the *bona fides* of applicants . . . has disappeared.' His Lordship added with massive understatement, 'I feel sure that this reply will come as a disappointment to you.'

An interview with the Colonial Secretary on 22 February had no effect. A week later a further blow descended: a letter from Lord Moyne to Dr Weizmann dated 4 March 1941:

> I am very sorry to have to tell you that the raising of the Jewish contingent has to be postponed. As you know I was anxiously considering certain details with a view to removal of minor difficulties, but the matter has now been shifted on to quite other ground, and the Prime Minister has decided that owing to lack of equipment the project must for the present be put off for six months, but may be reconsidered again in four months. . . . I can assure you that this postponement is in no sense a reversal of the previous decision in favour of your proposal.

Lord Moyne tried verbally to reassure him that nothing more than a technical postponement was involved; and on the eve of Weizmann's departure for the United States, Churchill engaged him in a conversation at 10 Downing Street where he had gone to say farewell to Brendan Bracken. The Prime Minister said: 'I am thinking of a settlement between you and the Arabs after the war. The man with whom you should make the agreement is Ibn Saud. He will be the lord of the Arab countries. But he will have to agree with you with regard to Palestine. Times are terrible for all of us and for you they are doubly terrible. I will see you through.'

Weizmann wrote this conversation down, put it in an envelope and sent it from the airport near Bournemouth to a friend in the country for safe keeping 'in case anything happens to me'. Air crashes were frequent on the Atlantic route in those days. But he reached his destination and plunged into a vigorous tour of communities in the midwest and California. On 25 May he assembled the American Jewish leaders and summoned them to the assumption of leadership in Jewish rescue. His discourse was of prophetic intensity: 'Victory will come and the Jewish problem will be brought before the great tribunal which will sit and carve out the new world after this terrible war. I believe in the eternity of Israel. . . . If that is religion, then I am religious. It was my lodestar all my life and it is now on this terrible morning.' He concluded with frank advocacy of partition and

a request to call American Zionists to a conference for the purpose
of enunciating Zionist post-war aims. 'There is an Arab nuisance
value,' he concluded cryptically—'Let us create a Jewish nuisance
value.'

Fortified by public support in America he returned to London and
indignantly charged Churchill with his responsibility for delaying the
Jewish Army project. 'Are the Jews so utterly unimportant', he wrote
to the Prime Minister in September 1941, 'as the treatment meted
out to them suggests? Let me feel, Mr Prime Minister, that our
friendship is not spurned nor our name obliterated at a time when
Hitler is endeavouring to obliterate our very existence.' In an article
in 'Foreign Affairs' published in October he asserted his formula for
the solution: 'It is for the democracies to proclaim the justice of the
Jewish claim to their own Commonwealth in Palestine.'

Lord Moyne had told him that the Jewish Division was only postponed. Now he delivered a harder blow. On 23 October he informed
Weizmann and Ben-Gurion that 'since the Government had to give
every aid to Russia it would not be possible to form a Jewish Division
... in view of the shipping accommodation which would be involved'.

'When troubles come they come not single spie but in battalions.'
The patient labours of two dark years were in collapse. To public
disappointment was now added the crushing burden of private grief.
On 10 February 1942, the eve of his departure for America on a
scientific mission requested by the United States Government, he had
a telephone conversation with his son Michael. 'He sounded quite
disconsolate,' wrote Weizmann later in his memoirs, 'but I tried to
cheer him up. I got in reply a sad laugh. It still rings in my ears.'
The next day found him and Mrs Weizmann in Bristol about to take
off for the Atlantic flight. They were informed by telephone that
Michael was missing after his squadron had carried out anti-sub-
marine duties in the North Sea and English Channel. Stunned with
grief, he and Mrs Weizmann returned to London.

Zionism had been his relentless master for fifty years. It had stirred
his youth, commanded his manhood and weighed down his aging
years. It had taken voracious toll of his energies and left him scant
time for the elementary private joys. His son, so often separated from
him in childhood, had now fallen in the service of allied armies
amongst whom no Jewish flag yet flew. His life had been touched
with great issues, exalted by responsibilities and monopolised by
duty. It was now illuminated by the cold light of sacrifice. The
friends who gathered about him in London during that grief-laden
February brought him tidings of unrelieved gloom. Singapore sur-

rendered. The *Struma* with a cargo of 700 Jewish refugees was refused admission to Palestine and blew up with the loss of all its passengers but one in the Mediterranean.

For some weeks Chaim and Vera Weizmann were paralysed by the weight of their sorrows. But a week after the news that Michael was missing Weizmann was at the Colonial Office to excoriate Lord Cranbourne for the *Struma* affair and warn him that broken British promises would not cancel the divine promise to Israel. 'Palestine', he said, 'will never again become an Arab country. The present policy merely creates a running sore. What is being done in Palestine is in flagrant contradiction to what is being said about a better world after the war.' Cranbourne, more sympathetic than Moyne, worked out a compromise whereby Jewish illegal immigrants who reached Haifa would, if detained, at least be held in Palestine and not turned away. But there was no movement on any other central issue.

On 2 March Weizmann attempted to break through the wall of Soviet hostility in a letter to the Soviet Government through Ambassador Maisky. Beginning with a stoical reference to his own personal disaster he emphasized the collective ethic at the root of the Zionist movement:

> Collective welfare and not individual gain is the guiding principle and goal of the economic structure. Equality of standing is established in the community between manual and intellectual workers; and consequently the fullest scope is provided for the intellectual life and development of labour.
>
> The vast majority of adherents of Zionism have close personal and family relations with the USSR, and a peculiar interest in, and special sympathy with, its people. . . .
>
> May I express my firm hope and belief that the Soviet arms, which have already achieved such brilliant results, will succeed in freeing their country from the enemy, and will thus contribute to lifting the pall of darkness now hanging over a distracted world, and that the forces of progress and freedom will then unite in order to undertake the work of reconstruction which will lie before them. I have no doubt that the Soviet Government and people will show sympathy and understanding for the vexed Jewish problem which has weighed on us and on Europe for so many decades.
>
> I would like to thank you personally for your kindness in receiving me, and in listening to our views.

In late March Weizmann reassembled his vitality, packed his bags, and took once more to the road—the envoy of a people, implacable and tenacious in duty. In April he again landed in the United States.

The American Ambassador in London, Joseph Winant, had urged him to concentrate seriously on his chemical work. Even here he met frustration. His contribution to the rubber shortage was obstructed by vested interests in the oil industry. Later the Vice-President of the United States, Henry A. Wallace, was to declare: 'The world will never know what a significant contribution Weizmann made towards the success of the synthetic-rubber programme at a time when it was badly bogged down and going too slowly.' When his production process was fully perfected he handed it over to a Philadelphia firm, and resumed the thread of his Zionist labours.

He was now in his sixty-ninth year and ill-health began to pursue him with growing frequency. But he made an effective appearance at the Biltmore Conference in May 1942, at which American Zionists united in support of a platform calling for a Jewish Commonwealth in Palestine. He was now under criticism by many leaders of Palestinian and American Jewry. In stormy sessions in New York Ben-Gurion criticized his tendency to conduct the Presidency with complete exclusiveness of decision. Ben-Gurion argued for a more collective and broadly diffused concept of political leadership in which the man of chief responsibility would not act or decide alone.

In an address to the American Zionists on 2 December, Weizmann reaffirmed 'his full agreement with the Biltmore Programme'. If he made little fuss about it it was because he saw no difference between its text and that of his article in 'Foreign Affairs' the year before. He may have underestimated the effect of Ben-Gurion's achievement in confirming these ideas as a banner and platform of Zionist action. Noting that at least two million Jews had perished under the Nazi terror he observed bitterly to his Zionist colleagues that it had not been possible to get this hideous fact published in the American press. He felt that the work in Washington was not sufficiently sustained. No permanent Zionist office existed there in constant touch with the State Department. He called for a reinvigoration of Zionist purpose in support of the Biltmore Programme and concluded 'Miracles can happen if you work hard enough for them.'

During the first part of 1943 the prospect of allied victory brightened. Palestine was now safe from invasion and the urgent business was to create a favourable climate for the post-war settlement. It was clear that the United States would play a decisive rôle, but the vehement support which the Jewish cause enjoyed in the public and in Capitol

Hill, was not reflected in the Department of State. Weizmann now engaged the leading American diplomats, including Sumner Welles and heads of the Near East Division, in a concentrated and patient seminar on the Jewish problem and its solution. Sharett and Goldmann joined him as powerful reinforcements. Departmental chiefs now added to their diplomatic experience by experiencing the sting of Weizmann's swift retorts. One of them expressed the view that the publicity of Congressional resolutions and statements injured the Zionist cause by exciting Arab hostility. Dr Weizmann replied that 'what mattered to Arab politicians was the fact of Jewish aspiration, and not the amount of publicity that they received'. The State Department official noted that not all American Jews were united in support of Zionist aims. Dr Weizmann: 'Why is it that in all democratic countries a majority decision is deemed adequate whereas from Jews one expects unanimity?'

These conversations marked an early stage in a long and unfinished dialogue between the Jewish nation and the State Department. In their support Weizmann enlisted powerful auxiliary forces. Henry Wallace, the Vice President, Henry Morgenthau, the Secretary of the Treasury, Judge Samuel Rosenman, Robert Nathan, Isidore Lubin and Ben Cohen formed a Washington group of informal but perceptive counsellors. At a little distance off-stage, as judicial propriety directed, Felix Frankfurter surrounded him with affection and epigrammatic advice.

The official American Zionists were more at home in Congress and in the press than in direct dealing with the State Department. With them too Weizmann cemented his contacts, establishing a political committee in New York to which he brought frequent and lucid reports. He tried hard to break the public silence on the Jewish holocaust in Europe. On 1 March he took the floor at Madison Square Garden to deliver an impressive cry of anguish.

When the historian of the future assembles the black record of our days, he will find two things unbelievable: first, the crime itself; second the reaction of the world to that crime. He will sift the evidence again and again before he will be able to give credence to the fact that, in the twentieth century of the Christian era, a great and cultivated nation put power into a band of assassins who transformed murder from a secret transgression into a publicly avowed government policy to be carried out with all the paraphernalia of State. He will find the monstrous story of the human slaughterhouses, the lethal chambers, the sealed trains, taxing the powers of belief.

But when that historian, overwhelmed by the tragic evidence, sets down the verdict of the future upon this savage phenomenon, unique in the annals of mankind, he will be troubled by still another circumstance. He will be puzzled by the apathy of the civilized world in the face of this immense, systematic carnage of human beings whose sole guilt was membership in the people which gave the commandments of the moral law to mankind. He will not be able to understand why the conscience of the world had to be prodded, why sympathies had to be stirred. Above all, he will not be able to understand why the free nations, in arms against a resurgent, organized barbarism, required appeals to give sanctuary to the first and chief victim of that barbarism.

Two million Jews have already been exterminated. The world can no longer plead that the ghastly facts are unknown or unconfirmed. . . . At this moment, expressions of sympathy, without accompanying attempts to launch acts of rescue, become a hollow mockery in the ears of the dying.

The democracies have a clear duty before them. Let them negotiate with Germany through the neutral countries concerning the possible release of the Jews in the occupied countries. Let havens be designated in the vast territories of the United Nations which will give sanctuary to those fleeing from imminent murder. *Let the gates of Palestine be opened to all who can reach the shores of the Jewish homeland. The Jewish community of Palestine will welcome with joy and thanksgiving all delivered from Nazi hands.*

On 7 May he saw Lord Halifax, now the British Ambassador in Washington, and reminded him that a deadline was approaching. The White Paper required that there should be no further Jewish immigration into Palestine at all after March 1944. 'Now, Lord Halifax, do you think you can really maintain that position? Somehow or other you have allowed everybody to get away with the idea that if one additional Jew enters Palestine there will be a revolution. For all I know there will be. But the Jews have nothing to lose. If you allow the position to drift it will lead to disaster.'

He carried the same warning to President Roosevelt on June 12. The President was full of smiling but non-committal charm. He proposed a Jewish-Arab conference with the possible participation of Mr Churchill and himself. 'Did you see Churchill here in Washington?' he asked. Dr Weizmann replied: 'No. Mr Churchill doesn't like to see me because he has very little to tell me.' Roosevelt predicted that it would now be different in London.

Weizmann had completed his sojourn in the United States—the longest and most systematically planned of all his visits there. The harvest was not abundant, but he had strengthened the foundation of a sustained and ordered Zionist diplomacy in the United States. On the eve of departure he wrote to Stephen Wise in irritation about the constant 'heckling and badgering' of his efforts by some Zionist colleagues in other lands. One passage in this letter tells the full story of his attitude on the vexed question of militance and moderation:

A dangerous tendency seems to be developing in our councils. Many Zionists in responsible positions seem to think that a mere affirmation of our aims constitutes an action towards the achievement of our objective. . . . I hope you will forgive me for saying this: it is obviously nothing but demagogy continuously to play the rôle of the maximalist in the confines of a small room and conversely when meeting with Government, or even with non-Zionist Jews, to speak in whispering timidity. *I have always preferred the reverse.*

The tide of war was now running strongly for the Allied cause. British and American troops swarmed out of conquered North Africa into Sicily and the Italian mainland. Weizmann returned to London and resumed his assault on Downing Street. In the summer he mourned two gallant friends, Victor Cazalet, a Conservative Member of Parliament, killed in an air crash and the veteran Labour statesman Josiah Wedgwood, a tenacious champion of Zionism in the British Parliament for thirty years. On 25 October he lunched with Churchill at Downing Street together with the Deputy Premier, Clement Attlee and Air Marshal Lord Portal. When the ladies retired the Premier presented Weizmann affectionately to the other guests and plunged into words of firm commitment about the Jewish future. 'When we have crushed Hitler,' he said with sonorous emphasis, 'we shall have to establish the Jews in the position where they belong. I have had an inheritance left to me by Balfour and I am not going to change. But there are dark forces working against us. Dr Weizmann, you have some very good friends; for instance, Mr Attlee and the Labour Party are committed on this matter.' Mr Attlee said, 'I certainly am.' 'I know the terrible situation of the Jews,' said Churchill. 'They will get compensation and will also be able to judge the criminals. God deals with the nations as they deal with the Jews. Of every fifty officers who come back from the Middle East only one speaks favourably of the Jews. That merely convinces me that I am right.'

Weizmann drove back to his hotel in a daze of crowded thought. The words that he had heard from Churchill in the hearing of his probable successor came from the great war leader at the height of his fame and power. Only a week ago Weizmann had spoken with his old friend General Smuts after a separation of eleven years. He had poured out a bitter tale of resentment against British policy. 'I have co-operated with them for twenty-five years and now everything is being done to drive me into opposition to them.' 'Dr Weizmann,' said the General, 'you have changed a great deal in the years since we last met. Do the Jews still follow you?' Weizmann replied that the Diaspora Jews still did. 'So far as Palestine was concerned it is some years since I have been with them and they might regard me as coming empty handed. But I think that they will still follow me.'

'There are all sorts of rumours flying about concerning partition,' he wrote to Meyer Weisgal at the end of 1943. He entreated his colleagues in Jerusalem to believe that an earnest debate on partition was now in full momentum in the highest reaches of British policy. Indeed these discussions were far more concrete and positive than any proceeding at that time in the United States where other Zionist leaders believed the centre of gravity to be. Weizmann was met by sceptical reactions and accusations of wishful thinking. Years later the published documents revealed who was right.

Prime Minister to General Ismay, for Chief of Staffs Committee
January 1944

I have now read the paper about British strategic needs in the Levant States. The Chiefs of Staff seem to assume that partition will arouse Jewish resentment. It is, on the contrary, the White Paper policy that arouses the Jewish resentment. The opposition to partition will come from the Arabs, and any violence by the Arabs will be countered by the Jews. It must be remembered that Lord Wavell has stated that left to themselves the Jews would beat the Arabs. There cannot, therefore, be any great danger in our joining with the Jews to enforce the kind of proposals about partition which are set forth in the Ministerial paper. . . . Obviously we shall not proceed with any plan of partition which the Jews do not support.

The very existence of such trains of thought demanded efforts to establish the Jewish flag amongst the banners of the victorious alliance. During the period of danger, when Rommel's forces stood at the gates of Alexandria, a remarkable episode of British-Jewish co-operation had formed an island of harmony in the general discord.

Groups of hundreds of Jews, the forerunners of the Palmach, the Israel Army's striking force, had been trained by the British Department of Special Operations, to offer underground resistance to the German occupation force if the Nazis should succeed in overrunning Palestine. The country had been mapped out into zones of guerrilla operations from which the commandos would set out to disrupt communications, eliminate Nazi leaders and Generals and sell their lives dearly. A camp had been established at Mishmar Haemek at which British officers were training young Jewish fighters in the varied arts of sabotage. They were later to put these skills to good use in a context for which most of their instructors had not bargained.

By the beginning of 1944 it was plain that these hundreds of trained commandos would not be called upon to fight on Palestine soil in revolt against German occupation. The Jewish Agency, in a letter from Moshe Sharett to the British Minister Resident in Cairo, Lord Moyne, submitted a proposal for the parachuting of trained Palestinian commandos into Bulgaria, Roumania, Hungary and Slovakia for the purpose of organizing Jewish resistance movements against the Nazi occupation forces. This offer was hesitantly accepted in the most minimal dimensions. Nevertheless, Palestinian Jews, including the martyred Hanah Senesh, performed acts of heroism in which they often gave up their lives.

While the offer of commando participation was under consideration, the attempt to organize a regular Jewish fighting force was renewed in a determined diplomatic movement led by Weizmann in London and Sharett in Jerusalem and Cairo. On 28 March 1944, Weizmann addressed the War Minister, Sir James Grigg, with a 'plea for the formation of a Jewish Fighting Force within the British Army to take part in the liberation of Europe'. . . . On 4 July he wrote to Churchill even more urgently in the same sense.

It required some resilience and optimism to renew this request after the high hopes and subsequent frustrations of 1940–42. But Roosevelt had not been wrong in predicting that Weizmann would now find a new spirit in London.

Prime Minister to Dr Weizmann

5 August 1944

I am sorry to find that I have not yet replied to your letter of 4 July about the question of the Jewish Fighting Force. I can assure you, however, that I have given my personal attention to your suggestions, with which, as you know, I myself have much sympathy. They have been under active consideration during the last few weeks, and the War Office will shortly be in a position to

discuss concrete proposals with the Jewish Agency. I hope it may
be found possible to reach agreement on a scheme that will be
satisfactory to all concerned.

About the flag. I should like to know what it looks like before
I embark on this contentious ground.

Dr Weizmann to Prime Minister

5 August 1944

Your letter of August 5th in reply to mine about the Jewish
Fighting Force has given me great encouragement, and I thank
you for it most warmly. In the first place, it is a renewed assurance of your personal sympathy with the desire of the Jews to
fight the Nazis under their own name and flag. . . .

The moment that the War Office is in a position to discuss concrete proposals, I and my colleagues will be more than ready. In
the meantime, I have the greatest pleasure in sending you a sketch
of the proposed flag—two horizontal blue stripes on a white background, with the Star of David in the centre. It is known to Jews
all over the world as their national symbol. You helped us to raise
it in Palestine a quarter of a century ago; its meaning has grown
with our growth.

These exchanges leave no doubt concerning the rôle of Weizmann's
influence and prestige in the approval secured in 1944 for the formation of the Jewish Brigade Group. The publication of Churchill's
papers in 1953 makes this point even more plain, and provides the
background for the 5 August letter.

Prime Minister to Secretary of State for War

12 July 1944

I am anxious to reply promptly *to Dr Weizmann's request* for
the formation of a Jewish fighting force put forward in his letter
of July 4 of which you have been given a copy. I understand that
you wish to have the views of General Wilson and Paget before
submitting to the Cabinet a scheme for the formation of a Jewish
Brigade Force. As this matter has now been under consideration
for some time I should be glad if you would arrange for a report
setting out your proposals to be submitted to the Cabinet early
next week.

Prime Minister to the Secretary of State for War

12 July 1944

I am in general agreement with your proposals (for a Jewish
fighting force) but I think the brigade should be formed and sent

to Italy as soon as convenient, and worked up to a Brigade Group there as time goes on by the attachment of other units.

I like the idea of the Jews trying to get at the murderers of their fellow countrymen in Central Europe, and I think it would give a great deal of satisfaction in the United States.

The points of detail which occur to me are:

I believe it is the wish of the Jews themselves to fight the Germans anywhere. It is with the Germans that they have their quarrel. There is no need to put the conditions in such a form as to imply that the War office in its infinite wisdom might wish to send the Jews to fight the Japanese and that otherwise there would be no use in having the Brigade Group. . . .

I will consult the King about this proposal (that the force should have its own flag). I cannot conceive why this martyred race scattered about the world and suffering as no other race has done at this juncture should be denied the satisfaction of having a flag. However, not only the King but the Cabinet might have views on this.

Please go ahead and negotiate with the Jewish Agency. Remember the object of this is to give pleasure and an expression to rightful sentiments and that it certainly will be welcomed widely in the United States. . . .

It might have been expected that Weizmann's mood would now be more buoyant than during his melancholy conversation with Smuts in July. The faith that he had reposed in Churchill was now being vindicated in eloquent word and convincing deed. If the Prime Minister had, however belatedly, honoured his commitment in the matter of the Jewish Force why should he not do so in the case of partition? One could hear the crunch of thawing ice.

But from Europe there came a stream of news which quenched any spark of Jewish satisfaction. In June Weizmann had addressed a closed meeting of Jewish leaders on the Jewish holocaust.

Germany, as you know, has occupied Hungary, and all the news reaching us suggests that the Nazis will deal with the Hungarian Jews as they have already dealt with the Polish. Indeed, we hear that the first train-loads of Hungarian Jews have already left for Poland. On the other hand, the 'Second Front' has opened across the Channel. Knowing the minds of the Nazi leaders—as bitter experience has taught us to do—we know that the nearer they see their doom approaching, the more hastily they will strain every nerve to carry their anti-Jewish policy to full fruition.

In July a Hungarian Jew, Joel Brand, reached Istanbul where he made contact with Jewish Agency emissaries. He brought a fantastic story. Eichmann, the Nazi officer charged with the extermination of the Jews, was now engaged in the liquidation of Hungarian Jewry. Much of the grisly work had already been accomplished, but hundreds of thousands of Jews still remained alive. Allied armies were converging on Germany and the doom of Nazism and its leaders was certain. Brand explained that Eichmann had told him, in the presence of Dr Kastner, the representative of the Jewish Rescue Committee, that if 10,000 trucks were made available to Himmler, the expulsion of Jews to the Auschwitz death camp would be stopped. Brand insisted that if he could return to Budapest with the reply that the offer was being seriously considered 'the mills of death would stop grinding'. Jewish representatives urged that despite all natural scepticism the macabre offer should be treated as genuine. There was an objective possibility that Himmler was seeking to curry favour with the advancing allies by belatedly saving Jewish lives.

Weizmann, joined by Sharett in London, urged the Foreign Office to act on Brand's proposal. On 30 June Sharett cabled his colleagues in Jerusalem:

> Weizmann myself saw Foreign Under Secretary Hall stop We urged [. . .] Brand should be enabled to return immediately stop When asked whether we would prefer Brand's returning immediately or waiting till major decision has been reached we replied best course would be reach decision within next day or two and authorize Brand refer to it otherwise Brand should be sent without delay and instructed report that message been delivered is under consideration highest quarter early action will follow stop Hall stated matter is before War Cabinet our suggestion will be transmitted immediately decision will be reached soon in conjunction American Government

On 6 July Weizmann and Sharett carried their plea to the Foreign Secretary Anthony Eden whom they found maddeningly hesitant. His main argument was that 'there must be no negotiation with the enemy'. Weizmann admitted that 'the Gestapo offer must have ulterior motives. It is not impossible, however, that in the false hope of achieving their ends they would be prepared to let out a certain number of Jews, large or small. The whole thing may boil down to a question of money and the ransom should be paid.'

On the following day Weizmann urged the Foreign Office to approach the Royal Air Force with the proposal to bomb the death

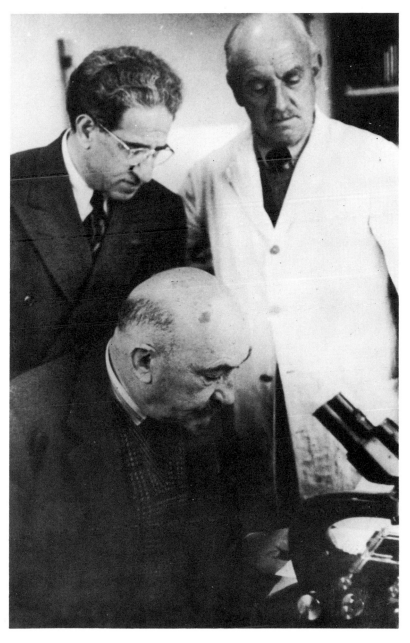

20   Weizmann in his laboratory with Weisgal and Dr Harold Davies

Israel

21 An Honorary Degree from the Hebrew University, 1947 (*left to right*) Mrs Weizmann, Weizmann and Dr J. L. Magnes

22 Weizmann reviews Druze volunteers in the Israel Army, 1948

23 Ben-Gurion, Weizmann and Yigal Yadin, Chief of Staff

24 Dr and Mrs Weizmann on their way to the Provisional State Council of Israel in Tel Aviv, 1948

25 After the assembly of the Provisional State Council of Israel, with (*left to right*) Joseph Sprinzak, Kaplan, Weisgal, Rabbi Maimon and Dr Michael Simon

camps at Auschwitz. He admitted that this measure might do no more than delay the extermination. But the bombing 'would have a far-reaching moral effect. It would mean that the allies waged direct war on the extermination of the victims of Nazi oppression'. 'Secondly', he added in a parenthesis of terrible import, 'it would give the lie to the oft-repeated assertions of Nazi spokesmen that the Allies are not really so displeased with the action of the Nazis in ridding Europe of Jews.'

The Foreign Office was living in the moral vacuum of which the White Paper was both a cause and an effect. Brand's mission was allowed to fizzle out despite Eden's assurance to Weizmann that there would be no objection to him going back. And on 1 September the Foreign Office informed Weizmann that his proposal for the bombing of the death camps had been rejected by the Royal Air Force 'for technical reasons'. Once more the British policy, in the test of administrative action, had been utterly incongruous with the declared attitude of its chief architect.

Prime Minister [Churchill] to Foreign Secretary [Eden]
11 July 1944

There is no doubt that this [persecution of Jews in Hungary] is probably the greatest and most horrible crime ever committed in the whole history of the world, and it has been done by scientific machinery by nominally civilized men in the name of a Great State and one of the leading races of Europe. It is quite clear that all concerned in this crime who may fall in to our hands, including the people who only obeyed orders by carrying out the butcheries, *should be put to death after their association with the murders has been proved.*

The prospect of retribution was small consolation to Jewish leaders whose eyes were on rescue. Weizmann sank into a deep depression in the days following the rejection of his bid for an effort on behalf of Hungarian Jewry. Indeed on 20 July he had a seizure which was believed to be dangerous.

The decision in favour of the Jewish Brigade Group had been publicly announced in September. Moreover, Weizmann's conversation with Churchill in October 1943 had set serious partitionist discussions afoot. Weizmann now prepared to make the visit to Palestine which had twice been postponed, first through his breakdown in health and then through the inability of Mrs Weizmann to make the journey.

On 3 November, he received an urgent summons from Churchill. On the following day the Prime Minister's car came to take him to Chequers. There he found the Premier's son Randolph Churchill, and his two secretaries Major Thompson and John Martin.

The Prime Minister said that he would not be able to make any public statement until the end of the German war which, in his view, was from three to six months away. He was worried by lack of support for his Zionist views in the Conservative Party and by prominent Jews such as Bernard Baruch. 'If people of this kind start talking in the same way as the military do, it only hardens my heart, but still I would like to have as much support as I can.'

Dr Weizmann showed Churchill a memorandum outlining the objections of the Jewish Agency to any partition plan which did not include the Negev. Churchill said bluntly that he was for the inclusion of the Negev. 'If you could get the whole of Palestine it would be a good thing,' he said, 'but I feel that if it comes to a choice between the White Paper and partition you should take partition. . . . America must give active support and not merely criticism. If Roosevelt and I meet at the Conference table we shall get what we want.' Churchill asked whether it was intended to bring in large numbers of Jews to Palestine. Weizmann replied that he had in mind about a million and a half in fifteen years 'as a beginning'. He then spoke of the large number of children who would have to be brought to Palestine. Churchill replied that the governments would have to worry about that, and mentioned financial aid. Weizmann was still concerned by rumours of an inadequate and crippling partition and attempted vainly to get Churchill to study maps with him. Churchill revealed that he had a committee sitting on the Palestine problem. He said that Dr Weizmann should see Lord Moyne in Cairo. 'He has developed a lot in the last two years.'

On 5 November the Colonial Secretary, Oliver Stanley, sent a car to Weizmann's hotel inviting him urgently to Whitehall. He then bluntly informed him that Lord Moyne had been assassinated in Cairo by Palestinian Jews. It later emerged that the assassins were members of the Stern Group. Killing Jews of opposing ideology had been amongst the occupations of this group; Lord Moyne was its first scalp amongst foreign statesmen. Weizmann thus had no opportunity to test Churchill's statement about Moyne's 'development'. The documents indicate that Moyne's mind had moved towards a solution by partition and that he was advising Churchill's Cabinet Committee in that direction. Weizmann never forgave Stanley for the brutal way in which he conveyed the news to him. A few days later he told one of Churchill's friends: 'Oliver Stanley is half my age and if he lives to be a hundred he will not do half of what I have done in my lifetime.'

Even now it is difficult to estimate the effect of the Moyne murder on the development of a partition solution along the lines intimated to Weizmann at Chequers on 4 November. From that date to the defeat of the Churchill Government in June 1945 all discussions on the final solution were suspended.

On the other hand it is not easy to accept the view that Churchill withdrew in cold rage from a course which he would otherwise have pursued. On 17 November we find him sending a minute to the Colonial Secretary warning against extreme anti-Zionist action since 'this may well unite the whole forces of Zionism and even Jewry throughout the world against us, instead of against the terrorist bands. . . . Dr Weizmann will no doubt join in the protests on the grounds that the whole community are being punished for the acts of a small minority.' This sober communication does not indicate that reason has taken flight before the assault of emotion. A more probable explanation is that Churchill's tentative resolve to push the issue was weakened by the increased strength gained by anti-Zionist forces.

Weizmann arrived in Palestine on 15 November.

It was a moving reunion. He had faced it with apprehension. His labours during the five preceding years had been clothed in a diplomatic secrecy made thicker by the exigencies of war communications. Not all his Palestinian colleagues had been at pains to portray his exertions in the best and truest light. He had not erred in telling Smuts that he was unsure how he stood in Palestinian Jewish eyes. Tangible successes had more than once seemed to be in his grasp; but all except the Jewish Brigade Group had slipped away. Nor was this single gain endowed with the political effect which would have adhered to it if it had been secured when first promised to him in 1941. But his perseverance had been unlimited, his tenacity unceasing. He could face the tense and embattled Yishuv with easy conscience. *Militavi Non Sine Gloria.* But would they understand?

The answer came in the storm of welcome which struck him from the moment of his arrival and attended him for twelve frenzied weeks. The Hebrew press poured out its affection in words of stately tribute. The community surrounded him with the emblems and ceremonies befitting a beloved Head of State. Indeed, anyone reading the newspapers of that period today would find it hard to believe that the Jewish State under Weizmann's presidency had not already been established. The British High Commissioner, Lord Gort, solemnly exchanged visits with him. Schoolchildren crowded into the streets to greet his coming. The farmers of Galilee endlessly displayed their smiling fields and plump livestock. At Rehovoth his scientific colleagues at the Sieff Institute saluted him with awe. The little township puffed out its chest and almost exploded with pride. A trainload of Jewish soldiers, enlisted in the Brigade Group over which he and Sharett had spent so much of their vital force, were shunted onto the Rehovoth platform to parade before the two men who had arduously laboured for their establishment.

He was moved by these tributes to the depths of his soul. His people had understood and respected the constancy of his labour. They knew that he could not guarantee victories. He could, at most, deserve them. This he had done through the five long years since the dark days of parting at Geneva. Venerable and immaculate, erect and majestic in bearing, he moved amongst them in towns and villages and talked in simple Hebrew words of the suffering which had bound them together and of the statehood which was their due. He spoke out with emphasis against the assassinations and bomb throwings of the dissident groups. As he retired each evening to the verdant beauty of his Rehovoth home the bitter, frustrated, persistent toil of foggy, bomb-ridden London seemed like a nightmare receding before the morning light. On 4 December—his seventieth birthday by the Hebrew calendar—the chorus of affection swelled to a new intensity. Addressing the Elected Assembly of Palestine Jews on Mount Scopus he analysed the political forces which would soon converge on the post-war Jewish problem. 'A drop of love and tenderness in a sea of bereavement and anguish,' wrote the daily *Davar*, 'this is what we seek on this day of greeting to the leader of our nation's liberation movement. . . . Every clod of soil in our homeland re-echoes with a prayer for redemption. . . .'

At a Zionist assembly in Tel Aviv, flanked by his colleagues, friends and erstwhile critics, he reaffirmed the claim for statehood in ringing words. He was home again, and his long absence, prolonged by compulsion or, perhaps, by an erroneous judgment of priorities, was forgotten in this the most ardent of all his reunions with the land and people in whose service he was pledged.

He returned to London early in March 1945. He was immediately affected by glaucoma and condemned to temporary blindness and to tense, agonizing operations. The first news to reach his bedside came from the American Zionist leader, Stephen Wise, reporting on a conversation with President Roosevelt on his return from Yalta. The talk had taken place on 16 March and Wise had no premonition that the President had entered his last month of life. When Wise congratulated him on his success at Yalta, Roosevelt had replied: 'I have had a failure. The one failure of my mission was with Ibn Saud. Everything went well, but not that, and I arranged the whole meeting with him for the sake of your problem.' The President went on 'Every time I mentioned the Jews he would shrink.' When Roosevelt had spoken of what the Jews had done for the reclamation of the soil Ibn Saud had said, 'My people don't like trees. We are desert dwellers.' With mischievous satisfaction Roosevelt told Wise that Churchill had launched all his rhetoric at Ibn Saud the next day for two hours—with equal poverty of result.

Thus came the end of the strange and unsubstantial Anglo-American illusion that Ibn Saud, the 'decisive' figure in Arab politics, would exert his influence for Arab-Israel understanding. It may be that the memory of the Feisal-Weizmann encounter twenty-five years before had sustained this romantic hope beyond any normal point of credulity.

The war with Germany ended in April 1945. Early in that month Churchill had written to Weizmann postponing a meeting with him on the grounds of intense preoccupation. This was unusual. Might it be an ominous symptom of uneasy conscience? Or the worried reaction of a statesman facing defeat? In the 16 March talk with Stephen Wise, Roosevelt had predicted Churchill's downfall in the June election. It is unlikely that Churchill himself was less well informed.

Weizmann now sent the Prime Minister a concise description of the situation. 'The position of the Jews in liberated countries is desperate. The political position in Palestine is becoming untenable. And so is my personal position as President of the Jewish Agency. This is the hour to eliminate the White Paper, to open the doors of Palestine and to proclaim the Jewish State.'

These six statements expressed all the themes to which he had devoted his exposition for the past six years. Those years had seen many moments of shock. Scarcely a month had passed without a telephone ringing or a cablegram arriving with some tidings of disappointment or doom. Sometimes it had been personal bereavement, as when he had learned of Michael's death; sometimes the loss of friends—Cazalet, Wedgwood, Wingate; and in his own official Zionist family—Dov Hos, Berl Katznelson, Eliahu Golomb. Then there were memories of conversations and letters in which hopes suddenly raised were just as suddenly dashed. But never was he to receive a document more full of disillusionment than the letter which came from Churchill on 9 June.

10 Downing Street,
Whitehall
9 June 1945.

My dear Dr Weizmann,
    I have received your letter of 22 May, enclosing a memorandum on behalf of the Jewish Agency for Palestine. There can, I fear, be no possibility of the question being effectively considered until the victorious Allies are definitely seated at the Peace Table.
                    Yours sincerely,
                        WINSTON S. CHURCHILL.

For months Churchill had been telling Weizmann that a substantive move would be made when the German war was over. Time and again he had emphasized his opposition to the White Paper. He had discussed partition ('If the choice is between partition and the White Paper you should take partition'). He had agreed that Israel should have the Negev. He had made solemn personal commitments ('I shall see you through'). He had lectured the Chiefs of Staff against the White Paper. He had talked of the past ('I have inherited something from Balfour')—and of the future ('If Roosevelt and I are at the Conference table, there is nothing that we cannot do'). He had given his Cabinet colleagues notice of his views ('The Jews must have territory'). And now he was winding up his historic ministry with the White Paper unabrogated, no commitment on the record and Weizmann left high and dry, standing before the Jewish people baffled, enraged, undermined and empty-handed. A week later Churchill was out of office. And a few months after that his voice, from the Opposition benches, castigated the new government for not giving Zionism its due.

    It is not easy to reconcile all this with the accepted view of Churchill's place in Zionist history. Did he believe that he would return to power in a few weeks and that there was no point in rushing the issue between the end of the German War and the election? Or was he brooding on the prospect of defeat and confident, after confronting Weizmann and Attlee at Chequers, that the Labour Party would not let the Jews down? These are the only suppositions which have any power of extenuation. But in view of his constant emphasis in every Cabinet minute on Weizmann's personal rôle one would have expected Churchill to be sensitive to Weizmann's reference to himself ('My position as President of the Jewish Agency is becoming untenable'). After all, it would have been easy to strengthen his hand. A statement declaring that Britain, with American support, would seek a solution other than the White Paper, and was actively deliberating on partition, would have given a solid starting-point for Zionist relations with the next government. This was not done. Weizmann's last letter to Churchill as Prime Minister speaks of 'great shock' and disappointment.

On the receipt of Churchill's letter, Weizmann immediately made preparations to resign his leadership:

Mrs Dugdale's Diary—27 June

In the morning long informal talk between Chaim, Berl Locker, Lewis Namier and self about his projected resignation and the means of informing the PM beforehand. He will . . . write a letter, but also use the best personal channels which would appear to be —Smuts, Randolph [Churchill]. Should this be before or after next Big Three meeting?

Weizmann had invested endless hope and toil in Churchill and Roosevelt. By the summer of 1945, Roosevelt was dead and Churchill swept from power. The two had been endowed with unchallengeable power to set the Jewish cause on the road to consolation and recovery. They had not used that power. When they left the scene which they had dominated for six years the Jewish people stood at the lowest point of its historic fortune—stunned with anguish, ignored, rebuffed and with no glimpse of light ahead. On 26 July the Churchill Government was defeated and the Labour Party returned to power. Palestine Jewry celebrated the advent of the 'friendly' government with joy. Weizmann suspended his resignation plans and returned to the fray. But the celebration had been premature. . . .

How many times can one go back to the beginning and rebuild a shattered fortress of hope? Weizmann must have asked himself this question many times as he drove to Whitehall to demand his people's justice from the new and mediocre Colonial Secretary George Hall and his well-meaning but weak deputy Arthur Creech-Jones. At the Zionist Conference in London in August he had held no promise of better days. That meeting had been moving in its many episodes of reunion, but quite indecisive on the political future. The Labour Party was committed to a pro-Zionist programme. Its policy, as formulated by Hugh Dalton only a few months before, had bravely declared: 'There is surely neither hope nor meaning in a Jewish National Home unless we are prepared to let Jews, if they wish, enter this tiny land in such numbers as to become a majority. There was a strong case for this before the war. There is an irresistible case now after the unspeakable atrocities of the cold and calculated German Nazi plan to kill all Jews in Europe...' The statement went on to propose a voluntary population exchange: 'Let the Arabs be encouraged to move out as the Jews move in.'

When Attlee formed his government he had first considered Hugh Dalton as Foreign Secretary and Ernest Bevin as Chancellor of Exchequer. In twenty-four hours the rôles had been reversed. It is tempting to speculate on the influence of this change on Zionist fortunes. Dalton is revealed in his papers and diaries published in 1962[1] as an ardent partitionist, pressing his case in Cabinet from 1945 to early 1947. At that stage he was so alienated by the Irgun's action in strangling two innocent sergeants and attaching booby traps to their corpses that, in his words, 'I went absolutely cold towards the Jews in Palestine and didn't care what happened to them.' A few weeks later, however, the papers show him again advocating a partition solution. Mr Dalton also records that his disposition would have been to accept President Truman's proposal for the entry of 100,000 immigrants in 1946. The irony is that if this friendly inclination had been put into effect the problem would have lost its unendurable tension, and it is doubtful if the state of Israel would have arisen.

Mr Bevin was destined to be Israel's George III, the perverse and unwilling agent of her independence.

How unwilling Bevin was to promote Jewish national survival became apparent during the first weeks of the Labour Government's life. At his first meeting with the new Foreign Secretary on 10 October, Weizmann found him in irritable resentment at President Truman's proposal for the admission of 100,000 Jewish 'displaced persons' from Europe. The President's suggestion to Mr Attlee had been made in August on the basis of a report by his special emissary, Earl Harrison, who had visited the concentration camps where the Jewish survivors lingered on in emancipation and dull despair. 'They want to be evacuated now,' said Harrison, 'Palestine is definitely and pre-eminently their first choice.... Only in Palestine will they be welcome and find peace and quiet and be given an opportunity to live and work.'

[1] Hugh Dalton, *High Tide and After* (Muller, London, 1962).

Bevin now told Weizmann that 'he doubted whether the grant of 100,000 permits would be the right way to set about the business'. This ominous negation was followed by a thunderclap on November 13. In a statement of policy, Bevin refused to cancel the White Paper, repudiated the Labour Party's Conference Statement of December 1944, observed that 'we cannot accept the view that the Jews should be driven out of Europe', and announced the appointment of an Anglo-American Committee of Inquiry to consider the position of the Jews in Europe and to propose a solution to the two governments. In subsequent speeches Bevin spoke insultingly of Truman, bluntly ascribing his interest in Palestine to the electoral position in New York State. (The Presidential election was three years ahead!) Bevin also suggested that Truman's action was motivated by a desire to see that no more Jews got into the United States, and referred offensively to 'a person named Earl Harrison' whose report on the aspirations of the Jewish refugees was described as 'having set the whole thing back'. It should be remembered that Mr Bevin's main responsibility at that time was to strengthen American-British relations.

In point of fact, President Truman's approach to Attlee in August 1945 had not been suddenly conceived. He had addressed Churchill on 24 July—a week before the British election—with a suggestion that the Palestine problem be discussed between them at the Big Three meeting at Potsdam.

Knowing your deep and sympathetic interest in Jewish settlement in Palestine, I venture to express the hope that the British Government may find it possible without delay to lift the restrictions of the White Paper on Jewish immigration into Palestine. I hope that you can arrange at your earliest convenience to let me have your ideas on the settlement of the Palestine problems so that we can . . . discuss the problem in concrete terms.

By the time that this note had reached London, Attlee had succeeded Churchill. Between July and November the Labour Government had paid no heed to the President's request. But Truman's persistence went far beyond all the deferential communications previously made from Washington to London. This led the Attlee government to associate the United States in the new Commission of Inquiry.

It was the first formal and active engagement of American policy in determining the future of a Near Eastern country. In their indignation at Bevin's malevolence, the Zionists probably gave too little weight to this revolutionary departure. Palestine was never again to move within the sole orbit of British jurisdiction.

Weizmann was in the United States when Bevin's statement was announced. On 27 November, his 71st birthday, he had addressed the Founders' Dinner of the Weizmann Institute of Science. Scientists and Jewish leaders had taken part in this splendid and august occasion for which the stage had been set by Meyer Weisgal, who had been Weizmann's chief counsellor in his political work in the United States as well as in his scientific enterprises. Rising to the homage of a large and distinguished gathering, Weizmann had digressed from his observations on the scientific theme to speak of the 'considerable bitterness' which afflicted him. 'We had every reason to believe that the White Paper which had been riveted on the neck of the Yishuv would, with the advent of the present government, probably be lifted. We have been bitterly disappointed.'

Meanwhile Bevin's callous statements had burst the dykes of Jewish restraint. British troops and Jewish resistance groups were now in almost daily conflict at one point or another of Palestine territory. Hope was focused more and more on American intervention. Weizmann found Truman an encouraging listener at their first meeting on 4 December 1945. He followed up this crucial contact with an eloquent memorandum to the President claiming a 'Jewish democratic Commonwealth giving shelter, sustenance and peace to Jews and Arabs alike'. After a brief stay in London, he set out for Palestine at the end of February 1946, to prepare his statement for the Anglo-American Commission.

'Today', wrote Richard Crossman in his diary on 8 March, [1] 'We had Weizmann, who looks like a weary and more humane version of Lenin, very tired, very ill. . . . He spoke for two hours with a magnificent mixture of passion and scientific detachment. . . . He is the first witness who has frankly and openly admitted that the issue is not between right and wrong, but between the greater and the lesser injustice.'

Few other members of the Anglo-American Commission had Crossman's sophistication or power of expression. But they all shared his verdict on Weizmann's sombre and moving address. The hearings took place in the YMCA Hall in Jerusalem under the chairmanship of Mr Justice Singleton, the British Chairman. Among the American members Bartley Crum and James MacDonald were in strong

[1] R. H. S. Crossman, *Palestine Mission* (London, 1947, New York, Harper and Bros., 1947).

sympathy with the Jewish cause. Reginald Manningham-Buller, Lord Morrison and Sir Frederick Leggett were responsive to the ideas of the Palestine Administration and the British Government. On the American side Professor Aydelotte and Ambassador William Phillips maintained the detachment usual to the academic and diplomatic disposition. A colourful southern Judge, Joseph Hutcheson ('Texas Joe'), enlivened the deliberations with a carefully contrived informality of ideas and expression.

It was strange that what Roosevelt, Churchill, Sumner Wells, Halifax, Attlee and Bevin had feared to decide, should now have been put on the shoulders of this able but not excessively distinguished group.

Arab witnesses stridently urged the end of Zionist development. Jewish spokesmen called for free immigration and land purchase and the eventual development of a Jewish Commonwealth. Behind the scenes Weizmann and Sharett openly hinted that an adequate partition plan would win Jewish support. Indeed, Weizmann told Crum and Crossman at luncheon in Rehovoth, that he saw no possibility of any continuation of the British Administration in Palestine.

'Somehow', wrote a British member of the Commission a year later, 'we like the Arabs even though they fight us; and we dislike the Jews even if our interests go together.' But when the Commission reached Lausanne to consider its judgment in the tranquillity of the Swiss lakes and mountains, the stress of argument went beyond these intuitive prejudices. Partition was considered and rejected as a 'counsel of despair'. In the glow of the post-war world there was reluctance to believe that any two peoples could not be made to live together—even when all the circumstances of history and sentiment proved that a 'desperate' solution was the only true answer to a desperate situation. Finally, the Commission announced its conclusions. The White Paper should be abolished, 100,000 immigrants should be admitted at once, land restrictions removed, and Palestine be prepared for trusteeship with no statehood either for the Jews or the Arabs.

The report had rejected Jewish long-term proposals for a sovereign state. But in the context of its time it was something of a break-through. The White Paper of 1939 was now smashed to pieces. The doors were to be opened, the humiliating pale-of-settlement land laws repealed and the doctrine of permanent Jewish minority status repudiated. The Jewish leaders were divided in their attitude. Some, including Ben-Gurion, stressed its negative findings on the constitutional future. Others saw it as a point of release for

pent-up energies and the prelude to a new spurt of intensive con-
solidation. With a great infusion of Jewish immigrants and a
broadening of the territorial structure, the prospect of a Jewish State
solution seemed greatly enhanced. Crossman wrote in his diary on
22 April:

> I cannot help seeing this report, if adopted by the Government,
> as a useful, indeed a necessary step to an ultimate partition. . . .
> The Arabs have lost the White Paper of 1939 and must look for-
> ward now to continued Jewish immigration, and, even more
> important, Jewish settlements being set up over the whole of
> Palestine, now that the Land Transfer Regulations have been
> abolished.

Zionists who compared the report with their hopes for the future
were disappointed. Those who compared it with the reality of the
present were elated. Twice—first in the Peel Report of 1937 and
now in the Anglo-American Inquiry of 1946—the aspiration to
thwart the dynamic of Zionism had been frustrated by a competent
and not over-sympathetic tribunal.

But it was hardly worth while for Zionist leaders to quarrel about
a report which the British Government refused to implement. President Truman swiftly published his support of the immigration proposal which was, by all accounts, the central innovation of the
report. But in sharp anger, Attlee and Bevin drowned the incipient
Jewish enthusiasm in a flood of cold water. They made the implementation of the plan dependent on American military aid and on
the disarming of the Jewish population. The disbandment of Jewish
defence forces had been proposed in the Anglo-American Commission's deliberations, but rejected by eight votes to four. Thus Bevin
had violated his promise to the Commission that he would accept
any verdict reached unanimously by its members; and Attlee had
attached a condition which the Commission had explicitly dismissed. In Bournemouth, a few weeks later, Bevin descended to new
depth of anti-Semitic invective in excusing his rejection of the
report.

For the Palestine Jewry the lesson was plain. There was no doubt
that the British Government would have carried out an anti-Zionist
report with pious fervour. Bevin's message to the Jewish people was
'Heads I win, tails you lose.' Acts of violence and sabotage in Palestine mounted in intensity and frequency. Dark despair descended on
the refugee camps in Europe. The Labour Government had shown
something not far from sadism in dispelling the hopes of rescue

which the Anglo-American Report had raised in tens of thousands of Jewish hearts.

Attlee and Bevin seemed bent on creating a crisis of revolutionary proportions. On 29 June the Palestine Government arrested the Jewish Agency leaders, Moshe Sharett, Dov Joseph, Rabbi Maimon and David Remez and other representative figures. The Jewish Agency headquarters were occupied and searched. The Jewish leaders were to be held at Latrun without any charge against them for over four months. The leaders of the activist groups whose excesses Sharett and his colleagues had castigated were left cheerfully unmolested! Even in the history of colonial misrule it would be difficult to find a more insane action than this desperate fling of the dying mandate.

It was evidently the hope of the Labour leaders and of the Army Intelligence officers under Colonel Martin Charteris that the way would be cleared for 'collaboration' with and by Dr Weizmann. Arriving at Government House the aged Zionist leaders shook the High Commissioner Sir Alan Cunningham out of his equanimity. In an address to the Actions Committee on 9 July, Weizmann excoriated the administration in words far stronger than those used by his 'extremist' colleagues behind the barbed wire in Latrun:

> When I am asked these days to use my 'restraining influence' my mind goes back some forty years or more to the day when a poor Jewish tailor shot the Governor-General at Vilna. We were called by Plehwe, and commanded to 'restrain' our young men, lest worse things befall us. And we told Plehwe that, much as we deplored such acts of violence, they were the inevitable result of the impossible conditions which Russia had herself created for her Jewish population and which deprived the leaders of the community of any influence they might otherwise have possessed. Looking back now, I see that the single shot fired by a little Jewish tailor was the first shot of the 'Great Revolution'.

He continued with irony and anger:

> Nothing could be farther from my mind than to suggest comparisons between the Tsarist regime and the British Government of today, but one's memory is sometimes irrational. . . . Ours is no less a struggle—Let my people go!

He went back to London. In the conditions of those pre-jet days the frequency and extent of his travel were a prodigy for a man 72 years old and weighed down by ill-health. On 22 July the news came that the King David Hotel had been blown up with fearful loss of British, Jewish and Arab life. Two days later the British Government published a White Paper showing that the Agency leaders, not excluding Weizmann, had been privy to the violent activism of recent months. On 29 July the press carried a violent circular by the Commander of British troops in Palestine, General Sir Evelyn Barker, bidding his troops act with 'hatred and contempt' towards all members of the Jewish 'race', and especially 'to hit them in the pocket where it hurts'. On 30 July, Weizmann was invited to see the Colonial Secretary. He refused to attend until the Palestine debate in the House of Commons was over. He suspected that the Government's intention was to claim that he had been 'consulted' in advance on its proposed statement of policy.

The respite offered by the Anglo-American Commission's Report had been squandered. Peace had come to Europe only to be disrupted in Palestine. Bevin had contrived to make an admittedly complicated situation even more complicated than it was previously thought to be. On 1 October Weizmann and his colleagues made a purposeful attempt to find a path of reason in the thickets of the Foreign Secretary's obduracy.

Weizmann said that he had come 'in the hope that it would be possible to hack out a solution which would stop the strife in Palestine'. The first need was to release the arrested Zionist leaders. Then the military command in Palestine should be restrained. 'I do not want to waste any words on a man like General Barker. Terrorism will not be stopped as long as the Army and General Barker do the things that are being done in Palestine. A solution can be arrived at. The solution I have in mind is partition.'

The soft answers did not turn away wrath. The Jewish leaders were now given a glimpse into the dark places of the Foreign Secretary's mind. The official record of the meeting continues:

Mr Bevin said . . . that as far as he could see the British were the best friends of the Jews, but he had never seen so much anti-Semitism under the skin as there exists now. . . . They did not segregate Jews in this country. The Jews were free here and had made a great contribution to the success of Britain in commerce, science, and so on. . . . More Jews had been taken into this country than any other of its size, but the treatment being meted out to them by the Jews was very bad. He thought that the Jewish Agency could have helped them earlier. The feeling in this country was that they had declared war on Britain.

. . . The Arabs would not accept partition. Was he to force it on them with British bayonets? He would try to get agreement, other wise they would hand the Mandate back to UNO. He wanted to work out a plan for a unitary state with democratic safeguards. He would like as the greatest triumph of his career to find a solution.

Mr Hall then reiterated the invitation to the Jewish representatives to attend the 'conference' then being held to find a solution. The Arabs had been in attendance for many weeks; but the Jewish Agency had refused to participate until its leaders were released.

As the Jewish leaders dispersed into the dark London streets their minds revolved confusedly on the medley of ideas that they had just heard. Would any other Foreign Secretary in British history have openly and persistently described such an issue in terms of his own 'career'? Yet this theme was never absent from Bevin's discourse. It seemed to set him apart from the style and tradition established by all those who had preceded or were to follow him in that room.

The 'plan' to which he referred later turned out to be a federal scheme propounded by a reluctant Herbert Morrison to the House of Commons. It involved the establishment of a tiny enclave, without sovereignty, in which Jewish immigration and settlement would be permitted. The Jews had no two minds about this idea; and there followed a warm and moving correspondence between the two leading figures in Zionism.

28.10.1946.—Letter from Mr David Ben-Gurion (Paris)
to Dr Weizmann (London)
(Translated from Hebrew)

I rejoiced to hear that your second [eye] operation succeeded and that you will soon leave hospital for a rest in Switzerland. I hope that you will be able to participate in full vigour in the Congress. I am sure that even those who do not agree with you in every respect have much to learn from your experience and your sagacity—and especially from your profound Jewish and Zionist intuition. . . .

I think that we have reached a political cross-road. . . . Even though there are a few in the Yishuv who believe that we should resign ourselves to the Morrison plan, since it gives a possibility of immigration and constructive work and may in the future lead to a State. I believe that we should oppose the plan with all our power, to the extent of boycotting any Conference which places it in the centre of its deliberations. Even more—we should go so far as to boycott the plan if the Government tries to impose it on the Jews and Arabs.

This is not because we should reject every compromise. On the contrary. . . . We should, in my opinion, be ready for an enlightened compromise even if it gives us less in practice than we have a right to in theory, but only so long as what is granted to us is really in our hands. That is why I was in favour of the principle of the Peel Report in 1937 and would even now accept a Jewish State in an adequate part of the country, rather than a British Mandate with White Paper rights in all the country. . . .

Our line should be the Mandate—or a State. For as long as Britain rules Palestine she must carry out the Mandate as the League of Nations intended. . . . If Britain is unable or unwilling to carry out the Mandate, she should agree to the establishment of a Jewish State, even if not in the whole of Palestine, but at once. . . .

I hope to find you in better health and able to bring your contribution to this Congress—a contribution that the providence of Jewish history has enabled only you to bring.'

Ben-Gurion concluded in words of eloquent tribute to his older colleague:

. . . Whatever your views are on all this you remain for me the elect of Jewish history, representing beyond compare the suffering and the glory of the Jews. And wherever you go you will be attended by the love, and faithful esteem of me and of my colleagues. We are the generation which comes after you and which has been tried, perhaps, by crueller and greater sufferings and we sometimes, for this reason, see things differently—but fundamentally we draw from the same reservoir of inspiration—that of sorely tried Russian Jewry—the qualities of tenacity, faith, and persistent striving which yields to no adversary or foe.

6.11.1946.—Letter from Dr Weizmann to Mr Ben-Gurion

My dear B.G.,

I was greatly moved by your very charming and friendly letter to me and touched by your considerateness in taking such pains to write it by hand and in big letters. I am sorry that, even so, I was unable to read it all myself, and had to have most of it read to me. My eyes are improving, but slowly. When I get my new glasses I look forward to reading it all for myself—I hope in a few days from now.

I am in cordial agreement with the main lines of your policy, though I think it would be wrong to abstain from the Conference, even if our point of view is not accepted beforehand. I believe the others will eventually come round to it.

A great deal will, of course, turn on the conversations between Byrnes and Bevin now going on. I can't help feeling that the inexorable logic of facts will drive them towards partition. I was very happy to see in the papers today that you are seeing Lord Inverchapel—he used to be a very good friend of ours, and I hope still is. I shall be much interested to hear of your conversation with him. . . .

We both send you and Paula our affectionate regards: may the future bring you every satisfaction, and some freedom from the cares which have oppressed us all so heavily in the last few years.

CHAIM WEIZMANN.

For fifty years the parliament of the Jewish people had wandered pathetically between hired halls in European lake-resorts and spas. Basle was its first home. Some Zionist veterans were still alive who could recall the top-hatted, white-tied Assembly in which Herzl and Nordau tried to introduce the Jewish people to the order and majesty of European parliamentarism. But by 1946 symbolism and formality were not the main purpose. Zionism had become a ramified enterprise with its banks, funds, companies and newspapers. Above all, the Congress was the arena for the political debate. Its discussions re-echoed with the appeal to remove Jewish history from its isolated compartment and merge it into the cosmic procession in which all other nations moved.

In the days before the Nazi holocaust all the colours of the Jewish spectrum were reflected here. Industrialists, professional men and Rabbis from America and South Africa mingled with dark-eyed Yemenites from Palestinian farms. East European Zionists, passionate and intense, poured out their dreams in public, while prosperous and cultivated German Jews would meditate on the more practical and urgent compromises of tomorrow. A small delegation of British Jewry would patiently accept its submergence in this flood, and then go back with relief to Great Russell Street where, by the grace of political geography, it counted for something beyond its mere numbers. In recent years Palestinian Jewry, with double representation in tribute to its special status, had come to dominate the Congress with broad and varied delegations which were almost a facsimile of the Jewish people itself.

On this stage Weizmann had been the leading star for thirty years. The appearance of the massive domed head and tall figure at the rostrum would hush the turmoil, as his soft, modulated voice came across the benches where the Jewish people sat, complete in its diversity.

And now he was probably going there for the last time. As he struggled in Lugano to regain his sight after the London operations he had heard little of the manœuvrings which were to drive him from his presidential office. The plain fact was that the Zionist movement had moved out of primeval innocence to taste the fruit of political knowledge—good and evil. There were ambitions, envies, caucuses, lobbies, jostlings and shovings—as well as the overriding conflicts of ideology and policy which gave legitimacy to all of these.

Weizmann had built no bridges and mended no fences in this internal political struggle. He had never campaigned or election-eered. The President of the Zionist Organization was a Prime Minis-ter, Ambassador and Tax-Collector rolled into one. The powers of the office had never been defined. But in the years in which it mat-tered most its main incumbents had been Herzl and Weizmann, with David Wolffsohn and Nahum Sokolow serving periods of manifest and avowed interregnum. The attributes of the two chief Presidents emphasized the authoritarian aspect of the office. Whatever one thought of Herzl and Weizmann, nobody could imagine them in any rôle but that of captaincy.

There can be no doubt that many leaders of the American and Palestinian delegations came to Basle with the fixed idea of remov-ing Weizmann from office. This, indeed, was the only original idea with which they came. The clash was of personalities, not of policies. Did Weizmann, behind the Biltmore formula, see the 'sinful' shape of Partition? Partition was precisely what his adversaries wanted and what, with his aid, they were going to get. Did they feel that the mandatory period had run its course and suffered no renewal? It was he who had told the Anglo-American Commissioners that 'some-thing had snapped' in the British Jewish relationship and a new solution by statehood was now imperative. Was the trouble with him that he always condemned the dissident activists? As soon as he was dismissed the Congress, by a large majority, adopted a resolu-tion 'opposing and condemning acts of murder and bloodshed of innocent people as a means of political struggle'. The resolution went on: '. . . The terrorist acts of certain groups in Palestine which have separated themselves from the community, violating the disci-pline of the supreme national institutions, distort the true character of the Yishuv in the eyes of the world and do not advance, but rather injure its just struggle. The Congress proclaims its full support of the Yishuv in its anti-terrorist efforts.'

The truth is that the Congress was torn between a deep affection for his person and a sentiment that he symbolized a policy which they—and he—no longer upheld, but with which a stubborn mythology had identified him beyond repair. Their resentment against Britain was nothing as compared to his. They felt politically frustrated. He felt personally as well as nationally betrayed. But a statesman remains a symbol of an attitude long after the attitude has passed away. The Zionist movement was entering a short but crucial phase of intense conflict with Britain. Weizmann's leadership of such a conflict would have diminished the credibility of the conflict itself. The logic which had led him to surrender his Presidency in protest against the first Government's betrayal in 1930 might well have been valid now. But instead of following this course, in harmony and consent, the Congress and he fell apart in a tragic atmosphere, of resentment on his part and furtive distrust on theirs.

And yet there was no Congress which he dominated so completely. 'The shadow of tragic bereavement is upon us tonight,' he said in the opening address, casting a glance inquiringly over the assembly, as if to wonder where German, Polish, Hungarian, Dutch and Belgian Jewry had gone. The voice was choked, the eyes tense and painful behind the dark glasses. 'The greatest malice in the annals of inhumanity was turned against us and found our people with no hope of defence. . . . European Jewry had been engulfed in a tidal wave. Its centres of life and culture have been ravaged, its habitations laid waste.'

The familiar voice continued, low in tone and incisive in formulation. He spoke of the White Paper: 'Few documents in history have worse consequences for which to answer.' He told of British ministerial promises which he had frankly believed: 'It seemed incredible that anybody could be playing fast and loose with us when we were so battered and exhausted.' He did not deny the existence of a strong anti-British current in the sentiment of the Jewish people: 'If there is antagonism directed against the British Government, its sole origin is indignation at Britain's desertion of her trust.' He spoke lucidly of Arab hostility: 'How can it be moderate for them to claim seven states and extreme for us to claim one? Sympathy belongs to those who have suffered. Restitution is the desert of those in need. The Arab people cannot compare with us in suffering and need.'

In an electric atmosphere he declared that he understood the motives which led many young Jews in Palestine to violence. 'It is

difficult in such circumstances to retain a belief in the victory of
peaceful ideals. And yet I affirm without any hesitation that we
have to retain it. . . . Jews came to Palestine to build, not to destroy.
. . . Massada, for all its heroism, was a disaster in our history.
Zionism was to mark the end of our glorious deaths and the beginning of a new path whose watchword is—Life!'

The debate went on, endlessly. Nobody rose to his level of feeling
or expression. Here and there criticism of his patience was expressed.
Some speakers committed the cardinal sin in his eyes—the confusion
between formulating a policy and indicating the road to its fulfilment. Little was said in collision with his views. But he was in a
strange de-humanized atmosphere in which younger men felt that
he was quite simply and personally in their way.

He reached a firm decision. Like the blinded Samson he would
grip the pillars of the Temple and bring it down upon his head. On
16 December he arose to perform the most remarkable of his ora-
torical feats at any Congress. With delicate scorn he lashed out at
those who recoiled from the necessity of patient toil, both in diplomacy and in development. He promised 'blood and tears'. There
was no shame in failure. 'My grandfather used to say that he never
made any mistakes in the letters which he did not write.' In the chanceries as in his own laboratories he believed in the experimental
method. 'Our suffering and anguish are not sufficient reason to
desert a rational path in favour of adventurism.' He was not interested in the debate between adherents of Silver and Goldmann about
credit for American support. 'There are enough credits around for
everybody to get his fair supply.'

An American Zionist leader had urged Palestinian Jewry to revolt
against Britain while American Jews 'would give full political and
moral support'. Weizmann was enraged by this formulation. He
would have none of this division between the battlefield and the
side-lines. He now uttered the rebuke which may have cost him the
Presidency: 'Moral and political support is very little when you send
other people to the barricades to face tanks and guns. The eleven
new settlements just established in the Negev have, in my deepest
conviction, a far greater weight than a hundred speeches about
resistance—especially when the speeches are made in New York
while the proposed resistance is to be made in Tel-Aviv and
Jerusalem.'

His voice was now stronger than anybody remembered it for a
long time. As he delivered his rebuke against vicarious 'activism' by
those who intended to stay far away from the gunpowder, a delegate

called out 'Demagogy'. He stopped his discourse, took off his glasses, and stood in stunned silence. Never had this happened to him. His age, infirmity, patient toil and sacrifice had been violated in a moment of dreadful rancour. The Assembly sat in horrified tension as he pondered his reply. The Congress protocol quotes him as follows: 'Somebody has called me a demagogue. I do not know who. I hope that I never learn the man's name. I—a demagogue! I who have borne all the ills and travail of this movement (loud applause). The person who flung that word in my face ought to know that in every house and stable in Nahalal, in every little workshop in Tel-Aviv or Haifa, there is a drop of my blood. (*Tempestuous applause. The delegates all rise to their feet except the Revisionists and Mizrachi*). You know that I am telling you the truth. Some people don't like to hear it—but you *will* hear me. I warn you against bogus palliatives, against short cuts, against false prophets, against facile generalizations, against distortion of historic facts. . . . If you think of bringing the redemption nearer by un-Jewish methods, if you lose faith in hard work and better days, then you commit idolatry (avodah zarah) and endanger what we have built. Would that I had a tongue of flame, the strength of prophets, to warn you against the paths of Babylon and Egypt. "Zion shall be redeemed in Judgment" —and not by any other means.'

No dramatist could have conceived a more overpowering climax. He left the hall never again to make a controversial address to a Jewish audience. Between the rows of applauding delegates standing in awe and contrition he made his way painfully, gropingly, into the street. A few days later he appeared to make a short farewell. 'If I have said harsh things to anyone, I did not intend to hurt. The Jewish people, especially those waiting in the camps, look to you to open the gates. I thank you all.'

The delegates arose, this time without exception and sang Hatikvah. Weizmann, the Zionist, had left the Congress arena for ever.

He had made his presidency dependent on freedom for the Zionist executive, if it saw fit, to attend discussions in London in a last attempt to concert a settlement with Britain. The Congress, by a small majority, rejected a Labour-Zionist resolution, proposed by Golda Meir, urging this course, and voted categorically against attending the London Conference 'in present circumstances'. This was tantamount to a rejection of his candidacy.

A month later with no change of 'circumstances' the new Executive attended talks with the British Government in London and attempted to reach an agreement—on the basis of partition. For the second time in two decades the Zionist movement had first dismissed Weizmann—and then followed his advice.

On 23 December he returned to London where he heard of his final defeat at Basle. His bitterness was sharp. It was directed both at the British Government which had betrayed his hopes and at his Zionist followers who had withheld the candour and appreciation which he thought that he had earned. He fell into an aggrieved solitude. In a letter to friends during January he mentioned a small group of Zionists who continued to keep him in touch with the pulse and spirit of events: 'Sacher, Simon Marks, Isaiah Berlin, Stein, Eban and a few others.' He ends his letter pathetically: 'Give my love to Lipsky and other friends (if any).'

Early in February 1947 he left for Palestine and gave himself actively to the work of the Weizmann Institute of Science. Eight months before amidst daily violence and tension, he had laid the foundation stone of the Institute in a short address, whose motto is monumentally inscribed today on the Weizmann Memorial Plaza: 'I believe that science will bring to this country both peace and renewal of its youth.'

He had given up the reins, but his ears were alertly tuned to the news from London. There, in a chilly room of the Colonial Office, with the electric light repeatedly going out owing to the fuel shortage, the last attempt was being made to reach a settlement by consent between Britain and the Jewish people. It was a populous and unwieldy negotiation between British representatives from the Foreign and Colonial Offices (Bevin, Creech-Jones, Sir Norman Brook, Sir Douglas Harris, Sir Thomas Lloyd, Beeley, Martin, Baxter, Trafford Smith, Armstrong) and a large Jewish Agency delegation (Ben-Gurion, Shertok, Brodetsky, Gruenbaum, Goldmann, Neumann, Locker, Horowitz, Eban, Linton, Rosenne). Not for a single moment did Bevin allow a conciliatory mood to take root. The discussion ranged from Partition, which Bevin professed himself as unentitled to impose, to various federal schemes based on the Morrison Plan, which Bevin had amended ferociously to the Jewish detriment. While constantly asserting that it would be wrong under partition to place 300,000 Arabs under Jewish 'domination', Bevin declined to explain why it would be right, under his proposals, to subject 700,000 Jews to the domination of the Arabs.

The Jewish leaders saw British policy at its lowest level of representation. It had neither the old imperial dignity nor the liberalism of the post-war age. It was incredible that the very Cabinet which stood paralysed before the Palestine issue had carried out the Indian Partition with such audacity and sweep.

Above all, it was the policy of a tired nation, weary of responsibilities beyond its power. As the talks proceeded into late February Bevin sank into a mood of cosmic despair. He began to declare that he would 'wash his hands of the whole business' and send the issue to the United Nations. The Zionist leaders reacted to this idea with scepticism and distaste. They believed neither that Britain would relinquish its trust, nor that the Jewish cause would triumph in the arena of multilateral diplomacy. But there was no other way out. Churchill had for several months been advocating the end of the Mandate. 'I cannot . . . recede from the advice which I have ventured to give, namely that if we cannot fulfil our promises to the Zionists we should, without delay, place our mandate for Palestine at the feet of the United Nations and give due notice of our impending evacuation of that country.'

Bevin had been won round to this policy by the failure of the February talks. On 18 February 1947, the decision came in a public announcement.

> His Majesty's Government have of themselves no power under the terms of the Mandate to award the country either to the Arabs or to the Jews, or even to partition it between them. . . . We have therefore reached the conclusion that the only course open to us is to submit the problem to the judgment of the United Nations.

In preparation for a substantive discussion in the autumn session, the United Kingdom requested a special session earlier in the year. On 29 April 1947 the General Assembly convened at Flushing Meadow, New York with 'the Palestine question' inscribed on its agenda—where it was to remain for many long years to come.

The Jewish cause had been anchored for four decades in British waters. For good or ill it was now set loose on the international ocean. The first sensation was of solitude rather than of exhilaration. The League of Nations had never played much of a rôle in the administration of the Mandate of which it was theoretically the master. British ministers, diplomats and colonial officials had reacted with condescension to the duty of reporting every year to amiable foreigners in Geneva, such as the Swiss Rappard, the Belgian Orts and their own luminary, Lord Lugard. It cannot be said that the Zionist executive during the late 1930's invested any great tenacity or optimism in cultivating Geneva as a possible counter-weight to

London. As the League's prestige declined in general, it sank in each particular problem submitted to it.

But now on the ruins of the League a new and seemingly more robust international organization had arisen, fortified by the membership of all the major powers, and enjoying American support to a degree that must have caused ironical anguish to the ghost of Woodrow Wilson. There was, of course, a danger that the special ethos and pathos of Zionism would be submerged in the torrent of global politics. After all, the slogan of self-determination had never been applied to an ingathering people not yet constituting a majority on its soil.

But there was also an opportunity. The Jewish claim would now be weighed on the scale of international justice, remote, to some degree, from the strategic interests of any single power. On 15 May 1947 the General Assembly voted to appoint a Special Committee to make recommendations to the General Assembly. It had heard an eloquent appeal from Rabbi Abba Hillel Silver.

> The Jewish people belongs in this society of nations. Surely the Jewish people is no less deserving than other peoples whose national freedom and independence have been established and whose representatives are now seated here. The Jewish people were your Allies in the war and joined their sacrifices to yours to achieve a common victory. . . . The representatives of the Jewish people of Palestine should sit in your midst.

Eleven countries, other than the Great Powers (Sweden, Canada, Iran, India, Holland, Australia, Guatemala, Uruguay, Peru, Czechoslovakia and Yugoslavia), were appointed to the United Nations Special Committee. The Jewish Agency announced the appointment of two liaison officers, Abba Eban and David Horowitz. The Arab Higher Committee, in a blunder of historic scale, boycotted the Committee and refused to be represented. The Jewish liaison officers were briefed by the head of the Jewish Agency Political Department, Moshe Sharett, to work for the creation of 'a Jewish state in a suitable area of Palestine.

Weizmann had been remote from all these affairs. In Rehovoth he had observed the debacle of the mandate, sharpened by the conflict between the Jewish community and the British administration. In a letter to Churchill's secretary, John Martin, he wrote: 'I was saddened to hear the report from Linton about the talks in London and partition being relegated to the back bench. I am quite certain that they will have to come back to it. . . . Being an optimist I believe that

Palestine will not go up in smoke. . . . If it does—I will go up with it.' To Richard Crossman he wrote in March: 'I do not believe in the UNO business. It will procrastinate matters and if it can be avoided everything should be done to achieve such a purpose.'

But nothing could be done—and the United Nations phase was in full and crucial swing. When the Commission reached Palestine the Jewish Agency Executive invited Weizmann, the private citizen, to enter the fray. The anomaly of his removal from the Presidency at Basle had now been revealed on three counts. First, no President had been elected in his place, and the responsibility oscillated between Ben-Gurion in Jerusalem and Silver in New York. Second, at every international crisis or opportunity his prestige and power of exposition were still regarded as indispensable. Third, the Jewish Agency was aiming at the very partition solution which he had supported unwaveringly for ten years and which the Agency itself was unable formally to sponsor. Officially its programme called for the solution, impossible in the short run, of a Jewish state in the whole of Palestine.

On 8 July 1947 Weizmann appeared before the United Nations Special Committee. 'I speak', he said, 'in my private capacity, but I believe I speak the mind of the overwhelming majority of the Jewish people everywhere. . . . The views to which I give expression here are the results of a long experience in one of the most intricate problems confronting the statesman of the world.' He went on to advocate partition as the only available solution combining the three qualities of 'finality, equality and justice'.

As a link with the heroic age of Zionism he was able to quote a letter from Field-Marshal Smuts which had reached him that week advocating a partition plan. One of the Committee members, Jorge Garcia Granados of Guatemala, has recorded the deep impression made on the Committee by Weizmann's dignity, eloquence and authority. [1] Even the usually violent interrogation of the Indian representative Sir Abdurrahman sank to a deferential whisper.

But his main impression on the UNSCOP discussion lay in a series of private conversations and luncheons, to which the Jewish liaison officers took the Committee members at his Rehovoth home. Horowitz has vividly described these occasions:

> The Committee in two successive groups visited Dr Weizmann's home at Rehovoth, where they dined and had long conversations. Weizmann sparkled, especially at the first conversation. With

[1] Jorge Garcia Granados, *The Birth of Israel* (New York), 1949.

masterful dexterity he interwove the story of his own early years
with the broad narrative of the Jewish people's past and destiny,
so that the latter appeared to focus on his own experiences. The
wonderful synthesis of Jewish wit and delicate irony of this fine
and gifted personality, who combined Jewish simplicity with the
highest values of the European spirit in the best sense of the term;
his tales about his father, the timber-merchant of Pinsk, and of
the school in which he studied in his youth; and thrown in casually, his references to meetings with the great ones of the earth,
completely captivated those present, who included Justice Sandstrom and Justice Rand.

Dr Bunche, who was greatly moved, referred to his feelings as
a Negro and the emotional identity that Dr Weizmann's description of Jewish destiny aroused in him.

As we motored down to Rehovoth, Sandstrom and Rand interrogated me at length on settlement and security matters. Driving
back to Jerusalem they sat silent and meditative, and only mur-
mured. 'Well, that's really a great man.' [1]

While the United Nations Committee was in Palestine some of its
members watched the squalid spectacle of Jewish refugees from
Europe being violently returned by British troops to the ship *Exodus*
and driven back first to France and then to Germany. It was difficult
to know what Bevin thought that he was doing. It is not surprising
that the entire Committee stated in its first recommendation that the
Mandate must come to an end. Its death had been advocated by
those who had given it birth—Churchill, Smuts, Weizmann. It only
remained to prescribe the alternative, and the majority suggested a
partition scheme which included the Negev in the Jewish state. At
an informal meeting at Sharett's house in Jerusalem Ben-Gurion had
openly discussed partition with the Commissioners at a meeting also
attended by Eliezer Kaplan, Golda Meir, David Horowitz, Abba
Eban and Leo Kohn.

As the Committee deliberated in Geneva it became more and
more captivated by the logic of the Peel Report, which had been
Weizmann's chief success in the thirty's. Members of the Committee
informed the Jewish liaison officers that they would not have been
able to recommend such an audacious solution if the 1937 proposal
had not lain before them, with the added force of a decade's experience to sustain it.

At midnight on 1 September the report proposing partition was

[1] David Horowitz, *A State in the Making* (New York), 1953.

handed to the Jewish liaison officers in the Palais des Nations at Geneva.

This was the authentic turning-point. But it was only potentially decisive. If the Committee had rejected the Jewish case, the United Nations would never have adopted a favourable recommendation. Now that it had advocated Jewish statehood there was at least a chance of General Assembly endorsement. A splendid gleam of friendship had lit up the Jewish solitude.

The arena now shifted to United Nations headquarters where the most crucial political struggle in modern Jewish history was joined. Everything depended on the possibility of uniting America and Russia in support of the Committee's proposal. At the outset this prospect was not certain. In 1946 the State Department had indicated, in a conversation between Assistant Secretary Dean Acheson and Dr Nahum Goldmann, that it would support a viable partition plan in preference to the Morrison Plan if this were proposed by the mandatory power. But this statement had not been followed up, and the United States had explicitly told the members of UNSCOP that it did not wish to determine the United Nations position in advance. In the event, it was UNSCOP which brought American support for partition, and not vice versa.

The Soviet Union, in a speech by Gromyko at the United Nations in May 1947 had included partition amongst the feasible solutions: but it had also expressed sympathy for the federal proposal which a minority of the UNSCOP members had recommended. Every resource of Jewish influence and statecraft would be needed if the springboard of the UNSCOP report were to be used for a victorious forward leap. And these resources manifestly included the Elder Statesman whose formidable shadow still dominated every scene in which he moved.

In October he arrived in New York—invited to join the struggle by those who had rejected him ten months before. The official attitude of the Jewish Agency, expounded to delegations by Sharett, Silver and a large band of helpers, had now unfrozen. The public support of partition was now official Zionist policy. By mid-October it was plain that American and Soviet support could be expected, but even then the two-thirds majority was not automatically assured. Weizmann's rôle was to make an impact on the uncommitted and wavering delegates who were being shaken by the strong blasts of Arab pressure. He wished his address to be carefully formulated. He knew that it might be his last appearance at the bar of the nations. But his eyesight was bad and the work of preparation agonizing. I find the following entry in my diary of the period.

October 16 (1947)

Saw Chief after he lunched with Henry M(orgenthau). Worked on draft for four steady hours. After each sentence was written in huge letters and agreed, he would go to lamp-stand and bring the text right to his glasses, endeavouring to learn it by heart. By the end of the session his eyes were watering as if in tears. Finally he said: 'We'll make this do—but how about a posuk (biblical verse) for the ending?' We looked for a Bible and eventually found one supplied by the hotel in the bedside table. Spent a half-hour on Isaiah, looking for 'Return to Zion' passages. Finally his mind was caught by the prophecy of 'an ensign for the nations'. As I left he said: 'Well, this is it. Over the top for the last time!'

The delegates of fifty-seven nations listened to him in suspense. He was more personal than usual. In describing a previous international assembly twenty-five years ago he said: 'I came from the council room in which the Mandate was ratified with the feeling that the most cherished ideals of our own history had been sanctioned by the conscience of all mankind.' He made light of Arab spokesmen's assertions that the Jews were the descendants not of the Hebrew Kingdoms, but of the Khazars of Southern Russia. 'It is very strange—All my life I have been a Jew, felt like a Jew—and I now learn that I am a Khazar.' He spoke of the prospect that Jews might be a minority in an Arab state. 'I will not discuss whether it is a good or bad fortune to be a minority in an Arab state. I would leave the Jews of Iraq, of Yemen and Tripoli—and the Christian Assyrians of Iraq to pronounce on that. Here I would say that this was not the purpose for which, under international auspices, we were encouraged to come to Palestine. . . . Those of us who made our homes in Palestine did not do so with the object of becoming Arab citizens of Jewish persuasion.'

He gave friendly delegates a paternal nod of approval: 'I must confess the deep satisfaction that I felt after so many years in expounding the ideals of our movement to hear so many impartial and disinterested nations from the old world and new, from the East and West, expressing the spiritual and liberal motives of Zionism with such sympathy and understanding.' And in conclusion—the reference to prophecy: 'The Lord shall set his hand the second time to recover the remnants of his people. And he shall set up an ensign for the nations, and shall assemble the outcast of Israel and gather together the dispersed of Judah from the four corners of the earth.'

But he had not played his last act in the drama. In the next five months he was destined to be the primary architect of two achievements—the retention of the Negev area in the United Nations' plan for a Jewish State, and the spectacular recognition of Israel by the United States. Two of Weizmann's brightest diplomatic victories were to be won from private status in support of a Zionist leadership from which he had been officially banished.

When it became evident that Jewish statehood would be proposed by the General Assembly, the opponents of Zionism moved away from wholehearted anti-partitionism towards a policy of truncating the Jewish area and making it unacceptable to Jewish opinion. Early in November the United States delegation, influenced by this campaign, pressed the Jewish Agency representatives to yield the southern Negev to the Arabs. American diplomats even hinted that without this concession they would abandon support of the Partition plan, which would thus be defeated in the Assembly vote. On 19 November Weizmann arose from his sick bed and went to Washington for a talk with President Truman. When he arrived at the capital he was informed from New York that the American delegation was going to exclude the Negev from the Jewish State in the partition resolution. He decided to concentrate entirely on the importance of the Southern Negev in his talk with Truman. He was warmly received and plunged immediately into his theme, illustrating it with a memorandum prepared under his direction by Eliahu Elath:

Akaba, which is found on the southern end of the Negev and the Red Sea, represents the only outlet for the Jewish State to the Indian Ocean, India, the Far East, Australia and New Zealand. For the Jewish State this outlet will be one of the important routes for commercial relations with that part of the world. The Jewish State, in order to absorb the refugees coming from Europe, will have to do its utmost to develop its industrial and commercial capacities and in this connection the importance of Akaba is much greater than just a piece of land on the Red Sea. . . .

Akaba has played an important rôle in Jewish history from the early days of the Jewish Kingdom, and the UNSCOP report giving this place to the Jewish State has recognized the historic connections of the Jews with this part of the Red Sea.

Akaba, in the hands of the Arabs, may be a permanent threat

in the rear of the Jewish State. The Arab States have an outlet to the Red Sea and the Gulf of Akaba through Transjordan, Egypt and Saudi-Arabia.

Weizmann kept Truman's mind riveted on this point alone. The President became fascinated by the unexpected excursion into a phase of remote political geography. Grasping the simplicity and force of the argument he gave his assent.

But there was a race against time. At three o'clock the next day the Jewish Agency representatives were invited to meet the American delegate Herschel Johnson in the United Nations' lounge in New York, to hear the State Department's verdict—against the retention of the Negev in the Jewish State. Ambassador Johnson faced Sharett and began to pronounce what amounted to a judgment of execution. In mid-sentence he was called to the telephone. He told the messenger that he could not be disturbed and sent his deputy General Hildring to take the call. The General returned to say that the President himself was holding on at the Washington end of the line.

Johnson leaped to the telephone booth like a startled and portly reindeer. Twenty minutes later he returned. Seating himself opposite Sharett and Horowitz he blushed out an embarrassed retraction. 'What I really wanted to say to you, Mr Shertok, was that we have no changes to suggest.' Horowitz records the Jewish reaction with quiet understatement:

We sighed with relief. Dr Weizmann's talk had been successful. The struggle for the frontiers ended in victory.

The way was now clear for the final vote. In the desperate unforgettable week-end of 27–29 November, Weizmann threw himself into the frenzied pursuit of wavering votes.The prospect of French abstention threatened to disrupt the West European front. In a cable to Léon Blum, Weizmann summoned the Socialist statesman to a supreme effort: 'Does France really wish to be absent from a moment unfading in the memory of man?' On 29 November, when the French vote for partition was announced, a gasp of surprise and a ripple of incredulous applause rang through the Assembly Hall.

He spent the day of 29 November in quiet contemplation at the Plaza Hotel. When the historic vote was announced Jewish representatives led by Sharett and the veteran Labour leader Sprinzak and Shazar, went to his suite and found him profoundly moved. That evening at a Labour Zionist rally in Carnegie Hall he raised his hands aloft to a cheering crowd in speechless joy. His dark glasses concealed his tears.

History had taught him that there was never any respite. Every victory was short-lived and had to be consolidated at once. A few days before the vote he had looked at the map of the Assembly vote and found that the new Jewish State had received almost no Asian support. Must it for ever live in isolation within its continental family? A thought had come to him—of startling prescience. He had written a letter, almost out of the blue, to Nehru proposing scientific and technical co-operation between Palestine and India. On 2 December Nehru replied welcoming Weizmann's suggestion and inviting scientists from Palestine to attend the Indian Science Congress in January 1948. It was the first premonition of Israel's integration in the Asian world.

Weizmann now bethought himself of the Oxford scholar who had first propounded the partition solution in the Peel Commission Report. Sir Reginald Coupland was surprised to receive an affectionate cable from Weizmann to which he made immediate reply:

It was kind of you to think of me at the moment of your victory, after so many and such perverse delays. I shall remember my association with Zionism as the most interesting chapter of my life—beginning with that meeting in the little room at Nahalal—and the best of it has been the privilege of your friendship.

You have now to impress your State with the stamp of your statesmanship—so that it can show the world what the Jews can do when restored to their historic home, and standing at last on an equal footing with other peoples.

Weizmann intended to spend a few weeks in London to wind up his affairs and then to arrive at Rehovoth at the end of the winter. He also planned a visit to Asia where he hoped to initiate scientific co-operation. During December and January, however, his tranquillity was dashed by the news of bloodthirsty clashes in Palestine into which Arab 'Liberation Troops' were pouring from all sides to reinforce the revolt of Palestinian Arabs against the United Nations resolution. The British Administration, formally responsible for law and order, was holding the door open to the Arab incursions and simultaneously harrying the desperate defence of the Jews. Mr Bevin was in a truculent mood. He was going to teach the international community a lesson for presuming to reject his advice. As it became apparent that the Arabs would not peacefully acquiesce in partition, second thoughts began to grip many members of the United Nations who had supported the plan. In Washington the State Department repented of its good deed on the very morrow of its performance.

Weizmann found it hard to believe that anyone could seriously envisage a reversal of partition. In his eyes the thing to be wondered at was the inordinate time that it had taken for the obvious and logical solution to be reached. In January he continued to plan large visions for the future Jewish State. Today, when assistance to newly emerging nations holds so large a place in Israel's policy, there is something impressive in the foresight which led Weizmann to correspond with the Government of Burma, which had invited him on 19 December 1947 to pay a visit to their country.

He wrote to Rangoon on 2 January accepting the Burmese Government's invitation. Three weeks later a reply from Rangoon proposed the dispatch of Burmese specialists to Palestine for work at Rehovoth.

These communications sound as though Weizmann already imagined himself to be involved in the practical deeds of statecraft. But many hurdles still remained. The news from the United Nations and Washington was bad. The vastest anti-climax in Jewish history was being prepared. Having been placed on the threshold of statehood the Jews were going to be urged back into the vacuum of tutelage. His friends amongst the Jewish delegation in the United Nations made an urgent appeal for Weizmann's return:

Cablegram, New York, 23 January 1948
Chaim Weizmann, Dorchester Hotel, London.

In view worsening situation advise you if possible reconsider decision to go Palestine January stop No conditions exist there your constructive political activity everything depending upon outcome negotiations here Lake Success and Washington stop Most crucial phase of all now approaches here in which we sorely miss your presence advice activity influence affectionately

EBAN

He refused to act on this appeal until it was repeated officially, although in less enthusiastic terms, by the Jewish Agency Executive in New York.

He arrived in a snow-covered New York on the Queen Mary on 4 February. My diary for that day concludes:

Dined at Waldorf with Chief and Mrs Weizmann. He opened belligerently: 'Why in heaven did you drag me to this frozen waste when I might have been in Rehovoth?' Told him of our danger at Lake Success and our position in Washington where not a single contact on high level had been possible since November. Truman furious wtih Zionist leaders and won't even see

26 Taking his first Oath of Office in Jerusalem, 1949

27 Weizmann and Lord Samuel at Rehovoth, 1951

Portraits

28 At Rehovoth

29 With his grandson, David

30 At a Zionist Congress   31 At the Weizmann Institute

32 With Toscanini

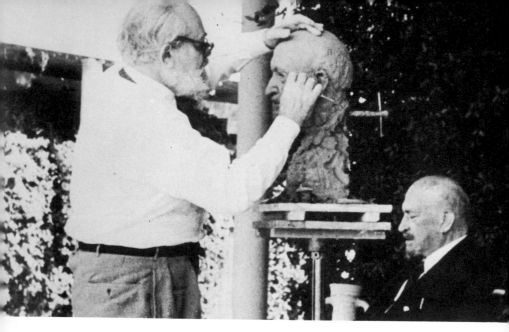

33 Weizmann sits for Jo Davidson, Rehovoth, 1951

34 Mourners at Weiz-
mann's funeral,
Rehovoth, 1952

them. Chief's contact with President our only hope at UN and Washington. Chief decided to seek interview with Truman this month.

President Truman in his memoirs frankly recounts his displeasure with the official Zionist leadership, some of whose spokesmen he considered wanting in moderation and in respect for his person and office. If Weizmann could achieve access and secure presidential intervention, the political victory of November 1947 might still be saved in time for the State to be proclaimed with unimpaired international authority during the early part of 1948.

It is difficult at this point of time to describe the choking suspense in which Jewish life was lived during those winter months. The community in Palestine was under violent attack by Arab invaders. The British authorities neither protected them, as they were legally bound to do, nor allowed them freedom of self-protection as moral duty commanded. The Five Power Commission, established to carry out the Partition plan, languished impotently in New York, rejoicing in the facetious but significant title of the 'Five Lonely Pilgrims'. The United States was in full flight from partition. It was having every sort of nightmare—from Soviet military intervention, to the massive influx of Communist agents in the guise of refugee immigrants to Palestine. The Jewish prospect had been incredibly transformed since the triumph of the previous November. The outlook was of political collapse and military defeat.

Weizmann's discussion with Truman was delayed by his own illness, by the President's absence on leave in the Caribbean, and, more ominously, by Truman's reluctance to have anything to do with Zionist leadership. At last, on 14 March, the opening appeared. To Weizmann's suite at the Waldorf came Eddie Jacobson of Kansas City who had been the President's partner in an unsuccessful clothing store in the 20's. He had a remarkable tale to tell. Stimulated by the leader of B'nai B'rith, Frank Goldmann, he had urged the President by cable to receive Dr Weizmann. Jacobson was a non-Zionist, but he could not escape the exhilaration of the times. And Weizmann was his hero-figure.

Receiving no positive reply from Truman, Jacobson had flown to Washington and burst into the White House on the plea of personal business. He had met with a cold reception from his eminent friend. For the first time Truman was freezing Jacobson, unfairly, with the blasts of his official dignity. In despair Jacobson noted the bust of Andrew Jackson on the President's desk. 'You admire him, don't you. Mr President?' he said. 'Well, my people has its founding father too. I admire him more than anyone else. He's old and ill and has come all the way, thousands of miles, to see you, and you won't see him. It isn't like you.'

The President looked out through the windows of the Oval Room over the rose garden. Jacobson feared that he was going to be withered by the storm. Truman turned on him with mock fury: 'All right, you bald-headed .... you win. Tell Matt [the appointment's secretary] to invite Dr Weizmann here.' Jacobson proceeded to New York and gave Weizmann the news. He was a loyal and humble Jew, meeting his hero for the first time. 'My feeling is,' he wrote later, 'that not another person in the whole world could have sold me as Dr Weizmann did that day.'

In his memoirs Mr Truman tells the same story, but with puritanical avoidance of expletive.

On 18 March Weizmann arose from his sick bed in New York and travelled by train to Washington. President Truman has written in detail about this meeting:[1]

> Dr. Weizmann, by my specific instruction, was to be brought in through the East Gate. There was to be no press coverage of his visit and no public announcement. . . . We talked for almost three-quarters of an hour.
>
> Dr Weizmann was a man of remarkable achievements and personality. His life had been dedicated to two ideals, that of science and that of the Zionist movement. He was past seventy now and in ill health. He had known many disappointments and had grown patient and wise in them. When he left my office I felt that he had reached a full understanding of my policy, and that I knew what he wanted.

The President gave his visitor a specific commitment. He would work for the establishment and recognition of a Jewish State, of which the Negev would be a part.

The following day, 19 March, was to become known in Jewish diplomacy as 'Black Friday'. Warren Austen, the American Ambassador to the United Nations, addressed the Security Council with a sensational request. All efforts to implement partition should be suspended. The General Assembly was to be convened in special session to work out a plan for temporary trusteeship. The dream of

[1] Harry S. Truman, *Years of Trial and Hope* (London, Hodder and Stoughton, 1956, New York, Doubleday, 1956).

Jewish statehood which had illuminated the winter months was now to be shattered through the timidity and inconstancy of those who had fostered it.

A frenzy of rage and disappointment rolled through the Jewish world. President Truman was, not surprisingly, assailed by the formidable armoury of invective which Zionism had perforce stored up during the dark, long years of failure. The only absent voice was that of the man who had the most right to feel betrayed. On Monday 22 March Weizmann called Eddie Jacobson on the telephone to express his irrational belief that Truman would still fulfil his promise. The President was never to forget this act of faith. In his apartment at the Waldorf, Weizmann organized his plan of action, beginning with a clear summons to his people: 'I would now urge the Jewish people to redouble its efforts to secure the defence and freedom of the Jewish State.'

A few days later he addressed President Truman with a reasoned argument against trusteeship and in favour of partition. He concluded with incisive words: 'The choice for our people, Mr President, is between statehood and extermination.'

April 9 (Eban Diaries)

After drafting letter to President, the Chief called me back to the hotel. Dave [Ginsburg] had told him from Washington that there was some thought in the State Department of asking the British to carry on with the administration despite their categorical statement that they would leave. Chief thought this the worst possibility of all. He decided to add a paragraph on the theme 'Britain must go' and we worked on this till late. . . .

The new paragraph in the letter to Truman expressed all Weizmann's pain and despair after forty years of co-operation with the mandatory Power:

I would sound a note of solemn warning against the prolongation of British rule in Palestine. As you may know, I have cherished the British-Jewish relationship all my life, I have upheld it in difficult times. I have been grievously disappointed by its recent decline. . . . I tremble to think of the wave of violence and repression which would sweep Palestine if the conditions and auspices of the recent unhappy years were to be continued under British, or indeed any foreign, rule. I also know how passionately the British people desire the end of this troubled chapter. Should your administration, despite all this, press for any prolongation of British tenure, it would mean a responsibility for terrible events. . . .

Truman was already in deep turmoil of spirit. In his book *The Man of Independence* Jonathan Daniels has recounted the story of Black Friday in the White House.[1]

> Truman called Clark Clifford [his administrative assistant] on 7.30 Saturday morning [20 March].
> 'Can you come right down,' he said. 'There is a story in the papers on Palestine and I don't understand what has happened.'
> In his office Truman was as disturbed as Clifford had ever seen him. 'How could this have happened? I assured Chaim Weizmann that we were for partition and would stick to it. He must think I am a plain liar. Find out how this could have happened.'

When the General Assembly convened in April it became evident that partition was not going to be killed easily at the United Nations. And in Palestine itself it was coming spontaneously to life. As British power receded Jewish and Arab authority began to assert itself in the vacuum, in rough approximation to the partition boundaries except that the Negev was still empty and cut off.

The Jewish political effort at New York now branched off into two roads. The Jewish Agency executive mounted an assault on the ill-starred trusteeship proposal. Addresses were made to the General Assembly and delegations were mustered to support the principle that an international judgment must not be overthrown by armed force. The fate of the League of Nations, and indeed of the pre-war world, offered portentous support of this theme. If the 1947 resolution could not be actively implemented it was essential at least to prevent the annulment of its revolutionary principle—that of Jewish statehood. And while the Jewish delegation pursued this task, Chaim Weizmann, a private citizen in a hotel suite, conceived a daring enterprise of his own.

He would induce the President of the United States to recognize the Jewish State whose establishment the United States Government was at that moment trying to prevent.

March, April and May 1948 were golden autumn months in Weizmann's political life. He had an objective from which he never wavered, and he pursued it with zeal. United Nations delegates who came to see him on the assumption that he was a 'moderate' who

[1] Jonathan Daniels, *The Man of Independence* (New York, 1950).

would make their retreat easier found themselves shrivelled by the fury of his assault. Austin, Jessup and Ross of the United States sat down on his hotel sofa and told him how dangerous it would be for peace if the Jews of Palestine proclaimed a State on 14 May. Weizmann replied that he was only a private Jew, but in his view 'Palestine Jewry would be off its head if it postponed statehood for anything as foolish as the American trusteeship proposal.' Typical of his uncompromising exposition in those days was his talk with the head of the French delegation.

March, 13, 1948 (Eban Diaries)

Lunched with Chief and Alexandre Parodi. Latter full of doubts about partition. Fears that if Jewish State is established its inhabitants will be massacred by superior Arab forces. 'How can a few hundred thousands of you stand up against millions?' Chief replied that numbers are not decisive. 'The trouble with the Egyptian army is that its soldiers are too lean and its officers too fat.' If Jews stood firm they would win through.

In a wonderful climax Josef [Cohn] put his head round the door with a copy of the *New York Post* telling of spectacular Jewish victory at Mishmar Haemek.

For Weizmann the importance of avoiding a vote for trusteeship was enhanced by his secret resolve to work for recognition. No American President would recognize a Jewish State after the United Nations had voted to place its territory under trusteeship. It was essential, at least, to preserve the vacuum. And on Passover Eve, April 23, the breakthrough came—to the knowledge of himself and of his closest circle alone.

He was due to go to his friends Siegfried and Lola Kramarsky for the Seder service. Before he set out he received an urgent request to see Judge Rosenman, one of President Truman's closest political advisers. Rosenman, like Jacobson, was outside the range of official Zionist contacts. But he was a willing victim of Weizmann's personal spell. Weizmann went to see him at the Essex House Hotel, as the judge was incapacitated by a leg injury. The two men talked with quiet concentration for an hour. On emerging from the hotel Weizmann was tense with excitement. He sat through the Seder service in a mood of far-away contemplation, and left early. At ten o'clock he gathered his friends about him and told them of Rosenman's report.

It seemed an incredible story. It contained a massive refutation of all the 'hard-headed' theories which deny the personal and human factor in international relations. The President had called Rosenman into the Oval Room and told him quite simply, 'I have Dr Weizmann on my conscience.' He had not realized on 18 March that the State Department had gone so far in abandonment of the Partition plan. The President would like to find his way back to the United Nations resolution. If the General Assembly session could be surmounted without reversing partition and if a Jewish State was declared, the President would recognize it immediately. Thus fortified by international legitimacy the new State could fight for its survival, not as an unregarded outcast, but as a member of the international family.

But the President stipulated one absolute condition. He would deal with Dr Chaim Weizmann—and with him alone. It was essential, therefore, for Weizmann to stay in America and be available for the unfolding of the plan.

There was a certain pathos in the President's eagerness to regain Weizmann's respect. Harry Truman had ordered atomic bombs to be used against Japan. He had boldly proclaimed the doctrine of intervention in defence of Greece and Turkey. He wielded supreme authority for the policies of the non-communist world. His political career had been full of tough battles and flexible compromises. Yet somehow he was moved to sentimental contrition by the thought that an aging Jewish leader, banished from office, might regard him as having dishonoured his pledge.

Weizmann lived the next three weeks in acute expectancy. Events moved towards a sharp transition. In Palestine, amidst furious fighting, the profile of a recognized Jewish authority began to emerge over much of the country. At Flushing Meadows the United Nations reacted to the American trusteeship proposal with a sharp distaste. But in the absence of an alternative solution there was always a chance that this would be adopted. There was an even greater peril that some Jewish leaders would be intimidated by the prospect of military invasion and political solitude into renouncing the idea of immediate statehood.

All Weizmann's efforts were now directed to the second danger. It was a strange rôle for the so-called 'moderate'—to be summoning the Jewish people to the utmost intransigence and tenacity. To Meyer Weisgal, telephoning from Nice at the request of Ben-Gurion to seek his views, he said briefly: 'Proclaim the State, no matter what ensues.' As Sharett flew home to advise rejection of Secretary Marshall's warning against proclaiming the State, Weizmann pursued him to the airport with an entreaty, 'Don't let them weaken, Moshe, it is now or never.' A military cease-fire was legitimate. But the 'political stand-still' which the State Department was suggesting was anathema. For this would impede any new political moves such as the declaration of Jewish independence.

Meanwhile he hugged his secret and waited for its consummation. As in 1917 he was without official standing, and yet the key of a political triumph was in his hands.

On 29 April the House of Commons enacted the termination of the British Mandate for 15 May. On 7 May a puzzled Bartley Crum came to see Weizmann with the 'strange story' that the President was going to recognize the Jewish State within a week. On 13 May Weizmann was on tenterhooks. Would the crucial twenty-four hours be safely surmounted at the United Nations? And would the State actually be proclaimed? He was frankly nervous:

13 May 1948 (Eban Diaries)

I was in the UN delegates' lounge when the Chief came on the phone and asked me to come round at once. He had heard a rumour that the UN was going to adopt a trusteeship proposal and appoint a High Commissioner after all. Was this the position? If so all was wrecked.

I said that he need have no alarm. We had blocked trusteeship. Since the Political Committee meeting on 5 May I had seen support for it dwindling. Gromyko had told me at a party in Trygve Lie's home, 'You have buried trusteeship.' The Assembly would at most appoint a Mediator, not a High Commissioner; and this would create no juridical fact incompatible with the proclamation and recognition of a Jewish State. I pleaded with the Chief to let me go back to the UN. We were very thin on the ground with Moshe away.'

He sat down and wrote a letter to Truman asking for recognition of the Jewish State; Josef Cohn took the overnight train to Washington and gave it to the White House. On 14 May a message came from the Executive Office that Truman was sitting with Marshall and Lovett and deliberating on Weizmann's letter. Clark Clifford had telephoned to Eliahu Elath from the White House saying that a more formal approach was necessary. Elath, responding to this approach, drafted a letter as representative, not of the Jewish Agency, but of 'the Jewish State' and sent it in due style and form to the White House in a taxi-cab. Before the cab reached the White House the news came that a State called Israel had been proclaimed in Palestine at a moving ceremony conducted by Ben-Gurion in Tel Aviv. Meanwhile, in the General Assembly, Dr Silver had broken in on the Committees' debate to announce that the State of Israel had been established.

In Weizmann's suite the minutes ticked by. Jonathan Daniels has told how the receipt of his letter in the White House had given Truman his chance. The President had summoned Marshall, Lovett, Niles, Clark Clifford and a State Department official, to consider Weizmann's letter. The meeting had dispersed several times—once in order to elicit Elath's formal letter announcing that the State referred to in Weizmann's request for recognition had actually been established. Finally, the decision fell. At 5.16 Truman authorized the recognition of Israel by the United States.

He had kept his word. 'The old Doctor will believe me now,' he said.

The representatives of the United States in the General Assembly knew nothing of the President's announcement. They were still advocating all kinds of proposals other than Jewish statehood. The news of Truman's recognition broke on them like a thunderbolt. Ambassador Jessup went into a telephone booth to check with the White House and then read the Truman announcement to an Assembly now plunged in a pandemonium of surprise.

Exhausted and triumphant Weizmann sank into bed. Egyptian troops bombed Tel Aviv while Ben-Gurion made his first broadcast as Prime Minister of Israel from an air-raid shelter. American recognition came to the embattled Jews of Palestine as an unexpected act of grace. They were no longer forsaken or alone.

As the tumult of Jewry's greatest day in all its modern history swept through the streets of New York, Weizmann lay silent in the darkened hotel room. The first cables from Tel-Aviv told of familiar Zionist leaders now bearing glamorous ministerial titles. But no news or greeting reached Chaim Weizmann. A sense of abandonment and ingratitude invaded his mood. Suddenly , a bell-boy appeared with a message from the Palestine Jewish leaders:

> On the occasion of the establishment of the Jewish State we send our greetings to you, who have done more than any other living man towards its creation. Your stand and help have strengthened all of us. We look forward to the day when we shall see you at the head of the State established in peace.
>
> BEN-GURION, MYERSON, REMEZ, KAPLAN.

He had led Israel for forty years through a wilderness of martyrdom and anguish, of savage oppression and frustrated hope, across the sharpest agony which ever beset the life of any people. And now, towards the end of his days, he had entered in triumph upon his due inheritance of honour as the first President of Israel—the embodiment in modern times of the kingly and prophetic tradition which once flourished in Israel and became an abiding source of light and redemption for succeeding generations of men.

Plutarch's life of Pericles concludes with these words:
He was indeed a character deserving our high admiration not only for his equitable and moderate temper which all along in the many affairs of his life, and the great animosities which he incurred, he constantly maintained; but also for the high spirit and feeling which made him regard it the noblest of all his honours that in the exercise of such immense authority he never had gratified his envy or his passion, nor ever had treated any enemy as irreconcilably opposed to him.

Mr Abba Eban is Minister of Education and Culture in the Israel Government, and President of the Weizmann Institute of Science. He was for ten years Israel's Ambassador to the USA and its chief permanent delegate to the UN.

CHAPTER TWELVE

BRIDGE TO STATEHOOD

JON KIMCHE

THE HISTORY of the State of Israel and of the Zionist movement that brought it into being is a singular confirmation of Clausewitz's celebrated remark that 'war is the continuation of politics by other means'. For the most extraordinary thing about the politics of Israel has been the division between the international, diplomatic wing of the Zionist movement, with which Weizmann's name is indissolubly associated, and the strictly Israeli, military wing, led by Ben-Gurion and the commanders of the Hagana.

The overwhelming importance of Weizmann's contribution to the setting of the political stage for the show-down out of which the State of Israel emerged is universally acknowledged.

However, all the available evidence indicates conclusively that Weizmann played little part in the war, and certainly none in the specific preparations for the war against the Arab invaders of Israel during the initial period of the formation of the State. Yet, at the same time, Weizmann's monumental contribution to the political decisions at the United Nations and in Washington also demonstrates the separation of the two activist wings of the Zionist movement in 1948 and ever since. In the crucial business of preparing for the war, and fighting it, there was remarkably little rapport, and not very much direct contact, between the diplomatic and the military wings. Each of them lived, operated, and fought in a distinct world of its own, the one for a favourable political decision in Washington and at Lake Success, the other for a favourable outcome of the war against the invading Arab armies.

Even when the two wings impinged on each other, as they were bound to do at times, it was, as Weizmann said in *Trial and Error*, the realities in Palestine that dictated the decisions at the United Nations. In Israel the only moments of significance in the outside world that received any attention were the beginnings and endings of the successive periods of war, cease-fire and truce, and the welcome recognition of the new state by the United States and the Soviet Union. For the rest, it was the course of the war that dominated the conscious existence of the Jews in Israel and of the march of diplomatic events at the United Nations in Washington.

From this Weizmann was to all practical purposes excluded; but why? It is too easy and too simple to seek the explanation in Ahad Ha'am's contrast of Priest and Prophet, of Aaron the Priest whose guiding principle was expediencey and who had to reconcile the ideal objective with the practical aim that was attainable, and Moses, the single-minded leader who would not abandon the struggle or swim with the tide. It was no more an explanation to see the cause of Weizmann's exclusion in the transfer of leadership from statesman to soldier, from politician to revolutionary, from the man of peace to the man of war, from Weizmann to Ben-Gurion. The explanation that the passage of leadership was conditioned by Ben-Gurion's better appreciation of the mind of the British labour movement may be partially true, but it also does not cover the crucial and decisive reasons for Weizmann's exclusion.

This was due in the first place to Weizmann's age and infirmity—in 1948, Weizmann was seventy-five and half-blind and Ben-Gurion was sixty-two, at the peak of his intellectual and physical faculties. It was due, in the second place, to geography—Weizmann was in the United States, Ben-Gurion in Tel Aviv. But it was not due to any fundamental difference in Weizmann's philosophy of Zionism from that of Ben-Gurion, or because of any basic division of opinion on matters of policy. There was no real distinction between Weizmann's and Ben-Gurion's attitude towards the British. If anything, because he knew them better and had more intimate contact, Weizmann had become the more critical of the two towards British policy and politicians. Both had hoped that it would yet prove possible to reach a friendly agreement in which the Jews of Palestine and the British would be associated, though Weizmann's disillusionment (during this critical final phase of the Mandate) had begun earlier and had gone deeper than had Ben-Gurion's. But both deeply suspected British intentions immediately after the war. Weizmann's hopes had been shattered by Churchill's letter of 9 June 1945; Ben-Gurion's remaining hopes were shattered by Ernest Bevin's press conference on 29 September 1945 when he announced that the Anglo-American Committee of Inquiry would be set up. Weizmann was convinced at this time that the British were actively preparing a new deal for the Arab nations which would be carried out at the expense of Palestinian Jewry.

This mood is reflected in the coded exchanges that passed between the Zionist leaders in Jerusalem and Weizmann and Ben-Gurion in London and which the Colonial Office subsequently published as a White Paper. Although this is only a very incomplete record, it reflects the continuing mood of impatience that had become evident at the London conference of the Zionist Organization which had been held in August. The Zionist leadership had held their hand; they had relied on the weight of their argument and on the justice of their cause to move the British Government to favourable action. They had produced no tangible dividends.

Then, on 15 September, confidential information reached the Zionist leadership in London that the Cabinet sub-committee of which Stafford Cripps and Ernest Bevin were members had concluded its consideration of the Palestine question. It had recommended that the White Paper should not be abrogated but that immigration certificates should be made available to the Jewish Agency at the rate of 1,500 a month until the Cabinet had finalized its Palestine policy. On the following day, it was the eve of the Day of Atonement, the news was broadcast in Palestine shortly before the commencement of the Fast.

An immediate exchange of opinion followed between the Zionist Executive members in Jerusalem and London. A week later, on 23 September 1945, Moshe Sneh, the Security Member of the Jewish Agency Executive in Jerusalem and the *de facto* political head of the Hagana, advised the members in London that he had proposed that they should not await the official announcement from the British Government but issue forthwith a warning to the British. It had also been suggested that they cause 'a serious incident' and make it clear to the British that this was a warning of what would follow if the British did not heed it. There followed an exchange of views between London and Jerusalem which the White Paper did not publish. Ben-Gurion was opposed to Sneh's proposal for an 'action-agreement' with the Stern group. Weizmann was concerned that the Hagana should avoid a general conflict with the British. In the end, on 12 October, Sharett cabled in the agreed code that both Weizmann and Ben-Gurion consented to isolated and specific operations which would serve to warn the British that the Hagana could disrupt at will the effectiveness of Palestine as a British military base.

What is interesting here is that both Weizmann and Ben-Gurion adopted very much the same attitude when it came to the use of force as a form of pressure once they had concluded that the diplomatic approach had proved ineffective in persuading the Labour Government to accelerate the entry of refugees from the camps in Europe. It was, however, the British who loomed largest as the enemy in 1946 and 1947, not the Arabs. The political and para-military activity of the Zionist leaders and the Haganah was therefore directed almost wholly against the British. So was their thinking, their planning, their policy-making—and it very nearly led the Jews of Palestine and the hopes of the Zionists into an irretrievable disaster.

Insofar as Zionists and the Jewish population of Palestine prepared themselves for the supreme effort, it was first and foremost focused on the contest with Britain and, next, on the contest to secure a majority at the United Nations for a Zionist solution in Palestine. There was neither serious thought, nor serious preparation, for a major military conflict with the armed forces of the Arab countries.

The attempt to force the hand of the British by a show of strength from the para-military forces at the disposal of Palestine Jewry resulted in three impressive demonstrations in which the Hagana, the Irgun Zvai Leumi and the Stern Group participated: railways, police boats, bridges and airfields were effectively sabotaged and paralysed at the end of October 1945 and in February and June 1946. But the operation ended in complete failure. The British were not intimidated, only annoyed. Instead of submitting to the demands of the Jewish Agency, they arrested the Jewish Agency leaders and many of the key personnel of the Hagana, the Irgun and the Stern Group. But even the limited operations carried out by the British against the Agency and Hagana leadership at the end of June 1946 had come as an unpleasant surprise. Only the High Commissioner's intervention, supported by the GOC Palestine, later averted the Cabinet's approval of far more drastic measures against Palestine Jewry which Field Marshal Montgomery had proposed. Both Weizmann and Ben-Gurion had been mistaken in their assumptions.

This error of judgment serves, however, to underline another error of which the Zionist leadership had been guilty in its diplomatic relations with the British Government; first with Churchill, then with Attlee and Bevin. As the war drew to its close, and the full extent of the Jewish tragedy came to be recognized, Weizmann and his colleageus were understandably bitter and impatient. Their thinking was wholly preoccupied by the necessity of saving the remnant of European Jewry. They were in no mood to consider the niceties of power politics or the hardships of the British Empire in dissolution.

But to the Labour Cabinet the priorities were reversed. They were under relentless pressure at home and abroad. Bevin and Cripps had jointly studied the demands which Weizmann had brought to Down

ing Street as soon as the Labour Government had taken office. But
other promissory notes were now also appearing on the Prime Minister's table. For the Labour Party had, in fact, distributed a whole
handful of 'Balfour Declarations' to expectant, dependent or
oppressed nations. All expected the promises to be met—at once.

Attlee's Government was quite unprepared for this. One after the
other the expectant friends were abandoned. Republican Spain was
the first, then came the others, including the Zionists. In justice to
the British Labour Government it must be said that they acted very
much under compulsion. They did not want to abandon the Jews in
Palestine, or in the camps. But they did not know what to do under
the conditions where they felt that Arab goodwill and Arab oil was
essential to Britain. There was, after all, nothing improper in such
conclusions, for the oil was of immense consequence. Unfortunately,
Weizmann in these later years had given up hope of a friendly agreement with the Arabs and, what was worse, the Zionist leaders had
written off Arab feelings as of no account. In the negotiations for the
Balfour Declaration, and later in the discussions on the Mandate,
Weizmann and his friends had shown great insight into the Arab
situation. They understood that it could not be ignored. But that
was no longer so, now that the second World War neared its close
and Labour prepared to take over. The Labour leaders had been
ably and completely briefed by their Zionist friends to the effect
that there was no Arab problem. 'Let the Arabs be encouraged to
move out, as the Jews move in . . .' proposed Hugh Dalton to the
Labour Party conference in December 1944. The resolution was
carried and became Labour Party policy.

This was not much help to the Cabinet when it had to face the
Palestine problem nine months later. Nor, for that matter, were the
endless complaints from Zionist leaders addressed to their friends in
the Cabinet—Morrison, Dalton, Greenwood and others. Soon they
ceased to understand each other; they were no longer talking the
same language. Weizmann, as one of them put it, had become a bore
to be avoided. There was moreover, yet another aspect of the breach.
Zionist 'diplomacy' had been directed almost exclusively at the
political wing of the Labour Party. The trades unions, which had
the decisive voice in the councils of the party, had been altogether
ignored. The Zionists were also completely out of touch with the
military advisers of the Cabinet. There was neither sympathy nor
understanding there: the soldiers could not comprehend the Zionists.

A few months later, Weizmann discussed the reasons for this at a
small private luncheon in Jerusalem. He had just been to see the
High Commissioner in an effort to get the Jewish Agency leaders

released from detention at Latrun. He had come back discouraged. He had not been able to make a dent in the man, he said. Then he began to talk about the extraordinary difference he had found between negotiating wtih Attlee, Bevin and their advisers and the negotiations he had in 1917 with Lloyd George, Balfour, Curzon, Milner and Sykes. They had treated the Jewish problem as stemming back to the Bible; they had been informed and understanding even when, like Curzon, they disagreed. But not so now. He was disgusted with the crudeness and the lack of dignity with which the talks with Bevin had proceeded. He felt neither sympathy, understanding nor intelligence.

But was it only Bevin who had changed? Had not Weizmann, too, come a long way from 1917? Was he not now inclined to romanticize those men who helped him to his remarkable achievement? Were they all he now believed them to have been? My doubts increased when I read the last-minute addition to that remarkable collection of documents on British Foreign Policy for 1919 in which Felix Frankfurter records a conversation in Balfour's apartment in Paris on 24 June 1919. Those present were Balfour, Mr Justice Brandeis, Lord Eustace Percy and Frankfurter.

Balfour began by saying that he was distressed and harassed by the difficulties of the Jewish problem (of which the Palestinian problem is only a fragment but an essential part). Moreover, the problem of the Jews in Eastern Europe was complicated 'by the extraordinary phenomenon that Jews now are not only participating in revolutionary movements but are actually, to a large degree, leaders in such movements'. Balfour added that a well-informed person had told him only the other day that Lenin also, on his mother's side, was a Jew.

Brandeis corrected Balfour and told him that he had reason to believe that Lenin on both sides was an upper-class Russian. He then expressed his belief that every Jew was potentially an intellectual and an idealist and the problem was one of directing him into constructive channels. As an example, he cited his own approach to Zionism. He had come to it wholly as an American, for his whole life had been free of Jewish contacts and traditions. As an American he was confronted with the disposition of the vast number of Jews, particularly Russian Jews, who were pouring into the United States year by year. After he had chanced to read a pamphlet on Zionism he made a study of the Jewish problem and reached the conclusion that Zionism was the answer. The same men who had sought their outlet in the revolutionary movements would find in Zionism a constructive alternative for their contribution to civilization.

At this point, Balfour interrupted Brandeis in order to express agreement, adding: 'Of course, these are the reasons that make me such an ardent Zionist.'

Weizmann, it is evident, never saw Balfour in this light because Weizmann would never have discussed Zionism on this level. To Balfour's perceptive, cynical and sceptical mind a man like Brandeis was much nearer to Edwin Montagu than to Weizmann, and he responded in kind. Frankfurter's notes of the discussion suggest that Balfour seemed almost relieved that he could discuss Zionism on this mundane level, as a lightning conductor for the Jews in the United States and a possibly powerful rival to the Russian Revolution. The reason why Balfour was so different a personality with Brandeis than when he was with Weizmann did not spring from his chameleon-like attitudes to different Zionist leaders but from the response which Weizmann's approach evoked in him.

It would be reasonable and natural to assume that the views which Balfour expressed were more accurately his real reasons for supporting Weizmann than the more profound and high-toned explanations he was later to adduce. And it is here that the secret of Weizmann's success is probably buried. He did not go to Balfour as an Englishman, as did Samuel; or as an American, as did Brandeis. He went as a Jew, an uncomplicated Jew, and he forced the discussion on this level; unlike Brandeis, Weizmann did not lower his sights. It was this that was the saving grace of Weizmann's political opportunism; it was always anchored to this fundamental position that no matter how much he had to turn and to twist, to beg and to plead, to trim and to retreat, he never lost his dignity as the spokesman of the Jewish people. In other words, it was not Lloyd George, Balfour, Milner and Curzon that ranged so much higher in 1917 than Attlee and his colleagues in 1945; it was Weizmann who then commanded their respect in a way he did not command the attention of Attlee, Morrison, Bevin and Bevan in 1945 and during the following two years.

I have often pondered over the difference of the impact which Weizmann made on the statesmen after the first World War and on those after the second. From what did it stem? Surely not from his person. If anything, he had grown in stature. There were men after the second World War who esteemed him as highly as any after the first: Churchill was one, Crossman another, and there were many more on both sides of the Atlantic. But not in the Cabinet at Downing Street. The answer, I believe, lies in Weizmann's diplomatic method. He was no organization man at any time. His negotiations over the Balfour Declaration were generally conducted alone and informally, under conditions in which his personality could best expand and make its fullest impact, untrammelled by colleagues or advisers. That was also the basis of his association with Churchill and Crossman; but not with Bevin or the Labour leaders.

Weizmann's negotiations after the second World War were conducted in company, often large company, which invariably had the effect of shrinking his personality and his impact. If, instead of exchanging legalisms and complaints over the green table at the Foreign Office, surrounded by Zionist and British officials intent on scoring points, Weizmann could have taken Bevin and Cripps for a walk round the orchards at Rehovoth, especially in the first weeks after Bevin's arrival at the Foreign Office when he was working on an idea of making Palestine the pilot project for the development of the Middle East, a great deal might have been different. But Weizmann was no longer in a position where he could play solo diplomat; he had to bow to the new Zionist democracy.

It nearly stifled him. But he rose above it when the time came and in his own manner in which he had excelled all his life, he returned to his solo diplomacy. He intervened decisively, though not often, with the President in Washington, with the United Nations in Lake Success. But he did not intervene in the war in Palestine. And yet, perhaps the most valuable part of his mantle had fallen on Ben-Gurion, who had learnt the lesson of Weizmann's experience, he, too, had to prepare for the hour of decision in Weizmann's unorthodox manner. Neither the Zionist Executive nor the Vaad Leumi would see that they had to prepare for a war on a much larger scale, as 1948 came near, and that it would be a war not against the British, but against the Arabs. Ben-Gurion had to take it on himself to initiate the necessary preparations and in his most critical hour, with responsibility heavy on his shoulders, and with that terrible feeling of loneliness in leadership, Ben-Gurion could recall Weizmann's example as a spur and a guiding light. Weizmann had handed him the torch, and that was the greatest contribution Weizmann could make to victory.

And Joshua the son of Nun was full of the spirit of wisdom; for Moses had laid his hands upon him; and the children of Israel hearkened unto him. . . .

This was Weizmann's contribution to the War of Independence. It

needs no reference in an index, no mention in the record. He just had
to lay his hands upon his Joshua. He did.

Mr Jon Kimche is the editor of the JEWISH OBSERVER AND MIDDLE
EAST REVIEW *and author of* BOTH SIDES OF THE HILL, *the
generally accepted history of the Arab-Israel war of 1948, and of
a number of other books including the best-selling* SPYING FOR
PEACE.

1949–1952

CHAPTER THIRTEEN

THE PRISONER OF REHOVOTH

R. H. S. CROSSMAN

FOR WEIZMANN the proclamation of the State was both a supreme moment and an anti-climax. As in the case of that earlier climax of his life—the publication of the Balfour Declaration—elation was mixed with anxiety and disappointment. For once again achievement fell far short of expectation. The Jewish State was now a reality; and, with American as well as Russian recognition granted within a matter of hours, its chances of surviving the Arab invasion were immeasurably increased. But only Weizmann and his immediate associates in New York knew by what a hair's breadth the race for recognition had been won. Quite literally, on that 14th of May, American support, without which the new State could not survive, depended on two men—Harry Truman, in the White House, and Chaim Weizmann, on his bed in the Waldorf-Astoria.

The full story of 'the Chief's' most desperate diplomatic battle and most personal victory has been told in a preceding chapter. At the time, the strictest secrecy had to be observed. Even when he sat down to draft the epilogue to his autobiography three months later, he could not reveal the details without which it was impossible for his fellow-countrymen to realize the unique contribution he had made to their military victory. It was Sir Charles Webster's judgment that the debt Israel owes to Weizmann's diplomacy is even greater than that owed by Czechoslovakia to Thomas Masaryk. But was not the achievement of May 1948 even more remarkable? Thirty years before, Weizmann was at the height of his powers, the British War Cabinet, with which he was negotiating, was at the zenith of its Imperial strength, and the tide of history was flowing in his favour. In 1948 these favourable factors had disappeared. He himself was old, ill and racked by spasms of deep depression. The links he had formed with Britain in order to achieve security for the National Home now shackled the Yishuv to a disintegrating Imperial system. And the colonial revolution was giving the new nations

325

of Africa and Asia a sense of affinity not with the Jews but with their Arab foes.

True enough, the Yishuv still enjoyed the staunch support of the American people, who sympathized with it as the victim of a latter-day George III. But the State Department and the Pentagon had always regarded this popular American Zionism as an embarrassment. Planning the policy of containment, they foresaw that America would in due course replace Britain as the protector of the Middle East, and they believed that, when this happened, the Administration would be compelled to adopt 'realistic' pro-Arab policies. Inevitably, the influence of these new American *Machtpolitiker* was greatly strengthened in February 1948 by the Communist *putsch* in Prague. Indeed, from that moment the man in the White House, with his simple belief that he could not let the Jewish people down, remained the sole link with the Yishuv, and Weizmann's contribution was to hold the President to his promise and thereby so to strengthen Mr Truman's will that he was able, by a rare exercise of his personal authority, to defy all his military and diplomatic advisers and accord recognition.

Weizmann was not a man who yearned for public appreciation. Indeed, he often took an impish pleasure in alienating his supporters and frustrating their applause. But on 14 May and the days that followed, he felt to the full the frustrations of secrecy and the isolation of his enforced exile. He was keenly aware that his absence from Palestine, when his people were fighting for their lives, would be misunderstood. But, since absolute secrecy had been imposed on him, the justification for his absence could not be given to the Yishuv until it was far too late to repair the damage done to his personal reputation.

Yet on 15 May he received a message from Tel Aviv, signed by the five Mapai leaders in the Provisional Government, David Ben-Gurion, Eliezer Kaplan, Golda Myerson, David Remez and Moshe Shertok (Sharett):

> On the occasion of the establishment of the Jewish State we send our greetings to you, who have done more than any other living man towards its creation. Your stand and help have strengthened all of us. We look forward to the day when we shall see you at the head of the State established in peace.

Two days later it was announced that he had been elected President of the Provisional Council of State. In his own words:

> This came as a complete surprise to me: I had not expected any

such suggestion to be made for some months to come—if then. I was deeply moved—it is always moving to be assured that one is needed—but I was also conscious of the shadows already gathering about the path of our infant State—and, as it now seemed, about my own, which would run beside it.[1]

The announcement from Tel Aviv cheered him; and his exhilaration was strengthened by many messages of congratulation, which included touching personal tributes from Felix Frankfurter, Albert Einstein and Louis Lipsky. 'Mine eyes have seen the coming of the glory of the Lord,' wrote Felix Frankfurter. 'Happily you can now say that—and can say what Moses could not. I salute you with a full heart—full of glad sadness or, rather, sad gladness.' Einstein's emotions too were mixed: 'I read with real pleasure that Palestine Jewry has made you the head of their State and so made good at least in part their ungrateful attitude towards you.'

For a few days he was able to enjoy the triumph. But he did not relax. Since the new State was still without official representation, he sent his friend Eddie Jacobson on the 17th to the White House to discuss three items—(1) the arms embargo, (2) a loan, and (3) the British pressure against the Negev. Jacobson returned to New York with an informal message that Weizmann should cancel his passage on the following Wednesday because the President intended to invite him to Blair House.

That official visit to Washington took place duly on 23 May. Weizmann and his wife Vera drove up Washington's Pennsylvania Avenue, bedecked with blue and white flags, to Blair House. On the following day he was affectionately received by President Truman and repeated the request he had made through Eddie Jacobson for a $100,000,000 loan for Israel's development. The request was granted. On the White House porch he handed Truman a symbolic memento—a Torah scroll, the gift of a sovereign Israel to her powerful friend, the first to recognize her in the moment of her solitude, adversity and pride.

On 25 May he sailed from New York. He had planned to holiday in London and meet old friends. But Britain was still Bevin's Britain, where the new President of Israel could not stay. And there was another reason why England was painful to him. On the day after independence, 'Baffy' Dugdale had suddenly died in Scotland. Niece of A. J. Balfour, she had become the truest and the most

[1] I take these words from the first draft of the Epilogue to *Trial and Error*.

intimate of all his Gentile friends. London would be empty without her.

On his arrival in Paris, after days of excitement in New York, he was once again beset by forebodings, which already centred round his future rôle in Israel. We now know that, from the first, Ben-Gurion held the view that the presidency should be modelled on the British Monarchy, in which the King has no effective power. The accident of Weizmann's physical absence from the State during its first days gave this concept of the Presidency some reinforcement.

Weizmann, in Paris, knew nothing of Ben-Gurion's views. At this time he expressed the hope in conversations that the relationship between himself and Ben-Gurion in the new State might be modelled on that between the President of the Zionist Organization and the Chairman of the Executive. On 26 June, in the course of a letter to Sharett which ranged over the main problems of foreign policy, he observed:

> With regard to the Presidency, I am in full agreement with you, that the American model would not suit our conditions, but I do not think that the French model is more desirable. I think that the middle course approximates to the Czech model. I am not thinking of it because I may have to serve as President, but more as a general proposition, in the interest of the State. There must be some institution not torn by party strife.

There was no positive response to this letter and in the course of the next weeks Weizmann became increasingly exasperated. His fury often exploded in letters and telegrams to loyal lieutenants anxious to shield him from the shock of disillusionment. Finally, on 30 July, he expressed his resentment to Meyer Weisgal:

> Since the establishment of the Jewish State, I have been trying to obtain some clear information both about policies and projects. I have been telegraphing and writing and so far I obtained no satisfaction. In fact, no reply has been forthcoming. Whether this is due to bad communications, as I am being told, or to some other causes, I cannot say. But I feel that it has reached the state that I must take a definite decision.
>
> From time to time, I get glimpses of a byzantine display of power and quasi-military strength but nothing else. As you know, these are things which produce no echo in my soul. I realize, that we are at war, but it seems to me, that the moloch of militarism is having everything and everybody in his grip. As far as I am

concerned, this cannot go on much longer, and as I do not see any hope of a change, I have decided to sever my connection with the office which has been foisted on me . . .

You will—I beg of you—send a copy of this letter to [Sharett] . . .

This draft was never signed or dispatched, but Weizmann meant its contents to become known. He therefore characteristically enclosed it in another letter to Weisgal, which explains that the receipt of a telegram from Sharett 'renders the sending off of the letter less urgent'. But the mood of depression persisted.

He was also concerned about the Constitution, but on this issue his agreement with the Government is shown in this letter to Sharett:

My advice would be, not to produce a fully fledged constitutional project but have for the time being something very general which would serve as a guide in the first two years and let experience teach us, what is the best form suitable to our conditions. We shall have for the first ten years a very heterogeneous population coming from all corners of the earth and it will not be easy to assemble them under the cover of one constitution which shall be drawn up now after such a short time of our existence. It is quite possible, that the very same ideas have crossed your mind and you may take mine for what they may be worth.

But, though he was deeply preoccupied by the problems of his homecoming, he was still the man of action, and his main concern was still to do all he could for the new State. Ever since his famous interview with Mr Truman he had made the fight to foil the British Government's plans and retain the Negev one of his main concerns. On 7 July he wrote a long letter to Truman, warning him against the intrigues of the British Foreign Office and suggesting that 'an indication on the part of the American Government to the British Authorities in favour of the Negev remaining within the Jewish State would go a long way towards stopping the propaganda for the detaching of the Negev from the State of Israel.'

But Bevin's pressure to detach the Negev continued unabated, and on 20 September Eban had to write from Paris that 'it would be only realistic to understand at this moment that at least a partial relinquishment of the Negev will be inevitable'. This roused Weizmann to send urgent cables to his two main White House contacts. Judge Rosenman and Eddie Jacobson, insisting that the Negev must remain Jewish.

Another subject which deeply concerned him was the need to plan for a new University, now that Mount Scopus was temporarily lost. Writing to Dr Senator, the administrator of the University, he remarked:

> It is a tragic fate of ours, that our capital and our unique University should fall outside the boundaries of the State. I am convinced, that we must begin to think of a second University. It does not mean, that we renounce Jerusalem but I think, that in a year or two Palestine could do with a second University. . . . In about two years we shall have 1 million Jews in Palestine. And therefore we could have another University in Tel Aviv. . . . I am only throwing out this idea for you and your colleagues to think about it.

The reply to this far-sighted proposal was wholly negative: Dr Senator felt that the 'strengthening of the Mt Scopus institutions' was needed for the 'strengthening of Jewish Jerusalem', and that it 'would be a serious mistake to propose the establishment of a second university for some time to come.' Weizmann retorted immediately by pointing out that Christianity, as well as Islam, had 'a great claim' on Jerusalem, and that the existence of the University in Jerusalem would 'always be precarious.'

Weizmann's argument was partially invalidated by the collapse of the plans for the internationalization of Jerusalem, but his conviction that a second University would soon be required has been confirmed by history.

These months of enforced delay before his return to Israel were physically and morally exhausting. He was still confident that he had an active rôle to play and he found it trying to concentrate his attention either on correcting the proofs of his autobiography or even on composing the epilogue, whose closing words are indicative of his mood:

> All that is written here is by way of introduction to the New History of Israel. Its writing has been for me a labour compounded of pain and pleasure, but I am thankful to lay it aside in favour of more active and practical pursuits.

Staying with him by the lake at Glion in Switzerland, I was impressed both by the stoic calm with which he treated the threat of blindness (at the end of the month he was to submit himself to an operation for cataract at a single day's notice) and by the confidence he displayed that his presidency might well have a determining effect on the early stages of Israeli democracy. In the Zionist Congress he had never been a politician jostling shoulders with other politicians. Not only had he stood head and shoulders above all his colleagues; he had proudly refused to concern himself with the detailed controls that normally enable a democratic leader to remain master of his political machine. If he was dismissed now and again from office, well and good. Without office, his complete personal ascendancy was demonstrated even more clearly. But the very loneliness of his eminence was bound to bring its own dangers, now that the politics of a real State had been substituted for the shadow politics of a mere Congress. Once the Government had been established, he could no longer exert his immense moral authority from outside or above its structure. The issue, therefore, of the powers which the President would possess concerned him deeply. What should those powers be? He knew that he himself was too old and too ill to wield effective power, but he did want to be consulted; and at this time he confidently expected three things—to have the right to preside, on some occasions at least, at the Cabinet; to have some influence on foreign policy and the appointment of Ambassadors; and, lastly, to have access to Cabinet minutes. For a man of his eminence and service, they were not outrageous demands. But, as we shall see, all of them were denied him.

As soon as he arrived in Israel, his anxieties were confirmed. He had flown home in the first Israeli civil aeroplane, and the initial reception by the Provisional Council of State was simple and moving. In his welcoming words, his old friend Sprinzak assured him that the Constituent Assembly would elect him as the first President of Israel. Weizmann replied briefly and calmly, but his voice broke as he recited the prayer, 'Blessed art Thou, O Lord our God, King of the Universe, Who hath preserved us until this day.' And shortly afterwards he left.

Next day he invited the press to visit him at Rehovoth and spoke wtih great candour to the assembled journalists:

> I have before my eyes two types of President. One type has no rights at all, except the quasi-rights of appointing the Prime Minister and presiding over the Cabinet. The other type, like the late President Masaryk, plays a rôle in the life of the country. I am certainly not so vain as to think that I am like President Masaryk, though I hope I am more than a figurehead, but I certainly have no intention of interfering in any way with the machinery of the Government. I would like to help, not to hinder.

He had a deep-seated foreboding that he might be excluded from the 'rôle in the life of the country' which he had hoped that he, like Masaryk, could play. In one of his first interviews with Ben-Gurion he asked if he could see the Cabinet minutes and received the reply that the Cabinet must be consulted. On another occasion he asked Sharett exactly what his duties, rights and privileges would be when the Provisional Government was replaced and he was élected President of the State. Sharett replied candidly that his importance would be 'symbolic', a word he felt to be an insult and never forgot. Soon, however, his relations with the Government were established as a regular routine. After the Cabinet meeting on Sunday, the Secretary of the Cabinet, Sharef, visited Weizmann each Monday and read to him the Cabinet decisions. But the stenographic record of the proceedings was denied to him. It was also Sharef's job to arrange visits by Ministers. In the case of his old and trusted friends, particularly Kaplan and Sprinzak, such arrangements were unnecessary; they visited him regularly. But for other Ministers special appointments were made whenever they had anything that might specially engage his attention. This routine was maintained after he had been elected President and the Presidential powers had been defined.

Denied any effective influence on affairs, his mind began increasingly to brood over the reasons why this should have happened to him. One particular. grievance loomed ever larger: he came to believe that he had been denied the privilege of signing the Declaration of Independence. Friends consoled him with the thought that he was not the only one absent: others, cut off in Jerusalem, had also been unable to sign. One of those who used to visit him regularly at this time was Yigal Alon, whose Headquarters as commander of the Negev troops was close to Rehovoth.

> He took a liking to me, [Alon writes] and from then on I always informed him about forthcoming operations before zero hour and also went to see him after the battle was over to tell him how things had gone. He enjoyed these visits enormously and he enjoyed particularly being briefed by a commanding general. After the occupation of Elath I invited him to make an official visit and inspect the troops. We made a special journey to Negba, where he met all my senior officers, and then to Beersheba, where I paraded a mixed force drawn from all the units in the Negev. When I left him at Rehovoth that evening, he said to me, 'This is the first time I have had the feeling of being Royalty.'

After this an intimate friendship sprang up between the old President and the young General. Alon recalls that, on half a dozen occasions, Weizmann repeated his complaint about the omission of his name from the Declaration. 'At the time I was intimate with B.G. and could easily have got him to act,' Alon adds. 'But when I suggested doing this, he always said no. He was too proud.' If only Alon had been permitted to speak! For this misunderstanding, which caused him so much pain, could have been cleared up at once, if only it had been brought to the attention of the Cabinet.

Weizmann seems to have assumed that the thirty-seven who signed the Declaration of Independence had been selected because of their personal eminence. But this was not the case. In fact, they were the members of a body named the National Council, which had been set up on 12 April 1948 in order to fulfil the requirements of a resolution of the United Nations Implementation Commission. This Commission had been charged with the task of forming a Provisional Government Council, to which power could be handed over when the Mandate ended, and the UN resolution laid it down that this new body must be 'responsible to Palestine Jewry'. In order to fulfil these requirements, therefore, it was decided that the membership of the National Council should consist of (1) the Jerusalem members of the Jewish Agency Executive, (2) the members of the Vaad Leumi, and (3) a number of additional members, representing bodies that refused to accept representation by (1) and (2). Neither the Jewish Agency nor the Vaad Leumi, for example, was accepted by the Revisionists or the Communists as representing them. When these additions had been made, the total membership of the Council came to thirty-seven. But on Independence Day only thirty-four of these were in Tel Aviv and space was left on the document for the signatures of the three who were absent.

It is quite clear, therefore, that the omission of Weizmann's name was not the result of a deliberate slight. Since at the time he was a member neither of the Jewish Agency Executive nor of the Vaad Leumi, he was not eligible for membership of the Provisional Government Council, and it was only after he had been elected President of it that his name could be added as its thirty-eighth member.

Not all the autumn was spent in vain regrets. As his health improved, the President reflected that there were two fields in which he could hope to serve the young State without being accused of interference —he could maintain his unique personal relationship with Mr Truman and help to re-establish good relations with Britain. Mr Truman's dramatic and completely unexpected re-election in November 1948 gave Weizmann the opportunity for a letter of congratulation. In this he pleaded at length with the President to intervene and put an end to the hostile manœuvres of Ernest Bevin. On 29 November Mr Truman used the occasion of the first anniversary of the UN partition resolution to send a cordial and intimate reply:

> As I read your letter, I was struck by the common experience you and I have recently shared. We had both been abandoned by the so-called realistic experts to our supposedly forlorn lost causes. Yet we both kept pressing for what we were sure was right—and we were both proven to be right. My feeling of elation on the morning of 3 November must have approximated your own feelings one year ago today, and on May 14th, and on several occasions since then.
>
> However, it does not take long for bitter and resourceful opponents to regroup their forces after they have been shattered. You in Israel have already been confronted with that situation; and I expect to be all too soon. So I understand very well your concern to prevent the undermining of your well-earned victories.
>
> I remember well our conversation about the Negev, to which you referred in your letter. I agree fully with your estimate of the importance of that area to Israel, and I deplore any attempt to take it away from Israel. I had thought that my position would have been clear to all the world, particularly in the light of the specific wording of the Democratic Party Platform. But there were those who did not take this seriously, regarding it as 'just another campaign promise' to be forgotten after the election. I believe they have recently realized their error. I have interpreted my re-election as a mandate from the American people to carry out the Democratic Platform—including, of course, the plank on Israel. I intend to do so.

This warm-hearted correspondence continued for some months and was only ended by Weizmann's increasing infirmity.

Weizmann decided that the best way of restoring Anglo-Jewish relations was to invite a select number of friends to visit him at Rehovoth and see for themselves the achievements of the young nation. To each of them—Leo Amery, Walter Elliot, Simon Marks, Lord Rothschild, Lord Melchett, Leonard Stein, Isaiah Berlin and Richard Crossman—he wrote a long letter, full of vivid and enthusiastic decriptions of what he had seen on his presidential tours. Throughout that summer he also tried to restore his personal relations with Churchill, which had been shattered in 1944 by the murder of Lord Moyne. But Churchill had sent no message to him either when the State was established or when he was made President. In July, after pressure from various well-wishers, Walter Elliot had extracted from him a verbal message:

The Palestine position now, as concerns Great Britain, is simply such a hell-disaster that I cannot take it up again or renew my efforts of twenty years. It is a situation which I myself cannot help in, and must, as far as I can, put out of my mind. But send Weizmann himself my warm regards.

Weizmann did not permit himself to be affronted by the offhand tone of this message. At once he dispatched a long letter, full of reminiscences of Churchill's past services to the cause of Zionism. But there was no response and, instead of writing again, Weizmann gave tactful instructions that his long letter to Leo Amery should be shown to Churchill. Walter Elliot may well have been right when he assured Weizmann that this indirect contact had helped, in the debate on 10 December, to obtain from Churchill a declaration in favour of *de facto* recognition.

This was a considerable advance. For, up to this point, the Conservative Party had supported Mr Bevin's Palestine policies— though in recent months with ever growing reluctance—and active opposition had been limited to the Government's own benches. Weizmann realized that the Labour Government would only be compelled to concede this demand when the Opposition abandoned its acquiescence and made up its mind to vote against the Government with the Socialist rebels.

He had not long to wait. The first Negev campaign ended the Egyptian threat to Israel; and the second was so successful that Alon's advanced units crossed the Egyptian frontier and threatened the British base at El Arish. On this occasion the Foreign Office was able to obtain the collaboration of the State Department in insisting that Israeli troops should at once be drawn back across the frontier. Negotiations began at Rhodes for an Israeli-Egyptian armistice. But still Bevin remained actively hostile, pleading unsuccessfully with the Egyptians to accept British assistance and persuading King Abdullah to permit Aqaba to be protected with British troops.

Eleven o'clock on 9 January 1949 had been agreed for the commencement of the armistice, and a few minutes later five British Spitfires flew low over the Jewish lines in the Negev. They were engaged by Israeli Spitfires and one was shot down inside the frontier at Nir'am. In the afternoon twelve more British fighters crossed the frontier—presumably to discover what had happened to the missing plane—and were engaged by four Spitfires, commanded by Weizmann's favourite nephew, Ezer. In this dog-fight, and in another which succeeded it, four British planes were brought down, without Jewish loss.

I was staying with Weizmann and returned that afternoon from Jerusalem to find him in his study, talking earnestly with Sharett and a couple of his lieutenants. 'We'd better tell him what has happened,' Weizmann said calmly, and when he had done so Sharett added that the BBC had announced that the British Fleet was preparing for action at Malta. 'Will Tel Aviv be bombarded tonight?' he asked dramatically. I replied, 'No! This is good news Bevin has overreached himself and this will bring you British recognition,' and Weizmann warmly concurred.

The sense of crisis put him on his mettle. He insisted that I should be sent next day to Nir'am to see for myself that the British planes had violated the frontier, and also interview the RAF pilots who had been captured. All this was arranged within a few hours, enabling me to publish a completely accurate indictment of Bevin on the Sunday before Parliament resumed.

For those few days of renewed activity, Weizmann was serenely happy, particularly when the news came in that Bevin had been isolated in the Cabinet, which, under the leadership of Stafford Cripps and Herbert Morrison, had agreed to concede *de facto* recognition in the course of the debate, due to take place on 26 January. But when the day came and the Foreign Secretary rose to speak, he amazed the Commons by launching into a passionate defence of the Arab position. After he had sat down, without making the expected announcement, Churchill at once announced that he was moving a vote of censure and then proceeded to reaffirm his Zionist faith, in terms which he had not used for many years and which greatly shocked many of his supporters. 'The coming into being of a Jewish State in Palestine,' he said, 'is an event in world history to be viewed in the perspective not of a generation or a century but in the perspective of a thousand, two thousand or even three thousand years. That is a standard of temporal values which seems very much out of accord with the perpetual click-clack of our rapidly changing moods and of the age in which we live.' And he went on to pay a personal tribute to Weizmann:

> I was glad to read a statement from Dr Weizmann the other day pleading for friendship between the new Israeli State and the Western world. I believe that will be its destiny. He was an old friend of mine for many years. His son was killed in the war fight-

ing with us. I trust his influence may grow and that we shall do what we can, subject to our other obligations—because we cannot forget those other obligations—to add to his influence.

Though Weizmann could not know it at the time, this was the end of Bevinism and the beginning of that restoration of Anglo-Israeli relations whose speed and completeness astonished even those of us who wanted it most.

In February 1949 Weizmann was still full of vigour, and deeply concerned with the development of British public opinion. He took part in an exchange with Lady Violet Bonham Carter, daughter of Herbert Asquith and still the most prominent leader of British Liberalism. Lady Violet is regarded as one of the most formidable controversialists in British public life, but on this occasion she met her match.

> I think you know how deeply I have felt the tragic wrongs and sufferings of the Jewish people [she wrote to the President]. You know that I have always tried to fight their battle both in public and private life. Yet to-day, alas! I can feel no friendship for the new State of Israel.

Having expatiated on the sins of the terrorists, she then went on to complain that

> the first act of the new State of Israel, under you, its great President, was to declare a general amnesty, embracing 40 members of the Stern Gang. . . . Israel will no doubt in time be 'recognised' —*de facto* and *de jure*. But it has lost the *hearts* of all its truest friends in this country.

And she concluded.

> I am sorry to have to write you this letter, but, remembering our old friendship and all the hopes and all the sorrows we shared, I think it is right that you should know the bitter disillusionment some of us are living through.

Despite his own passionate hatred of terrorism, Weizmann, in his reply, conceded nothing.

> I am very sorry [he began] that you should have fallen a victim to the campaign of vilification that is now being waged against our young State. British people have a reputation of being able to see the other side even in times of conflict and tension. There is little evidence of this where we are concerned. You use strong language

about our terrorists and their deeds. Has it occurred to you that there might be grievous reasons for the appearance of so unbeliev-able and unprecedented a phenomenon as 'Jewish terrorism'? The Jews are not a people given to violence. For many centuries force has not been our weapon. Our colonisation in Palestine was an outstanding achievement of non-violence.

Having rehearsed once again the provocation to which both the Yishuv and the Jews of Europe were submitted, Weizmann turned to the question of the amnesty.

You are annoyed with Israel and its Government for having declared a general amnesty which benefited also the terrorists. It so happens that I had nothing to do with this matter because it is outside my province, although I share the responsibility for it, but you are very much mistaken if you think that this decision implies any truckling to terrorism or any fear of its agents.... If the Government have now decided to proclaim a general amnesty, it is because they felt—and presumably had good reason to feel— that that was the most effective way of liquidating, not the ter-rorists, but terrorism. It may be that they were mistaken: only the future can tell. But if the assumption is correct that this evil thing was the result of a holocaust such as the world has not seen and of the heartless policy of those who bolted the doors of Palestine against the victims, there may be ground for hoping that the normalisation of our national life may eradicate this cancer more effectively than savage punishment, however well deserved by ordinary standards. The hangman and the jailer, on which the British Administration relied for fighting terrorism, have as you know certainly not produced results. This is not an age of humanists, but speaking for myself I still believe that there is boundless wisdom in Goethe's great dictum that if you want to change the hearts of men, treat them as though they were already what you want them to become.

On 7 April he left for the USA, aware that he had a real job to do there but deeply unhappy that Israel's first President would be absent from the country on the first anniversary of Independence. Immediately after he became President he had promised Weisgal that he would come to the States on 9 January 1949 in order to be the guest of honour at a dinner for the Weizmann Institute, but his reluctance to leave the country, emphatically concurred in by the Government, was reinforced by his ill-health. As month after month went by, the pressures generated in America by the supporters of the Institute grew overwhelming. Weizmann finally saw that he had to keep his promise and go, and the Government gave him their blessing and placed a special plane at his disposal.

But parallel pressures had also been building up in America from the Jewish community in general. The leaders of American Jewry could not be put off, and Weisgal had to give up his prize attraction in favour of the central fund-raising organization. A compromise was finally agreed on between the supporters of the Institute and the Jewish community as a whole, plus the Israel Government; the funds collected at the Weizmann Institute dinner were to be devoted to the purposes of the new State.

The dinner was a staggering success. Money poured into the large basket in front of Weizmann in an endless cascade of cheques and cash. By the end of the evening the extraordinary sum of $38 million had flowed from the throng that attended the dinner. For days afterwards Weizmann had his right arm in a sling, undone by the fervent handshakes of the masses of Jews for whom he coined an enduring term—the *Hinterfolk* of the State of Israel.

Weizmann delivered two notable addresses on this trip. He chose the Weizmann Institute dinner as the occasion for giving the stamp of his personal approval to the policy of non-identification, which was then the official Israeli foreign policy and which has since been abandoned. 'A policy of friendship to all the nations', were the words he used to describe it, 'whether or not they diverge amongst themselves in other aspects of their policy.' And he concluded with a passionate reassertion of the 'deep sense of regional responsibility' which he believed that an Israeli statesman should show and the hope that 'the Arab peoples would soon join in the common pursuit of peace and welfare'. A few days later, he started a great address in New York with the statement:

> When our Declaration of Independence was issued, some of us in Israel did not know whether we were signing the birth certificate or the death warrant of the Jewish State.... The General Assembly had laid down its blueprint for Jewish statehood. We were determined that it was to be our Magna Carta.... And so we went to war.

He went on to talk with quite unusual candour about the problems of immigration, warning his American listeners that, without adequate assistance, 'we shall be forced to consider the possibility of regulating and limiting the flow of new immigrants, if we are thrown upon our resources'. But the warning was followed by inspiration, and in his concluding paragraph he coined yet another unforgettable phrase when he said, 'always and steadily we are narrowing the confines of the impossible'.

His efforts had completely exhausted him. On Independence Day he was in one of his blackest moods when he was suddenly informed by Weisgal that a great demonstration was waiting to see him in Madison Square Garden. Weizmann always suffered from a form of stage-fright when on the verge of making a public speech. He had always had to be cajoled into confronting a large audience. Now in his state of exhaustion, he was more refractory than ever. He angrily told Weisgal that for once he was going to let him be taken for a liar. But the devotion of the American Jewish masses, to whom he had always been tenderly attached, was too much for him. His faithful body-guard Joshua rushed in and told him that not only was Madison Square Garden itself packed tight 'like herrings in a barrel' but that literally tens of thousands of people, estimated at about 150,000, were hanging about the streets outside all absolutely determined to wait for Weizmann. They had been waiting hopefully since morning, not in order to hear the various speakers, but for his sake alone. When Weizmann heard this his resistance evaporated at once. He summoned up all his physical and nervous reserves and was taken to the Garden, where his entrance provided a thrilling climax to the greatest mass-meeting in Zionist history.

Wherever he looked in the political scene there were frustrations and personal anxieties. But was there not one area where he could feel himself master in his own house? Could he not regard the supervision of the Institute at Rehovoth as the main continuing responsibility of his declining years? In the second World War, as in the first, Weizmann had never permitted his political activities to halt his scientific work. In 1939 he stationed himself in Paris in order to give his assistance to the French Government. But by February 1940 his political instinct told .him that something was desperately wrong with French morale. At once he sent David Bergmann, who had accompanied him to Paris, back to Palestine in order to keep things going in the Daniel Sieff Institute. 'Possibly there will be no communications after the German victory,' he said to Bergmann in a mood of acute pessimism, just before he left on his journey to the Middle East. But in March 1940 Bergmann received a telegram ordering him back to London, and for the rest of the war he worked with Weizmann in Britain and America, while Dr Bloch remained in charge at Rehovoth. There, as is well known, a most remarkable war service was contributed by what was still a small research institute, very modestly equipped and desperately short of staff. It was largely owing to the Daniel Sieff Institute that a local pharmaceutical industry was established in Palestine, which, after the Middle East was cut off in 1940, showed itself capable of supplying both soldier and civilian with drugs previously imported from the West.

Though this war work inevitably involved a diversion of energy from the proper functions of a research institute, Weizmann gave it his wholehearted approval. But before the war was over he had returned to Palestine and spent four months reorganizing the Institute, planning the money-raising effort and, most important of all, making arrangements for the new building and new staff required if the Sieff Institute was to expand, as he was determined it should, into an institute of pure and applied science that could stand comparison with the best in the Western world.

The work started extremely well, and if only he had been able to stay on at Rehovoth and ensure that the foundations at least were built to his satisfaction, much unhappiness and distress would have been avoided. But it was not to be. Once again politics forced him not merely to leave Palestine but to suspend the close personal supervision which he had intended to give to the development of the new Institute. Nevertheless, even during his most harassing political tribulations in London, New York and Washington, the tension of his emotions was relaxed by detailed attention to what was going on at Rehovoth. Despite the delays occasioned by a suspicious British bureaucracy in 1947, immigration permission was being obtained for new staff and the first of the new buildings was at last under erection.

In March he consulted his business and scientific directors, Dr Bloch and Dr Bergmann, about the possibility of an early return. When they gave him contradictory advice, he sent Meyer Weisgal to make a personal inspection. On 14 April Weisgal sent him a vivid description and an unambiguous answer to his question:

This brings me to the question of your returning home. I know how your heart longs for Rehovoth and for your home. I walked through your grounds yesterday and I prayed to God that you might be given some surcease to be able to return to that beautiful place and enjoy the comfort of home and the fragrance of your gardens. But I am afraid it cannot be done. Every responsible person I spoke to—and I spoke to all of them—to B.G., to Kaplan, to the High Command, all of them are of one opinion: They understand your desires, they appreciate your anxiety, they all know what it would mean to the Yishuv for you to be in their midst, and yet they think it unwise and imprudent to come back at this time.

Weisgal's letter reached Weizmann at one of the darkest periods of his New York exile, just three days before the Passover eve on which Judge Rosenman arrived in his room in the Waldorf-Astoria with his secret message from President Truman. He was in one of his black moods and, in a characteristic reply to Weisgal's letter, he wrote:

> It was an absolutely futile waste of time here. I have seen some people, but really, it was not worth while for the sake of this sort of activity to go through the ordeal of a crossing in mid-winter and of being sick, and at the end, to add insult to injury, you are not giving me a visa to come to Palestine. I am still hoping to find a telegram when I come to London that I may come, because the military situation may improve. This would compensate me for all the heart-breaking experience here.

His letter to David Bergmann, written on the same day (20 April 1948), is equally characteristic. He thanks him for a detailed report about the research activities of the Institute and then goes on:

> My own criticism of it is that it is too many-sided and too much for a limited group of people, and unless you have a very considerable number of collaborators, it doesn't seem wise to attempt so many things at once. However, you know best, although my experience has shown me that you overstrain yourself and overestimate the limit to which you can go. I would, therefore, advise most energetically to curtail some of the work, which does not seem to me to be of equal importance or of equal character, and from so many subjects one could select some which have priority, leaving the others aside for the time being.

In the weeks following Independence, the invading Arab armies came close to Rehovoth and the news that Weizmann received from the Institute was both stirring and disturbing. On Independence Day itself Bergmann wrote:

> I would have loved to stay in Tel Aviv for the birth of the State of Israel, but I had to go home and to organize all the work we had to perform within the next few days. The Institute was completely silent, only the pumps and the machines were making their noise—but everybody was in his place—and everybody means 75 people! (We are now working 7 days a week and 24 hours a day). At 5 minutes to 4, everybody spontaneously began

to move to our physics lab. We have our own wireless transmitter and receiver, so that we are in constant touch with the scientific department in Tel Aviv, and it was very moving when at 4 pm the Hatikvah resounded from the set. Our 35 soldiers (in uniform) stood automatically to attention; it was like a wave going through the room.

He continues his report in a letter of 31 May:

We are shifting the intensity of our work to the night hours which so far have been free from air attacks. The windows in the ground floor of the Sieff Institute and the doors are protected by brick walls so that we will be protected against blast; otherwise, we can only hope that the staff will get accustomed gradually to the frequent air raid warnings. . . . We are fortunate that the Arabs are relatively primitive in their technical experience, even though they have a tremendous amount of material at their disposal. As I wrote you once before, we are very far behind them in long-range weapons, and we have very little protection against air attacks. . . . I often wonder whether we have done right in doing in the Institute the sort of research we have carried out in these fourteen years, instead of preparing the country chemically and mechanically for the most refined of modern warfare methods.

The references to emergency war work become ever more frequent in each of Bergmann's successive letters. On 22 June, for example, he writes:

The truce has become a very uneasy proposition; we expect nothing from the efforts of Count Bernadotte, and I believe everybody is convinced that we will have to go on fighting. Therefore, I do not think that we will be able to go back to peaceful research for some time to come. There are many questions which have to be solved during the period of truce and many preparations which have to be made in anticipation of the possibility that the war continues. Perhaps in the end it will have been an unnecessary effort, but I hope that you will agree with me that as long as we are not sure of the future, we must be prepared for the worst. The other day the Scientific Department of the General Staff had a small exhibition of all the work which has been done and of all the things which have been and are being produced under its auspices. I think it was a great success, and the Institute was very conspicuous. Of course, the number of people who have seen this exhibition was very small, and some of the exhibits were only made accessible to ten people.

To this series of letters, Dr Weizmann replied, on 6 August, with what for him was an unusual and exemplary control of the passionate resentment and disapproval to which his young lieutenant's reports had aroused him.

> I will not go into all the details of your interesting project but I would like to give an expression to a certain amount of scepticism regarding the size and the scope of the project. I think you are planning too much. You know very well that you will meet with very little response on the part of the government even if it is our own government. Governments never have much understanding for scientific research, and whereas they are prepared to waste considerable sums on munitions in buying them from other places, they cannot be brought to understand that it is much more economical to do fundamental research, which would enable them to produce the material on the spot and, in the long run, to save a great deal of money.
>
> Be it as it may, it would take a long time to build up a central laboratory and a workable organization. . . . And therefore, my advice is—for the present at any rate—to try and do all you can in the buildings, which are ours. I am happy to hear, that you have quite a number of good young men and no doubt, under your guidance you will be able to train them and bring them into shape, so that they may be useful for the future.
>
> You know my deep aversion to anything which deals with war. It is a waste, it is cruel and it does not suit us at all. I know, we are compelled in self-defence to do a great many things, but I would like you to feel, that I am anxious to reduce it to a very minimum. If such a war industry is to be created, it should be done exclusively under government auspices. We can help and advise and give them guidance, but we must take no responsibility.

What damage to the Institute did these emergency wartime activities do, and what compensating contribution did they make to Israeli victory? Anyone who attempts to answer these questions faces two obstacles. First, he finds himself circumscribed by the official secrecy with which certain aspects of Israeli weapon development during the war of independence are still surrounded. To the present writer, however, an even graver difficulty is the conflict of loyalties that arose out of this controversy. Yet anyone intent on giving a truthful picture of the last years of 'the Chief's' life cannot suppress this episode.

As soon as he returned to Israel he assumed once again his position as Head of the Institute and soon found that in reality things had gone a good deal farther than Dr Bergmann had been able to reveal in his letters. Deeply affronted by his exclusion from any kind of responsibility for affairs of State, he was all the more passionately concerned to ensure that, in his own scientific Institute, it was he who gave the commands. But an ironical fate had decreed that even this would be denied him—until late in 1949, when age and illness had impaired his powers of administration and compelled him to leave to others the control of the Institute that by now bore his name.

This tragic situation had developed not, as he was wont in his last months to fancy, owing to the personal conspiracies of those in whom he had put his trust but as an inevitable result of the Arab invasion. It is characteristic of the Israeli people that one of the first decisions made by the military leadership as soon as the war was seen to be unavoidable was the recruitment of a scientific research unit from among the young scientists in Jerusalem. Of course the Haganah had always had access to Israeli scientists. In 1936, for example, its commanders had asked Weizmann for a chemist who could help them to produce on the spot an effective high explosive. At the time, all they had was dynamite, which, owing to sweating, was dangerous in the climate of Palestine. Weizmann detailed David Bergmann to do the work—and he proceeded to recruit four other members of the staff.

The work was done outside the Institute and the details were not known to Weizmann. Nevertheless, in 1939 Bergmann was instructed to bring to Paris the sample of the new explosive they had developed, so that it could be shown to the French authorities. Later, when the Middle East was cut off from Britain the Institute, as we have seen, was devoted almost entirely to war production; and the return of normal research—inaugurated by Weizmann in 1944—had scarcely been launched when the Haganah leadership was faced with the imminent threat of Arab invasion. Moreover, in the spring of 1948 Mount Scopus had been seized by the Arabs and the scientific departments of the Hebrew University were in disarray. It was inevitable, therefore, that the military scientific research unit, which was forced to leave Jerusalem when it had scarcely been established, should migrate to Rehovoth. For there were available not only the laboratories of the Sieff Institute and to some extent those of the neighbouring agricultural research station. In addition, the first building of the Weizmann Institute was nearing completion, though it was still unable, owing to lack of equipment, to sustain normal research. The Israeli Army therefore took the unfinished building over, in addition to the laboratories of the Sieff Research Institute, which were soon teeming with soldier scientists.

How this take-over was made is vividly recalled by a distinguished scientist, now a Professor at the Weizmann Institute but in 1948 a junior research worker in the Sieff Institute, with a far higher rank and more responsible status in the Haganah. 'I was working,' he writes, 'on a problem utterly remote from war, and I can recall how little impact the partition decision of November 1947 made on my daily life. At the Haganah headquarters we knew of the danger that impended and I was concerned that it had no effect on my daily work. I knew that the Institute was an important target and posed a tremendous security problem. Camouflage against aerial attack was almost impossible and it was wide open to ground attacks from the Arab village of Bi'Salim and, farther off, from Ramleh. Surrounded by orange groves, it provided an ideal objective of surprise attacks. I can remember the day in February 1948 when the mandatory power withdrew and we realized we were on our own. That morning information reached us that Iraqi troops had seized the hills surrounding the Institute. At once we began to build fortifications around the town and the Institute, which included strongpoints on the roof of the new building. In March the first groups of young scientists arrived from Jerusalem and I remember how Dr Bergmann called me on the phone and told me that the Institute would be transformed into a military scientific centre. I was left with the alternatives of going on active service or staying at the Institute for active scientific duty. But the choice was made for me. I remained at the Institute. The place started buzzing day and night. Chemical problems were tackled hastily; products were confiscated or abandoned; stores were assembled from various places; pilot plants were organized in different corners of the new building. Every inch was used and the whole area resounded with the explosions of new weapons and experimental mixtures. My war-time experience at the Institute, however, only lasted for a few weeks. Then I was sent to another unit near Tel Aviv and only returned when the war was over.'

The story is taken up by another scientist, who arrived at the Institute in the summer of 1948. After four years as a British artillery and staff officer in the Far East, he had taken his chemistry finals at Oxford that June and a few weeks later found himself a member of the military research unit at Rehovoth. 'We were housed', he writes, 'as a self-contained military unit, using the classrooms of the agricultural college across the road from the Weizmann Institute as dormitories, storerooms and offices. We ate in soldiers' canteens in Rehovoth, either walking back and forth or hitching rides on military transport. When I arrived, Rehovoth was quite near the front line. There were still air raid alarms and infrequent air raids. The canteens where we ate were often filled with soldiers going off to battle or returning from it. This was our only contact with war.

'Our research was done by small groups in different sheds, stores and outhouses and in parts of the as yet unfinished Weizmann Institute building, which was covered with a camouflage net of eucalyptus leaves. Since many of the new recruits were somewhat unskilled and often over-enthusiastic, the number of fires and serious accidents was quite high. There was no shortage of laboratory equipment, since much of the Weizmann Institute's new equipment had arrived in large crates and was available to us.

'These incidents, the lavish use of equipment and the general high spirits were looked on with some disfavour by the old staff of the Sieff Institute, most of whom had been trained in the strict discipline of German science and were continuing their peace-time research. The unit's first task was to produce stop-gap solutions to many problems. But, as conventional weapons became more readily available, the research became more abstract and much of it a somewhat impractical attempt to lay the foundations of military science with theoretical studies of ballistics, communications and electronic controls.

'None of this, however, had any influence on later developments at the Institute. When the unit was finally disbanded, the physicists were released to go abroad for study; the engineers were transferred elsewhere and most of the rest of us were asked to join the Weizmann Institute and now form the core of the senior staff. Most of us, when released from military discipline, settled down to do Ph.Ds set by our supervisors and have continued in these or related fields. Very few of us managed to complete our formal education. Many were granted all sorts of exemptions in their finals and yet the standard of their later work was, I think, appreciably higher and certainly more imaginative than that of the regular science students who went through university in the usual way after the war. In comparing these veterans with later generations at the Institute, I think their broader outlook and ability to cope with major scientific problems was born of the responsibility suddenly thrust on them in 1948.'

To these two impressions, provided by present members of the Institute, it may be useful to add some examples of the actual scientific problems which were dealt with at Rehovoth by the military research unit.[1]

(1) It seemed a simple task to produce large quantities of sterile saline (physiological salt solution) for injections to wounded soldiers; but nobody had any experience with the phenomenon of pyrogens, toxic substances formed in the course of sterilization, and a group of young biologists and biochemists had to work day and night to find a solution to the problem of pyrogen-free saline.

(2) Very soon, it became clear that the quantities of morphium available in the country would not be sufficient for the rapidly increasing needs of the armed forces, and it became imperative to produce a synthetic substitute. It had just become known that this problem had been solved elsewhere by the discovery of Methadon. One of the young scientists who had come to Israel not very long before and occupies today a very important position in Israeli science was given as his first task the elaboration of a practical method for the synthesis of Methadon. He solved the problem satisfactorily.

(3) The problem of emergency rations was one of prime importance. In Israel it was more difficult to solve than in other countries because of the lack of certain foods, particularly animal proteins, which under the Mandate had been largely imported. A solution was sought along the lines of one of the studies to which Weizmann had devoted some effort before and during the second World War. Plant proteins which were relatively easily accessible were digested by the proteolytic enzymes of yeast and converted in to a soluble mass which in flavour and in nutritional value approached, at least, the unavailable meat. The ingenious solution devised for this problem was one of the favourable exhibits for occasional visitors to the laboratories.

(4) The British blockade had made the acquisition of aircraft fuel extremely difficult and attempts were made to produce a substitute. Here the size of the problem was undoubtedly underestimated. However, the solutions proposed were rather interesting; they resulted in a memorandum on aircraft fuel production submitted to the Israel Ministry of Defence and—from the scientific point of view—in some good publications.

Two methods were proposed. (a) There was available in the country in relatively large quantities a by-product of the citrus industry, limonene. This compound could be converted by a simple method into cymene, an aromatic hydrocarbon which was known to have a

[1] In order to ensure accuracy and avoid breaches of security, this passage has been submitted to the Israel Ministry of Defence.

very high (about 140) octane number and therefore could be used to improve the qualities of the—rather bad—gasoline available for motor cars. (b) There existed some indications that the German tanks in the Africa campaign had used methyl isobutyl ketone to improve their fuel. This compound can be made from acetone, and a process was worked out on a pilot plant scale for the production of that ketone; the process could be combined successfully with the production of limonene. This method seemed so promising that the conversion of the alcohol-producing plants in the country into plants for the fermentative production of acetone was seriously considered.

(5) One of the first units to be established was the electronics group; it was—suitably—housed in the part of the Weizmann Institute which was destined for the electronic computer. In this large hall, the foundation was laid for the present electronics section of the Ministry of Defence which can be considered as one of the best scientific groups of the country. In fact, this group had already carried out successfully a major task; it had constructed and commissioned the first Israeli radio station, which was ready in time for the first broadcast of the Prime Minister and for the first performance of the Hatikvah.

(6) Not less serious than the complete absence of experience in electronics at the outbreak of the War of Independence was the fact that the country was not able to produce the classical explosives and propellants (gunpowder). Thus, one group had to adapt the existing know-how on a very ineffective type of explosive, the Cheddites, to the problems at hand. These explosives are based on potassium chloride, one of the few materials abundantly available in the country. Thus the first plastic explosives were designed and produced.

Even more serious was the situation with regard to propellant powders. In this field, it became apparent that a fundamentally new approach had to be made, and it was decided to begin the development of rockets based on synthetic propellant compositions. A large effort was devoted to this problem: a group of physicists worked on its theoretical aspects—some of them, who are today in high positions in civilian science, will perhaps not want to remember that this was the beginning of their scientific career—and a number of chemists began to develop then what is now considered one of the major achievements of Israeli applied science, the synthetic rocket propellant.

Now that it can be seen in retrospect and without the exaggeration of partisan controversy this record of the Institute's contribution to the military victory is impressive enough. But at the time the reality of the scientists' achievements was inflated by the myths of friend and foe alike. The secret weapons that Arab rumour was constantly ascribing to the Jewish armies had a disastrous effect on the morale of their own civilians and soldiers. Who can forget how Safad was saved from what in military terms was unavoidable surrender by a panic fear of a Jewish atomic cannon, which in sober truth was nothing but a home-made mortar? And, on a larger scale, the sinking of the Egyptian flagship with all hands and in a few minutes was quickly ascribed throughout the Arab world to yet another secret product of Dr Weizmann's armoury at Rehovoth.

There was a similar process of myth-making among Israel's friends. Before 1948 the Yishuv had scarcely heard of the Research Institute at Rehovoth; it was widely assumed that, as practical men, with no time for theories, they would have to rely on the Jewish scientists of the Diaspora. It was in the war of independence that many Israelis realized for the first time how essential science was to their survival. Perhaps it was a pity that the lesson which brought this home to them was a legend about the secret weapons produced by what was later to become the Weizmann Institute. Nevertheless, it remains true that this legend did much to popularize the Institute among the Yishuv and to deepen the respect it felt for Dr Weizmann's scientific powers.

Moreover, the work of the military research unit had important material advantages for the Institute. Thanks to these activities, the new buildings, half-finished at the outbreak of war, were completed as a matter of urgency. Staff who would otherwise have been dispersed were retained and increased by a notable influx of young men. As a result, the Institute emerged from hostilities with its manpower, its buildings and its popular image all enhanced.

Alone in Israel, Weizmann really understood *both* politics and science. Unlike his academic colleagues, he appreciated that politics is the art of the second best and never demanded the impossible of the men with whom he worked. But, unlike the politicians, he appreciated that in science nothing but the best is of any avail, and he was determined, whatever it cost him, to exclude from his Institute those political and governmental influences which would lower scientific standards in the name of practical expediency. If Rehovoth was to be the home of a Jewish scientific research unit equal to the best in the Western world, then the Weizmann Institute must be liberated from the governmental influences which in war time had inevitably taken over control of its activities. To this task of achieving his Institute's complete independence he devoted a major part of the last energies available to him. Never again was he to have such physical strength or sustained powers of concentration as he showed in the months of 1949 whose climax was reached when on 2 November the new Institute of Physics and Physical Chemistry was dedicated and the cornerstone was laid of a new Institute for Biology and Biochemistry. It was with special pleasure that Weizmann must have listened to the following passage in the speech of Professor Brodetsky, President of the Hebrew University:

> It is very significant that in the State of Israel the President of the State is also the person so completely identified with scientific research. . . . The scientist often has the feeling that the results of his work are afterwards exploited and prostituted by the politician. . . . I know that in the State of Israel the chief aim is peace. The fact that our President Weizmann is also the scientist Weizmann means that we can expect that the Weizmann Institute, together with the other great institutions of learning in Israel, will serve the people of Israel as well as humanity, in the interest of the peaceful co-operation of all mankind.

The significance of the occasion enabled David Ben-Gurion, too, to express his deepest feelings about Weizmann. In an obviously sincere and moving speech he summed up Weizmann's qualities by referring to the 'Crown of Wisdom and the Crown of Dominion' as being rightfully his.

Weizmann replied in language whose magnanimity and wisdom can only be appreciated in terms of the controversy that had gone before:

> You will all no doubt have asked yourselves, What is the purpose of the Institute? It is a fundamental question. We here in Rehovoth are primarily engaged in pure research. If, as a result of our research into, say, foodstuffs, soils, pharmaceuticals, and cogent related projects, practical application becomes possible, we are only too happy. But we do not start out with the thought of making discoveries.
>
> We have been working steadily, without let or hindrance. In fact, as already mentioned, the Institute was actually in operation and able to play its part in last year's War of Independence long before the building was completed. Our scientists and the scientists of the Army of Israel were able to use the facilities then available to contribute a vital chapter to the magnificent epic of resistance.
>
> We live, as you know, in a pioneering country. We are pioneering in the wilderness, in agriculture, and in industry. But here in

Rehovoth we are also engaged in a peculiar kind of pioneer work
—we are pioneering in Science. There are many problems to be
solved in our land, many difficulties to be overcome. There are
also many dangers still to be met. But to meet them, we must not
rely only or chiefly on physical force. We have a mighty weapon
which we must utilize with ingenuity and skill, with every means
available to us. Science is that weapon, our vessel of strength
and our source of defence.

Though none knew it at the time, this was the last great personal
declaration that Weizmann was to make. A few days later the occasion of his 75th birthday was celebrated in London by a great
dinner, at which Field Marshal Smuts was the chief speaker. In a
remarkable concluding passage, Smuts said:

> We are passing through a tragic period such as perhaps has no
> parallel in history. It reads like some tragic Odyssey, not of one
> man but of man, of the human race. . . . Mankind . . . stands per-
> plexed and confused before the future, with no clear light upon
> the way before it. It is at such a time . . . that we may derive com-
> fort and guidance from the case of Israel. . . . The soul, spiritual
> force, is the answer to the machine. What little Israel could
> achieve, in spite of Hitler, and against almost unimaginable odds,
> surely this Western world of ours may achieve on its larger scale.
> The unconquerable reserve of man is his will to victory, his deter-
> mination to win through at all cost. And once the peoples of the
> West make up their mind to sacrifice minor comforts and benefits
> . . . the wide prospect of fulfilment will stretch out before them. . . .
> Such an all-out effort was made here in the Battle of Britain, and
> repeated in the resurrection of Israel in Palestine. I bracket them
> together as among the human highlights of our epoch. Let us
> repeat that supreme effort and our European civilization will
> enter upon perhaps its most glorious epoch of history. We thank
> Israel for having once more reminded us of that last, that only
> way to salvation. And especially do we think of Chaim Weizmann
> tonight in honour and gratitude for his great leadership and in-
> spiration to the world looking for leadership and inspiration.

It was a fitting tribute by the greatest philosopher statesman to the
greatest scientist statesman of our century.

After the inauguration of the Weizmann Institute, the shadows
thickened fast. Even in the life of a statesman there are periods
which should remain closed to the public eye because they contain

nothing of political significance and much whose publication would be painful. Such a period is that between his 75th birthday on 27 November 1949 and his death almost exactly two years later. There were times of positive happiness, especially when the school holidays came round and he could enjoy the presence of his grandson. There were also days of sad serenity, when he sat on the terrace looking out to the Jerusalem hills and, in the presence of a trusted friend, recounted ever more slowly, his favourite stories or brooded quizzically —sometimes with a flash of his old intellectual ferocity—over the past. One of Weizmann's stories, contributed by Mr Sharef, will describe, more aptly than any biographer, the last phase of his life.

He had been asking Sharef about the attitude of the *sabra* to the older generation. 'What do these young people think of us?' he asked. 'How do they talk about the old Zionists? What do they say of me?' Taken aback by the question, Sharef replied that nobody associated him with any single group. In their minds he was in a class by himself. To this Weizmann replied: 'I would like to tell you something that happened to me. In 1931, after the Zionist Congress at which I had not been re-elected as President (he would often bring up this fact reproachfully), the movement was short of funds and I was asked to travel to South Africa. I went. After the tour had ended, Mrs Weizmann and I, together with a guide, visited Kruger National Park. At one of our stops, I saw a buffalo resting in the shade of a rock. I asked the guide, 'Why is the buffalo sitting there?' He explained to us that buffaloes travel in herds and that, when one grows old, he is forced out of the herd. When an old bull has been rejected by the herd, he looks for a place in the shade of a tree or a rock. There he lies, no longer going in search of food but waiting patiently for death to overtake him. As we were talking, a herd of buffalo passed by, not far from the old bull. He raised his head as if to call them. A pair of young bulls paused for a moment, turned their heads towards the old buffalo, and then went on. I saw a world of sadness in the eyes of the old buffalo. . . .'

Weizmann's was not a forgiving nature. He was unable either to show magnanimity to those colleagues whom he wrote off as clerks and subalterns or to feel any confidence that they could manage without his supreme direction. In the first months after his return to the country, he was mentally and physically capable of taking an active part in public affairs: after that the decline of his health excluded anything but spasmodic and irregular interventions. Yet to his dying day he girded against his rôle as presidential figurehead. He had always been moody; but in these last months, as one of his doctors put it, 'the changes of mood were linked with the ups and downs in his physical health and his illness took on ever more obsessive forms'. Increasingly he felt himself a captive and on more than one occasion talked about himself as 'the prisoner of Rehovoth'.

To what extent was this prison without bars, in which he felt himself confined, created by the Government's decision to make his office symbolic and to what extent was it an imaginary product of his own frustrations and physical infirmities? Looking back now, it is difficult to blame the Government for excluding him from any effective power. In the circumstances they could justify their action by the state of his health. But it is also true that, if he had returned to Israel strong and vigorous, the case for excluding him would have been even stronger.

For between the President and the Prime Minister there had grown up a certain tension. It was to grow less and less, and ultimately to dwindle away altogether, but at this time it had both personal and political roots. After Independence Day the personal friction between the two men was aggravated by differences of political emphasis. At first the Government's adherence to non-identification left little for Weizmann to criticize in its foreign policy. As passionate as Ben-Gurion in his opposition to Bevin and his determination to retain the Negev, Weizmann at this time found himself surprisingly in accord with such young activists as his nephew Ezer Weizmann and Yigal Alon. Before they got to know him, they had been inclined to write him off as 'pro-British' and 'pacifist'. But, when they became frequent visitors to Rehovoth in the winter of 1948, the old President impressed both of them as a man of action, who understood the need for backing diplomacy with military strength.

Yet Weizmann continued to envisage the future of Israel in the old terms of 'a Middle Eastern Switzerland' and to regard non-identification as the only method not merely of continuing the flow of refugees from behind the Iron Curtain but also of breaking down Arab opposition. Before Abdullah was murdered, Weizmann was convinced that the King and he—if the politicians on both sides had given them a free hand—could have achieved an understanding between Jordan and Israel; and he blamed the Government for forbidding him to attempt a personal approach to the Court of Amman. He was equally critical of Ben-Gurion's decision that the Israeli vote should be cast in favour of United Nations action against North Korea. It was not that he was blind to Communist aggression. But Weizmann shared Pandit Nehru's philosophy. He believed that, whereas Israel's military strength was bound to be insignificant, the new Jewish State might well develop an important rôle in the cold war as a mediator, unattached to either side.

Would it be fair, therefore, to claim, as some of his friends do, that there existed a Weizmannite peace policy, which could be regarded as a true alternative to the activism of Ben-Gurion? The factual answer to this question is that, after he became President, he had neither the political opportunity nor the physical strength to develop a constructive foreign policy. But there can be little doubt that, with good health and a measure of presidential power, he would have evolved an alternative that would have brought him into conflict with Ben-Gurion. The constitutional decision to make the President powerless was not taken on its merits but as a precaution against an otherwise inevitable clash between two great and completely incompatible personalities, the first President and the first Prime Minister of Israel.

It was because he knew that Ben-Gurion had foreseen this peril and coolly taken steps to prevent it that Weizmann could never acquiesce in his rôle of constitutional monarch. If he had been able to do so, he would not only have enjoyed happiness in his declining years but exerted the kind of influence on public affairs which an experienced King in Scandinavia or Britain builds up over the years. But it was not to be. After a life of political struggle, what he cared about was not advice and influence, but effective power, and that was not forthcoming. He had accepted the ceremonial duties of a Presidency that made its holder impotent to champion the policies in which he believed.

After his death, those policies suffered a rapid and progressive decline. Instead of pursuing non-identification between the warring blocs, the Government sought to attach Israel to such Western organizations as NATO and the Common Market; built up the nation's military strength by an intimate alliance with France; and, in the Sinai campaign, collaborated with Britain in an attempt to overturn Colonel Nasser. The mature, internationalist aspects of Zionism that Weizmann personified were gradually ousted by a youthful Israeli nationalism that sometimes brought the new State into conflict not only with the United Nations and international law but with the traditional Zionist ideas of the Diaspora.

Yet Weizmann's ideas live on in Israel and there may well come a day when leaders inspired by them will once again be needed to rescue the nation from an isolation imposed by the self-centred use of military power. Meanwhile the home of the 'prisoner of Rehovoth' has achieved the symbolic significance that the Government tried unsuccessfully to give it in 1948.

As long as he lived, Weizmann refused to be a constitutional monarch. An ironic fate has decreed that, lying in his grave in Rehovoth, he should play in death the rôle he refused so stubbornly to play when he was alive.

Mr R. H. S. Crossman is one of Britain's foremost parliamentarians, authors and political commentators. He was a member of the Anglo-American commission of inquiry on Palestine in 1946 and has stayed in the country on extended visits many times since.

INDEX

Abdulla, Emir, 190, 193
Abdullah, king of Jordan, 335, 354
Aberson, Zvi, 23, 24
acetone. *See* Weizmann process
Adler, Dr. Cyrus, 219
Adler, Nahum, 99
Agricultural Research Station, Yavne, 116, 122, 233
Ahad Ha'am (Asher Ginsberg): influence and views, 22, 25, 26, 72, 84, 102, 133–5, 147, 149, 197, 207, 315; friendship with W., 31, 35, 37, 104, 159, 165, 198; 'Slavery in the Midst of Freedom', 102
aircraft fuel, 348
Aleichem, Sholom, 71, 72, 175
Alexander, D. L., 34
Alexander, Professor Samuel, 32, 91, 146, 148, 156
Alexander II, Tsar, 18, 21, 65
Allenby, Field Marshal Lord, 37, 173, 174
Alliance Israélite, 30
Alon, Yigal, 332–3, 335, 354
American Jewish Committee, 214
Amery, Lord, 34, 163, 245, 253, 334, 335
Anglo-American Commission of Inquiry on Palestine, 52, 281–4, 315
Anglo-Jewish Association, 30, 34, 156
Anglo-Palestine Club, 227
Aniline Dyes, 91
Arabs: fear of Jewish antagonism with, 34, 39; reaction to Balfour Declaration, 37, 163, 164, 191; nationalism, 166, 180, 188, 199, 206, 250; attitude to Mandate, 190, 192; views on partition, 48, 49, 51, 155, 263, 287; riots in Palestine, 46–8, 52, 177, 189, 190, 195, 205, 206, 214, 219, 223, 224, 235, 236, 241, 243; at St James' Palace Conference, 244; at Anglo-American Commission, 283, 284, 315; at United Nations, 296, 299, 300, 301; at Yalta, 277; British policy regarding, 50, 52, 165, 280; W.'s policy regarding, 44, 174, 176, 193–4,

197–8, 200, 202, 227, 238–9, 244, 261, 263, 265, 291, 318; war with Israel, 55, 56, 303, 305, 314, 317, 321, 325, 336, 342, 343, 350. *See* Churchill's Statement, Sykes-Picot Agreement
Arlosoroff, Chaim, 201, 219, 233
Asch, Sholem, 219
Asquith, Herbert, 32–4, 157
Attlee, Clement, 52, 254, 267, 278, 280–1, 284–5, 317–19, 320
Auschwitz camp, 272
Austen, Warren, 306, 309
Aydelotte, Professor, 283

Bakstansky, 255
Balfour, A. J., 30, 32–5, 39, 42, 90, 93, 95, 145, 174, 319, 320
Balfour Declaration: opposition to, 35, 194, 242, 244; W.'s achievement of, 33, 78–9, 95, 99, 102, 104, 118, 119, 143, 148–68, 254, 260, 321; publication of, 36, 89, 177; reactions to, 173, 175, 184, 187–91, 193, 202, 213, 225, 226, 250; and Palestine Mandate, 39, 235
Barker, General Sir Evelyn, 286
Barness, Dr, 21
Baruch, Bernard, 274
Basch, Victor, 33
Bentwich, Herbert, 31, 96, 149
Ben-Zakai, Rabbi Yochanan, 133, 175
Ben-Gurion, David: at St James's Palace Conference, 49; discussions in England, 294, 316; Biltmore Resolution, 51; attitude to England, 53, 257–9, 262; at founding of Jewish Agency, 219; and 1939 White Paper, 283; proclaiming of Israel, 55, 143, 310, 312; conflicts with W., 264, 332, 354; friendship with W., 249, 287–9, 312, 326, 351; authority of, 297, 314, 315, 317, 321, 328, 341, 355; and partition, 298
Berenson, 19
Berger, Judah L., 20
Bergmann, Dr E. D., 111, 340–6

357

Meyer W. Weisgal

Born in Poland, Meyer Weisgal came to America as a boy. He attended public schools in New York City and Columbia University. A delegate to the World Zionist Congresses since 1925, Mr. Weisgal was national secretary of the Zionist Organization of America for nine years. 'Among other capacities in which he has served are those of secretary-general, American Section, of the Jewish Agency, and vice-president of the American Financial and Development Corporation for Israel. He has served the Weizmann Institute since 1947 as executive vice-chairman of the American Committee, and since 1949 as chairman of the Executive Council. He has edited several newspapers and books of Jewish interest and produced plays, including Franz Werfel's *The Eternal Road.* Mr. Weisgal commutes between Israel and New York.

Joel Carmichael

A native of New York City, Joel Carmichael attended Columbia University and received two degrees at Oxford, where he was a Scholar in Oriental languages. During the war he served as a naval officer attached to the Office of Strategic Services, specializing in research and intelligence about Germany and the Middle East. Following the war, he became a correspondent in Germany for the *Nation* and later became a Fulbright Fellow in Islamic Studies. Mr. Carmichael, who has traveled in Palestine, Syria, Lebanon and Transjordan, now is a free-lance writer. He translated, abridged and edited N. Sukhanov's memoir of the Russian revolution and published *An Illustrated History of Russia,* as well as numerous articles.